# Lords
# of the
# Harvest

# Lords of the Harvest

*Biotech, Big Money, and the Future of Food*

Daniel Charles

BASIC
BOOKS
A Member of the Perseus Books Group
New York

Copyright © 2001 by Daniel Charles
Previously published by Perseus Publishing
Published by Basic Books, A Member of the Perseus Books Group

Library of Congress Control Number: 2002113414
ISBN-10: 0-7382-0773-X   ISBN-13: 978-0-7382-0773-5

Find us on the World Wide Web at http://www.basicbooks.com

Books published by Basic Books are available at special discounts for bulk purchases in the U.S. by corporations, institutions, and other organizations. For more information, please contact the Special Markets Department at the Perseus Books Group, 11 Cambridge Center, Cambridge, MA 02142, or call (617)252-5298 or (800)255-1514, or e-mail special.markets@perseusbooks.com.

Text design by *Brent Wilcox*
Set in 11-point Sabon by the Perseus Books Group

First paperback printing, November 2002

# CONTENTS

*To Brigid*

# Acknowledgments

This book demanded resources far beyond what I alone could bring, and I'm grateful for the goodwill and generosity of those who made it possible.

My agent, Katinka Matson of Brockman, Inc., saw promise in a half-formed idea. Amanda Cook and her colleagues at Perseus Books were brave enough to place a wager on the efforts of a writer from the world of radio, and unfailingly supportive throughout the project. Marianne Ginsburg and her colleagues at the German Marshall Fund of the United States came to my rescue with funding that allowed me to embark on this expedition.

Many veterans of the struggles over agricultural biotechnology went out of their way to help me understand their story. I'm grateful in particular for the aid of Fred Gould, Mary-Dell Chilton, Paul Heisey, Eric Van Dusen, and Tom Urban, who checked parts of early versions of the manuscript for accuracy. A number of former and current employees of Monsanto were generous with their time and memories. I'd especially like to thank Philip Angell, Will Carpenter, Charles Gasser, Rob Horsch, Ernest Jaworski, Harry Klee, and Steve Rogers. Thanks are due a number of others who wished to remain unnamed. Margaret Mellon and Jane Rissler at the Union of Concerned Scientists allowed me to look through some of their accumulated papers from a decade's devotion to this issue. Others to whom I'm especially indebted include Detlef Bartsch, Andrew Baum, Peter Carlson, Robert Colwell, Donald Duvick, Cary Fowler, Rebecca Goldburg, Robert Goodman, Richard Hellmich, John Howard, Kenneth Moonie, Michael Morris, Peter Raven, Mike Roth, Ann Jennings Shackleford, and Tray Thomas. Special thanks to Audrey Schneiderman, who allowed me to look through her late husband's personal notebooks, and to Cheeze and Peppy, who opened their home to me during visits to St. Louis.

My friends and former colleagues at National Public Radio and *New Scientist* have been a constant source of encouragement and good advice. Thanks in particular to Anne Gudenkauf, who always received news of my shifting career plans with good humor and support, and Christopher Joyce, who persuaded me by example that writing books was a worthwhile occupation, even if one ended up living on beans while waiting for that final installment of the publisher's advance. Thanks also to Rob Gurwitt, who helped carve the manuscript into shape.

Some of the material that I've included in the second half of the book was collected while reporting for National Public Radio from 1993 to 1999. An invitation to speak at a meeting of the Wisconsin Academy of Arts and Sciences in the fall of 2000 provoked the thoughts that later grew into the epilogue.

My greatest debt of gratitude is owed my family. My parents, who taught me how to see the world, then let me go explore it for myself, have been my most loyal readers. The sharp and wise judgments of Brigid, my lovely in-house editor, freed me repeatedly from thickets of technical minutiae, even at the temporary cost of marital harmony. Molly and Nora, banging on the door of my room or sliding their latest drawings underneath it, were a constant reminder of all the things in life that are more important.

# Prologue

I grew up in the middle of the American agrarian ideal, on a small family farm in Pennsylvania just like those that serve as the centerpiece of so many nostalgic children's books. My brother and his family live there now, and it hasn't changed much. Beside the house, there's a big garden and a small orchard of apple and pear trees, plus some blueberry bushes. The tall wooden barn is hung on a frame of enormous rough-hewn beams, carefully pieced together in the old style with notches and pegs by long-dead craftsmen. About fifty Holstein cows wait patiently to be milked, half a dozen barely domesticated cats find shelter in the straw, and a dog paces distractedly. In back of the barn, a grassy pasture slopes gently toward a creek where my older sister and I built dams out of rocks. To the north, there's more pasture and a hill perfect for sledding. To the east lie alternating strips of corn, soybeans, and alfalfa. It's a tidy eighty acres, tiny by today's standards, but for two hundred years it's been enough for a succession of families to make a living.

Across Donerville Road to the east is the farm where my father grew up. From that farmhouse, you can look to the north and east and see the farms where my grandfather, great grandfather, and great-great grandfather were born.

I'm attached to my memories of that place, more attached now than I was as a boy who preferred reading books to baling hay. Yet anytime I'm seized by the temptation to wax poetic about the purity of rural life, it does me good to shake my father's hand. That hand is rough, hard, and slightly disfigured. Twine from hay bales has cut into it. Steel pipes, broken by freezing water in the middle of winter nights, have chafed it raw. A cable from the barn's gutter scraper once caught that hand, tore through skin and muscle, and ground manure into raw flesh. My father could not extricate his hand from the machinery. A neighbor finally heard his cries for help. My parents drove to the hospital; I stayed home to milk the cows. The wound healed remarkably well, but my father was never again able to bend his right index finger.

LAST SPRING, as my brother David was planting corn, he ran out of seed. He drove up the road to a neighbor, the local Pioneer dealer. It was already late in planting season, so he needed a kind of corn that would mature quickly. There wasn't much to choose from. "How about trying some of this 'Bt' corn?" asked the dealer. "Now it does cost a little more." (The extra cost amounted to ten dollars for an acre's worth of seed.)

"You think it's worth the money?" asked David. The dealer figured it probably was. And as simple as that, my brother carried home the latest in agricultural technology.

One gene—out of perhaps fifty thousand genes in each microscopic cell of a corn plant—made this corn seed different. Twenty years ago, scientists had discovered that this is the gene that makes certain bacteria poisonous to many caterpillars, including caterpillars that feed on the stalks of corn. (The bacterium is called *Bacillus thuringiensis,* hence, "Bt corn.") Almost ten years later, in the laboratories of a company called Monsanto, scientists redesigned that gene, creating a new version that worked better when it was inserted in plants. A year or two after that, the gene was blasted into a clump of corn cells growing in a petri dish, and new corn plants containing this gene grew from that clump of cells.

The plants that grew in my brother's fields last year descended from one of those seedlings. When the seed sprouted, the Bt gene went into action. Throughout the plant, from roots to tassel, the plant's cells manufactured the new protein. If a European corn borer were unlucky enough to attempt to feed on one of these plants, it would die.

But animals or humans who ate the corn wouldn't notice. Suppose one of these plants were put through a chemical wringer, and all of its Bt toxin extracted. The result would be only a tiny speck of powder—like all pure protein, white and tasteless—weighing perhaps a hundredth of an ounce. Scientists have fed this powder to colonies of mice. Each day, the mice ate about a tenth of an ounce of it for every pound of their body weight. To consume an equivalent dose, a person weighing 150 pounds would have to eat about fifteen hundred whole raw corn plants. The mice suffered no apparent ill effects, either visibly while they were alive or when they were dissected and studied afterwards. This is what the people conducting these tests expected to see. When this Bt toxin enters the digestive system, it breaks down into small fragments, short strings of amino acids indistinguishable from any other digested protein that enters the body. Based on this knowledge, government regulators are convinced that Bt toxin is harmless to humans.

Most corn grown in North America ends up in animal feed. A portion of the harvest, however, processed into cornstarch or corn meal, does become an ingredient in food on supermarket shelves. Soybeans, meanwhile, the other major crop that's been genetically engineered, provide oil, meal, and emulsifiers that end up in a host of processed foods from chocolate to soups.

As it happened, there weren't many hungry caterpillars in my brother's cornfields last year. None of the plants appeared to suffer much damage, whether they boasted the new Bt gene or not. The new, more expensive corn seed probably wasn't worth the extra money, but David isn't fretting too much over an extra ninety dollars for three bags of seed.

My brother knows more about the biology of plants than your average farmer. He has a university diploma in horticulture hidden away somewhere in the house and spent several years as a county agricultural agent, advising fruit and vegetable farmers. But he's a bit mystified by genetically engineered corn and soybeans. When he heard I was writing this book, he wanted to know: "So how *do* they put those genes into plants?"

Anyone who reads on will learn the answer. There's also another, to me, even more compelling question at the heart of this book: *Why* do they put those genes into plants?

I watched the rise of agricultural biotechnology not primarily as a farmer's son, but as a journalist covering science and technology. The high-tech community has its own view of the world and of history, nurtured by stories of its great triumphs. Engineers and scientists really believe that they have the power to change the world. Individual companies and particular technologies may stumble and fall, but this community is sustained by a powerful faith in the ultimate triumph of technological progress.

From the 1980s onward, this faith burned brightly at biotech companies and in particular at Monsanto, a St. Louis-based company with a long history in the chemical industry. At those times when they were most caught up in enthusiasm for their technology, Monsanto's executives promised a revolution in agriculture. They sometimes spoke as if plants soon would become putty in the hands of science. There would be more productive corn, more nutritious rice, and tastier tomatoes. These plants, they suggested, would produce more food on less land not just in North America but all over the world. Biotechnology would relieve world hunger and allow poor farmers in Asia and Africa to stop destroying precious forests and grasslands.

I came to believe that this was not simply the product of an overheated public relations machine. Many people at Monsanto want this to be true, and they believe that it still could be true. They dream, as all of us do, of doing something significant, of making a difference in the world. Naturally, they hoped to do enormous good in the world while also profiting handsomely themselves. Some of the more ambitious ones dreamed of ascending to that Pantheon of technological pioneers who change the world.

Yet that hoped-for revolution could only be sustained through profits, and profits required control of products—genes—that are singularly difficult to control. So even before most of Monsanto's dreams of improved plants were close to reality, the company set out to dominate the businesses that provide genes to farmers—the seed industry. This attempt provoked similar moves on the part of Monsanto's corporate rivals.

When my brother buys seed corn these days, the bags still carry familiar company labels: DeKalb, Pioneer, or a small local company called Doebler's Pennsylvania Hybrids. But DeKalb now is owned by Monsanto. Pioneer is owned by DuPont. Doebler's breeds its varieties from parent varieties that come from a company in Iowa called Holden's Foundation Seeds. Monsanto, in turn, owns Holden's Foundation Seeds. Seed companies have become extensions of corporate laboratories in St. Louis or Wilmington, Delaware.

There was something deeply mystifying about the rush of big biotech and chemical companies into the seed business, about Monsanto's headfirst dive in particular. These companies love control, efficiency, and predictability. They've grown rich from the carefully tuned operations of climate-controlled factories that pump out products, rain or shine, according to fixed schedules. But agriculture is a holdover from an earlier era; it is dirty, messy, and unpredictable. Farmers are notoriously cranky and difficult to manage. Plants growing in open fields are subject to drought, disease, and windstorms that simply blow them over. Prices are set in far-off commodity markets; the farmer has no control over such things. It is not, in the lingo of Wall Street, a high-margin business. There is not a lot of extra cash sloshing around small farming towns in Indiana or Illinois.

Yet Monsanto spent at least a billion dollars on research before it had a single genetically engineered plant to sell, then billions more to control a handful of seed companies. At this writing in spring 2001, the company's annual revenues from genetically engineered plants add up to a few hundred million dollars—but Monsanto spends more than that just on research aimed at creating new genetically engineered crops. The payoff seems embarrassingly meager. If this is a business, something about it doesn't add up.

ROBERT POST, a historian at the University of Maryland and former president of the Society for the History of Technology, isn't one bit mystified.

"People believe that technologies are driven, more often than they really are, by completely rational considerations and particularly by the idea of maximizing profits," he says. "But I am firmly of the view that technologies are driven by irrational considerations."

Take plans for defense against missiles, known as "Star Wars," says Post, or NASA's planned International Space Station, or a good proportion of the nation's computer purchases. There is no convincing rational reason for any of them. But there seems to be a powerful force behind them all. Call it the romance of new things or the irresistible attraction of unexplored terrain, a place where—who knows?—dreams may come true.

"A big aspect of it is something you see all the time in the history of technology, what we call 'technological enthusiasm'; simply getting caught up in the fun of it all," says Post. His grin suggests that this is by no means the most base of human motives.

FOUR THOUSAND miles away, in a small restaurant in North London, Zoe Elford has a name for the stalks of Bt corn in my brother's fields: "Living pollution." Taking a gene from bacteria and putting it in corn is, first of all, just "really odd, really unnatural," she says. Second, it's taking liberties with nature. No one knows what the results might be.

Elford is an earnest, mild-mannered, yet determined young woman in her twenties with long brown hair. She works for a nonprofit group that works with poor communities around the world, trying to end injustice. The thought strikes me that in an earlier age, she might have entered a cloister.

Her views on genetically altered crops are, by now, well practiced. She's spent years picketing grocery stores and talking to shoppers about genetically engineered food. In 1998 she was arrested, along with several of her friends, for uprooting genetically altered plants in one of Monsanto's trial plots in Oxfordshire. The case has since wandered in and out of several courtrooms. "I felt the urge to stop the stuff growing, because when you release genetically altered plants up and down this country, those are sites of living pollution, and that pollution will replicate itself. Once it's out there, you can't get it back, so it's a kind of now-or-never sort of situation. It's an immediate threat."

That threat, the possibility of unknown consequences, is the theme of Mary Shelley's tale about the fateful curiosity and ambition of Victor Frankenstein, a scientist who could not withstand the lure of knowledge. Heedless of the consequences, Frankenstein created new life, a creature that returned to haunt and destroy him.

Shelley's tale turns a mirror on modern society's love affair with the new, capturing it and reversing the image. Where so many are captivated with the possibilities of technology—"caught up in the fun of it all"—others are caught up in anxiety about where such ventures might lead. Shelley's tale is fiction. But Chernobyl really happened, and DDT, once hailed as a savior from malaria and insect pests, did poison fish and birds, even as insects developed resistance to it and it became ineffective in its original purpose.

Fear of technology's unforeseen consequences courses through debates and conversations about genetically engineered plants, especially in countries with strong environmental movements. In England, consumer protests and fears have forced most grocery stores to ban genetically modified ingredients from their shelves. It's an enormous triumph for committed campaigners like Zoe Elford.

"Does this place serve food from genetically modified crops?" I ask her. It's a vegetarian establishment where Elford goes regularly for lunch across from the Archway tube station.

"I don't think so," she says, looking slightly surprised at the idea. "Did you ever ask?"

"No. I have less of a problem eating it," she confesses. "I just think, yeah, it may harm me, but so what? I'm worried more about the big picture really."

What bothers Elford is not so much the technology itself as the forces she sees behind it, the "grotesque juggernaut" of companies like Monsanto. "We are rapidly losing the natural world to multinational corporations and governments complicit in their myopic, manic scheme," she wrote in 1998 explaining her decision to rip out some of Monsanto's plants. She called on her fellow citizens to "act for democracy, for diversity, and to restore a land lush with fields, free of genetic pollution, and free of genetic contamination."

FROM THE vantage point of the farm, some of this rhetoric is as mystifying as the dreams of the biotech industry. Agricultural fields such as my brother's are not "lush" and "free of genetic contamination," and they haven't been for centuries. Wherever crops are grown, competing vegetation is suppressed. Agriculture, in fact, is the single human activity that has most profoundly erased "nature" from the planet, with no help whatsoever from genetic engineering. The world's grasslands have been plowed under and forests cut down, sacrificed for the purposes of food production for humans. The world's major food crops, more often than not, grow in fields thousands of miles removed from their native habitats. Soybeans came from China, corn from Central America, and wheat probably originated somewhere in southwestern Asia. Perhaps such plants represent the original "genetic contamination" of Europe and North America. What's more, none of these plants are anything like their wild ancestors. They've been manhandled, genetically speaking, to the point where they often could not even survive in their current form without human aid. So if all of agriculture is shaped by human hands in such profound ways, where does nature end, and intolerable human manipulation begin?

WHEN I first started working on this book, I thought my most difficult challenge would be to get people interested. I'd written about the science and business of genetically engineered crops for ten years, and for most of that time few people seemed to care. Then "Frankenfoods" exploded onto the front pages, and the partisan debate that engulfed them became a blessing and a curse. People started to care about this topic, which I liked. But I sometimes felt as though I'd wandered by accident into a no-man's-land between two hostile barricades. Each side wanted to pull me to safety behind their particular fortress of ideology, information, and logic. I tried to resist them. It was confusing out there in the middle, but the view was better.

This book is not an argument. It's the product of a personal search for understanding. The result of that search is not a set of conclusions, but a story of how genetically engineered foods came to be, and why.

There is plenty here for the cynic: ambition, rivalries, battles over profits, and calculated exploitation of public anxieties. Yet again and again, surprisingly, it's a chronicle of idealism and conflicting ideas about the shape of a better world.

The combatants in this street battle over genetically engineered foods, in fact, often seem caught up in their own romantic visions. On the one side are those who ascribe a purity and wholesomeness to the production of food and a threatening novelty to human intervention in nature. Their nightmares are of scientific hubris and of unnatural creations akin to Frankenstein's monster. On the other side are scientists and companies, convinced that they hold in their hands the genetic tools that will solve agriculture's problems and unlock a glorious new age of plenty.

Again and again in this story, such dreams are rudely contradicted by reality, yet they never fall dead to the ground. Like ghostly apparitions, they reform into new shapes, their power over the human imagination as great as ever.

# 1

# The First Transformation

*January, 1983*

Potentates of the laboratory brought a temporary stir of life to the dilapidated glitz of a former Playboy Hotel in Miami Beach. Their conversations were charged with competition, smoothed by camaraderie. They had gathered to trade tales of scientific accomplishment at the annual Miami Winter Symposium on Molecular Genetics of Plants and Animals.

A short, quiet man with brown hair moved unnoticed among them. He was barely thirty years old and looked more like eighteen. Glances fell on him and slid off again, fixing themselves to personalities more dashing and colorful. Yet behind this modest figure lurked financial and legal resources that eclipsed those of most scientists in the room.

His name was Rob Horsch. He was a tinkerer in the natural world. As a youth, he'd taken cars apart and put them back together again, growing bored with those that ran perfectly and never demanded his attention. Even more passionately, he was a gardener. "I was fascinated by rich soil. I loved the smell of it, the heat of it," he says. "My goal was always to grow things better than what I could find at the grocery store."

Horsch had found his calling in the field of "tissue culture." He spent long days coaxing a clump of plant cells in a petri dish to form roots and shoots and grow into a whole plant. Tissue culture is a somewhat mysterious skill, as much art as science. "Every great tissue culture person I've known has a kind of artistic side," says one scientist who's known many of them. "This sensitivity to color and texture—to be able to look at bumps on the callus [a mass of plant tissue] and say, 'This one will be a leaf.'"

"I would grow the plants on a special light cart with a southeast-facing window," Horsch recalls. "I could pick the individual leaves and tell by the opalescent quality of the underside epidermis that it was going to be good." Fragments of "good" leaf would grow easily and predictably back into plants.

Horsch is a man who respects patience, hard work, and seriousness of purpose. When it came time to find a job, he took one with a company that seemed to exemplify such qualities: Monsanto. Monsanto, in a fit of desperation, boredom, or genius (you could find people at the company who believed each version), had decided to place a bet on the dicey new field of genetic engineering. In order to accomplish the genetic engineering of plants, the company needed experts in tissue culture. It needed Rob Horsch.

Those efforts had prospered. Now the time had come to announce the company's first great triumph in biotechnology. The privilege had fallen, almost by accident, to Horsch. In his pocket was a sheaf of papers, a manuscript that listed him as coauthor.

At that moment, though, Horsch didn't know exactly how he was going to present this paper. He wasn't listed on the schedule of speakers. He went looking for Edward Cocking, a genial Englishman from Nottingham University in England. Cocking was to chair a session on possible ways to insert new genes into plants, a goal that had eluded scientists for more than a decade.

Horsch found Cocking and announced that he wanted a place on the podium. Horsch recalls the moment: "I said, 'I have these really significant new results, and I'd like to be added to the program.' Cocking looked at me as if to say, 'Who . . . are you?'"

"This is a highly unusual request," Cocking responded. "I think you'd better give me a copy of your paper."

Horsch handed over his papers. Nothing opens doors in the world of science like fresh data. Hours later, Horsch was sitting on the podium, facing several hundred of the world's leading figures in his scientific field.

"I was scared to death," Horsch says. "I'd never even given a talk to twenty people before."

COCKING'S SESSION featured a pair of scientific superpowers. Mary-Dell Chilton, from Washington University in St. Louis, was a tart-tongued, intense researcher who'd battled her way into the predominantly male bastion of science. From across the Atlantic came her rivals, Jozef "Jeff" Schell and Marc van Montagu, two Belgians whose collaboration had begun in the ferment of student politics in the aftermath of World War II. The competition between these two laboratories was fierce.

As each scientist proceeded to the podium, it became clear that each was pursuing the same goal, with almost identical tools. Each was working with a tool that had been discovered in nature, a remarkable type of bacteria called *Agrobacterium tumefaciens*. This microbe was able to splice several of its own genes into plant cells, causing them to grow into tumors on the plant. The researchers were trying to take advantage of this unique ability. They hoped to convert *Agrobacterium* from a disease-causing germ into a pack mule, ready to carry new, foreign genes into plant cells.

But before the scientists could use this microbial beast of burden, they needed to accomplish two things. First, they needed to "disarm" the microbe, ripping out the piece of it that caused tumors, without crippling the microbe altogether. That task had just been accomplished. They also needed a way to locate the cells in which the microbe had deposited its new genes and to nurture these genetically "transformed" cells into thriving plants.

To accomplish this second task, each group of scientists had chosen a gene that was known to protect cells from the toxic effects of an antibiotic called kanamycin. Any cell that contained this gene could grow and survive, even in the presence of the antibiotic; the gene served as a kind of bodyguard for genetically transformed cells, enabling them to survive a drug that would kill off all normal cells. So the strategy, in principle, was simple: Include this gene among the packages carried into plant cells by the pack mule, *Agrobacterium*, and it would allow scientists to select only those plant cells into which the mule had carried its cargo. Then scientists could grow those cells into complete, genetically altered plants.

The principle was simple. The execution was not. No one had yet reported success in getting this bodyguard, the kanamycin resistance gene, to function in plant cells.

Mary-Dell Chilton went first. She'd made it to the conference on sheer willpower. Two days earlier, she'd been in the emergency room of a St. Louis hospital, afflicted with a debilitating headache. "Scott [her husband] drove me out to the airport and practically carried me onto that airplane, because I knew I had to be at that meeting," she says.

She'd received a friendly warning from a colleague at Monsanto just a few weeks earlier. The company's researchers, he told her, would deliver some important news regarding gene transfer into plants at the Miami symposium. Chilton's competitive instincts were activated. She contacted her former postdoctoral student Michael Bevan at the Plant Breeding Institute in Britain, urging that he allow her to report on their collaborative work lest they be scooped by Monsanto. Bevan gathered the latest data from his experiments and dictated them over the phone. Chilton summarized the data into a single transparency for an overhead projector. It was a breathless dispatch from the front lines of scientific discovery. Bevan had succeeded in ferrying a kanamycin resistance gene into his tobacco cells, she reported, and the gene was alive and working.

Jeff Schell took Chilton's place at the podium. (Van Montagu remained in the audience.) Schell was "a kind of kingly presence," recalls Chilton. "Always in possession of the land he stood on. He was a brilliant lecturer. Spellbinding. Hypnotic. My feelings for him were admiration, respect, almost a sense of awe."

Schell reviewed the recent history of research on *Agrobacterium*. The real news came in a brief section at the end of his talk. The Belgian researcher reported that his lab soon would be publishing new work very similar to Chilton's and Bevan's. They also had introduced antibiotic resistance genes into plant cells, and the genes appeared to be working. He did not reveal more details, or detailed data.

Then came Horsch, voice quavering, hands shaking. Monsanto's scientists, he said, had done much the same thing. They had inserted the kanamycin resistance gene into snippets of a petunia leaf. Not only that—Horsch had brought along evidence that the gene was working: charts, graphs, and even photographs of pale green clumps of petunia cells growing in petri dishes containing kanamycin. Horsch didn't reveal it at the meeting, but his group also had managed to regenerate whole petunia plants from these clumps of cells. Back in Monsanto's laboratories, those plants were taking root.

The scientists had grasped a locked door and swung it open. Suddenly, a wide vista of experimentation seemed within grasp. This pack mule and bodyguard might also deliver additional genes with much more valuable functions; genes, for instance, to make a plant more productive, or immune to diseases. Any plant that was susceptible to *Agrobacterium*—tomatoes, potatoes, cotton, squash, poplar trees—suddenly seemed within the reach of genetic engineering. "Everybody could see that the gates were opening," recalls Cocking. "It was almost self-evident at that point that it was only a matter of time until other genes were inserted."

Van Montagu and Chilton would always maintain that all three scientists at the meeting in Miami presented the same results. "We were frustrated because Monsanto monopolized the media," van Montagu recalls. "We all had the same story, but no one listened to our story. We were part of the show but not part of the show." Horsch was accompanied to Miami by a representative from the company's public relations department. Monsanto had sent out a press release. Within days, the front page of the *Wall Street Journal* credited Monsanto with a scientific breakthrough.

Among the other scientists, there was also chagrin. After all, Schell and Chilton had devoted their lives to this field. They'd lived and breathed *Agrobacterium* for a decade, while Monsanto's scientists hadn't touched the microbe until two years earlier. Almost overnight, Monsanto had forged to the forefront of their field. And Chilton and Schell, more than anyone else in the room, knew the sources of Monsanto's success. They had only to look in the mirror.

Since the late 1970s, both of them had been engaged as consultants by Monsanto and rewarded with hundreds of thousands of dollars in research funding. Horsch and his comrades from Monsanto had wandered freely in and out of their laboratories. Schell and Chilton had passed along advice and even crucial snippets of DNA that ended up in Monsanto's petunia cells. This was how Monsanto quickly put all the pieces together and was poised to dominate the field.

The scientists in Miami may not have realized it immediately, but in that moment their field had changed. The solitary genius of the independent scientist had given way to the organized, collective, purposeful genius of corporate institutions. It echoed other such turning points in the history of technology. There was the moment during World War II, for instance, when the American military organized a ragtag band of theoretical physicists into the scientific-industrial enterprise known as the Manhattan Project, dedicated to creating an atomic bomb. Similar shifts in power and control took place during the rise of radio, or the telegraph, or, for that matter, the Internet.

Monsanto was not the only company intent on mastering the genetic manipulation of plants in the early 1980s. DuPont had set up laboratories to work on plants, as had Pfizer and the Swiss firm Hoffmann–La Roche. Venture capitalists had financed a raft of small startup ventures. Peter Carlson, founder of a small company called Crop Genetics International, called it "nervous money," rushing to join the latest investment fad.

Yet Monsanto would outrace the large companies and outspend the small ones for most of the next decade. The trio of names on the paper that Horsch delivered in Miami—Steve Rogers, Robert Fraley, and Robert Horsch—would become a familiar incantation, linked forever on a steady stream of scientific papers, and on patents giving Monsanto exclusive rights to new tools of genetic engineering and plants with unprecedented powers.

The ultimate fate of this research would remain uncertain throughout the 1980s. There would be no products to sell for more than a decade. Most of the "nervous money" would run out of patience, sell out, and move on. But a small cadre at Monsanto would stick with their bet, and double it. In their own eyes, they had successfully caught a monster wave of technological innovation, and they were riding it into a bright, clean, hopeful new world.

MONSANTO, LIKE most American companies born in the age of railroads, grew up in the heart of a great urban center. The company's eight-story redbrick headquarters dominated South Second Street along the Mississippi River in downtown St. Louis. In the 1970s, Monsanto retreated from downtown, constructing an insular "campus" in the suburb of Creve Coeur. The low-slung, modernist buildings, laid out in geometrical format and each named with a letter of the alphabet, seem built to withstand the elements. Indeed, it's possible to move from one building to another through a series of tunnels, never encountering the outside world. That physical fact, some say, reflects a mental inclination. Monsanto has been a company that is focused inward.

In the lobby of Building A waits Ernest Jaworski, a diminutive, grandfatherly figure who is probably the single most important reason why Monsanto introduced the world to genetically engineered crops. Jaworski has agreed to lead the way to his old laboratories on the fourth floor of Building U, the place where Jaworski's team of scientists first transported new genes into petunia plants. But Jaworski insists on a small detour, to a modest single-story building next door. We find our way blocked by a ribbon of tape; there's construction under way. But Jaworski seems oddly reluctant to move on or let that building out of his sight. "That was the cell biology building," he says, and there's a note of nostalgic satisfaction in his voice. As Jaworski tells his story, I gradually come to understand: Long before the glory days of biotechnology, that building was Jaworski's kingdom, the first vindication of a solitary, contrarian vision.

Ernest Jaworski had a nickname at Monsanto, rarely mentioned in his presence: "Ernie the Cork." Monsanto was a tumultuous place that chewed up talent and tossed it aside. The company had a reputation for pouring money into new programs, only to chop them down a few years later, sending scores of employees looking for other jobs. Earnings soared and crashed with the fortunes of a few blockbuster products. But after every shakeout, every breaking wave of pink slips, Ernie the Cork somehow bobbed to the surface.

Jaworski possessed a combination of ambition and caution that came naturally, perhaps, to a child of immigrants. His parents sailed from Poland in 1925 and settled in Minneapolis. Ernest was born in

January of the following year. "Maybe I came along on the boat," he says.

He joined the company in 1952 with a freshly pressed doctorate from Oregon State University, and never left. Colleagues remember him as a decent man, a "good-hearted soul," and a hard worker. Some, however, suspected that he was more dedicated to his scientific reputation than to Monsanto's corporate goals. According to one, Jaworski "was trying to be an academic scientist in a corporate environment." His dream, some said, was election to the National Academy of Sciences. At home, he played classical guitar and helped raise several children, none of whom followed him into science. One son became a sculptor.

Jaworski collected few enemies in those early years; more often, potential rivals had a hard time taking the short, enthusiastic man with the crooked grin seriously. Jaworski's head was filled with dreams that sounded quirky, if not downright disloyal to the fraternity of chemists. But those dreams proved irresistible to a succession of Monsanto executives who were looking for new frontiers for an old chemical company.

In the early 1970s, Jaworski was supposed to be working on the next generation of herbicides for farmers to spray on their crops. Instead, he became fascinated by the plants themselves. The idea with herbicides is to kill every kind of plant except those the farmer wants to grow. Unfortunately, chemicals aren't usually that precise; if they leave corn unscathed, they probably do the same to all plants that are similar to corn, and that includes all weedy grasses. "We spent all this money getting selectivity in herbicides. Why not get selectivity in the plants?" Jaworski wondered. Perhaps it might be possible to find—or create!—a gene that allowed corn plants to survive a dose of herbicide that normally killed all vegetation. (Monsanto had just invented such a "broad-spectrum" herbicide, called glyphosate. It would hit the market in 1976 under the trade name Roundup, and its booming sales would astonish the industry.)

None of Jaworski's immediate colleagues seemed interested in this approach; Monsanto was, after all, a chemical company. It employed hundreds of scientists skilled in manipulating chemicals. None of them knew the first thing about manipulating plants.

But Jaworski's steps increasingly followed the distant drum of biology. The tools available for tinkering with plants in the mid-1970s were admittedly crude. Researchers exposed plant cells to chemicals that induced random genetic mutations in the hope that one in a million of these mutations might turn out to create a more valuable version of the plant. Others treated plant cells with enzymes that dissolved their rigid cell walls, creating so-called protoplasts. With these protective barriers out of the way, protoplasts from different plants were fused so that all the genes of both species were combined in one cell. That cell was then placed in a petri dish filled with nutrients, a "cell culture." If the researchers were lucky, they could coax the cell to multiply, form plant tissue, and eventually grow into a new plant, a hybrid that could never have occurred in nature. Thus was born the "pomato," a cross between the tomato and the potato. It was a bit like throwing all the disassembled parts of a car and a tractor into a workshop, hoping that the mechanics could reassemble those parts into a single vehicle that combined strengths of both. More often, one ended up with hybrids that wouldn't even sprout, much less produce fruit. The Pomato, for instance, produced neither tomatoes nor potatoes worthy of the name.

These were speculative ideas, with no guarantee or even probability of success. But Ernie the Cork turned out to have a gift for capturing the imagination of powerful men far above him on the corporate ladder. In 1975, they awarded Jaworski his very own research program on the biology of cells and built the small annex off of Building T for him to use. Jaworski had a team of about thirty researchers practicing protoplast fusion and cell culture.

There was just one problem. Years went by and nothing very useful emerged from Jaworski's laboratory. "He was a master of avoiding deadlines," says one former superior. "In the agricultural division, he was pretty generally thought of as a lightweight." One former executive says Jaworski avoided getting fired only because executives decided "it wouldn't look good." Some called him "Mr. Second" behind his back; he was always the second person to do something, replicating another person's discovery.

But Jaworski did two remarkable things in those years. He became a fixture at scientific conferences, chatting with any scientist who was exploring the inner machinery of plants. While Jaworski's own science faltered, he seemed to have a gift for recognizing talent in others.

"Ernie Jaworski showed up in my lab in 1975," recalls Richard Meagher, now a professor at the University of Georgia. "I was really anxious at the time. I wanted to work with plants, and absolutely no one was interested. And Jaworski told me, 'Don't worry; it's going to happen, and you're going to be in the right place when it does.' It was really important to me. He was a really positive person." In a similar way, Jaworski became acquainted in the mid-1970s with the pioneers of *Agrobacterium,* Mary-Dell Chilton, Jeff Schell, and Marc van Montagu. He nurtured those contacts. Eventually, when the time came, he would exploit them.

JAWORSKI'S HOUR arrived with the great biotechnology craze of 1979 and 1980, which washed across the American business landscape like a giant wave. It began in the summer of 1979 with the announcement that scientists had managed to splice a useful gene—the human gene that produced the body's growth hormone—into bacteria, turning those bacteria into factories for the precious hormone.

Murmurs of an impending revolution grew in volume on June 16, 1980, when the U.S. Supreme Court ruled that living organisms created by the human hand—in this case, a genetically altered microbe—could be patented. The case had been in the works since 1972; a researcher named Ananda Chakrabarty, working at General Electric's Schenectady laboratories, had managed to squeeze genes from one type of bacterium into another, creating a new strain that promised to be useful in cleaning up oil spills. The methods Chakrabarty used quickly became obsolete, but by the time the case bearing his name arrived at the Supreme Court, fortunes were riding on the outcome.

Patent applications covering techniques for modifying bacteria, and the modified bacteria themselves, had been piling up in the chemical division of the patent office. Patent officials refused even to examine them until the Chakrabarty case was decided.

The Supreme Court decision "was a signal that this industry was going to be recognized. And intellectual property rights were going to be recognized," says Kate Murashige, a lawyer and pioneer in gene patenting, who worked for Genentech, one of the original biotech startup companies, in the early 1980s. "The management of Genentech, when I worked there, was convinced that, were it not for patents, they could not survive as a company. It was always considered an essential part of the business plan."

Soon after, the first biotech bull market roared its assent. On October 14, 1980, Genentech offered a million shares of stock for sale at $35 a share. Frenzied buyers bid the price up to $89 within hours. By the end of the day, the company was worth half a billion dollars. It still didn't have a product to sell.

The scientific heart of this first biotech boomlet lay in California, along the San Francisco Bay, in the laboratories at Stanford and the University of California. The boomlet's spiritual heart lay there too, in a place where a great tide of explorers washed up against the continent's western coast, stared at the day's dying light, and contemplated new frontiers beyond the merely geographic. Certainly, small companies devoted to agricultural biotechnology also emerged elsewhere, in Colorado, Wisconsin, and Texas. Yet the early prophets of biotechnology did fit the California stereotype. They were restless and enthusiastic. Sometimes they blithely disregarded cautionary lessons of experience and history. And they had one other significant thing in common: They were relative strangers to agriculture. They promised to transform a world that they barely understood.

"All things seemed possible," says Peter Carlson, who cofounded a small company called Crop Genetics International in 1981. "For the first time, a good story was as important as performance in the marketplace." He adds, with a grin: "It's easier to weave dreams when you don't know the roadblocks ahead."

It was indeed the day of the dream weavers. Among them was David Padwa, a precocious child of New York City who'd made his first few millions in the computer business before he dropped out during the 1960s, traveled the world, and dabbled in environmental causes. He spent 1981 on the road, talking to potential investors, pitching the dream of an agricultural revolution. He raised $55 million and set up a company called Agrigenetics. Admiring reporters wrote that Agrigenetics would have "miracle crops" in hand within five years.

In San Carlos, California, scientist Martin Apple received a stream of visitors at another fledgling company, the International Plant Research Institute, or IPRI. "We are going to make pork chops grow on trees," Apple told the *New York Times*. When that quote appeared in the newspaper, Apple was mortified. He meant, of course, that engineered plants might produce the same nutrients that one finds in a pork chop, not an actual hunk of meat hanging on a tree. Besides which, as an observant Jew, he'd never touched a pork chop in his life. He called the chairman of his board, asking how they might get the *Times* to print a correction. The chairman was amused. "Don't worry about it," he told Apple. "It's great publicity."

In Davis, California, Professor Ray Valentine joined forces with Norman Goldfarb, the son of a prominent Silicon Valley entrepreneur. Goldfarb had been a junior executive at Intel Corporation, but he was restless. He wanted to follow in his father's footsteps and start a company. Within months, the two had founded a free-wheeling, high-spirited, very Californian venture named Calgene.

On the far side of the Atlantic, in the historic Belgian city of Ghent, the explosion of American entrepreneurship awakened Marc van Montagu's sense of European patriotism. Van Montagu was, besides being one of the original pioneers of genetic engineering in plants, a well-connected aristocrat, carrying the inherited title of Baron. In 1983, he helped establish Belgium's own biotech startup, called Plant Genetic Systems.

Meanwhile, in St. Louis, Monsanto's leaders went looking for a new chief scientist, someone who might lead the company's researchers toward this new scientific frontier. They came back with Howard Schneiderman, a big Californian with irrepressible enthusiasm, a member of the National Academy of Sciences and a top administrator at the University of California–Irvine.

Schneiderman soon met Jaworski and decided that this was someone he could trust. The boisterous newcomer made Jaworski his trusted deputy and told the thirty-year Monsanto veteran to start hiring new talent.

THE GENETIC engineering of plants rests on three scientific pillars. First, there is the manipulation of DNA, those impossibly long, impossibly tiny chemical strands, in order to snip out genes that might be useful. Second, there's the matter of transporting those genes into plant cells. Third comes tissue culture, the art of regenerating whole plants from those genetically transformed cells.

During 1980 and 1981, Jaworski assembled all three pieces of the puzzle. They arrived in the form of three scientists: Stephen Rogers, Robert Fraley, and Robert Horsch. All were young. All were bright and driven. But only one harbored oversized ambitions and visions of a business empire in the making.

Horsch certainly did not. The mild-mannered, unassuming expert in tissue culture signed on with Monsanto, he says, because the company seemed "serious." "Everybody else was living in dreams and generalities. Monsanto had a systematic approach." But Horsch was willing to be patient. Genetically engineered plants, he thought, weren't about to come into being overnight, or even within a few years.

Nor was Steve Rogers a man for grand visions. Rogers was a scientist's scientist, a "gene jockey" most comfortable at the laboratory bench, manipulating unseen strands of DNA inside an array of small test tubes. Power and money meant little to him; the ambitions that filled his mind were those of discovery and knowledge. He wasn't looking for a job; he already had one, as an assistant professor at Indiana University. When Ernie Jaworski sent him a letter, Rogers tossed it in the trash. At his wife's urging, he retrieved it and answered, more out of politeness than interest. But when he visited Monsanto, he realized that the company offered incomparably more resources and even, in some ways, more personal freedom to pursue his scientific goals.

Robert (Robb) Fraley, a preternaturally self-confident twenty-eight-year-old, possessed an altogether different, more formidable temperament. He pursued Jaworski, rather than the other way around, and caught up with the Monsanto executive in Boston's Logan Airport one day in 1981. Jaworski still remembers one piece of that first conversation. "I asked him what he'd want to do next. And he said, 'I'd like your job!'"

In fact, Fraley wanted more than Jaworski's job. His ambitions, according to people who knew him during those years, stretched beyond science into business and global agriculture.

Fraley was a farm boy from Illinois. Years later, he would often volunteer that bit of his biography to show his long-standing connection with agriculture. But Donald Lueking, who shared a laboratory bench with Fraley during graduate school, saw little evidence of a hankering for life on the land. Fraley, in fact, was "a little wild," smoking cigars, driving a big Lincoln, shooting pool, and drinking beer. "I remember him saying, 'I don't want to ride that tractor back and forth for days at a time, ever again,'" says Lueking.

Jaworski hired Fraley because he promised to solve the problem of how to ferry genes into plant cells. He'd done his postdoctoral research on liposomes—small fatty structures that are able to move freely through the membranes of plant cells. Fraley thought liposomes could be a kind of shuttle bus for genes. The idea was, if one put bits of DNA into liposomes, the liposomes could carry those genes into plant cells.

Liposomes, unfortunately, turned out to be a scientific dead end. Fraley's real skill proved to be organizing teams of scientists and driving them toward a common goal. He had, as Mary-Dell Chilton put it, "a big wide stripe of leadership right up the middle of him."

"The man is driven," says one scientist who worked at Monsanto in the mid-1980s. "He's the most driven man I've ever interacted with." He was impatient. "I used to want to kill him," says Steve Rogers. "He'd come down daily and ask me about results from an experiment that takes two weeks." He had an instinct for power, how to acquire it and how to use it. He also developed a taste for the trappings of success in the corporate world, showing up on occasion in expensive clothes and a sports car.

But most of all, Fraley possessed unshakeable confidence in the power and future of genetic engineering. "In Monsanto, there's a lot of bright guys, but they didn't exactly know where they were going," says one veteran of the biotechnology industry who's monitored Fraley's entire career. "You dump in Fraley, and he knew where he wanted to go. He was, in my opinion, the best thing that happened to Monsanto."

None of Jaworski's new hires arrived at Monsanto possessing any experience with the organism on which they would build their scientific reputations: *Agrobacterium tumefaciens*. Nor did they possess crucial pieces of DNA that would make it possible to transform plants. Those pieces of the puzzle Jaworski bought. In these transactions, no price was ever named. The currency involved was part cash and part friendship.

AGROBACTERIUM TUMEFACIENS is a wanderer between worlds. It navigates the gulf that divides two great forms of life: prokaryotes and eukaryotes. Eukaryotes account for every life form we can see with the unaided eye: animals, worms, sponges, trees, mosses, and even slime molds. All are made up of cells with certain common characteristics—a nucleus, for example, where tightly wrapped strands of DNA form chromosomes. Prokaryotic life includes the vast realm of bacteria. Prokaryotes consist of a single cell, without a nucleus. When it comes to the structure of cells, humans are closer to slime molds than slime molds are to a prokaryote like *Agrobacterium*.

For most of this century, *Agrobacterium* was like a familiar neighbor who harbors profound secrets behind a slightly irritating facade. Two researchers at the U.S. Department of Agriculture identified and named it in 1907. They discovered that this rod-shaped microbe caused crown galls, tumorlike growths that sometimes sprouted from the stems or trunks of infected plants. Forty years later, Armin Braun, at the Rockefeller Institute for Medical Research, decided that there was something odd about these growths. How, he wondered, could a bacterium cause tumors in plant cells? Experimenting with crown galls, he found something odder still. Tissue from these tumors could survive and flourish on a simple diet of salts or sugar. They didn't need the growth hormones that normally are required to keep plant cells alive. Apparently, *Agrobacterium tumefaciens* permanently altered the plant cells it infected.

Creative minds on both sides of the Atlantic found this discovery intriguing. Some suggested that the bacteria induced a genetic change in the plant cells. A few even wondered if this odd microbe transferred genes directly into the chromosomes of the infected plant cells. In the early 1970s, three groups of researchers led the way in unlocking the secrets of *Agrobacterium*. At the University of Leiden, in the Netherlands, there was Rob Schilperoot, a charismatic figure given to inspired hunches, although his experimental techniques sometimes were faulty. At the University of Washington, in Seattle, there was the team of Eugene Nester, Milton Gordon, and Mary-Dell Chilton. And the Free University of Ghent probably had the largest group, led by the Belgian duo Marc van Montagu and Jeff Schell.

These groups still argue, mostly with good humor, over their respective accomplishments. A scientist working with Schell and van Montagu discovered that the genes responsible for *Agrobacterium*'s special powers were harbored on a giant plasmid, a ring of DNA separate from the microbe's main chromosome. Mary-Dell Chilton and her collaborators, meanwhile, usually get credit for finding specific stretches of DNA from that plasmid firmly anchored within infected plant cells. The experiment that led to this discovery was an enormously complicated race against the clock. "I have never experienced such completely committed teamwork in my entire career, before or since," Chilton recalls. At its conclusion, *Agrobacterium*'s secret stood revealed. Genes were indeed crossing the great biological divide from bacterium to plant and functioning in their new environment. Chilton, Nester, and Gordon wrote years later: "At the time of our discovery there was controversy over the safety of recombinant DNA experiments, but here was a bacterium that was a natural genetic engineer, operating outside the National Institutes of Health guidelines."

Harry Klee, who later went to work at Monsanto, was a graduate student at the University of Massachusetts when he read Chilton's paper establishing the transfer of bacterial DNA to plants. His imagination went into overdrive. "I said to myself, 'This is great! All we have to do is use this to piggyback genes.'" Klee says that paper set the course for his scientific career. "This is what I want to do for the rest of my life," he remembers thinking. He applied to join Mary-Dell Chilton's research group at the University of Washington. But by the time Klee arrived in 1980, Chilton had left, frustrated by her inability to get a regular faculty position at the university. At precisely that moment, Monsanto had decided to begin a crash program on biotechnology, and Mary-Dell Chilton, queen of *Agrobacterium*, landed right on the company's doorstep, at Washington University in St. Louis.

"THERE'S NOTHING like intensity," says Mary-Dell Chilton. "I'm driven. I've always been driven." When she arrived at Washington University, Chilton drove her laboratory toward the forefront of efforts to transfer foreign genes into plants. "You can't imagine how hard I worked during those years," she says. She remembers long nights in the laboratory, tapping away at grant proposals on her IBM Selectric typewriter.

Ernie Jaworski dropped in from time to time. He'd followed Chilton's work through the 1970s, and he'd helped smooth the transition to Washington University by offering funds to support her research. Chilton became a Monsanto consultant. Her laboratories were located in the university's Monsanto Hall, just five miles to the east of Monsanto's headquarters. And Jaworski and his researchers had full access to Chilton's research. One former researcher in Chilton's laboratory recalls his very first day there. At a meeting of the laboratory staff, he looked around and was startled to see Monsanto's Robb Fraley sitting in the corner.

Chilton wasn't the only beneficiary of Jaworski's largesse. The Belgian duo of Jeff Schell and Marc van Montagu also were Monsanto consultants. (Van Montagu cut his ties with Monsanto when he helped set up Plant Genetic Systems, which became a competitor to Monsanto.) There were no formal conditions placed on this funding; today, researchers look back fondly on those days, when scientific collaboration with a major company could be so uncomplicated. "We weren't even required to write a report," says van Montagu.

By 1981, with Howard Schneiderman in place as Monsanto's vice president for research and with the company pouring millions into biotechnology, these relationships became more formal. In his 1981 Plan for Biotechnology, Schneiderman wrote: "We are in the process of establishing long-term and exclusive collaborative programs in fields of intense interest to us, with . . . key researchers at different institutions. . . . This group of collaborators could give Monsanto exclusive access to some of the most powerful and creative talents in these areas of molecular biology today."

The old guard at Monsanto thought the company might lose more secrets than it gained from these scientific collaborations. Nick Reding, head of the Monsanto Agricultural Company, sent Schneiderman a memo suggesting that he might reconsider this "heavy reliance on consultants": "The issues on my mind are ones of security, property, and exclusivity rights."

Reding may not have understood just how much Jaworski's young researchers depended on the academic scientists, and especially on Mary-Dell Chilton. Robb Fraley and Steve Rogers became regular visitors to the Chilton lab. "We talked to those guys two or three times a week," recalls Michael Bevan, the lean, energetic New Zealander who joined Chilton's research team in 1981.

Chilton didn't merely contribute the general idea of using *Agrobacterium* to transform plant cells. She, and her collaborators, also contributed specific snippets of valuable DNA that helped get Monsanto's scientists started down the path toward a genetically engineered plant.

One crucial roadblock was the difficulty of persuading genes that were taken from bacteria to work in plants. For instance, the researchers wanted to use a bacterial gene that protected cells from the toxic effects of an antibiotic. They wanted to put that gene into plant cells; it would be the "bodyguard" that would allow genetically engineered cells to survive and grow into complete, genetically altered plants. But genes that were taken from bacteria didn't work in plants because bacteria and plants recognize different snippets of DNA as the signals, or switches, that turn a gene on or off.

Those signals include the "promoter," a short sequence of DNA that precedes the gene itself, and a "termination sequence" that is attached to the end of the gene. Scientists realized that they had to combine the bacterial gene with plant-type promoters and terminators; the combined strand of DNA—half-bacterial, half-plant—was called a "chimeric" gene, after the mythical chimera, which was part goat, part lion, and part serpent.

In 1981, there were no plant promoters or termination signals in hand. So Michael Bevan, in Chilton's laboratory, decided to take a risk and use a promoter and termination sequence from *Agrobacterium* itself. These signals were part of the baggage that *Agrobacterium* transferred into the plant cell. Even though they originally came from bacteria, these signals appeared to function just fine inside a plant cell.

Bevan set to work finding the most crucial element, the promoter. "Here's where I gave what I think was the key information," he says. He told the Monsanto researchers exactly where the promoter was located. "Having that information, they could then make chimeric genes." Bevan also passed along copies of these pieces of DNA for the Monsanto researchers to use.

"YOU KNOW, Mary-Dell and Monsanto had a falling out at some stage," says Michael Bevan. We're sitting in the elegant lobby of the Waldorf Astoria, on Park Avenue in New York City. Bevan assures me that the hotel wasn't his choice; corporate sponsors who want to learn about the future prospects for biotechnology have flown him to New York and put him up in this place. In the years since his lonely days working in Mary-Dell Chilton's laboratory, Bevan has risen to become one of the scientific leaders of the United Kingdom's John Innes Centre, which some consider the world's most accomplished center of research on plants.

"In the end, I think Mary-Dell realized that Monsanto was shadowing her work, doing it themselves, and patenting it," Bevan says.

"And claiming it as their own? Unjustifiably?"

"The law has settled that, that their claims were justified." Bevan is impassive. "I was terribly naive in those days," he explains. "I don't think I knew what a bloody patent was. I had sort of a British attitude; 'crass commercialism' and all that."

"I assumed that Mary-Dell knew about it, condoned it; that it was just part of the deal that she had established with Monsanto. They were paying for her lab, and the quid pro quo was they got the stuff." He pauses. "I expect that that's a legal fact as well."

PATENTS INSPIRE resentment. They are the no-trespassing signs that block what one presumed to be a public path; the fences between hungry boys and orchards heavy with ripe fruit; the privately owned waterfront real estate. They allow monopolies that are no less profitable for being limited to the span of a generation. And they are the bedrock on which the biotechnology industry is built.

When Howard Schneiderman arrived at Monsanto from the world of the university, he assumed that his job was to create a fertile ground for fresh ideas and new discoveries. The company's executives quickly taught him that there was something else to consider. Discoveries were useful only if they led to a "proprietary position"—in plain words, something approaching monopoly.

On April 6, 1982, Monsanto's president, Richard Mahoney, sent Schneiderman a pointed letter: "What plans do we have to protect our technology—to permit a reward for high-risk research?" And a few months later, Schneiderman took careful notes as another top executive, Lou Fernandez, added another tutorial: "Where are opportunities for proprietary position? For such margins, you need a proprietary position. If you have a good idea, and you can't protect it, it's not a profitable idea."

For young scientists arriving in Monsanto's laboratory from academic laboratories, the procedures for securing the company's intellectual property were eye-opening. Each page of their laboratory notebooks was to be signed and dated, not just by the scientist but by a witness as well. The notebooks had to stay in the laboratory. Every publication had to be cleared by Monsanto's legal staff, lest it disclose information that should first be included on forms filed with the patent office. In fact, if the legal staff had had its way, the scientists would have published as little as possible.

"It was a real shock" to discover that not publishing new findings was a real possibility, remembers Rob Horsch. He eventually came to believe that patents were valuable because they allowed him to publish. If Monsanto's lawyers first filed a patent "disclosure" on some new discovery, establishing the company's claim to exclusive rights, then scientists could freely publish those results. "I'd come to the position, if we file patents, I can talk. I like to talk, so patents are good," says Horsch.

In 1982, the company hired Patrick Kelly as the first patent lawyer devoted solely to biotechnology. "Within a month, I was working double shifts," recalls Kelly. There was feverish activity up and down the long corridor where Jaworski's troops worked. All the pieces were coming together: the kanamycin resistance gene; Michael Bevan's promoter; the pack mule, *Agrobacterium*. By the end of 1982, Monsanto's breakthrough was in hand. Jaworski noted it dryly under "Technical Highlights" in his monthly report: "Development of a proprietary high efficiency transformation system for the introduction of DNA vectors into plant cells." *Agrobacterium* had been tamed and was ferrying antibiotic resistance genes into circular bits of tobacco and petunia leaf. And Rob Horsch was beginning to grow some of those genetically transformed cells into plants.

Now the lawyers swung into action. The Miami Winter Symposium was just a few weeks away. The scientists wanted to announce their successes, and Patrick Kelly wanted to assure that Monsanto maintained a monopoly over their discoveries. "We knew that Schell and Chilton were going to be there, and they were going to generate a set of publications that would be held as prior art," he says. "To get the best patent coverage, we had to get our applications in before that." Kelly recalls those weeks as an "extraordinary" time; "I doubt that I will ever surpass that in an intellectual experience. These are vivid memories that will stay with me forever."

Kelly wrote three patent applications. They arrived at the U.S. Patent Office in Washington on January 17, 1983. A day later, Horsch joined Chilton and Schell on the podium in Miami Beach. (It was Jaworski who'd had the courtesy to call Chilton and let her know that Monsanto would have something important to say in Miami.)

Monsanto's scientists believed that they had won the race. They were confident that the Patent Office eventually would validate their claims, name them the inventors of genetically engineered plants, and grant them exclusive rights to the use of *Agrobacterium*. It was not to be.

Chilton and Schell, it transpired, had learned to play the patent game as well. All of them had submitted their own patent applications. Mary-Dell Chilton's applications were based on work she'd finished a year earlier. She and her collaborators had created genetically engineered plants without resorting to a "selectable marker" such as the antibiotic resistance gene. It was an awkward technique and, in hindsight, not terribly practical, but there they were: the first genetically engineered plants.

Chilton hadn't been able to get Washington University's patent lawyers interested in her accomplishment at first. Her father, a corporate executive in New York, advised going over their heads, meeting instead with the university chancellor. Chilton followed her father's advice, taking along her department chairman for added support. "We sat with Chancellor [William H.] Danforth for about half an hour," she recalls. "I remember [my department head] saying, 'She's invented the wheel! You can do all these things with it!' That was Friday afternoon. Saturday morning, a patent attorney was in my office. We started writing."

Jeff Schell's application was submitted by his employer, the German government's Max Planck Society. Its documents reached the U.S. Patent Office on the very day that Schell appeared in Miami, one day behind Monsanto. Schell's application for a European patent, however, arrived at the European Patent Office in Munich before Monsanto's.

Each of the applicants claimed to have invented much the same thing: the use of *Agrobacterium* in the genetic engineering of plants. The European patent office, because it grants patents strictly based on who files an application first, awarded inventorship rights to Schell's group. In the United States, which awards patents based on who has first invented something, the Patent Office still has not made a decision in the case as of this writing, eighteen years later. Instead, the Patent Office has declared an "interference"—a kind of adjudication procedure—to resolve competing claims from the different inventors. Hundred of millions of dollars could be at stake in the eventual outcome, and each inventor's cause is represented by a different large multinational corporation.

ERNIE JAWORSKI says he doesn't know of any hard feelings harbored by the company's academic collaborators. On the contrary, "I think they were pleasantly surprised that we weren't the ogres that industrial scientists were made out to be." Michael Montague, a longtime associate of Jaworski's, says there really weren't grounds for conflict because Monsanto's scientists and their academic counterparts had different priorities. "Our scientists are rewarded for an economic return," he says. "Academic scientists are rewarded and promoted based on publications."

Yet when Monsanto's former collaborators reminisce about these days, about how they helped to create knowledge and tools to which Monsanto then laid legal claim, there is a mixture of emotions ranging from sympathetic admiration to betrayal. Bevan still counts Rogers, Fraley, and Horsch as friends. Chilton says her feelings toward Monsanto are "some terrible mixture of jealousy and respect and admiration and anger."

Almost fifteen years after the Miami Winter Symposium, as genetically engineered crops spread across the American agricultural heartland, Monsanto nominated Jaworski, Fraley, Rogers, and Horsch for the National Medal of Technology, an award presented annually at the White House. Monsanto officials solicited letters of recommendation from several of the former academic collaborators. Nam-Hai Chua, from Rockefeller University, declined to provide a recommendation. Since he had been the beneficiary of financial support from Monsanto over the years, he wrote, it would be inappropriate for him to recommend the company for such an award. Jeff Schell wrote a warm letter of recommendation, crediting Jaworski with being the first to recognize the revolutionary potential of techniques for introducing new genes into plants. Asked how he remained on such good terms with Monsanto while Chilton did not, Schell responded simply, "The difference is that she was a lot closer to them." Monsanto's representatives did not contact Mary-Dell Chilton.

# 2

# Marching on Washington

Of all the accusations aimed at the genetic engineers, the one that strikes the deepest chords in Western culture is the claim that scientists are engaged in "playing God." It conjures up visions of humans rushing in where they should rightly fear to tread.

The authors of Monsanto's success in biotechnology were by all accounts a hungry, driven crew. Yet their ambitions were strikingly earthbound, the normal ones of success, prestige, and the satisfaction of a job well done. Their transcendent beliefs were the assumptions of modern science: Knowledge is useful; innovation brings progress; progress is good.

Rob Horsch, the company's artful expert in tissue culture, has to be persuaded to speak in religious terms about his work, but he rises to the challenge. Was he "playing God" in coaxing plants to grow from a genetically transformed lump of tissue? No, he says. "If you want to use that language, God gave plants these properties. And he gave us the intellect to plant and harvest, and cook, and select, and breed . . . "; Horsch pauses. "And do tissue culture. All we're doing is harnessing those gifts."

These young genetic engineers did believe that their work would be good for the planet, possibly making it easier to grow food or reducing agriculture's dependence on chemicals. Some of them, working inside chemical companies, often saw themselves as "green" revolutionaries fighting against the entrenched power of the chemists, whom they dismissed as "nozzleheads." They had gone through university and graduate school during the 1970s, in the heyday of environmentalism. They'd seen DDT banned and Earth Day celebrated. Chemicals represented a dirty and regrettable past, and biology was the savior.

At Monsanto those views "came from the very top," says Pam Marrone, a researcher at Monsanto during the late 1980s. "I remember having lunch with [then-CEO] Dick Mahoney and him saying, 'Because of parathion [a particularly hazardous insecticide], I don't ever want to be in chemicals again. And that's why we're in biotechnology.'"

"During these years, all of us who went into biology were influenced by the wave of environmentalism," says Willy de Greef, who worked first for Plant Genetic Systems in Belgium, then the Swiss company Novartis. "The idea was reduce chemicals with biologicals or with genetics." Fred Perlak of Monsanto says much the same thing. "We were all children of the sixties and the seventies. We'd all read *Silent Spring;* we knew the connection between 2–4-D [a common herbicide] and 2–4–5-T, Agent Orange." Yet this self-image held a hazard. Those who occupy, in their own minds, the moral high ground are usually the least able to accept criticism or even comprehend it. When the genetic engineers found themselves attacked by a new generation of environmentalists, they were incredulous and hostile.

LEONARD GUARRAIA was Monsanto's head of regulatory affairs for much of the 1980s, assigned to charm and cajole officials in Washington. He was perfect for the part, a jovial, profane, oversized man who loved a good dinner, a good story, and a good laugh.

One day in the early 1980s Guarraia returned to St. Louis from Washington with a videotape in his hand. It was a tape of biotechnology's most vociferous and implacable foe, Jeremy Rifkin, rousing an assembly of environmentalists into action. Guarraia took the tape up to Monsanto's executive suite on the top floor of D Building, known as "The Kremlin."

Monsanto's executives were of the old school, hard-bitten and gruff. The era had not yet arrived in which it became fashionable for an executive to cultivate informality, break down office walls, or be seen at a keyboard. Cussedness was permitted—in some cases, encouraged. Not long before, two feuding vice presidents with adjoining offices had gone years without speaking directly to each other.

They all were men, all in suits; they gathered around the television screen and listened to a description of themselves that they could not have imagined. They were used to being reviled as polluters or defilers of the landscape. They knew how to respond to such charges. But Rifkin's diatribe was something new. It was particularly shocking because as far as these executives were concerned biotechnology barely existed. For most of them it was merely a research project with highly questionable commercial prospects. Yet already it appeared to have struck fear and anger into the hearts of the people depicted on this videotape.

The exact text of that particular speech no longer exists, but Rifkin made many such speeches in the early 1980s. Loquacious, self-aggrandizing and self-mocking at the same time, he was more responsible than anyone else for awakening popular fears about the consequences of biotechnology. Rifkin infuriated scientists and fascinated journalists. He recognized few political boundaries. A nonobservant Jew with a background in leftist causes, he managed to form coalitions with creationists, religious conservatives, and family farmers.

Genetic engineering, Rifkin announced, could "very well pose as serious a threat to the existence of life on the planet as the bomb itself." Its goal was the reduction of life to its smallest component parts, which then could be manipulated at will. DNA, proteins, cells, and whole organisms would simply be the cogs of new biological machines, shaped to conform to human desires. If genetic engineers had their way with bacteria today, Rifkin argued, they would engineer new kinds of dogs tomorrow, and human beings soon after that. "Bioengineering is coming to us not as a threat but as a promise; not as a punishment but a gift," Rifkin wrote in his book *Algeny*. Who could turn down the chance to create more productive crops or heal genetic diseases? The price, he insisted, was the human soul. In this new world, creation would no longer be sacred. Human life would no longer have intrinsic worth. All of creation would be a *human* creation, subject to no higher law or morality. In a bioengineered world, "we are responsible to nothing outside ourselves, for we are the kingdom, the power, and the glory, for ever and ever."

The Monsanto executives were dumbfounded. "Is this real? Do people really believe this stuff?" they asked. Then, "Mahoney's gotta see this."

When Dick Mahoney, Monsanto's chief executive, arrived, he was in a foul mood. "This better be good," he snarled. "I've got three minutes."

Twenty minutes later, he was still watching.

"Gentlemen," said Guarraia, "this is what we're up against."

WILL CARPENTER was perhaps the one person in the room, apart from Guarraia, for whom the videotape held no surprises. Carpenter is a son of Mississippi, a gracious, courtly man who cultivates friends and knows how to hold his tongue in the presence of adversaries. For many years, he served as a kind of diplomat for Monsanto, meeting with government officials and representing the company at various councils of the chemical industry. He'd been following the early debates over biotechnology closely. He desperately wanted to avoid what he considered the chemical industry's past mistakes when it came to dealing with government regulation.

Carpenter says he "accumulated a lot of scar tissue" during the chemical wars of the 1970s, which pitted environmentalists against industry. He was tired of being the bad guy and, on top of that, losing.

"The chemical industry's history was: faced with regulation, it would just throw rocks," Carpenter says. "It made enemies, and regulations were passed anyway."

With biotechnology, Carpenter saw the chance for a new beginning. During strategy sessions within Monsanto in 1983 and 1984, Carpenter pressed his case. The only way we'll bring biotech products to the market is if the public is assured that they are safe, he argued. That means we need the government's stamp of approval. So let's not repeat the futile battles of the past. This time let's *ask* for regulation! We'll be on the inside, helping to shape those regulations so we can live with them.

Carpenter, of course, wanted a particular kind of regulation. He wanted an efficient and predictable process, one that gave companies the assurance that if they fulfilled a clear list of requirements their products could enter the marketplace. Carpenter did *not* want entirely new laws drafted to cover biotechnology. There was no telling what mischief might result if Congress got involved.

But when Carpenter took this message to Washington, he entered a surreal new environment. Ronald Reagan was in the White House; regulations were out of favor. Carpenter ended up arguing not just with small biotech companies like Genentech, which opposed any special regulations for biotechnology, but also with government officials themselves. True-blue Reaganites and even some career civil servants took the view that a drug produced using genetically altered bacteria should be regulated just like any other drug. And a tomato produced with the aid of gene-splicing should be regulated just like a tomato created through traditional breeding methods—which is to say, not at all.

An official at the Food and Drug Administration (FDA) named Henry Miller led the opposition to any special regulations aimed at biotechnology. Miller was the FDA's designated spokesman on biotechnology. Unfortunately for his own career, when Miller got involved in heated debates, he felt an irresistible urge to call his opponents insulting names. Environmentalists critical of biotechnology were "troglodytes" or "intellectual Nazis," not to mention ignorant of essential scientific facts. The entire Environmental Protection Agency in Miller's view was "science-challenged." Miller also came to believe that Monsanto's campaign for regulations on biotechnology was really intended to squeeze out smaller, more nimble but less well funded competitors. Monsanto could easily afford to spend millions of dollars to test a new product; small startups like Calgene could not.

"Henry has more or less called us traitors. He gets very intense," says Carpenter. "He really thought he was helping us. But I told him once that we couldn't stand much more of his help."

Guarraia is less polite. "Henry Miller," he says grimly, "did more harm to biotechnology than Jeremy Rifkin ever did. He put the government completely at odds with the critics."

Those critics, a diverse group that included Rifkin, several environmentalist groups, and a few Democratic leaders in Congress, pushed for an entirely new set of regulations to govern biotechnology.

Their leader on Capitol Hill was a young congressman named Albert Gore. Gore had crafted an image of pragmatism; political observers numbered him among the "Atari Democrats," who rejected ideology in favor of pragmatic, workable solutions. The "Atari Democrats," as the name implied, liked new technology. It seemed to offer new possibilities for overcoming entrenched divisions rooted in an earlier era. But Gore's fascination with technology went beyond pragmatism. He sometimes sounded like an amateur futurist, preoccupied with visions of a radically different world in the making. This tendency gave rise to an odd alliance across the aisle with the "conservative revolutionary" Newt Gingrich. Together, Gore and Gingrich sponsored several bills calling on the government to pay closer attention to the impact of new technologies.

During the early 1980s, Gore became one of Congress's leading watchdogs on biotechnology. He cast a skeptical eye on gene-splicing, on the rush of private investment into this new technology, and on the Reagan administration's fitful, often reluctant efforts to regulate it. For too long, Gore declared, government had arrived on the scene of technological innovation long after its course was set, sometimes after lasting damage had been done. Here was a chance to assert the public's interest during a technology's infancy. In different ways, Gore's hopes meshed with those of Monsanto's Will Carpenter: New technology seemed to offer the possibility of a fresh start, a chance to do things better, redeeming the sins and failures of the past.

Such naive hopes were dashed. The 1980s witnessed a series of vicious battles between environmentalists and the Reagan administration over biotechnology. Those battles left behind a perception, rooted partly in reality, that the government had to be dragged unwillingly into any regulatory role at all.

The Reagan administration eventually unveiled its plan for regulating biotechnology in 1985. It was close to what Monsanto had wanted all along. The plan called for no new legislation. Biotechnology was a new way to produce the same old things, the government said, so existing laws covering food, pesticides, and plants were sufficient. Under this "coordinated framework," the Food and Drug Administration would make sure that foods produced through biotechnology were safe, the Environmental Protection Agency would approve any new pesticides, and the Department of Agriculture would watch for any special risks that genetically engineered crops might pose to the environment. Environmentalists immediately condemned the plan as weak and full of holes. In their eyes, the government had lost its credibility as a guardian of the public, and no government "seal of approval" obtained under this system would carry much weight.

Yet for all the emotions aroused by this battle, it was confined to a small group of Washington insiders. Occasional firestorms of controversy erupted over proposals to release genetically altered versions of microscopic bacteria into the environment and over future prospects for altering the genetic makeup, or even the possible cloning, of human beings. Such things seemed threatening and ominous, closer to Jeremy Rifkin's vision of the world to come. The idea of altering the genetic makeup of plants, however, failed to arouse great passions. Soybeans or tomatoes growing securely in a field seemed relatively innocuous. Field trials of genetically engineered crops generally came off without a hitch.

Perhaps the most fateful consequence of the early debate over biotechnology had nothing to do with government policy or legislation. It was instead a matter of language. Journalists, biotech opponents, and corporate officials alike referred to "genetically engineered organisms" or "genetically modified organisms." When such a plant was grown outside a sealed greenhouse, it was said to be "released" into the environment. Regulations spoke of "deliberate release." Such words created mental images of forms of life that were different in some fundamental and possibly threatening way. Such "organisms" required control lest they proliferate and devour.

Scientists and biotech entrepreneurs sometimes cursed such terms and blamed Rifkin and his allies for promulgating them. In fact, the enthusiasts of biotechnology had mostly themselves to blame. It was the genetic engineers, after all, who called the splicing of one or two genes into a cell "genetic transformation." This choice of words revealed their pride of authorship and implied that they had indeed "transformed" a plant, creating something new, different, and (with a wink toward Wall Street) uniquely valuable. Inevitably, those who were wary of biotechnology would turn this notion on its head, sensing a threat where others perceived only promise.

# 3

# "Everything Was Worth Doing"

For a few years in the early 1980s, the pioneers of genetic engineering were simply caught up in the fun of it all. They sometimes spoke as though genes were becoming mere playthings in their hands.

Mary-Dell Chilton abandoned the academic world. In the spring of 1983, she left St. Louis for Research Triangle Park, North Carolina, where she set up a new biotechnology operation for Ciba-Geigy, the Swiss chemical giant. "The solutions are coming very fast now," she told *Business Week* in 1984. "In three years, we'll be able to do anything that our imaginations will get us to."

Ernie Jaworski dubbed the fourth floor of U Building, the lair of Monsanto's genetic engineers, U-4ia. The spirit of the place was indeed euphoric. Many of those who worked there look back on the years 1983 to late 1985 as a kind of golden age. They felt—they *knew*—that, when it came to knowledge about the inner workings of a plant's genetic machinery, they lived at the center of the scientific universe.

A laboratory picture from 1985 shows a scruffy band of researchers, their average age a mere thirty-one. Rogers, Horsch, and Fraley, the elders, already have the look of managers. Fraley, the undisputed leader, is turning prematurely bald. Contemplating the camera with a calculating gaze, he looks a bit like Lenin. Fraley was the scientist most drawn to the language of business and the goals of the company's leaders, who were paying the bills. It was Fraley who conducted impromptu inspections of laboratory notebooks to make sure that each page containing significant data was signed and countersigned in preparation for possible courtroom challenges to Monsanto's patents.

Among the most disheveled, unpolished faces is that of Harry Klee, who arrived at Monsanto in 1984. "I had sworn I would never work in industry," Klee recalls. "But when I got to Monsanto, it was just instantly apparent that if I wanted to do plant biotechnology, this was the place to be." It wasn't just that Monsanto offered superior resources, Klee says. Paradoxically, it was also a much more collegial place. In academia every colleague is also a competitor; every collaboration involves a negotiation over credit. At Monsanto, Klee says, much of that was stripped away. "There was less ego involved."

The genetic transformation of plants rapidly became routine. Genetically altered petunia plants filled the laboratory with a splendid array of colors. Those petunias remain Jaworski's strongest memory of that time; it was a "thrill," he says, "knowing that all of them had our genes in them."

"Anything was worth doing because it was new," says Steve Rogers. Almost every conceivable question needed answering. No one could be sure, for instance, whether new genes would be inherited normally by future generations of plants or rejected as unnatural additions. No one knew how the genes would respond to different growing environments or whether the effects of inserting a new gene would be identical from plant to plant. And no one knew exactly where *Agrobacterium* deposited new genes.

The petunias answered those questions. Generation after generation of these plants carried the foreign genes; they were inherited as reliably as floral colors. By analyzing the pattern by which the genes were inherited, researchers also deduced that foreign genes were inserted purely at random into a plant's chromosomes. Steve Rogers collaborated with Nam-Hai Chua, at Rockefeller University, in a series of experiments with a gene from the common pea plant that responded to light. The question was, would it behave the same way in a different organism? The researchers transferred the gene to petunias, and, as it turned out, the gene behaved exactly the same way. The "unity principle" propounded by the pioneers of molecular biology stood vindicated: Genes maintained their function without regard to the organism in which they were found. "A lot of these things where people now say, 'Oh, of course that works'; nobody knew that then. They were important questions," says Rogers.

THE EARLY days of genetic engineering revealed other phenomena that plant engineers often prefer not to talk about, perhaps because these phenomena undermine the image of this enterprise as "engineering" at all. Engineering implies something very precise and predictable. Yet it became obvious that, when genetically altered *Agrobacteria* transferred their genes into petunia plants or tomatoes, the results varied enormously.

Monsanto's genetic tinkerers discovered, for instance, that the random placement of new genes in plant chromosomes created random variation in how those genes functioned. One transformed plant "expressed" its new gene powerfully; in another the gene barely whispered its presence, and in a third the gene was completely silent. The variation apparently was due to something scientists call, with deliberate vagueness, "position effects." Some parts of the chromosome seem to be more active than others: If the new gene lands on a particularly active part of the chromosome, it will surge into action like a seed landing on fertile soil. Other parts of the chromosome, perhaps because of their physical structure, produce less dramatic results. In some cases, the cell will recognize the new gene as a foreign import, swing into action, and "silence" it.

Then there were the odd genetic mutations that resulted from growing plants from a few cells rather than seeds. Some plants that emerged from the transformation laboratories were stunted in their growth, or had odd-shaped leaves and flowers, or exhibited other genetic abnormalities. The cause of these effects also is unknown; some speculate that the shock of forcing a plant cell to grow under these conditions unleashes bits of DNA called transposons, which are capable of jumping from one spot to another on the plant's chromosomes, sometimes disrupting other genes in the process.

Colin Tudge, the erudite British writer about all things biological, proposes ditching the idea of genetic "engineering" entirely and using instead the term "genetic gardening." A gardener may plant, weed, and water her garden, but the harvest remains uncertain. Like the plant cell, a garden is a complex system that remains just beyond complete human control and outside the predictability of "engineering."

MONSANTO'S DOMINANCE, both real and imagined, of genetic engineering in plants provoked much envy and rancor among rival scientists. And few subjects aroused more resentment than Monsanto's claim of ownership over a powerful genetic tool called the 35S promoter.

A promoter is a short strand of DNA that activates the gene to which it is linked. The 35S promoter was discovered in a disease called the cauliflower mosaic virus, which infects cauliflower and many other related plants. Early in the 1980s, scientists who studied this virus noticed that when the virus infected a plant cell the virus's genes went into overdrive. Somewhere in the virus's DNA there appeared to be a powerful engine—a promoter—driving those genes. The hunt began to find that promoter, and tame it.

Many scientists in laboratories scattered from Paris to California had a hand in searching through the virus's DNA and locating the promoter. One of them, Richard Gardner, worked at Calgene alongside a flamboyant Italian scientist named Luca Comai. Comai, who now teaches at the University of Washington, is convinced that Gardner gave Monsanto a valuable hint by "blabbing" about an experiment showing that the 35S promoter, rather than several other promoters within the virus, was a superior gene engine. "Sometime in 1982, the Monsanto guys came by," says Comai, who seems to find the story more entertaining than painful. As Comai recalls the scene, Gardner proudly showed off his data, and the visitors from St. Louis were transfixed. "Their eyes were popping out of their sockets. It's a very vivid memory of mine," says Comai.

But the job of snipping that particular bit of DNA out from the rest of the virus seemed painfully laborious to Gardner and Comai. They decided to look for something a little easier. Comai still believes that this decision, born of frustration at the prospect of months at the lab bench, cost Calgene sole ownership of the 35S promoter.

Monsanto had the manpower to throw at this problem, however, and it also had free access to research carried out by one of the leading experts on promoters—Nam-Hai Chua of Rockefeller University—who was a Monsanto consultant. Together the scientists not only isolated the promoter but also ran a series of trials pitting several different promoters against each other to see which had the most power. "They had the horses to do it," says one of the company's consultants. "Monsanto would compare them side by side, and they wouldn't tell you what the results were. But they proved conclusively that the 35S was by far the best in many different kinds of plants."

On April 13, 1984, Monsanto sent a new package to the U.S. Patent Office, claiming rights to any man-made genes incorporating the 35S promoter. The company's claims would be granted nearly a decade later.

THERE'S AN official history of Monsanto's foray into agricultural biotechnology, written in 1997 and published in *Monsanto* magazine. It includes a photograph of the company's first field trials of genetically engineered plants. In the background are billowing white clouds. In the foreground is a machine for planting seedlings. Sitting on it are four young men, each with a box of tomato seedlings. Three of the four are company heroes: Steve Rogers, Robb Fraley, and Rob Horsch. The fourth is not identified.

That man's name is Roger Beachy, then a young assistant professor at Washington University in St. Louis. Beachy collaborated closely with Monsanto's scientists over many years, and few people understood better the blessings and curses that accompanied such a close relationship with the emerging juggernaut of plant biotechnology in St. Louis.

Beachy was, and remains, a gregarious, athletic man brimming with enthusiasm. He'd struggled to find a job in the academic world, having burned through two postdoctoral research positions before finally finding a job at Washington University. In the early 1980s he was anxious to make his mark.

Beachy had long been intrigued by the ways that plants develop resistance to certain viruses. When a plant is exposed to one virus, it sometimes becomes immune to infection by other viruses. Scientists had named the phenomenon "cross-protection," but they didn't understand how it worked, and they didn't know how to induce it without first subjecting the plant to disease.

Beachy's idea was that, since there was something about the virus that blocked further infection, perhaps he could induce the same effect by inserting pieces of the virus, one gene at a time, into a plant. By themselves these genes should be harmless, but Beachy was hoping one of them would activate the phenomenon of cross-protection. Any gene might have worked, but Beachy decided to start with the most obvious piece: the gene that produced the virus's protective surface, or "coat protein."

Beachy proposed the idea to the U.S. Department of Agriculture, but officials there turned him down. "They said, 'No, it won't work and it's not worth the effort,'" Beachy recalls. Beachy then turned to Monsanto against the advice of some academic colleagues. "There were people who said, 'Don't talk to them; they'll steal everything you've got,'" says Beachy.

Unknown to Beachy, another group of scientists in England was beginning exactly the same quest. In a blind race with each other, the two groups located the gene for the coat protein of a virus that infects tobacco, snipped it out, hooked it up to different promoters, and shuttled the gene into tobacco plants.

In England the technique failed. In Beachy's hands it worked. Tobacco plants that contained one gene from the tobacco mosaic virus did develop resistance to infection, exactly as he had hoped.

The difference between the two experiments, between fame and a footnote, lay in one fact: Beachy's gene, it turned out, produced about fifty times more protein than the English group's. It did so in part because Beachy had access to Monsanto's genetic toolkit. Beachy's gene was linked to the 35S promoter, and the promoter was driving the gene harder, causing it to spin out more copies of the virus's coat protein. That success launched Beachy's career, eventually landing him a spot in the National Academy of Science.

Those were the benefits of riding the Monsanto tiger. There were days, though, when Beachy wondered how the ride would end.

Monsanto began its own program of research on virus resistance, dwarfing Beachy's own, and Monsanto officials often described virus resistance as the company's own invention, leaving Beachy out of the picture entirely. "I was truly offended," says Beachy. "But part of the culture I come from is one of looking past it. It doesn't do any good to stay dissatisfied or angry; you sort of make the best of where you are and move forward. And after a while I realized this is just the way it is. They are good collaborators. They had to feel that they were owners of it in order to promote the company. And then you say, 'That's what companies do!' You forgive and you go on."

The "culture" that Beachy refers to is a religious one. He grew up the son of a Mennonite pastor (who died unexpectedly when Beachy was in high school). It's a pacifist tradition, one which celebrates sixteenth-century martyrs as heroes and which until recently forbade members from using the courts to remedy wrongs or recover damages. Beachy went to Goshen College, a small school in Indiana which has as its motto "Culture for Service."

Beachy exudes that sort of idealism. He's most passionate when talking about the uses of biotechnology in bettering the diet and lives of the world's poor. But Beachy also has a powerful pragmatic streak and a taste for the jet-setting life. If success required giving up some credit, and much of the control, over a discovery, so be it.

The story of virus resistance then took an unexpected turn. The tiger simply walked away: Virus resistance, for all its allure as a scientific phenomenon, promised minimal profits. Viruses simply aren't big problems for the major crops of commercial agriculture such as corn, cotton, and soybeans, and Monsanto's business executives didn't consider virus-resistant versions of tomatoes or papaya worth the effort. Monsanto lost interest in Beachy's innovation.

For Beachy it was another frustrating lesson in the ways of business. Within Monsanto, meanwhile, the genetic engineers were learning similar lessons, in spades. It was becoming brutally clear that scientific exploration wasn't enough. Their masters, the company's managers and owners, wanted at least the promise of numbers on the bottom line.

RICHARD MAHONEY became CEO of Monsanto in 1984, before he turned fifty, and two years later made *Fortune* magazine's list of "America's toughest bosses." Mahoney didn't seem to mind. "Forgiveness is out of style, shoulder shrugs are out of fashion. Hit the targets on time without excuses," he told *Fortune*. Fifteen years later, he's still blunt and opinionated.

He recalls trying to drum some business sense into his scientists. "I used to go down there and address the researchers," he says.

"I'll never forget the first time I used the phrase 'We are not in the business of the pursuit of knowledge; we are in the business of the pursuit of products.' You could have heard a pin drop. They were furious."

Mahoney finally came up with an image for what he wanted from his scientists. "You know, I've just come back from Germany, and I've got a metaphor for technology research," he told them. "We were driving down the Autobahn at about 150 miles an hour toward Frankfurt. Every twenty kilometers or so there was a sign for an exit ramp that said *'Ausfahrt'* [German for 'Exit']. That reminds me of our R&D. We're barreling along with all this expensive equipment, but we've got to get a product every now and then! An *Ausfahrt!*"

For all his toughness, Mahoney in fact had a soft spot in his heart for the biotechnology project. Many others at Monsanto considered it a foolish, harebrained boondoggle. Much of the hostility was aimed at Ernie Jaworski and his boss, biotechnology's cheerleader at Monsanto, Howard Schneiderman.

Schneiderman, who died of leukemia in 1990, is now firmly lodged in Monsanto's hall of fame. People describe him as "mesmerizing"; a "magical figure." But in truth Schneiderman is revered more now than he was at the time. He was a foreigner at Monsanto, a Jewish scientist from Brooklyn in a company filled with Midwestern engineers, a Democrat among Republicans, and a lover of ideas in an enterprise that valued money-earning results. "I thought he was a buffoon," says Robert Kaufman, Schneiderman's archrival, who headed research within Monsanto's agriculture division. "Still do."

The rivalry was rooted at least partly in the men's contrasting scientific backgrounds. Kaufman is a chemist to his core. Schneiderman, who'd made his reputation studying insects, considered chemistry a played-out science, and thought that the sooner Monsanto abandoned it for the possibilities of genes and cells, the better.

"He kept saying, 'It's a new biological world!' I'd say, 'No, it's a chemical world!'" says Kaufman, sitting in the conference room and library of Gateway Chemical Technology, a small company he founded after leaving Monsanto. Kaufman doesn't seem bitter about old battles waged and lost, but he also hasn't revised his opinions. "Schneiderman didn't realize in his strange biological arrogance that genes were just chemicals getting other chemicals made," says Kaufman.

But the feud, at least in Kaufman's view, also divided scientists from the sort of people Kaufman calls "salesmen." Kaufman considered himself the scientist, his feet firmly set on the hard, uncompromising facts of the natural world; Schneiderman was the salesman, "all California wonderful," a big talker with a bubbly personality.

Kaufman had his own biotech program, led by scientists who'd spent decades in the company. They were Monsanto men, most of them chemists by training, with a sense for what it takes to keep a company in business. They resented the money flowing into Jaworski's laboratories filled with fragile petunia blossoms. Those flowers symbolized everything that was noncommercial, impractical, and pointless about Schneiderman's operation. The petunias, recalls Kaufman, "made everybody in [Monsanto's agriculture division] insane."

Jaworski's scientists knew what people thought of their petunias and joked about it. As part of the evening entertainment at the laboratory Christmas party in 1984, Robb Fraley displayed a picture of a plate covered with a sumptuous salad of petunia leaves and flowers. The caption read, "New Marketing Strategy: Eat more petunias!". The laughter, however, contained an undercurrent of foreboding.

Act I of Monsanto's quest for genetically altered crops, the era of untrammeled scientific exploration, was about to end. The curtain finally came down at the end of 1985. Monsanto lost nearly a hundred million dollars that year. It was also the year that Mahoney bought the drug maker G. D. Searle & Company for $2.7 billion. Searle represented Mahoney's long-sought foothold in the pharmaceutical business, but the transaction took Monsanto deep into debt. Mahoney also was fed up with the constant bickering between his company's rival biotechnology programs.

Mahoney, who never minded playing the tough guy, called Howard Schneiderman into his office, together with Robert Kaufman's boss, the president of the agricultural company. "I told them, 'You guys have got to combine these programs, or I'll do it," he recalls. "So they came to an accommodation."

On November 4, 1985, Schneiderman scrawled a few cryptic notes into one of the small black notebooks that he often carried with him that escaped Monsanto's shredders after his death: "Dreadful meeting with Dick Mahoney. Destroy Central R&D." Two days later, he found himself spitting up blood. Alarmed, he went to the doctor, who could find nothing wrong. As the bleeding subsided, the doctor decided that a blood vessel in Schneiderman's throat had burst, probably from stress.

Schneiderman and his proteges, however, emerged from the blood-letting in better shape than their rivals. Robert Kaufman, Jaworski's adversary, realized that he was being shown the door. "It was a question of which group would go," he says. "There was no compromise with Schneiderman. He was going to get rid of the chemists. They must have canned sixty people." The layoffs happened just before the end of the year, and some called it a "Christmas massacre." Kaufman himself was gone within six months.

The two groups were melded into one by force. From that point on, the researchers knew that their survival at Monsanto hung on their ability to create genetically modified plants that weren't just interesting but valuable. The search was on for blockbuster genes, gifts from nature that the scientists might be able to claim as their own, transfer into plants, and sell for hundreds of millions, if not billions, of dollars.

It was a demanding standard. The fact was that, despite their ambitious promises, genetic engineers still couldn't do very much, and those things they *could* do—such as induce virus resistance—often weren't commercially valuable. The genetic engineers were not yet masters of creation. They were more like intruders in an unfamiliar darkened house, walking only where haphazardly placed windows shed bits of light. There were many competing bands of intruders in this house, all trying to grasp the same few enticing treasures.

# 4

# The First Useful Gene: *Bacillus thuringiensis* and Its Many Inventors

If life followed myth, Wayne Barnes might have become the inventor of genetically engineered, insect-proof plants. Barnes is by most accounts one of the more creative scientific minds among the biochemists and molecular biologists at Washington University in St. Louis. He is also cantankerous and headstrong. "Wayne has more good ideas than he knows what to do with," says one colleague. "But I don't collaborate with him." Barnes is an example of that classic American hero, the solitary genius inventor, etched in the public's mind by tales of Thomas Edison, Alexander Graham Bell, and Eli Whitney. In the myth that they represent, the individual triumphs over the organization, new demolishes old, and an endless frontier of opportunity beckons. But reality isn't always that simple.

In the spring of 1982, Barnes found unwelcome worms at work in his yard. "I had two apple trees beside my house," he says. "They were just defoliated. My father's an entomologist, so I said, 'Dad, what can I use against these insects?'"

"He went through a list of insecticides, parathion and so forth. I wasn't too interested in them. And then he said, 'Well, you can always use Bt.'"

"I'd never heard of it!" said Barnes, still exasperated after all these years. He blames his instructor in bacteriology at the University of

Wisconsin, who never bothered to mention *Bacillus thuringiensis*. Poor education, Barnes thinks, cost him at least half a year in the race to capture one of biotechnology's most valuable prizes.

Barnes went to the library. *Bacillus thuringiensis*, he learned, was a species of bacteria that lived in the soil. Japanese scientists identified it in 1901 as the source of a mysterious epidemic among the nation's silkworms. The microbe secretes a protein that is deadly to many caterpillars. When a caterpillar ingests the protein, an enzyme found in the insect's gut cuts the protein in two, activating it. The activated toxin then eats away at the insect's digestive system, and the caterpillar shrivels up and dies. There are many different strains of the bacteria, and different strains are effective against different kinds of insects. Barnes also discovered—to his delight—that just the year before, scientists at the University of Washington had isolated the gene that produced Bt's toxin.

As it happened, Barnes in his professional life had been looking for exactly this sort of thing: a useful gene that he could transfer into plants. The laboratory of his faculty colleague Mary-Dell Chilton wasn't far away. Barnes, with his expertise in working with DNA, had even helped Chilton work out some of the details of *Agrobacterium* and how to use it as a tool for inserting new genes into plant cells. "Mary-Dell and I were talking to each other all the time," says Barnes. "We were finishing each other's sentences for a couple of months there. And I thought, now what gene could I express in plants that would be interesting? When I found out about Bt, the search was over. I decided to try it."

Splice the gene from Bt into plants, Barnes thought, and voilà!—the plants would poison caterpillars.

Unfortunately for Barnes, he had a host of competitors. *Bacillus thuringiensis* was too perfect a target for the fledgling biotechnology industry to ignore. "It was there for the taking," says Pam Marrone, an entomologist who worked at Monsanto in the mid-1980s. It was a single gene that promised immediate and dramatic effects. It promised to fend off insects that preyed on corn, tomatoes, potatoes, and—the biggest prize—cotton. Cotton farmers spent hundreds of millions of dollars each year fighting the tobacco budworm and the cotton bollworm. Biotechnologists could imagine a day when those farmers spent that money instead on high-priced, genetically engineered cottonseeds. Barnes, because of his apple trees and his collaboration with Mary-Dell Chilton, had a head start. But he was just one scientist, competing with such companies as Agracetus, Agrigenetics, Plant Genetic Systems, and Monsanto.

Undaunted, Barnes plunged into the project. First he needed a Bt gene. Each strain of Bt had its own form of the toxin gene. But getting one's hands on any of them was no trivial matter in 1984. Barnes couldn't use the gene that had been isolated at the University of Washington several years before; that research had been partially funded by the Cetus Corporation (the parent company of Agracetus), which as a consequence owned the rights to it. (The restriction was a mark of the changes that biotechnology was bringing to biology. Up to this point, the many strains of Bt had been freely available to all.) Barnes started collaborating with a researcher in Idaho who claimed to have a Bt gene, but after half a year of work, Barnes decided that the gene was damaged goods. Finally, he acquired one from a scientist at Purdue. He set about linking this gene to the necessary pieces of DNA that have to go on the front and the back of it so that a gene from bacteria will work in plants.

Barnes managed to transfer the whole package into tobacco plants in 1985. But when he unleashed caterpillars on the plants, they dashed his hopes. "The insects didn't seem to notice" his Bt gene. They devoured the genetically engineered plants.

In October of 1985, Barnes wrote a paper detailing these disappointing results and flew off to a Savannah, Georgia, to a meeting of molecular biologists working on plants. It was the first time a scientist had spoken publicly about efforts to put Bt genes into plants. Barnes may, in fact, have been the first researcher to put a Bt gene in a plant—an accomplishment that's become one of the pillars of an entire industry. "He probably had [the competition] skunked by twelve months at one point," says one industry researcher.

Yet Barnes's efforts were quickly surpassed. The task turned out to require new knowledge about bacteria, insects, DNA, and the tissue culture of plants. No solitary researcher—no matter how creative—could compete in all these areas against half a dozen hungry biotech companies.

MONSANTO'S RESEARCHERS had a head start in the crowded race for Bt but stumbled badly. The work had begun during the days when Monsanto's biotech research was divided between two warring factions, and the hostility probably didn't help matters. The company's agricultural division had acquired a Bt gene back in 1983 but lacked experience inserting the gene into plants. Jaworski's rival petunia-growing research group was probably the best in the world at putting new genes into plants, but it couldn't, or wouldn't, help much with the agricultural division's Bt project.

Scientists in Monsanto's agricultural division also made one unfortunate choice. They chose to work with a full-length Bt gene rather than a "truncated" gene that produced only the shortened, active form of the toxin. They tried to put their gene into tobacco. This seemed reasonable; tobacco is easy to transform, it grows quickly, and it had become the standard "lab rat" for plant scientists. Unfortunately, for some reason a full-length Bt gene simply will not work in tobacco. (It would have worked fine in other plants, like tomatoes, as the researchers learned later.) The young Monsanto scientists ran into this blind alley again and again, transforming tobacco plants with an ineffective Bt gene.

THROUGH 1986, Wayne Barnes's Bt gene continued to misfire. Barnes hitched the gene to a new promoter, one derived from a plant virus which he'd wangled from another university researcher. "It did work at first," Barnes recalls. "When the plants had two to four leaves, they'd kill caterpillars. So here I am all excited. Leaf number 6? Nothing. Leaf number 8? Nothing. They'd basically only express [the toxin] right after I put them in the dirt."

Finally, late in 1986 or early in 1987, Barnes hit on a good combination of regulatory signals for his gene. "Pow! High expression! Caterpillars dying right and left! Those plants have seeds; their daughters kill caterpillars!"

The taste of triumph was fleeting. During the first week of July 1987 Barnes got his copy of *Nature* in the mail. On page 30, Mark Vaeck and several collaborators at Plant Genetic Systems (PGS) in Belgium announced their own success with Bt in tobacco. They had used almost the same combination of DNA sequences as Barnes, and their results were much more conclusive. "I was pretty much knocked out of the water," Barnes says. "I immediately got depressed." (Needless to say, lawyers for PGS had already filed many patent applications claiming inventorship of plants containing Bt genes.)

In fact several companies in the Bt race got their gene working at around the same time, and all of them, while trumpeting triumph, realized to their dismay that their ultimate goal remained out of reach. The plants were producing pitifully small amounts of Bt toxin, enough to kill the extremely susceptible caterpillars used in laboratory tests but far short of what would be required to fight off hardier pests like the cotton bollworm. They estimated that in order to protect cotton plants, the genes would have to produce fifty times more toxin. Something was wrong, and they didn't know what.

The experts on gene expression at Monsanto were mystified. "The experiences from the corporate group were that the expression of genes in plants went very, very well," says Monsanto's Fred Perlak. "This gene did not go well. You could see some activity and detect the presence of the protein, but it was very, very small."

According to documents released in the course of later court battles, each company arrived independently at a similar strategy for overcoming this problem. Scientists surmised that there was something about the makeup of the Bt gene that plants found disagreeable. The scientists also suspected that they knew what it was. Already in the early 1980s researchers had pointed out that the genetic code of plants and bacteria showed subtle differences. The two seemed to prefer different ways of creating particular amino acids. It was almost as though they spoke the same language but with different dialects.

The letters of this language are "bases," individual links in the long chain of DNA that makes up a gene. The letters of a gene are "read" in triplets. Each set of three letters is a "word" called a codon. Each of these codons is translated by the cell into a particular amino acid, and the amino acids in turn are strung together to form a protein. (You might think of the protein as a whole paragraph.) But just as different words may express the same idea in ordinary language, several different codons can be translated into the same amino acid. Scientists observed that bacteria seemed to prefer some codons that plants avoided and vice versa.

The scientists speculated that the Bt gene might work better in plants if it were rewritten, substituting codons that plants appeared to prefer. This new gene would express the same "thought"; it would create the same protein, but it would use "words" or codons that were part of a plant's vocabulary.

All the companies had the brainpower to solve this problem. Only one of them had the financial muscle to get it done in short order. "We decided to synthesize a whole new gene, completely start over," says Monsanto's Fred Perlak. Perlak came up with a new sequence that the team hoped plants would like, then ordered that new sequence from three "gene factories" in the United Kingdom. Each of the three labs was assigned to deliver a separate piece of the gene; the pieces would be assembled in St. Louis.

By midsummer of 1988, the genes were assembled. By the second week in August, they were in tomato cells.

"I still remember Roy Fuchs coming into the lab; it was about ten o'clock in the morning," Perlak says. "He just walked up to me and said, 'Congratulations, Fred, you've done it.'"

"And I said, 'Done what?'"

"He says, 'We've got extremely high levels of Bt expression.'"

The levels were, in fact, astonishing. They were one hundred to five hundred times higher than anything Perlak and his colleagues had seen before in a plant cell. In the margins of his laboratory notebook, beside the test results, Roy Fuchs wrote: "Super!" "Perfect!" and "Novel Demonstration! Novel Information! Novel Constructs!"

If the gene worked that well in real crops such as cotton or corn, it would kill the tobacco budworm, the corn earworm, the cotton bollworm, and the European corn borer. It was, potentially, a billion-dollar gene. The effect was electrifying. "It was as if the oxygen content in the building suddenly went up," says Perlak.

ALONG WITH the excitement of discovery, the hotly contested Bt race produced moments of low comedy. Few could top the strange saga of the Bt strain called *tenebrionis*, or *san diego*.

*Tenebrionis* appeared first in a German journal of entomology, *Zeitschrift für angewandte Entomologie,* at the very end of 1983. Translated, the title read: "*B. thuringiensis,* var. *tenebrionis*; a new pathotype effective against Coleoptera larvae." It reported a new strain of *Bacillus thuringiensis,* one that didn't just kill caterpillars; it was also deadly against a class of insects that includes certain beetles. It had been discovered in the same way the first strains of Bt had come to light. Researchers at the University of Würzburg had been working with a colony of insects, in this case the meal beetle, when they all started dying. They sent several of the infected insects to the German government's Institute for Biological Crop Protection in Darmstadt. There, scientists isolated the new strain of Bt and discovered its peculiar toxicity to beetles.

Wayne Barnes in his offices in St. Louis heard about the discovery and leaped into action. "I wrote to the guy. Asked him for the strain," says Barnes. "When the reply came back from Germany, I set it down on a sterile bench, put on sterile gloves, opened up the envelope with sterile scissors, and without even reading it, I swabbed the envelope and streaked it on a plate in the hopes that I would get a spore." Barnes's hopes were dashed. The letter was sterile.

"The letter also said no," Barnes continues. "Or *Nein.* Apparently the guy got about seventy-five requests. He wouldn't give it to anybody."

The concept of patenting useful microbes had made its way to Germany by this time. One of the discoverers of the new strain, *Bacillus thuringiensis,* var. *tenebrionis,* had a research contract with a Germany company called Boehringer Mannheim. The lawyers at Boehringer rushed to apply for patents. They even persuaded the publishers of the *Zeitschrift für angewandte Entomologie* to delay the appearance of their journal for four weeks until the patent application was filed.

As it happened, a new company in California called Mycogen was looking for such discoveries. Mycogen was led by Jerry Caulder, who'd left Monsanto in order to run his own company. "My prediction was there wouldn't be a transgenic plant in the fields before the year 2000," Caulder says. But he had a strategy for making money in the meantime. Like the early U.S. railroads, which made their profits selling land rather than by carrying passengers or freight, Caulder decided the near-term profits in agricultural biotech lay in intellectual real estate. "My strategy was simple," Caulder says. "Let's find as many genes as we can and patent them. We'd jump ahead and build intellectual property." Caulder saw the early competition in biotechnology as a kind of Oklahoma Land Run, a race for property rights. This new form of Bt discovered in Germany looked like valuable property indeed.

Mycogen contacted Boehringer requesting a license to use the new strain of Bt, but the two companies couldn't agree on terms. Then in late 1984 a scientist from Mycogen, Corinna Herrnstadt, called one of the discoverers of the new strain, Aloysius Krieg. She was visiting Germany, and wished to visit Krieg in his laboratory at the Federal Biological Research Center for Agriculture and Forestry in Darmstadt.

Herrnstadt grew up in Germany, and the two scientists spoke German during their visit. "I was very open," recalls Krieg, who is now retired. "I showed her everything. I wanted to help her so she could get ahead."

Then, astonishingly, Corinna Herrnstadt announced her own discovery of a strain of Bt less than two years later. This strain also killed potato beetles and related species. Since it apparently had been found in Mycogen's labs, the new strain was dubbed *Bacillus thuringiensis san diego*. Mycogen also applied for a patent on it. In its application Mycogen noted tartly that the similar German strain "is not available for side-by-side comparison"; therefore, the German publication "is not a valid patent law reference under U.S. law."

As information spread about the two strains of Bt, scientists were struck by how similar they seemed to be. At Monsanto, where scientists wanted to obtain a license to use one or both of them, scientists carried out detailed analysis of the genetic structure of the two strains. They appeared to be identical.

In Darmstadt, Germany, Aloysius Krieg suspected microbial larceny. He tried to reconstruct Herrnstadt's visit in his memory. "She was alone in the laboratory when I went to do the photocopying," he recalls. Perhaps the microbes had hitched a ride on the publica-

tions that Krieg gave to his visitor. "They were lying in the laboratory, and we were producing massive quantities of these bacteria, so
the whole area was a bit contaminated."

Boehringer sued Mycogen, claiming that the San Diego company
had stolen *Bacillus thuringiensis,* var. *tenebrionis,* and claimed it as
its own. Boehringer then sold its rights to the bacteria to Novo
Nordisk, a large Danish company. Lawyers for Novo Nordisk began
tracking down former employees of Mycogen, asking them what
they knew about Bt *san diego.* Some of them knew or had heard
quite a bit.

They testified in depositions that Corinne Herrnstadt had taken
with her on a trip to Germany a petri dish for growing cultures of
bacteria. They repeated stories that they claimed Herrnstadt had recounted; how she'd slid her hand along the surface of a table in
Krieg's laboratory, then wiped her fingers on the petri dish hidden in
her purse; how she'd brought that dish back to San Diego and there
"discovered" Bt *san diego.* The tale was apparently part of the common lore at Mycogen. Jerry Caulder, though, says there never was
any solid evidence that the story was true. The original source of the
story, he says, was a former employee with a grudge against Mycogen. Caulder says he asked Herrnstadt about the story, and she denied it.

Years later, the case was settled out of court, but terms of the set-
tlement were made public, and they left little doubt regarding the
winner. Mycogen agreed to pay Novo Nordisk more than $4 mil-
lion, conceded that the original *Bacillus thuringiensis "san diego"*
was actually *Bacillus thuringiensis tenebrionis,* disclaimed its patents
on this strain of the bacteria, and assigned several other Bt patents to
a subsidiary of Novo Nordisk.

WAYNE BARNES is a determined man.

Ten years after he lost the race to insert a Bt gene into a plant,
Barnes was asked to testify about his work in a patent dispute. Novartis, a Swiss company, had been sued by Plant Genetic Systems,
which owned a patent on the use of Bt genes in plants. Novartis
hoped that Barnes's account of his early work on Bt would undermine PGS's claim to have invented the technique.

Barnes, who verges on the cranky under the best of circumstances, refused to help a multinational drug and chemical company. Finally, Novartis obtained a court order forcing Barnes to provide a video-taped deposition.

When the lawyers arrived with their video cameras, Barnes was ready for battle. He hung a banner out the window of his office: "Novartis Seeds, Inc.: Taking others' work by exploiting weaknesses in the federal court system." He wore a T-shirt bearing the same slogan. Then, when the videotape began rolling, he started taking his clothes off.

Barnes's lawyer, agitated, headed off the incipient nakedness by warning Barnes that disrobing would be tantamount to refusing to appear at all, and he'd be in contempt of court. But Barnes had a backup plan. He hauled out a baseball umpire's mask and put it on. His lawyer, perhaps feeling overwhelmed, called his boss, then informed Barnes that this too would be a violation of court rules. Barnes decided simply to refuse to look at any of the lawyers or the video camera. He sat, face resolutely aimed at the tabletop, and began to recount the story of Bt genes in plants.

# 5

# Gifts of God

When the locomotive of *Bacillus thuringiensis* first started rolling, the tracks it followed led straight toward scientific terrain occupied by Fred Gould. From such serendipity careers are made. Gould, a quick-witted, ponytail-wearing New Yorker who'd found a professional home at North Carolina State University, became a national figure in the debate over biotechnology.

Gould was a child of Darwin, a student of evolution. He'd made himself an expert on the ways that insect populations evolve when confronted with man-made pressures, such as attempts by farmers to drive insects from their fields. What happens, he wondered, when farmers buy new varieties of wheat that are unpalatable to the Hessian fly, which likes to feed on young wheat shoots? How soon do new strains of Hessian fly emerge that find even the new wheat varieties delectable?

To Gould they seemed like eminently practical questions, and he imagined that the people who fund research at the U.S. Department of Agriculture might be happy to fund his efforts. He was mistaken. "I went and talked to them, but they said, 'Really interesting work, but we hardly have money to keep our plant breeding going. Come back when you have money.'" Breeders of new wheat varieties didn't know how soon the Hessian fly would adapt, but in the end they didn't care whether the answer was five years or fifty years; it still was worth the effort to breed such crops.

Then a new kind of insect-resistant plant—or at least the promise of one—appeared on the horizon. Gould heard about the attempts by genetic engineers to splice Bt genes into plants, making those plants poisonous to pests. But this time, because it involved genetic engineering rather than plant breeding, many were fascinated and ready to spend money examining the effects of this technology. "Suddenly people cared," says Gould.

Gould's world—the world of evolutionary biology—is a universe apart from the commercial drives that motivate companies like Monsanto. Even language divides them. Take, for instance, the idea of inserting genes from *Bacillus thuringiensis* into plants to make the plants poisonous to certain insect pests. The genetic engineers spoke of "permanent solutions" to insect problems.

But evolutionary biologists don't believe that permanent solutions exist in biology. There is only adaptation, moves and countermoves in a game of chess that never ends. For them, dreams of technological solutions, so common among chemical companies, are the standard object of ridicule. "It's just another silver bullet," they say dismissively. Silver bullets never work for long. DDT, for example, became useless against many insects long before its harmful effects on birds and fish were widely recognized. The chemical merely selected from among nature's genetic diversity the insects that were immune to DDT's effects. Those insects mated with each other, producing a new, resistant generation. The population of such insects exploded, and soon the pesticide was useless.

Gould was sure that if companies and farmers covered millions of acres with Bt cotton or corn the DDT scenario would be repeated. It would be a tragedy, he said, because the toxin from *Bacillus thuringiensis* was a gift of God: "There just aren't a lot of compounds that are so wonderful that you wonder why they're on Earth." No one knows why this toxin kills only caterpillars, leaving other species unharmed. But it does.

Such a gift can be used for humankind's good; in fact, it should be used, Gould told his audiences, but only with care. Deploy Bt with abandon, heedlessly, and you will use up this gift of God. Within a few years, it will be gone, forever.

Gould retooled his computer models to study the ways that insects might adapt to crops that were engineered to resist insects. His star rose brightly in the academic heavens. Gould soon was flying on a regular basis to Washington, advising the Department of Agriculture and the National Academy of Sciences on biotechnology. He also cut off his ponytail. "I thought, if I go in there with a ponytail, I immediately stereotype myself as antitechnology, antiestablishment. If I'm going to say these things and be ineffective because I'm wearing a ponytail, what's the point of that?"

Gould's message to industry was one of self-interested restraint. For the first time in history, he argued, companies should limit the use of a pesticide (in this case a pesticidal plant) in order to keep plenty of vulnerable insects alive and delay the emergence of resistant strains. He had several suggestions. Companies might sell mixtures of seed in which only half was engineered to produce Bt toxin. Or perhaps the genetic engineers should create plants that express the toxin weakly so that insects got a severe stomachache and ate slowly but survived.

This was not what the companies developing Bt products—Monsanto, Agracetus, Ciba-Geigy, Plant Genetic Systems, and Agrigenetics—wanted to hear. Gould's proposed restraints on the use of Bt amounted to restraints on the profits that could be earned with it. The agricultural chemical industry did not aim merely to discourage pests and limit their damage; it promised to vanquish enemies that were stealing farmer's crops. Indeed, the industry's roots lay in research that began in the military during World War II, and its early marketing campaigns were filled with the martial language of total victory and annihilation of the insect enemy. At one point, Monsanto commissioned an investigation of Gould's background; the investigators reported back that Gould was politically suspect since he "supported socialistic agricultural policies."

Yet times had changed, and so had American industry. Gould had a secret ally within Monsanto, a self-described rabble-rouser and maverick named Pam Marrone. Marrone was an expert on insects; she was assigned to feed bits of genetically altered plants to caterpillars and see how many died. But she also was spirited and gregarious, freely sharing opinions on matters that went well beyond her lab assignments.

Marrone walked the halls of Monsanto spreading the treasonous idea that if Bt was too successful and if plants producing this insecticidal protein were planted across large areas, insects would rapidly develop resistance to it. "I was told many times: 'Don't be so idealistic; don't be so idealistic,'" Marrone says. When Marrone and her colleagues carried out experiments demonstrating that insects can develop resistance simultaneously to several different strains of Bt toxin, the company prevented her from publishing their findings for almost a year. But company executives soon realized they had to take the issue seriously; every time they went out to give talks about their plans for Bt, they had to answer questions about the potential for insect resistance.

By the summer of 1988 Marrone got permission to set up the biotech industry's own committee aimed at finding ways to avoid or at least delay the emergence of insects resistant to Bt. The committee included representatives from every company trying to develop Bt products. It was a remarkable step; for the first time, companies that killed insects for a living were discussing ways to limit the reach of their own weapons. Monsanto even asked Gould to conduct research on some of the company's genetically engineered plants. (Apparently, some executives then got cold feet; Monsanto sent the check for $15,000, but the transgenic plants that Gould needed for the experiments never arrived.)

Long and contentious arguments over exactly how to prevent the emergence of resistant insects lay ahead. But Gould had won a fundamental victory. For the first time, evolutionary biology had begun to intervene in agriculture's war on insects and enforce a kind of arms control.

ACCORDING TO some, biotechnology posed a potential threat to many other gifts of God that were less easily recognized and appreciated than Bt. These were the gifts encompassed by the diversity of natural life on Earth, with its intricate ecological webs. It was thus no accident that the earliest and broadest scientific challenge to genetic engineering emerged from the academic field of ecology—the study of how different living species interact. And among ecologists, the most formidable, intellectually nimble critic of genetic engineering was Rob Colwell, from the University of California–Berkeley.

Colwell had grown up in Denver, but every summer and most weekends during the rest of the year his family moved to a cattle ranch high up in the front range of the Rocky Mountains, five miles from the Continental Divide. He loved that land, which his family still owns. Colwell's father was a lay minister in a small Congregational church nearby. "I was raised to believe that God made us stewards of the earth and not exploiters," Colwell says. "That's my parents' teaching; it runs through everything I think."

Ecology is not the same as environmentalism. When ecologists publish their results, they resolutely avoid moral judgements about the value of one sort of ecosystem over another. But Colwell knew that he and most of his fellow biologists secretly *did* make moral judgements. In casual conversation they would speak of ecosystems being "destroyed" by human activity, and each of them understood what was meant: This was tragic, even evil.

One of the most famous phenomena in ecology is that of "invasive species," organisms that, when transplanted to a new environment, suddenly run wild, taking over the new ecosystem and driving native species into extinction. Such invasive species include rabbits in Australia, sparrows and starlings in North America, and chestnut blight, a fungus that came to North America from Japan at the beginning of the twentieth century and began wiping out one of the continent's dominant trees.

Colwell imagined a disturbing scenario. It was conceivable, he thought, that in the future invasive species might not arrive on boats; they might emerge from the laboratory.

Seemingly minor genetic changes, Colwell said, can produce large ecological effects. Let's say you inserted a gene into poplar trees being grown plantation-style for lumber production, he said. Suppose that gene made poplars unpalatable to caterpillars, which feed on the trees' leaves. He reminded people that domesticated poplar varieties are related closely enough to wild poplars, aspens, and cottonwoods that they can fertilize each other and produce fertile offspring. "So what? So, the wild poplars now have a new adaptation—resistance to caterpillars." Over time, he suggested, these trees might have an advantage over other species of trees and come to dominate the forest.

That would unleash a cascade of effects on the rest of the ecosystem, from the underbrush and bacterial life in the soil to insects, birds, and other animals both large and small.

Colwell's hypothetical scenario raised two types of questions. The first questions were concrete and practical: Would a specific type of genetic alteration create new weeds, growing where they weren't wanted or invading neighboring ecosystems? Would these traits migrate into wild relatives? Would they alter existing ecological systems?

Most of the time, Colwell admitted, the answer was probably that they would not. Genetically modified corn growing in Iowa, for instance, has no wild relatives growing within a thousand miles. The corn plant itself, modified by thousands of years of human selection, has become like a house pet; the chances of it becoming a weed or invading wild ecosystems nearby seems remote indeed. But a single exception, he pointed out, could produce enormous damage, and the risk of such effects could not be ignored. Look at novel species of plants that have overrun the landscape, like kudzu. Or, more realistically, look at close relatives of widely planted crops that are considered noxious weeds, such as wild carrots or red rice.

Many defenders of biotechnology scoffed at such concerns. We're making the tiniest of genetic alterations, they argued, changing only one gene out of tens of thousands. "Kudzu is not a single-gene change," said one of them. The function of any new gene would be well-known, so the ecological impacts would be obvious in advance.

Ecologists like Colwell were not convinced by these assurances. Even subtle genetic changes can have profound and unpredictable effects, they argued. Suppose a gene was discovered that made rice much more hardy and vigorous, and then because of cross-pollination the gene migrated into red rice, a closely related weed. That weed then might become even more viable and spread more quickly in wild habitats than it had before.

The bottom line, the ecologists said, was that genetic engineering might produce unpleasant ecological surprises, so genetically engineered crops should be regulated. This became the official position of the Ecological Society of America. Before any such crop was approved, said the ecologists, it should be subjected to a host of field studies carefully examining the new crop's interactions with its surrounding environment. That environment might include beetles that feed on the plant, insects that pollinate it, and wild relatives with which the plant might exchange genes. Separate tests might be necessary for each area in which farmers planned to grow the crop. Only when such tests were completed should a company be allowed to sell such genetically altered plants on the open market.

To companies that were counting on quick approval from regulators these were onerous and unrealistic demands, far beyond what anyone developing new varieties of crops had ever faced in the past. Such tests could delay the commercial launch of a product for years. One scientist from Calgene, after listening to Colwell speak at a scientific conference in 1985, returned to the company and wrote to his colleagues: "Ugh. A meeting designed to raise issues rather than find answers. Ecologists . . . repeatedly got up and described how little they know. A few essentially said research in the area had been underfunded for a long time and the ecologists were going to hold recombinant DNA projects hostage." Ecologists would oppose biotechnology research, in other words, until they got more research funding. The Calgene scientist also called Colwell "the most articulate and potentially troublesome for smooth regulatory review of plant releases." (Informed of this comment years later, Colwell seemed delighted. "Good for me! I like to be troublesome. I think it's the right thing to do!")

Biotechnology's defenders also felt that Colwell was trying to impose a higher standard on all of agriculture. After all, traditional plant breeding had also created new traits of ecological significance. When breeders developed strains of wheat that were resistant to the Hessian fly and farmers planted them over millions of acres, did anyone look into whether these genes might be transferred to wild relatives? Of course not. For that matter, did government regulators step in when farmers cut down hedgerows on their property or plowed up vast expanses of prairie? All of agriculture, they argued, had been so invasive and technological that the advances of biotechnology amounted to a tiny blip in history.

True enough, Colwell admitted. But the fact of past wrongdoing was no excuse to keep repeating it. People used to defend slavery too. Times had changed, and with a new era came a higher standard for agriculture.

The arguments raised by ecologists also raised deeper philosophical questions that few people bothered to address. These had to do with underlying values and assumptions: How valuable was Colwell's hypothetical forest of wild poplars and aspens, and how much effort should be spent protecting it from human intervention? Which ecosystems merited such protection? Only those previously untouched by human intervention, or managed ecosystems as well, such as wheat fields and roadsides?

Even if few people asked such questions, Colwell found them worth thinking about. In the fall of 1988, he spoke about "human responsibility and the natural order" in a Swiss castle, to an audience made up mainly of philosophers. The assignment forced him to examine his own assumptions about the value of nature and proper limits on human intervention in it.

As Colwell told his audience sitting amid the castle's grand surroundings: "Biologists behave, speak (usually off the record) and sometimes write in ways that reveal that they attribute intrinsic value to species." Living creatures, closely observed, inspire wonder; they exist independent of our powers, and they are irreplaceable. The same is true—perhaps even more so—for entire ecosystems. And something else, Colwell added: "*The intrinsic value of a species is diminished by its genetic alteration through human intervention. I strongly suspect that most biologists would agree with this proposition—but only for human intervention in the genetics of 'natural' (wild) species living in reasonably 'natural' ecosystems*" (emphasis in original).

So Colwell saw nothing inherently objectionable about manipulating the genetic makeup of strawberries or orchids or wheat, as long as the genes didn't migrate into wild species. These are domesticated plants; they have evolved over millennia through human selection and breeding into instruments for the satisfaction of human desires. They are not "natural," and changing their genetic makeup through modern gene-splicing (as opposed to, say, cross-breeding by hand in a greenhouse) would be no more problematic than putting an addition on your house.

Yet Colwell found the idea of creating genetically altered poplar trees that would intrude into a wild forest reprehensible. Manipulating the genetic makeup of a wild plant or of an ecosystem would be akin to vandalism, Colwell said. It would alter something of intrinsic value that is not of our own making. And even if it didn't create new weeds or destroy things with clear economic value, doing this was wrong and shouldn't be allowed.

Colwell admitted that "natural" ecosystems are difficult to define. Strictly speaking, if human beings are part of nature, then anything they do is "natural." But Colwell argued that humans have removed themselves from nature. They no longer exhibit the types of interactions with other species that are characteristic of other living things. Alone among the living creatures of the earth, humans have escaped the restraining forces of our environment. In fact, he said, the only way that most other species will survive is if we humans learn to restrain *ourselves* and the technology that we invent.

# 6

# Genes That Love Poisons

One day in the early 1980s, not long after Robb Fraley arrived at Monsanto, he met with two veterans of the company's pesticide business. One of them suggested a project for Fraley's team of genetic engineers. The company, he said, had found some bacteria that appeared to survive in the presence of Roundup, Monsanto's new herbicide. Why didn't Fraley and his gene wizards somehow find the gene responsible for this and splice it into plants? Plants that could similarly tolerate doses of Roundup could open up vast new markets for the herbicide. If farmers could plant Roundup-tolerant soybeans, for instance, they could spray Roundup on those fields, killing all the weeds without harming the crop.

Fraley, according to one of the Monsanto veterans, reacted with scorn. "If all we can do [with biotechnology] is sell more damned herbicide, we shouldn't be in this business." It was a response rooted in the genetic engineers' sense of moral superiority. Chemicals were dirty. Biotechnology was clean.

Yet within a few years Fraley was singing a very different tune. Roundup tolerance became the project that bankrolled Monsanto's pursuit of genetically engineered crops. It was a massive effort; one Monsanto scientist proudly described it later as "one of the most incredible and successful stories in all of biotechnology." It was the project on which Fraley built his career within the company, and it brought biotechnology and pesticides to the marriage altar in a fateful embrace.

At least one other company considered a similar union and rejected it. When Mary-Dell Chilton was in the process of building a biotechnology program for the Swiss company Ciba-Geigy, she put together a list of potential products from such research. She included the possibility of creating plants that could tolerate a dose of the herbicide atrazine. Ciba-Geigy sold substantial quantities of atrazine; if crops could be made resistant to this chemical, the reasoning went, that market would grow.

"I can remember the immediate reaction of the Swiss bosses was, 'That's an ethical problem, we'll never be able to sell that,'" says Chilton. "They saw that it would be a problem to sell the chemical with the plants, and especially if you were trying to sell them as a package. They said, 'It'll never fly; there'll be tremendous opposition to this.'"

Monsanto had no such concerns. But the St. Louis company also had a very different chemical to work with. Roundup, for many reasons, was the perfect mate for herbicide-tolerant plants.

ROUNDUP, KNOWN to scientists by its chemical name, glyphosate, is peculiar, both as a chemical and as a business phenomenon. When Monsanto brought this chemical onto the market in the 1970s, the entire industry scoffed. It violated all the rules for successful herbicides. Herbicides were supposed to kill weeds immediately. But the effects of Roundup couldn't be seen for a week or more. Successful herbicides were expected to be selective, killing as many weeds as possible, while leaving the crop unharmed. Roundup killed almost everything that was green and growing. The most valuable herbicides were those that persisted in fields for months, so farmers didn't have to keep spraying. (Otherwise, herbicide experts were fond of saying, why use chemicals at all? Why not just spray a field with boiling water?) Roundup, however, barely persisted in a field at all. It degraded quickly when exposed to sunlight and rain.

Yet Monsanto's marketers discovered, or created, a huge market for it. In any location where people simply wanted to control all vegetation, where they once had hoed or mowed, they now could use Roundup. In addition, Monsanto turned the chemical's low toxicity and the fact that it didn't persist in the environment into selling points. People sprayed it on roadsides, along fencerows, in orchards, and on the cracks of sidewalks. Farmers used it as part of "no-till" cultivation methods, which minimize erosion and conserve topsoil. They sprayed Roundup to "burn down" all vegetation, then planted corn or soybeans right into the unplowed ground. By the mid–1980s, Roundup had become the biggest money earner in Monsanto's agricultural division.

Imagine the market if we could spray it on crops, Monsanto executives mused. When Monsanto's scientists created glyphosate, they knew exactly how the chemical affected plants but not why. During the 1970s Ernie Jaworski, the wily, visionary Monsanto scientist, started figuring out exactly how glyphosate worked. He discovered to his fascination that he could reverse glyphosate's lethal effects. He could revive dying plant tissues that had been exposed to glyphosate by supplying them with certain essential nutrients. It was as though the plant cells were starving because the herbicide had prevented them from creating those crucial amino acids. Jaworski concluded that glyphosate was somehow disrupting a set of chemical reactions that produced those nutrients.

A scientist in Germany finally uncovered glyphosate's secret in 1980. He reported that the chemical bound to a crucial enzyme within each cell of the plant, rendering the enzyme inactive. This blocked the formation of essential amino acids, as Jaworski had suspected. This enzyme—glyphosate's target—doesn't occur in humans or animals, so glyphosate has little effect on these organisms.

This molecule, this tiny point of weakness where Roundup fastens its lethal grip, became an obsession for Ernie Jaworski, Robb Fraley, and almost everyone who worked for them. It was like a companion in their lives with its own personality—the Target. Somewhere in the chromosomes of each plant cell lay the gene that produced the Target. In it lay the secret to Roundup's lethal power. Alter that gene or kick it into overdrive, and Roundup might prove powerless.

This gene bridged the hostile universes that existed within Monsanto, the old world of chemical sales and the new one of gene-splicing. Find the Target, make it immune to Roundup, and everyone would be happy.

Scientists outside Monsanto had already identified the Target in bacteria. It wasn't surprising that bacteria should have this gene as well—they too must create these essential amino acids. (Humans eat protein instead.) One of the first things Steve Rogers did when he came to Monsanto, well before he'd succeeded in splicing new genes into plants, was to play around with that bacterial gene. "It was possible to put, say, twenty copies of the gene in a cell," Rogers says. "Now, is that cell resistant to glyphosate?" In fact it was. The bacteria were, with all these extra genes, prolific producers of the crucial enzyme; like a football team playing with extra men on the field, the enzyme could overwhelm a small amount of glyphosate and keep the cell alive. It was not of immediate practical significance, but, as far as Rogers knew, his genetically altered bacteria were the first organisms that had ever been rendered tolerant to Roundup through genetic engineering. In the summer of 1982, Rogers summarized his experiment on a large sheet of paper for a so-called "poster session" at a conference at the University of California–Davis.

It turned into a memorable and startling event. Rogers was standing beside his poster, as is the custom at such events, ready for other scientists to wander by and ask questions. One of the first was Luca Comai, a free-spirited Italian from Calgene, the small biotech company in Davis, California.

Comai's greeting was almost a challenge. "So. This is how you guys are doing it."

"Yeah," said Rogers, wondering why Comai would refer to this topic with such offhand familiarity.

"Well, that's okay, but there's a better way," said Comai. To Rogers's astonishment, Comai pointed to his own poster just across the aisle.

LUCA COMAI didn't really want to work for a biotech company. In January of 1981, he'd applied for a teaching job at the University of California–Riverside. As he made the rounds of the faculty, politely professing deep interest in all their research projects, one of them mentioned a fascinating new finding that had just emerged from a lab in Germany. It was the discovery that glyphosate killed plants by inhibiting one particular enzyme.

"My ears perked up," says Comai. "Glyphosate was kind of a mystery at the time. Ten different plant people would have ten different opinions about it." Comai filed the information away in his mind.

Comai didn't get the Riverside job. Six months later he went to work at Calgene in Davis, California. He was one of the very first employees. Calgene had millions of dollars in venture capital and only the vaguest notion of what to do with it.

"We met with the science board in June," says Comai. "I proposed, hey, we should engineer resistance to glyphosate. The strategy would be to get a mutation [in the gene] to alter the enzyme, so we could get resistance." Comai thought that glyphosate might not bind as well to an alternate form of the enzyme. But the Calgene advisors, most of whom had little or no experience with practical agriculture, couldn't see why this would be useful. Why should they make plants resistant to some other company's herbicide? Comai was disgusted. They should realize, he thought, that the plant itself would be valuable, not just the herbicide sprayed on it. "I was pretty cocky and young; I thought these were a bunch of old fogies," he recalls.

Comai set to work on the project anyway. He doused colonies of *Salmonella* bacteria with chemicals that induce random mutations in DNA. Then he poured small amounts of glyphosate into the colonies. Most died, but a few bacteria—those with a mutated form of the crucial enzyme—did survive. As Comai had hoped, this mutant form of the glyphosate target wasn't nearly as vulnerable to the herbicide.

These were the results that Comai showed to Rogers in the summer of 1982. According to Comai, "Rogers was just floored; they let this rinky-dink outfit [Calgene] in Davis beat them."

Rogers remembers his reactions a little differently. "My first thought was, holy criminelly, why would these guys be working on glyphosate? What's in it for them? And then the second one was, is that going to work better than what we're doing?"

Comai's method was in fact superior, but still not quite good enough. Solving the glyphosate tolerance problem would take far longer and consume far more resources than either scientist imagined at the time.

ROB HORSCH, Monsanto's gardener and biotech cofounder, is a cautious, play-by-the-rules kind of fellow. But he's also devoted to his experiments, and company rules were not going to keep Horsch from tending one of the most crucial experiments in his life.

The experiment was in some ways just like hundreds of others that Horsch had carried out over the last few years. Once again, there were little disks of petunia leaf in petri dishes filled with colonies of *Agrobacterium tumefaciens*. But the bacteria in this case were carrying a gene that was intended to produce petunia plants that could survive a dose of Roundup.

Horsch and his colleagues at Monsanto had spent almost two years coming up with this gene. Within petunia plants, they'd isolated the enzyme that Roundup locks in its lethal embrace. Then they'd worked backward step-by-step from the enzyme to the petunia gene that produces it. They'd taken this gene and replaced its "engine"— the piece of DNA called a promoter—with a more powerful one. Now they were ready to insert the souped-up gene back into a petunia to find out if it would make the plant immune to Roundup.

Yet just as this experiment was beginning during the summer of 1985, Horsch was supposed to leave for Cold Spring Harbor Laboratory in New York, a legendary site in the history of biology, where Nobel laureate Max Delbrück formed what one writer later called "a republic of the mind." Horsch was supposed to teach a course there on the molecular biology of plants.

"I thought, 'I can't leave this behind.' So I boxed it up and took it with me," Horsch says.

Horsch decided to take only a sample from the dozens of petri dishes; the rest stayed in St. Louis. He didn't tell anyone. The transgenic plants were tightly guarded intellectual property of Monsanto, and they were weren't supposed to be grown outside of a contained laboratory. But in this case, off they went to Long Island.

"Late at night after class was over, I'd go up to the lab and look at it under the microscope," Horsch recalls. He was looking for tiny green bumps around the edges of the small disks of petunia tissue.

They would signal that transformed cells were growing and multi-plying, even in the presence of glyphosate.

By the last week of the course, Horsch could see the signs of success. "Complete inhibition of the nontransformed cells; absolutely nothing growing anywhere. And dozens of little colonies coming out of the leaf disks in the transformed cells," he says.

It meant, at the very least, that they were on the right track; they had located the Target, and they'd created plants that were at least somewhat able to ingest Roundup and survive. Horsch couldn't keep this to himself, but he also didn't want to tell Fraley or Rogers what he'd done. He called Harry Klee, then a young molecular biologist in the lab.

Horsch: "Have you looked at the tissues?"

Klee: "Yeah. I didn't see much."

Horsch, his voice dripping with significance: "You should look harder."

Klee couldn't imagine what, or who, had taken possession of Monsanto's senior expert on plant tissue culture. Had the Angel Gabriel appeared to him and proclaimed the success of his experiment back in St. Louis? Then Horsch blurted out what he'd done.

"I told Harry not to tell anyone until I came back because I knew I'd get a lot of grief," Horsch continues. "But Harry did tell. So the last night of the course, we have this lobster banquet, and just as we were eating the shrimp cocktail appetizer, a bottle of champagne plops down on the table next to me. I look up and there's Robb and Steve." Fraley and Rogers had been scheduled to fly through La-Guardia Airport that evening. Instead of catching their connecting flight they drove to Cold Spring Harbor.

Horsch and his visitors didn't tell the other people at the banquet what the champagne was all about. "They just thought we were crazy," says Rogers.

AFTER THE triumph, as so often, came a sobering reassessment. The petunia plants turned out to be tolerant to small doses of Roundup but not to the amounts that farmers typically spray on weeds. The "overexpression" route—driving the gene harder with a more powerful promoter—would not be enough for a commercial product.

As if to drive the point home, Luca Comai whistled another shot past Monsanto's bow just a few months later. In October of 1985 he and several colleagues at Calgene published a paper in *Nature* describing their own glyphosate-tolerant plants. These contained the mutant gene from *Salmonella* bacteria that he'd described to Steve Rogers three years earlier. The tolerance to glyphosate didn't result from driving the gene harder, producing more of the plant's natural enzyme and overwhelming glyphosate's effects; instead, these plants created a slightly different form of the enzyme, one shaped differently so that glyphosate couldn't bind to it so tightly. Comai's paper was a professional embarrassment to Monsanto. Roundup was supposed to be their house specialty; they owned the patent on this chemical. And here was this "boutique" in California snaring the first publication on Roundup-tolerant plants. One Monsanto scientist described the reaction to a Calgene competitor over drinks at a conference several months later: "These dipshits from East Jesus were never going to beat Monsanto on its own product again."

On top of this came Monsanto's 1985 financial crunch, and massive layoffs at the end of the year. Robb Fraley called a council of war. Harry Klee still remembers the grim message: "We do not have the luxury of doing this the right way. We are going to do this the way that gets it done the quickest, because our entire future depends on the success of this program.'"

"We had to make this work." recalls Charles Gasser, another member of the group. "This was the one project that the administration of the company understood."

Fraley assigned experts on bacteria to look for mutant forms of the target gene, as Luca Comai had done. At the same time specialists on promoters had to find ways to drive the gene even harder— make it produce even more of the crucial enzyme. Others were assigned to work on ways to get the enzyme into the parts of the plant cell where it was most needed. "It was like the Manhattan Project," says Klee. "The antithesis of how a scientist usually works. A scientist does an experiment, evaluates it, makes a conclusion and goes on to the next variable. With Roundup resistance we were trying twenty variables at the same time: different mutants, different promoters, multiple plant species. We were trying everything at once."

It spelled the end of much research into scientific phenomena that were interesting but not urgent. "When I first came to Monsanto, it was a world leader in plant molecular biology," says Gasser. "You'd go to the academic meetings; there might be twenty-five speakers, and five of them would be from Monsanto. But this Roundup tolerance problem turned out to be so hard and so important, it slowly subsumed everything else. And it led to Monsanto no longer being a leader in that basic science. So when I left, there would be maybe one speaker [at scientific meetings] from Monsanto."

But year by year, as Monsanto assaulted the problem with its concentrated intellectual power, success edged closer. The company's scientists discovered a new variant of the target gene in bacteria. Like Comai's mutant, this gene produced plants that were somewhat resistant to Roundup. Unfortunately, the plants didn't grow very well either. (Comai's gene had the same effect.) Apparently, mutant versions of the enzyme that were unresponsive to glyphosate weren't very good at their normal job; they didn't provide a healthy stream of nutrients to the plant.

Fraley's troops spent the late 1980s reconstructing the exact shape of their target enzyme. They hoped that this picture of the molecule might give them clues to the shape of an ideal version of the enzyme, one that would do its normal job well while still repelling glyphosate. In 1989, they created a second mutation in the gene that delivered much better performance. They were tantalizingly close to their goal.

Then they discovered that nature had trumped all their efforts.

FIVE HUNDRED miles south of St. Louis, just west of New Orleans, lies Monsanto's Luling plant. It covers fifteen hundred acres along the Mississippi River. Along with massive chemical factories and waste ponds there are thick forests. The area is in fact registered as a Wildlife Habitat Council site.

Luling manufactures glyphosate, millions of pounds of it. There are glyphosate residues in the ponds, in the mud at the bottom of the ponds, and in the soil alongside. Those residues exert a steady pressure on the population of microorganisms in the water and the soil, eliminating those that are sensitive to glyphosate and selecting those that are less vulnerable.

By the early 1980s Roundup-tolerant bacteria were already there, flourishing despite the presence of herbicide residues. As part of their routine monitoring work, scientists from Monsanto's chemical waste division came to Luling and collected samples of the sludge. They were hoping to find bacteria that could use glyphosate as food, breaking it down into less harmful chemicals. They hoped such bacteria might help them clean up the environment.

The samples sat in the waste cleanup division of Monsanto for years. Finally the genetic engineers heard about these collections and began studying them. One group of scientists was assigned to look for new forms of the target gene. And one day a scientist from that group came down the hall, walked into the offices of the people who led the Roundup tolerance program, and said, "Guess what? This thing is perfect."

The new gene looked radically different from any target gene they'd seen before. But it performed its function in the plant cell and proved to tolerate Roundup far better than any gene the scientists had created in the laboratory. The long search for a Roundup tolerance gene was over.

WHILE MONSANTO'S scientists struggled to create Roundup-resistant plants, an alternative and competing version of herbicide tolerance emerged on the far shores of the Atlantic. European competitors offered their own herbicide and their own gene for creating herbicide-tolerant plants. This European alternative became the mirror image of Monsanto's Roundup Ready project. The goal was the same, but the path toward it followed almost exactly the opposite trajectory. These two genes, linked to two different herbicides, would come to represent competing industrial rivals and different continents, sales strategies, and philosophies regarding the value of biotechnology.

As in the story of Roundup resistance, the herbicide came first. During the 1960s, Japanese and German scientists who were examining soil samples from Africa came across some odd bacteria, members of the *Streptomyces* family. The microbes killed all plant life nearby. The scientists discovered that these bacteria exuded a chemical that blocked the ability of plants to digest ammonia, an essential byproduct of photosynthesis. As a consequence, ammonia accumulated in the plants and killed them. (Insects and mammals are able to get rid of ammonia in other ways, so the chemical is relatively non-toxic to them.)

Two companies saw commercial potential for this chemical. Meiji Seika in Japan filled fermentation vats with the bacteria, skimmed off the plant-killing chemical, and sold it as the herbicide Bialaphos. The German company Hoechst figured out a way to synthesize the key chemical subunit of Bialaphos in its factories. In the early 1980s, it began selling this herbicide in Europe under the trade name Basta.

Scientists in both companies occasionally asked themselves what allowed the microbes to survive the effects of their own poison, but for years no one pursued the question in any systematic way. Neither company in the early 1980s made the necessary mental leap; neither one looked at the herbicide-resistant bacteria in their hands and saw the possibility of herbicide-resistant plants.

By the early 1980s, both Meiji Seika and Hoechst wanted to find ways to produce their herbicides more efficiently, and both independently decided to look more carefully at the way the microbe itself manufactured its herbicide. Meiji Seika signed a contract with the Geneva laboratories of the small U.S.-based company Biogen, and Hoechst, starting in 1983, funded research at the genetics laboratory of the University of Bielefeld in Germany.

Months of tedium gradually unmasked the microbe's secret. Scientists in both laboratories squirted DNA-cutting enzymes into arrays of tiny test tubes, chopping up the microbe's DNA into ever smaller sections. They spliced the separate sections into other bacteria, trying to figure out which biological functions—which genes—were located on each particular pieces of DNA.

Around 1985 both laboratories came upon the same startling discovery. One small fragment of DNA, when transferred to other bacteria, made those bacteria immune to the effects of Basta. The gene just "popped up," says Günter Donn from Hoechst.

It was the starting gun to a scientific race, a sprint to find the gene and transfer its power to plants. It was an unequal contest, matching a small startup company against a giant chemical company and its academic collaborators. But in this case money was not a limiting factor; intensity and urgency won the day.

Biogen's researchers faced a quandary. They'd discovered the gene, but they had no experience working with plants, and neither did their corporate sponsor, Meiji Seika. But the world of biotech startups is small. One of Biogen's scientific leaders was a good friend of researchers at Plant Genetic Systems in Ghent. He called PGS.

The news of Biogen's gene went through PGS like an electric shock. At the very least, thought Jan Leemans, the company's scientific leader, the gene promised to be a superior tool for genetic engineering of plants. Genetic engineers had been working with tools borrowed from the world of bacteria; they'd been using antibiotics and antibiotic resistance genes as their system for selecting the cells that were genetically transformed. But when handling plants, wouldn't it make more sense to use herbicides and herbicide resistance genes? And beyond the laboratory, Leemans could imagine the commercial potential of crops that were immune to the effects of Bialaphos or Basta.

Leemans suspected that this one project by itself could mean the difference between success and oblivion for his small company. He threw all of the resources that PGS could spare into an all-out effort to create Basta-resistant plants. Leemans himself led the effort, working around the clock to convert the bacterial gene into one that would work in plants, then employing *Agrobacterium tumefaciens* once again to ferry that gene into tobacco cells.

For Hoechst, by contrast, the project was exciting, but it had nowhere near the same urgency. It was more of a scientific plaything, an intriguing venture worthy of attention but not obsession.

Günter Donn and his colleagues at Hoechst also wanted to do things right the first time. They wanted to learn from the mistakes that so many had made with *Bacillus thuringiensis*. They decided to take their time and synthesize a new version of the gene, translating the genetic code from the version preferred by bacteria into one preferred by plants. That effort probably slowed them down by several months and turned out not to be necessary.

For whatever reason, Hoechst lost the race. By June of 1986, PGS had transferred its gene into tobacco plants, and the natural gene, as it turned out, worked just fine. The PGS researchers called their gene the *"bar"* gene, for "Bialaphos resistance," and immediately filed patent claims in Europe and in the United States covering their gene and its use in plants.

One could hardly imagine a greater contrast to Monsanto's experience with Roundup resistance. At Monsanto dozens of scientists struggled for most of a decade trying to create a gene that would make plants resistant to Roundup. In addition, success in one crop often didn't translate into success in another. Creating Roundup resistance in corn, for instance, was a struggle that continued well into the 1990s.

Basta resistance, on the other hand, was a snap. Within three years after beginning to dissect the DNA of *Streptomyces viridochromogenes*, researchers at PGS and at Hoechst had Basta-resistant plants. The *bar* gene worked right out of the box. Even when the gene was only weakly active, it was enough to protect plants against standard doses of Basta.

The difference lay in the way the two genes carry out their task. Monsanto's scientists were forced to play defense against Roundup. They looked for an alternate form of the plant's vulnerable spot, the enzyme that Roundup attacks. This altered enzyme, because it is shaped somewhat differently, is less vulnerable to the herbicide; it fends off Roundup and keeps working. But the task is difficult; the plant continually has to fight off Roundup's challenge.

The *bar* gene works according to a completely different principle. Instead of playing defense, it attacks. It produces an enzyme that attacks the herbicide and breaks it down into harmless smaller molecules. (Monsanto's scientists had searched for genes that would "detoxify" Roundup in a similar way; they found one, but it was of limited utility. When it degraded Roundup, a chemical was released which tended to poison the plant.)

In theory these two genes should have been direct competitors in the marketplace. Both Roundup and Basta kill almost all growing vegetation; both of them are relatively nontoxic to humans. They offered similar advantages to farmers who sprayed such herbicides on their fields.

Hoechst's and PGS's resistance gene was in many respects superior, but Monsanto had other advantages: Roundup was already familiar to farmers, and it was much cheaper to produce. Such technical differences aside, the two companies had quite different ideas about the commercial potential of herbicide-resistant crops, and they pursued very different strategies. For Monsanto, Roundup was already the cornerstone of its empire, its top-selling agricultural product. The company wanted to build on that success, and quickly. It envisioned Roundup-resistant crops as blockbuster products, adding hundreds of millions of dollars, if not billions, to the company's profits. It moved aggressively and urgently to turn those genes into streams of revenue, working hardest to create Roundup-resistant versions of America's most valuable crops: soybeans, corn, and cotton.

Hoechst, which eventually bought PGS, rarely seemed to be in a hurry. For one thing it had less riding on the outcome; Basta was new on the market and accounted for less than 5 percent of Hoechst's sales of agricultural chemicals. Hoechst's executives entertained more modest dreams of Basta-resistant specialty crops like sugar beets and canola.

Over the following two decades, these two genes and two industrial empires would encounter each other at almost every step. The competition between them revealed contrasting cultures and attitudes, each with characteristic strengths and weaknesses. Hoechst's European caution was on occasion self-defeating. And Monsanto's American-style impatience, and confidence in the transforming power of technology, would sometimes prove self-destructive.

# 7

# Triumphs of Tinkering

Corn and soybeans dominate American agriculture. Together they cover 150 million acres of farmland in the United States, almost as much as all other crops put together. Every year, the fields pour forth about $20 billion worth of corn and $15 billion worth of soybeans. The wheat harvest, by contrast, is worth $7 billion and total tomato production less than $2 billion. Most other crops fall far behind. In the pungent aphorism of Will Carpenter, Monsanto's former head of agriculture research: "If you're collecting manure, you follow elephants, not sparrows. Corn and soybeans are the elephants of the crop world."

Those elephants proved to be obstinate, unyielding beasts. For years, Monsanto's genetic engineers tried to insert new genes into these plants and failed. Procedures that worked routinely in petunias or tomatoes failed completely when applied to these "recalcitrant crops." The more valuable the crop, the more recalcitrant it appeared to be.

Corn refused to accept any new genes at all; it spurned every advance by nature's genetic engineer, *Agrobacterium tumefaciens*. Soybeans offered some hope; *Agrobacterium* was able to infect soybean cells and transfer its foreign genes. Problems emerged consistently at the next step, however, when cells carrying the new genes had to be separated from those without. Untransformed cells had to be killed off, usually with a dose of antibiotic. Yet soybean cells, in a kind of suicide pact, refused to be separated. As untransformed cells were exposed to the antibiotic and died, they poisoned the genetically transformed, antibiotic-resistant cells as well. Rob Horsch, Monsanto's tissue culture expert, had even coined a name for the phenomenon: "colloperative death," death from cooperative collapse.

Until these plants could be brought to heel, the long-promised revolution in agriculture remained a distant vision, perhaps even a mirage. It remained so until a new invention arrived on the scene, accompanied by gales of laughter.

THE IDEA came, as they say, out of left field. Actually, it hurtled into the field of biotechnology like an unwelcome projectile from the bleachers, from a bystander, an amateur plant engineer named John Sanford.

Sanford is a gentle man, soft-spoken, earnest, and deeply religious. He affects modesty, but underneath the surface there lives a powerful, eccentric self-confidence. "Most people, I think—or a lot of people—have the dream of making a difference in the world. And a lot of people think that's naive. But if you don't try, you never will," he says.

In 1980, Sanford earned his Ph.D. in plant breeding and took a job at Cornell University's Agricultural Research Station in Geneva, New York. But Sanford became fascinated by a far more speculative endeavor, the project of inserting foreign genes into plants.

"It was my good fortune to be both naive and rather poorly informed," wrote Sanford many years later. "If I had known how many brilliant, well-trained, and well-equipped scientists were way ahead of me, perhaps I would not have even bothered."

Sanford possessed only the most rudimentary laboratory equipment. He knew next to nothing about manipulating DNA or regenerating plants from tissue cultures, the two most crucial pillars of genetic engineering in plants. In short, he had no business playing in this game.

He tried anyway. While other researchers employed *Agrobacterium,* Sanford attempted a cruder, more mechanical approach. He tried drilling tiny holes in the wall of a cell with a laser, hoping that bits of foreign DNA would seep through. It didn't work. But the attempt led to a conversation in the fall of 1983 with Edward Wolf, then Director of Cornell University's National Submicron Facility.

The Submicron Facility (later called the Nanofabrication Facility) had little to do with biology. Engineers there deployed beams of ions or electrons to etch electrical circuits far smaller than the wavelength of light into wafers of silicon. Sanford wanted to know if such beams might be used to cut holes in the walls of plant cells. Wolf, after some thought, said no. He calculated that such beams would produce an electrical discharge powerful enough to destroy the cell.

Yet the problem awakened Wolf's imagination. He'd grown up on a wheat farm in western Kansas, for one thing, and he had a weakness for odd, intriguing problems. He and Sanford took to calling each other on the phone, suggesting alternative ways to propel DNA into a cell. Wolf's thoughts turned to some tungsten powder that he happened to have on hand; Sanford meanwhile had his mind on guns, since he was engaged in a personal battle with marauding squirrels at his home. Between them the idea emerged: Perhaps they could soak microscopic particles of metal with DNA and simply shoot them into plant cells!

So it was that three grown men—Sanford, Wolf, and a machinist on Wolf's staff—carried a toy pistol into Cornell's Submicron Facility during Christmas vacation 1983. They donned white gowns, booties, and hair-hugging hats, as required by the facility's rules. Then, standing amid various million-dollar ion beam accelerators, they proceeded to blast whole onions with charges of tungsten beads. (Sanford chose onions because they have such large cells, easily examined.)

"We would pump up the pistol, load a bit of tungsten powder into the end of the barrel, aim, close our eyes, and fire," recalls Sanford. "The air reeked of onion. Onion juice and bits of onion splattered over our sophisticated high-tech frocks." At the right distance and with the right load of air pressure, the cells weren't destroyed. Through a microscope, Sanford could clearly see tungsten particles inside some intact cells. So far, so good. The next step would be to find out whether the beads could carry DNA, whether plant cells could survive such treatment, and whether the plant would accept that DNA as its own.

Sanford wrote a description of his idea, and sent it to Cornell's Biotechnology Institute, asking for funding. "I learned later that the evaluating panel's first response was laughter and ridicule," he says. Fortunately for him, a single member of the committee spoke up in support of the idea, pointing out that this was exactly the sort of risky, innovative exploration that the institute had been set up to support. The institute approved enough money for Sanford to hire an assistant, a graduate student named Ted Klein, who ended up devoting the next six years of his life to perfecting the gene gun.

Laughter was in fact the standard response when scientists first heard about the gene gun. "It was just beyond the realm of the reasonable," recalls one researcher. "Like a hunter's idea of how you transform a plant." Respectable researchers were trying their own novel approaches, to be sure. Some inserted DNA directly into cells with microscopic needles. Others used electrical charges to open small pores in the cell wall, allowing bits of DNA to flow in. But shooting plants with a gun? It sounded like the punch line of a joke.

Sanford often describes himself as naive. He sometimes leaves the impression of a man who'd rather avoid grubby details of commerce, whose ear is tuned to a distant, otherworldly drummer. But in his handling of the gene gun, as it came to be called, Sanford proved to be sophisticated, protective of secrets, and distrustful of those who might wrest control of his invention away from him.

Almost immediately after the experiments in the Submicron Facility, Sanford sat down to write a patent application. And in search of financial support, he went to Monsanto. The St. Louis company was the obvious place to start, he says. "They'd blown open the field, and everybody was beating a path to their door." In the fall of 1984 he flew to St. Louis and presented his idea to a small group of researchers. But the timing was wrong; in this early, exuberant period, Monsanto's researchers didn't think they needed any outside help. Sanford meanwhile had no evidence that the gene gun would work and no reputation in the field. "The general feeling was this is crazy. It just sounded silly," says Harry Klee, who attended Sanford's seminar. In hindsight, he says, that reaction is instructive. Scientists like to think of themselves as creative, freethinking types operating at the very boundary of knowledge. In fact, he says, "it's often a more conservative approach to life than we like to admit."

It would be two more years—month after month spent shooting defenseless onions—before the corporate world showed the slightest bit of interest in the gene gun. During that time, Sanford and Ted Klein redesigned the gun. In this version, tungsten beads soaked in DNA were painted onto a larger plastic projectile. When the gun fired, it drove this projectile into a plate that contained a small hole. Microscopic beads of tungsten flew through the hole and into the plant cells. The lab, Sanford recalls, smelled like a combination of a McDonald's (due to all the blasted onions) and a firing range (due to the gunpowder).

But success eluded them. The plants' cells, when bombarded with DNA, consistently died. Even when cells did survive, Sanford and Klein couldn't detect any evidence that the genes were active. At one point several years into their project Sanford went to Klein and suggested that "perhaps he might want to look for a less shaky career path." His graduate assistant disagreed. The pair trudged stubbornly onward.

Cornell's research foundation, which, as the employer of Sanford and Wolf, owned the rights to their invention, let companies know that they could acquire exclusive rights to the gene gun for $75,000. There were no takers.

What Sanford and Klein needed desperately—and they may not have fully realized it—were worthy collaborators. The gene gun needed to fall into the hands of scientists who were more experienced in the manipulation of DNA and in the art of nurturing plant life within petri dishes.

Eventually, the gene gun did move onward, following two very different paths. One route led to corn; the other to soybeans.

BY 1986 two researchers at Pioneer Hi-Bred, the largest seed company in the world, were ready to try something new. The two researchers, Arthur Weissinger and Dwight Tomes, were part of a tiny group of scientists at Pioneer pursuing the possibilities of biotechnology. It was exciting out there on the cutting edge of science, but Weissinger and Tomes were nagged by the suspicion that most of their colleagues were snickering at them behind their backs. "I likened it to riding a motorcycle when you're feeling all cool," says Weissinger in the accent of his native Alabama. "People looking at you may feel a twinge of envy at your freedom. But when you wreck the motorcycle, they'll gather around and call you a dumb SOB."

Weissinger and Tomes were in the process of wrecking their motorcycle. For five years they'd been trying to transform corn using electric shocks to open tiny holes in the walls of corn cells. They'd been able to get DNA through those holes into cells, but they couldn't get the cells to regenerate into whole plants. The cells that were capable of regenerating, meanwhile, wouldn't accept foreign DNA. Weissinger and Tomes were coming to the conclusion that their approach was a scientific dead end.

They were visiting Cornell one day and happened upon a presentation about John Sanford's gene gun. Weissinger went back to Des Moines, drew up sketches of the device, and presented the idea to his managers at Pioneer. "They all declared we were idiots and that we'd clearly gone off the deep end," Weissinger recalls. Weissinger fared no better among the company's plant breeders. "They found it hysterical. They shook their heads and wished us well in our next life."

But Weissinger and Tomes decided that pursuing a crazy idea was better than continuing to bang their heads against a brick wall. "We very quietly got plane tickets and got in touch with John Sanford," Weissinger says.

Sanford didn't let the men from Pioneer actually see the gun or watch it work until they signed an agreement to keep secret everything they'd seen in Sanford's laboratory. "He was very anxious about that," says Weissinger. "He sort of saw industry as the great thief."

Weissinger and Tomes provided two crucial bits of biological material that Sanford lacked. Tomes brought cultures of corn tissue that could be regenerated into whole corn plants. (These cultures were among Pioneer's most treasured secrets.) And Weissinger, through a collaboration with researchers at Stanford University and in England, had access to genes that were much more likely to work in corn. Researchers were discovering that grasses such as corn spoke a slightly different genetic dialect from broad-leafed plants. The 35S promoter, for instance, which worked so brilliantly in tomatoes or tobacco, didn't do nearly so well in corn cells.

The researchers worked night and day, interrupted only by brief naps and trips to a Perkin's restaurant, the only one nearby that stayed open all night.

In the following weeks, Weissinger and Tomes monitored these cultures, looking in vain for evidence of genetic transformation. "We were about to throw the cultures away and call it a bust," Weissinger says. "And I was sitting there talking on the phone, with the cultures in front of me. I opened one up and was playing with it with a dissecting needle. And all of a sudden I saw this little spot in there. I told the person I was talking to that I'd call them back. I threw it under a dissecting scope, and lo and behold, it was a tetrad." A tetrad is a group of four cells, the offspring of a single cell. And this tetrad showed a blue stain, a signal that a new marker gene in those cells was alive and working. It was like a radio signal from outer space, a sign that life existed in previously unknown spaces. "We photographed those little cells as if they'd been rock stars," says Weissinger, who's a guitar player himself. He plunged back into his work.

WHO CAN describe the path of a migrating idea? It moves at the pace of conversation and the speed of human imagination. Without John Sanford's knowledge, his idea also took root in a back corner of the biotech company Agracetus in Madison, Wisconsin. The idea grew into the concrete shape of another gene gun, one that looked nothing like Sanford's.

"So we were having this meeting in Monterey in 1986," says Dennis McCabe at Agracetus. "The meeting was over, and we were sitting around getting inebriated. Ken Barton was there and some other people. And Ken was talking about crazy ol' John Sanford."

Sanford was starting to talk, guardedly, about his invention at this point. Ken Barton, who also worked at Agracetus and was John Sanford's former paperboy, had been among the first to hear about his former neighbor's invention. Barton thought it was weird but interesting. McCabe, on the other hand, was captivated. "I thought, Wow!" McCabe says. "If you could really do that, that would be neat!"

McCabe is a boy's man, a rangy, plain-spoken free spirit who never lost his enthusiasm for explosives and other dangerous toys. "I have about half a radar station in my basement," he says. "Barb hasn't made me throw it out yet. They were selling off the parts when I was at the University of Iowa. Big, huge stuff! Twenty-five cents a pound!"

Sanford, plagued by squirrels, had imagined a gun complete with barrel and explosive charge. McCabe, his basement full of electrical equipment, thought of high voltages.

Venturing into his basement, McCabe excavated a big capacitor— a device that can store up an electrical charge then release it all at once. "My idea was I'd take this huge capacitor, charge it up, and then dump it across a narrow arc gap," he says. Twenty-five thousand volts of electricity flashing across this quarter-inch gap produced a lightning bolt and a crack of man-made thunder. "I put a drop of water in the gap. The power vaporizes that drop, and you get a nice shock wave that you can do things with." McCabe thought the shock wave would be perfect for blasting DNA into plant cells. Telling the story, his eyes shine with enthusiasm just remembering the eardrum-endangering fun of it all. "I knew I could get a lot of energy out of this. The trick is to avoid killing yourself."

This was not how McCabe was supposed to be spending his days. He was a technician, part of a team assigned to develop genetically engineered soil microbes that were supposed to help provide nutrients to the roots of crops, boosting their productivity. But McCabe found he had plenty of spare time to work on his water-drop blaster.

In about a week McCabe and a coworker named Brian Martinell had a crude device working, at least a little bit. They first tried putting DNA-covered beads onto pieces of a rubber glove. The exploding water was supposed to drive the strip of rubber against a metal screen; the beads would fly off the rubber, through the screen, and into the plant tissue. Unfortunately, rubber wasn't tough enough. It disintegrated and ended up "on the ceiling," says McCabe.

One day Martinell came walking in with a bag of potato chips from the building's vending machine, and McCabe's eyes fell on the bag. He remembered that such bags are made of Mylar, a flexible, tough material. On a whim, he decided to use a piece of that bag instead of rubber as the carrier for DNA. It worked perfectly. "For about a year and a half, we used potato chip bags, and the funny thing was it couldn't be just any bag. It had to be ones from the vending machine," McCabe says. "I was thin before this project started," chimes in Brian Martinell, grinning.

But which plant was a worthy target for this gene gun? Most researchers pursued corn, the world's most valuable crop and the one that seemed hardest to transform genetically. But Agracetus's scientific director was fixated on soybeans. Soybeans became McCabe's prey.

McCabe and his colleagues tried to blast gold particles coated with DNA into particular kinds of cells, called meristems, found inside the tips of soybean shoots. Meristem cells are a kind of growing embryo inside the plant; if they are genetically transformed, they can grow to become a whole new plant. It was a way of avoiding "colloperative death"; the Agracetus scientists wouldn't bother trying to kill off the cells that weren't genetically transformed. Instead they'd simply shoot thousands of these meristems and let them grow into whole plants, hoping that a few plants would turn out to carry the new genes and pass those genes on to their offspring.

It was a tedious, labor-intensive process. Shooting genes into meristem cells was like placing thousands of bets on horses that are sure to lose. But even a ten-thousand-to-one bet is likely to pay off if it's placed ten thousand times. By April of 1988 McCabe and his colleagues had in hand their first soybean plant that demonstrably possessed a new gene and had passed it along to its offspring. In order to secure that single plant, scientists at Agracetus had searched through nine thousand soybean shoots grown from meristems bombarded with foreign genes.

With that plant in hand, McCabe and his colleagues published their accomplishment. The news of genetically transformed soybeans caught the attention of John Schillinger, veteran breeder of soybeans and president of Asgrow, one of the country's leading soybean seed companies.

THE BIBLE lies open on John Schillinger's kitchen table. A visitor and talk of a life devoted to soybeans has interrupted his morning devotions. Schillinger retrieves the book, returns it to its accustomed place in a nearby closet, and begins his story.

Schillinger is among the century's most accomplished breeders of soybeans. In the late 1970s he created a variety of soybean that surpassed anything then available and turned Asgrow into the leading name among soybean seed companies. But he continued looking forward, this time toward the possibilities of genetic engineering.

When Schillinger heard of Agracetus's success, he traveled to Wisconsin for a visit with the company's scientific director, Winston Brill. "I remember he was superprotective, very secretive," Schillinger recalls with a chuckle. "He wouldn't let us back in the lab. We had to meet out in a conference room."

Brill was willing to turn his gene gun loose on Asgrow's soybeans for a million dollars. Schillinger approached the leadership of Asgrow's parent company, the drugmaker Upjohn. He convinced them—he's not quite sure how—that it would be a great thing to introduce the world to a genetically engineered version of soybeans.

*But engineered to do what?* Agracetus merely had the gene gun; it didn't have any genes that were worth blasting into soybean plants. "The heat was on me to find a gene," Schillinger says.

So Schillinger took another trip, to St. Louis. He met with Monsanto's leading scientists and toured the company's laboratories. He saw rows and rows of scientists and technicians trying to regenerate soybean plants from tissues that contained a gene for resistance to Roundup. The procedure was working but not very well, and Monsanto's Rob Horsch, who was in charge of the project, was losing patience with it.

Schillinger told Horsch that Asgrow and Agracetus, working together, had inserted genes into several of Asgrow's best new soybean varieties. He suggested that they might be able to create Roundupresistant soybeans quite a bit faster if they all worked together. The idea got Horsch's attention. If Agracetus held the key to genetic transformation of this crop, Horsch was willing to swallow his pride and turn that part of the job over to Dennis McCabe's gene gun.

The three companies struck a deal in 1989, and all of the three parties to it walked away after signing with queasy feelings in the pits of their stomachs.

The scientists at Agracetus worried that they'd promised Monsanto more than they could deliver. "We were really scared," says

Brian Martinell. "We knew we could deliver a random plant. But we'd never had to generate them on a schedule. And Monsanto wanted hundreds of plants."

Horsch meanwhile had to shut down much of Monsanto's in-house research in order to pay Agracetus. He didn't know for a fact that Monsanto's genes for Roundup resistance would even work. Meeting with the Asgrow executives, Horsch exuded a confidence that he did not feel and thought to himself, "I just hope this works!"

For Asgrow's John Schillinger, meanwhile, signing a deal with Monsanto meant giving up control of the project. It was one thing to collaborate with a small company like Agracetus, which needed his money. It was quite another thing to rely on the goodwill and the promises of a giant company like Monsanto, which had dreams for biotechnology that outstripped even his own. Schillinger wanted to be able eventually to sell Roundup-resistant soybeans, and with this deal Asgrow had purchased the right to sell Monsanto's genes. But Monsanto's executives secretly wanted much more; they wanted to see Roundup-resistant soybeans growing on every farm in America, not just those of Schillinger's customers.

JOHN SANFORD's original version of the gene gun, meanwhile, had emerged from obscurity on May 7, 1987, when Sanford and his collaborators published an article about their invention in one of the world's great scientific journals, *Nature*. The paper didn't show convincing evidence that the gene gun could genetically transform a cell, but many scientists seemed to feel, after they stopped chuckling, that if *Nature* was willing to take the gene gun seriously, perhaps they should, too. Peggy Lemaux was a researcher at the Carnegie Institution of Washington at the time. She and her colleagues, she says, "just hooted! Like, 'Oh, Right! Oh, ho, ho, ho!' But then I actually read the article, and the more I read, the more I felt it was worth a try."

A small stream, then a flood of requests for gene guns poured into Sanford's office at Cornell. Sanford set up a small business to manufacture and deliver the contraptions. Many requests came from laboratories pursuing the grand prize of plant transformation: creation of the first viable, genetically engineered corn plant. With the gene gun in hand, the race for corn turned into a mad sprint.

Peggy Lemaux joined in when she moved to the research laboratories of DeKalb Genetics in Mystic, Connecticut. DeKalb was not favored to win this international competition. The smart money would have bet on Pioneer or on several prominent researchers assembled at the USDA's Plant Gene Expression Center in Albany, California, who were collaborating with Monsanto. Yet through sheer serendipity, DeKalb's group made surprisingly fast progress.

Lemaux made one crucial contribution. She decided to switch to a new "selectable marker gene," the tool that allows researchers to select only those few cells in which a new gene is present and working. The new tool was the *bar* gene (*"bar"* for Basta resistance), which had just been discovered by researchers in Europe. One of the discoverers of that gene happened to visit DeKalb's laboratories soon after Lemaux went to work there and described his work. Lemaux asked him for a copy of the gene. "I can't give it to you," he replied. But Lemaux quickly realized that one of her old friends at Stanford, an expert on these types of bacteria, had independently isolated the same gene. A few phone calls, and the *bar* gene was on its way to Mystic. This gene proved to be far superior to previous selectable markers.

The most challenging task, more difficult than getting new genes into corn cells, was to coax these cells to grow into whole fertile plants. Corn tissues tended to degenerate quickly; if one waited too long, the tissues would grow into plants that no longer were fertile.

Hanging over the whole enterprise was the forbidding, nay-saying image of a European researcher, a Swiss biologist named Ingo Potrykus. Potrykus had made a career of shooting down the claims of scientists who claimed to have succeeded in transforming cereal crops, including corn and wheat. No mere sign of hope satisfied Potrykus. He demanded proof; he rarely found other scientists' evidence convincing, and sometimes he suggested that other scientists were faking their data. Even more infuriating, Potrykus often was right. Time after time, scientists announced successes that turned out to be illusory. "Potrykus was the evil empire," says one American scientist.

At DeKalb, Lemaux and her colleagues compiled a list of "Potrykus postulates"—the evidence required to prove beyond all doubt that corn plants had been genetically transformed. As their experiments proceeded, they checked off the "postulates" one by one. The group's expert on corn tissues perfected a method for freezing these tissues in order to keep them fresh, then bombarding them with the gene gun and quickly growing them back into whole plants. As new corn plants emerged, each one got a name from an alphabetized list. The first seven plants turned out not to be genetically transformed. A few days before Christmas 1989 the eighth plant, Henry, passed the test. It contained the foreign gene. As weeks passed, the researchers held their breath, hoping that Henry, not the most spry and healthy looking of plants, would produce seeds. One Potrykus postulate remained: Would Henry pass the new genes on to his offspring?

Lemaux had learned from her time rubbing shoulders with the founders of biotechnology at Stanford to take scientific competition seriously. "Part of what I brought to the group was an attitude of, we're going to get this out right now!" she says. Even before the final tests were done, the DeKalb group had an article already written, ready to submit to a scientific journal. "We just had to do this one last test," recalls Lemaux. "We got the ear, took the embryos out, and germinated them." Those shoots, like Henry, contained the foreign gene. The researchers checked off their last Potrykus postulate, added this final piece of evidence to their paper, and on April 8, 1990, sent it off to a journal called *The Plant Cell*. The report, sporting glossy, full-color photographs, appeared in July.

When the report arrived on the desk of Dwight Tomes at Pioneer Hi-Bred International, the mild-mannered, wispy-bearded researcher was "angry, to put it mildly." He was angry, he says, "because we had the knowledge of how to put those pieces together, and we didn't get those pieces put together." By custom, the scientific community gives precedence and honor to the first published, fully documented report of an accomplishment. By that standard, DeKalb had won the race. Monsanto's collaborators at the USDA's Plant Gene Expression Center in Albany, California, had reached the goal at almost the same time but published their results a few months later.

Yet in the view of the U.S. Patent Office neither of them had actually won the race. On the day in April 1990 when Peggy Lemaux and her colleagues at DeKalb checked off the last Potrykus postulate and dropped their article in the mail, examiners in the Patent Office already had spent several months studying a patent application covering almost exactly the same technique, filed by an unheralded group in Minneapolis called Plant Science Research. This group, the research subsidiary of Biotechnica, Inc., preferred to file a patent application rather than publish its work in a scientific journal.

It did, however, announce news of its breakthrough in January 1990 to the *Wall Street Journal*. Several DeKalb executives, in the wake of their own triumph, decided to pay the Minneapolis company a visit to see what real accomplishments lay behind the vague press reports. They found a company facing imminent bankruptcy and more than willing to entertain the possibility of a buyout. According to former executives at Plant Science Research, DeKalb claimed to be interested in acquiring the smaller company's research staff; once the sale was completed, however, DeKalb began laying off scientists. All that DeKalb really wanted, it appeared, was ownership of Plant Science Research's patents.

BUT IT turned out there were several paths to transformed corn. The gene gun turned out not to be necessary after all.

In the summer of 1990, as DeKalb's researchers basked in the glory of their triumph, several of the company's executives had an idea. The *bar* gene, which had been so useful in helping DeKalb's researchers create a genetically transformed corn plant, was now firmly lodged in the corn plants filling up the company's greenhouses. As a consequence, those plants were resistant to the herbicide Basta, sold by the German company Hoechst. Hoechst, they realized, might be *very* interested in this resistance. Basta-tolerant corn, if planted on a substantial portion of America's corn acres, could turn Basta into a blockbuster herbicide, with sales of hundreds of millions of dollars each year.

Hoechst should be willing to pay quite a bit to get its hands on such corn plants, the DeKalb executives reasoned. They sent an emissary to the headquarters of Hoechst in Frankfurt. There the DeKalb representative met the scientist Günter Donn. Donn was polite but seemed curiously uninterested in DeKalb's presentation. He

invited DeKalb's representative to take a tour of Hoechst's greenhouses. There, he revealed his secret: row upon row of corn plants,
all completely resistant to Basta. None had been created with the
help of the gene gun.

THE STORY of these plants had begun far to the east, in the Hungarian city of Szeged. Szeged is remote, even by Hungarian standards. It
lies several hours south of the country's intellectual center of Bu-
dapest, the last stop in Hungary before a traveler enters either Ro-
mania or Yugoslavia. But by happenstance it had become home to
Hungary's foremost scientific institute on the biology of plants.
Here, throughout the 1980s, with the Iron Curtain still erect though
wobbling, Denes Dudits and Sandor Morocz tended their corn
plants.

Dudits, the senior scientist, had spent part of the 1970s and 1980s
in Canada and the United States. By chance, during those years, he'd
become acquainted with Hoechst's Günter Donn, who also was visiting North America. The two scientists stayed in touch when they
returned to Europe. Morocz was Dudits's young student, still in his
twenties, hardworking and eager to establish himself.

The institute didn't have lots of money, but plant breeding and tissue culture don't require lots of money. They do require something
else, something in critically short supply in the hotly competitive laboratories of the West: a long attention span.

Careers moved more slowly in Eastern Europe during those years.
The work in Szeged was less buffeted by scientific fads or pressure to
break new ground constantly. Year after year, Dudits and Morocz
pursued the same goal. They were searching for varieties of corn
that displayed a powerful urge to regenerate from individual cells,
growing back into whole fertile corn plants.

Dudits and Morocz crossed different lines of corn that they obtained from China, the United States, and Hungary, looking for superior varieties. They also experimented with different methods for
handling their tissue cultures.

In 1987 a call came from Frankfurt. Günter Donn and his colleagues at Hoechst had discovered their gene for resistance to Basta.
They had been able to insert the gene into plants that were easily

transformable, such as canola and sugar beets, but corn was beyond their grasp.

Donn asked if Morocz could come to work in Frankfurt for two years. (It was the maximum period of time for which a visitor from Hungary could obtain a work permit.) Donn wanted to see if any of the Hungarian materials could be regenerated from the most stripped-down form in which a plant cell can exist, a so-called protoplast.

Protoplasts are plant cells that have had their rigid walls stripped off with chemicals. Once these walls are gone, foreign bits of DNA can infiltrate the cell, and some of that DNA will end up knitted together with the cell's natural DNA. It was a well-known technique for working with bacteria, but it didn't work well with plants. Most plant cells won't grow back from protoplasts, especially not if they are subjected at the same time to poisons intended to select those cells that have accepted the desired gene.

But Günter Donn wanted to try it. After all, no other technique had worked with corn either. It would work, though, only if Sandor Morocz could deliver corn cells with an unprecedented will to live and grow.

Morocz worked during those two years like a man possessed, cross-breeding, selecting, and studying his varieties of corn. His deadline was June 30, 1989, the expiration date on his work permit. Just a few weeks before that date, he produced one particular line that was superior to any he'd ever seen in the preceding decade of work. Morocz and Donn divided the cultures in half; Morocz took a set home with him, and the rest stayed in Frankfurt.

It was time for the crucial experiments. Donn took the corn cells, stripped off the cell walls with chemical solvents, then immersed the protoplasts in a solution containing bits of DNA. These were the Basta-resistant genes, hooked to a promoter that any plant would recognize as a signal to activate the genes.

The rest was stunningly, laughably simple. "The protoplasts did most of the job, not myself," says Donn. "We just delivered the DNA, kept them happy, gave them the right growing conditions." Protoplasts that contained the Basta-resistant gene grew and prospered. They formed shoots, then roots. They grew and produced ears filled with kernels which, when planted, sprouted into plants that also withstood many times the normal lethal dose of Basta. They filled growth chambers, then entire greenhouses. These were the plants that Donn showed to his visitor from DeKalb. Donn took secret pleasure in the crestfallen look in the American's face.

IT HAD been almost a decade since visionaries of biotechnology had promised genetically engineered crops in the field. Finally, companies were ready to deliver on their promises. In field after field, novel genes turned skeptics into believers.

John Schillinger, from the Asgrow seed company, has a field of soybeans etched in his memory. The field had been sprayed with Roundup. All around him were plants wilting and dying except for several rows of Roundup-resistant soybeans, which stood there green and robust as ever. "Things like that just stick in your mind," Schillinger says.

A Monsanto executive named Paul Johanson remembers a visit to the USDA research station on Long Island. The Colorado potato beetle had overrun Long Island, nearly driving potato production out of the area. The USDA outpost was trying out various new insecticides that purported to control the beetle, along with Monsanto's potatoes containing the Bt gene.

"I introduced myself and said I'd like to see our potatoes," says Johanson. The station manager gestured toward a large glass window in back of his desk, looking out over a series of test plots. "Look out across this field," he said. "The only thing green and growing out there—that's yours. There isn't anything else alive in that field."

"I walked out to the field," Johanson recalls. "There were vines wrapped over each other, and the vines from plants next to our plants were just completely stripped. And I pulled some of those vines out, and the parts of neighboring plants that were lying inside our plants were still green. The insects, once they got a bite of our plant, had stopped feeding."

The drama of genetic engineering in plants was ready to move beyond laboratory experiments and field trials. The stage was lit; players for the second act were waiting for the curtain to rise. Corporate executives in St. Louis, Des Moines, Frankfurt, and Basel, Switzerland, were ready for battles over what value to place on these genes, who should control them, and who should capture the profits from them. And in Washington, Brussels, Bonn, and in countless town halls and private homes on several continents, another battle continued, a struggle for the sympathies of the voters, consumers, and government officials who held the fate of this technology in their hands.

# 8

# Forces in Opposition

At the close of the 1980s, conflicts over genetic engineering of plants were becoming sharper, the lines of disagreement more clearly drawn. Will Carpenter, the genial Mississippian who was in charge of Monsanto's "public policy program" on biotechnology, noted the shift in a memo to fellow Monsanto executives early in 1989. "Environmental organizations clearly are becoming more activist in the area of biotechnology," he wrote, "and the predominance of press articles and editorials, while not wholly negative, are more questioning in tone and less supportive than they have been in the past."

Like geese flocking to a pond, people with disparate, sometimes idiosyncratic objections to biotechnology found their way to each other, forming a recognizable political force. By 1989, a leading antibiotechnology coalition called the Biotechnology Working Group included representatives from the Wisconsin Family Farm Defense Fund, the Pesticide Action Network, the National Wildlife Federation, Consumers Union, the Committee for Responsible Genetics, the Environmental Defense Fund, the ecology department of the University of Minnesota, and the United Methodist Church's lobbying office in Washington, among others. Various of these people had campaigned in earlier years against toxic waste, against the destruction of wilderness areas, in defense of small-scale agriculture, or against the commercial exploitation of genes and seeds. Their backgrounds were diverse, yet they shared common attitudes toward nature and toward politics. They saw genetic engineering as a perilous

*Monsanto's genetic engineers received permission to plant their creations in the open air for the first time on a sunny day in June 1987. On the planter, behind trays of tomato seedlings, from left to right: Stephen Rogers, Robert Fraley, Roger Beachy (from Washington University in St. Louis), and Robert Horsch. (Courtesy of Monsanto)*

*On April 27, 1999, the pioneers of Monsanto's venture into biotechnology gathered once again, this time in the White House, to receive the National Medal of Technology. From left to right: Stephen Rogers, Ernest Jaworski, Robert Horsch, Robert Fraley, President Bill Clinton. (Courtesy Christy Bowe)*

Monsanto's researchers benefited enormously from close relationships with university researchers, including Mary-Dell Chilton, a professor at Washington University in St. Louis.
(Courtesy Washington University in St. Louis)

John Sanford, inventor of the "gene gun," with a later version of his invention.
(Courtesy John Sanford)

Robert Fraley, here speaking at a conference of the National Cotton Council, became the driving force behind Monsanto's assault on the seed industry.
(Courtesy National Cotton Council)

*Tom Urban, (right with two of his customers) led Pioneer Hi-Bred, Monsanto's nemesis, during the 1980s and early 1990s. (Courtesy Pioneer Hi-Bred International, Inc.)*

*Roger Salquist, CEO of Calgene, showing off some of his company's Flavr Savr tomatoes, in a field near Dixon, California. (Courtesy Richard Gilmore)*

*Jeremy Rifkin, an activist and futurist, was one of the earliest and most vociferous opponents of genetic engineering. He introduced Benny Härlin to the issue. (Courtesy of the Council of Europe)*

*Benny Härlin (center, wearing leather jacket) at the front lines of Berlin's Haüserkampf, the Battle of the Houses, on September 27, 1981. During this period, police battled repeatedly with youth who occupied more than a hundred of the city's abandoned houses. (© Paul Glaser)*

*Benny Härlin leaves prison on August 19, 1983, ready to take his seat in the European Parliament. (© Paul Glaser)*

*In the late 1990s, Benny Härlin coordinated Greenpeace's international campaign against genetic engineering. (© Greenpeace/Novis)*

*Robert Shapiro's vision of global sustainability inspired many within Monsanto. After listening to Shapiro speak at a meeting called the Monsanto Global Forum in 1995, one Monsanto employee approached Shapiro and hung her name tag around his neck. Dozens of others then did the same thing. (Courtesy of Monsanto)*

A protestor in Paris holds a sign featuring the image of Monsanto's CEO. (Agence France Presse/Francois Guillot)

John Losey's dead Monarch butterfly larvae caused a worldwide sensation, and resentment among some of his scientific colleagues. (©Robert Barker/Cornell University Photography)

David Hoisington, director of biotechnology at the International Center for the Improvement of Wheat and Maize in Mexico (shown here with researcher Natasha Bohorova) has spent years trying to convince biotechnology researchers in "Europe and North America" to share their treasures. (A.M. Sanchez/CIMMYT)

Bruno de la Luz (second from left), a farmer in the tropical highlands of Mexico, has just started buying hybrid corn seed from Monsanto's seed companies. To the right of de la Luz are Olga Haas and Guillermo Alafita, who work for Monsanto in Mexico. (Courtesy Daniel Charles)

*Protestors in London take to the streets against genetically engineered food. (© David Hoffman/David Hoffman Photo Library)*

*British police lead away protestors clad in white garments, a symbolic protection against the "dangers" of genetically modified organisms, after the protestors began destroying fields of genetically engineered oilseed rape plants. (© Nick Cobbing/David Hoffman Photo Library)*

intrusion into the natural world, and they nurtured a visceral skepticism toward the motives and trustworthiness of large companies that were doing most of the intruding.

The emotional and ideological roots of this antipathy gave the movement stamina and determination, but such motivations weren't easily translated into effective political action. Opponents of biotechnology had to use the levers that were available to them, and the main levers within reach were existing laws intended to protect the environment from destruction or consumers from harmful food.

As a consequence, the battles over biotechnology were fought over details, not fundamental convictions and motives. Opponents and proponents of genetic engineering spent long days discussing such arcane matters as the rate at which genes might migrate through cross-pollination from genetically engineered crops to related wild plants and whether the wild plants might then become more "weedy." A few groups suddenly evidenced a new interest in the government's system for regulating food. The National Wildlife Federation declared in one press release that lax regulations on biotechnology were "turning food safety into Russian Roulette."

These were, for the most part, proxy arguments, the visible expression of motives that lay much deeper. Both the representatives of industry and biotechnology's critics knew this, and that knowledge fed cynicism. Each side grew increasingly inclined to dismiss the other's arguments as tactical ploys, intended merely—depending on the argument—to promote sales of genetically engineered products or to block their progress.

The tone was set by a conflict over the first product of Monsanto's biotech laboratories, which wasn't a food at all but a hormone that could be injected into cows. It was called bovine growth hormone, or BGH (Monsanto preferred the term *bovine somatotropin*, or *BST*), and was a version of a cow's own natural growth hormone, produced instead in fermentation vats filled with genetically engineered bacteria. Injected into cows, this hormone shifted their milk-making machinery into a higher gear.

"I remember sitting and talking with [prominent antibiotech activist] Jeremy Rifkin about this in the mid-1980s," says Margaret Mellon, who was in charge of the National Wildlife Federation's work on biotechnology at the time. "I just couldn't see how you could make it an issue." There didn't appear to be any serious safety problems with BGH; cows would just get more of a hormone that they have in their bodies already. *Cows* had good reasons to protest, but consumers had never seemed to care too much about the misery of cattle.

"And Jeremy said, 'I'll *make* it an issue!'" Mellon recalls. "I'll find something! It's the first product of biotechnology out the door, and I'm going to fight it!"

Indeed, one could hardly have imagined a more inviting target than BGH, a product without redeeming social value. Dairy farmers were producing too much milk already. The government was buying up the surplus in order to keep the price from falling. Biotechnology now offered a way to produce even more! Some economists predicted that if the hormone worked as advertised and milk production increased by 20 percent, the surplus would grow, prices would gradually fall, and small farmers in particular would be driven out of business.

Opposition was especially stiff in dairy states with a populist tradition such as Vermont and Wisconsin. The only people who were really enthusiastic about BGH, in fact, appeared to work at Monsanto.

But BGH taught opponents of biotechnology an unkind lesson. It wasn't enough to show that a product was unnecessary or unpopular or even irrational. (The same is true, after all, of most consumer gadgetry.) They had to show that BGH was dangerous.

The opponents of BGH did their best. They claimed that the use of BGH would raise levels of particular hormones in milk that some scientists believe are linked to certain cancers. They unearthed evidence that cows treated with BGH might be more prone to certain illnesses due to stress and that this would result in lower-quality milk. The Food and Drug Administration did delay approval of BGH for several years while it reviewed all the evidence, but in 1993 the agency declared that BGH presented no serious threat to human health. (The product was accompanied by warning labels, but only regarding possible effects on the health of cows receiving the treatment.) The agency also barred retailers from advertising their milk as "BGH-free." Such claims amounted to false advertising, the agency said. First, there was no way to verify the claim, since there was no way to distinguish between natural and injected growth hormone. Second, the claim itself was misleading, the FDA said. Milk was milk; its character did not change because the cows that produced it had been injected with hormones produced by genetically engineered bacteria.

So Monsanto won, but CEO Richard Mahoney wondered if the battle had been worth it. "It's come out all right, but if I'd known the public furor and the difficulty we'd face, I wouldn't have done it at all," he said years later. "We got into BST like we got into a lot of things. We'd been making agricultural chemicals for years. You increase the productivity of the farmer; you keep half [of the profits] and give him half. So what's the big deal? There wasn't even one discussion of the social implications. I never thought of it."

REBECCA GOLDBURG and Margaret "Mardi" Mellon insist that they never intended to become professional Cassandras, calling out unceasing warnings about biotechnology's dangers.

"I thought biotechnology was going to be a great thing!" says Mellon, who collected degrees in molecular biology and in law before setting up a biotechnology project in 1987 at the National Wildlife Federation in Washington, D.C. Goldburg for her part went to work at the Environmental Defense Fund in 1986, after earning her Ph.D. in ecology, simply because "I didn't think a research career was for me. You spend ten weeks in the field and you get kind of lonely. I wanted a wider focus."

Both Mellon and Goldburg owed their jobs to the Joyce Foundation, in Chicago, which decided in the mid-1980s that agricultural biotechnology deserved close scrutiny. The foundation did not, however, support out-and-out opposition to biotechnology. Mellon's first successful proposal to the Joyce Foundation promised to "assure that the technology is developed with the proper environmental controls" and suggested that even the biotechnology industry might benefit from active involvement of environmental groups: These groups, enjoying much greater credibility in the eyes of the public than industry, might help assure the public that particular products of biotechnology were indeed safe.

"We weren't talking about stopping the technology; we were talking about how many controls to put on a field test," says Goldburg. While Jeremy Rifkin stood atop the antibiotech ramparts shouting slogans, Goldburg and Mellon practiced subtler tactics. They demanded that the public have access to the same information that government regulators saw when giving approval to new biotech products. (Companies often declare much of this data "confidential business information.") They called for more comprehensive federal regulation and more public funding of ecological risks posed by biotech crops. Instead of blanket condemnation they raised questions. More and more questions. It drove biotech companies crazy.

"Mardi was the first one I met," says one Monsanto scientist. "I was naive enough to think, okay, she's asking some questions, she wants some answers. So here are the answers. Of course there was a lot more to it than that."

Mellon and Goldburg weren't in the business of accepting answers. Their job was to keep asking more questions, always alert for potential dangers either to the environment or consumers. Their natural allies were government regulators and the news media; their natural adversaries, profit-driven private companies. Success was measured by tighter government regulations passed, more press coverage obtained, and more grant requests funded. What started out as a cautiously cordial relationship between the environmentalists and industry gradually deteriorated into thinly veiled enmity.

Leonard Guarraia, Monsanto's former chief of regulatory affairs, was most irked by the environmentalists' claim to represent a higher public interest. ("She gets to be Joan d'Arc," he snorted, speaking of Goldburg.) The reality, Guarraia insisted, was that the environmentalists, too, served private interests: their own. Only by warning of public dangers could they generate publicity, raise money, and further their own careers.

Goldburg and Mellon for their part were angered by industry's use of political influence to achieve favorable regulations; they also became more cynical about the commercial forces driving biotechnology forward. No product exposed those forces better than the drive to create herbicide-tolerant plants. This, they asked, was the point of genetic engineering? To make fields safe for the spraying of more herbicides? For environmentalists raised on *Silent Spring,* Rachel Carson's exposé of DDT's dangers, it was as if biotechnology had married Satan himself. "It drove home to environmentalists that the agrichemical industry was going to continue being the agrichemical industry and keep promoting the same old practices," says Goldburg.

Monsanto's representatives could talk themselves blue in the face about the environmental benefits of spraying Roundup instead of more hazardous chemicals. Environmentalists were having none of it. In 1990, a coalition of activists including Goldburg and Mellon produced a report on these crops and named it *Biotechnology's Bitter Harvest.*

Herbicide-tolerant crops also drove biotechnology straight into the middle of older, larger arguments about the consequences of industrial agriculture. Chemicals replaced hoes, enormous machines replaced "hired hands" and neighborhood threshing bees, rural communities shrank and even disappeared, as farms became ever larger and ever less dependent on hand labor. And topsoil, the paper-thin, irreplaceable layer on which all life depends, continued to wash down the Mississippi faster than it could be replaced, as it had since plows first ripped open the Midwestern prairie.

Many mourned the social and environmental effects of this century-old phenomenon, but none had figured out a way to reverse it. In fact, critics of these developments often couldn't even get a hearing. Rural leaders from the U.S. Department of Agriculture on down had invested too deeply in technological "advances" to question them, and suburbanites barely cared how their food was grown.

Genetically engineered crops, in the eyes of the critics, represented the forces that had driven agriculture down an unsustainable path. Once again agriculture was about to use technology to override nature, and it was being controlled by the same large companies that had promoted herbicides and insecticides in years past. Opposition to biotechnology became a way of opposing agribusiness and promoting an alternative vision of agriculture.

The vision went by the name "sustainable agriculture." Over the years, as Margaret Mellon struggled to move beyond simple opposition to biotechnology and articulate what she was *for,* she settled on this vision of "a fundamentally different agriculture." Pesticides would be used sparingly, if at all. Vast areas covered with a single crop would give way to a mosaic of much smaller plots. Mass production in agriculture would be replaced by the more labor-intensive, smaller-scale farming methods prevalent before World War II.

JACK DOYLE'S crusade against corporate control of seeds, genes, and agriculture began in 1979 with a visitor from North Carolina and a cup of coffee. Doyle was a campaigner for the Environmental Policy Institute, "just a working-class guy looking for a fight." His visitor was Cary Fowler, thin, curly-haired, soft spoken, and a complete novice in the ways of Washington. Fowler worked for the National Sharecroppers Fund, an activist group originally set up to promote the interests of tenant farmers in the South. He'd also coauthored a best-selling book called *Food First*. The book condemned the social and economic impacts of the Green Revolution, which boosted food production in parts of the Third World by replacing traditional varieties of wheat and rice with new, high-yielding varieties.

Fowler was on a quixotic, highly improbable mission. He wanted to stop passage of an obscure piece of legislation, a proposed amendment to the Plant Variety Protection Act of 1970. The PVPA allowed seed companies to claim ownership rights over the plant varieties they developed. A new amendment would expand these rights to six kinds of vegetables that had been left out of the earlier law. The amendment was strongly supported by seed companies, and its sponsors in Congress assumed that no one else really cared.

But Cary Fowler cared. Over a cup of coffee, he told Jack Doyle about dramatic developments in the traditionally slow-moving seed industry. Large seed companies like Pioneer Hi-Bred and DeKalb were buying small ones. Small, family-run seed businesses were vanishing into the jaws of multinationals like Ciba-Geigy, ITT, Occidental Petroleum, Pfizer, Sandoz, Union Carbide, and Upjohn.

The reason, Fowler explained, was the ten-year-old PVPA, which was now about to be broadened. Until that law passed, there had been little promise of profits in seeds (with the notable exception of hybrid corn). The reason was that seed companies hadn't "owned" their products. Every variety, whether Beefsteak tomatoes or

Williams soybeans, had been public property, available on equal terms to all. Before the PVPA arrived, any "improved" variety that a seed company developed could be sold as well by competing seed companies or even by other farmers. (Corn was different because creating high-yielding "hybrid" varieties was a complicated business not easily duplicated, allowing companies like Pioneer and DeKalb to maintain control over their products.)

Once the PVPA came into force, a company could develop a new variety and claim exclusive rights to sell it, just as a pharmaceutical company could develop a new drug and through patents claim exclusive rights to it. The PVPA brought the scent of profits to the seed business, and corporate giants came prowling.

Fowler painted a frightening vision of growing corporate domination over plant life. Private interests, he told Doyle, were seizing control of the seed, the most crucial, irreplaceable resource for feeding humanity. Fowler foresaw a day when seed barons would reap monopoly profits from their proprietary varieties, thousands of mom-and-pop seed businesses would disappear, and with them the storehouse of freely distributed, "folk" varieties.

"I was blown away," says Doyle. These issues would dominate his life for the next decade.

Fowler and Doyle lost their battle against the proposed amendments to the PVPA, after an intense debate that shocked the seed industry. And as it turned out, many of Fowler's fears did not materialize, at least during the 1980s. Seed prices did not skyrocket, and traditional varieties of tomatoes loved by home gardeners did not disappear. In fact, if there was a "seed baron" strategy, it fizzled. Most seed companies remained only marginally profitable, and some of the large corporations that bought seed companies during the 1970s, such as Upjohn, Shell, and ARCO, got out of the business again a few years later.

But Doyle caught a glimpse of a second wave of consolidation in the seed industry rising in the distance, potentially more threatening than the first, fueled by enthusiasm for genetic engineering. The skirmish over the PVPA in fact was merely a preview for later battles over genetically engineered (and patented) crops, with many of the same people and arguments lined up on either side.

Doyle listened to David Padwa, the visionary founder of the biotech company Agrigenetics, speak of seeds as "envelopes" for the delivery of genes created in the laboratory. Those genes could be patented, a much tighter form of control than Plant Variety Protection. Padwa believed in owning not just the genes but the seed companies as well; they were the "turnstiles" where he could charge for his genes. Farmers would line up and pay high prices for seeds that contained genes to protect corn from insects or that turned tobacco plants into small factories for the production of industrial enzymes. "Seed barons," in this vision, were merely useful tools, vassals of the new powers, the gene moguls. Doyle's book on the emerging new powers in agriculture, *Altered Harvest,* was published in 1985.

"Today, the premier natural resource is not land or oil; it is DNA," Doyle told his audiences. "What is emerging, I believe, are huge multinational 'life sciences' conglomerates; unprecedented entities that will use genes just as earlier corporate powers used land, minerals, or oil." Which is to say, he suggested, that companies will exploit them with little regard for the public good. "In the long run, the big issue in biotechnology is going to be about economic power—about who owns and controls this technology, about who owns and controls the genes. The central issue is going to be about who is in a position to dispense biotechnology's miracle cures, or its productive powers in agriculture." Doyle knew who he did *not* want in control of biotechnology: big business in general and chemical giants like Monsanto and Ciba-Geigy (later Novartis) in particular.

THE DEBATE over genetic engineering had produced one positive result from Monsanto's point of view. It had produced a "regulatory framework" for products of biotechnology, consisting of a set of existing laws with specific requirements. This created the outline of a path toward legal approval of the company's products.

Europe had created a similar path. In 1990 European authorities in Brussels approved a "directive" that laid out how each national government should regulate the products of biotechnology. At first glance, these regulations seemed no stricter than those in the United States. But Monsanto's Steve Rogers, cocreator of the company's first genetically engineered plants, soon realized that first impressions didn't tell the whole story. Rogers spent fourteen months in Europe during 1990 and 1991 visiting officials in European capitals. He had the distinct impression that government officials preferred avoiding the issue. Perhaps biotechnology was too sensitive a subject, or perhaps European officials thought genetically engineered products lay too far in the future. "Most of the authorities were like, 'Oh sure. Well, come back in a few years when it happens,'" Rogers says. "You could just tell that it was going to take a while."

Rogers, with his enthusiastic, gregarious, very American personality, was struck by something else during that time. "In the U.S., something new comes along, and there's just an immediate acceptance, or at least a curiosity and a willingness to say, 'Hey, this is neat!'," he says. "The attitude in Europe was, 'Why should I try something new? What I have is working just fine.' There was a lot more tradition and suspicion of the new."

Those impressions stuck in Rogers's mind, even after he returned to the United States. As he helped plan Monsanto's march toward the market with its genetically engineered crops, he often raised his voice to warn of potential problems in Europe. "You've got to remember that the Europeans are not as gung ho as we are. You have to assume that it's going to take a greater amount of time," he told his colleagues. It was a lonely point of view. "It finally got to the point where I didn't have to say anything anymore," he recalls. "They'd just look at me and shake their heads. They knew what I was going to say."

IN NO country was the debate on biotechnology more strident and more divisive than in Germany. There were several reasons. A powerful antiestablishment youth movement had emerged in the country, hostile to mainstream commercial culture, big business, and technological solutions of all sorts. The Green Party was its political voice. Among other parts of the population, biotechnology awakened traumatic memories of Germany's recent past, in which modern science and technology became tools of military conquest and racial purity. And for whatever reason, German culture nurtured a profound— some called it romantic—attachment to nature, and a conviction that it was threatened by modern technology.

Opponents of genetic engineering had planted a bomb at the laboratories of the Max Planck Institute for Plant Breeding Research. A researcher had narrowly escaped injury when it exploded. They had picketed, and destroyed, field trials. And in 1989, when European plant breeders emerged from a meeting in the university town of Göttingen, they found tires slashed on all the out-of-town cars parked within several blocks.

In Berlin, a sociologist named Wolfgang van den Daele decided to turn this deep social and political chasm into a field trial of his own, a "participatory assessment" of genetically engineered crops. In an extraordinary human experiment, he brought the hostile parties into a room together for days at a time in a relatively peaceful debate that lasted more than two years. He built, at least temporarily, an island of calm conversation in the midst of rhetoric that had been both messianic and apocalyptic.

Van den Daele inhabits a spacious office within the Social Science Research Center of Berlin, near the city's old center. The building is a bizarre construction. The facade is pure Prussian bombast, all stone and stately geometry bearing the marks of gunfire from Soviet troops who fought their way through this area in 1945; attached to it, however, is a postmodern structure of curvaceous whimsy, each floor painted different pastel shades of orange, green, and blue.

Van den Daele too is not all that he appears to be. The lean, casually dressed, bushy-haired man fits every image of an ivory-tower academic. Yet he possesses a keen appreciation for the gritty details of politics and business and the confidence to play those games, too, if given the chance. As he once phrased it memorably, "I am not a political eunuch."

Van den Daele persuaded the German government to fund his project in 1990, but the more difficult task was persuading representatives from both hard-line environmental groups and from industry to participate. "We played them off against each other," he says, threatening to go ahead with only the opposing side represented. "And Monsanto played a very crucial role" by immediately agreeing to participate. Only then did German and Swiss companies, including Hoechst, Ciba-Geigy, and KWS, Germany's leading seed company, agree to send representatives. (Monsanto then participated only sporadically, in part because of language barriers.) Several of the country's most important critics of biotechnology agreed to participate, as did prominent academic researchers on both sides of the issue. On February 1, 1991, about fifty people gathered at a retreat center maintained by Germany's Lutheran Church in the small town of Loccum in northern Germany.

This meeting was the first of many filling ten days in all, spread over more than two years. Between the meetings, there were occasional smaller gatherings on specialized topics, and administrators at van den Daele's institute duplicated and distributed a blizzard of scholarly papers, memoranda, and arguments.

The social scientist admits that he harbored his own prejudices. "I was pretty sure that risks were not really the issue," he says. This placed him at odds with most of biotechnology's critics. Yet he also held scant sympathy for the biotechnology industry. Van den Daele chose to focus the group's attention on an aspect of genetic engineering that he considered "a mad project," the development of herbicide-resistant crops. Manipulating plants in this way, he says, "is crazy. It's against the environment and against all common sense."

What happened in the course of these meetings was partly a rational process, as van den Daele had envisioned. Differences were hammered to the ground in methodical, German-style manner. Whether considering potential risks to the environment, risks to human health, or potential benefits, participants were forced to search for the boundaries of fact and opinion and to distinguish what was known for a fact, what remained unknown, and what was simply unknowable.

This was exactly what van den Daele had hoped would happen. "This is an old idea, that argumentation is the glue of society," he says. Among sociologists, there were some who believed that this glue was gone forever. Rational conversation had been replaced by soapbox rhetoric transmitted through the mass media. Van den Daele wanted to see if the glue could still function.

During the meetings at this remote location, van den Daele noted, "they could not go anywhere." The participants were forced to present evidence for their positions, respond to contradictory information, and reveal hidden assumptions. The process was intended to test the limits of knowledge and reason when dealing with a subject that aroused powerful emotions. It was, in fact, more than that. It was a test of the modernist faith in science as a tool for the discovery of common truth.

But the meetings also were influenced by subjective, human factors. On the very first evening, as logs burned in the fireplace of the retreat center, participants sat transfixed by televised images of war in the Middle East. Operation Desert Storm had begun with a U.S. air assault on Baghdad. The shock of war began to break down some of the barriers that divided the group.

In the rhetoric of public debates, van den Daele notes, there is often a moralistic quality, a tone of judgement and condemnation. In the meeting rooms at Loccum "this was checked very early on. There was a reference to herbicides as 'chemical weapons.' There was a sharp response, and that sort of thing vanished. And the tendency to respect the other side grew over time." One scientist employed by the government, a specialist on water quality who was highly critical of biotechnology, found himself falling in love with a representative from industry. (They later married.)

Günter Donn from Hoechst, one of the inventors of plants resistant to the herbicide Basta, found himself reflecting on his anger when confronted with what he considered ignorant criticisms of biotechnology. "Our anger was considered arrogance. The arrogance of knowledge," he says. "And it made people furious."

"I made some mistakes during that process by making some emotionally driven statements," he continues. "But sitting together with these guys for three or four days, after a while you feel that you are human beings! You have feelings!" A helpless laugh escapes from the German scientist.

After two years, van den Daele decided that it was time to bring the discussions to a close and draw conclusions. With the assent of the participants, he assembled a committee of seven, representing all factions. They became a kind of jury, evaluating the mass of evidence and issuing verdicts point by disputed point.

It was a brutal process. The committee member who represented the environmentalist groups (she worked for the Pesticide Action Network) broke down in tears at one point when forced to abandon a long-held position. She hadn't wanted it to come down to such ruthless decisions about truth. She'd advocated a report that would simply have lined the opposing viewpoints up against each other. It would have presented the conflict as a matter of competing *beliefs,* subjective and irresolvable. But van den Daele wanted none of it.

"You have to say this was not a mediation procedure," van den Daele says. "If we'd done mediation, we'd have said, we'll stop this because carrying it further would hurt strategic interests of a particular side. But we said, it's in the interest of social science to take argumentation to its conclusion."

So over the weeks and months, van den Daele and his group of seven systematically dismantled some of the arguments that were most cherished by supporters and critics of biotechnology alike.

They dismissed industry's claims that herbicide-resistant crops offered significant benefits to society. Such crops, the group decided, were of little benefit to the environment. Nor would these genetically engineered crops be of much use to the world's poor and hungry, since subsistence farmers in the developing world didn't have the money to buy commercial seed.

The group also decided that foods containing genetically engineered ingredients should bear labels informing consumers of this fact. Consumers wanted this information, and they had a right to it.

But van den Daele's jury also rejected the environmentalists' arguments that genetically engineered crops presented new and different risks to human health and the environment.

Opponents of genetic engineering had long argued that this technology carried with it the possibility of unforeseen risks. The very first field trial of genetically engineered plants in Germany had delivered spectacular evidence that seemed to buttress the point. Researchers had planted thirty-one thousand petunia plants during the field trial, which was carried out during the summer of 1990. The petunias were naturally white, but researchers had inserted a foreign gene which they expected to turn almost all the plants brick red.

The plants grew and produced the anticipated red flowers, although some of the flowers, as they grew older, tended to fade in color. Then, after a midsummer heat wave, practically all the flowers turned shockingly white, and later in the summer the plants produced a mixture of red and white flowers.

None of these results had been anticipated. Further research showed that heat had chemically disrupted the structure of the 35S promoter, which controlled the inserted gene. The white petunias became a powerful image illustrating the gaping holes in science's understanding of genetic processes within plants.

But van den Daele's group decided that such phenomena were not fundamentally new. Similar genetic processes had been occurring in the world's fields and forests since the origins of plant life. Plant breeders regularly experience surprises of their own in the course of their own work. When crossing two plants, they cannot know how each of the offspring will grow and develop. New combinations of genes can produce unexpected effects. Genetic mutations can occur at any time, and naturally occurring "jumping genes" sometimes insert themselves randomly within the plant's chromosomes. So the risks posed by unexpected side effects of genetic engineering, though unpredictable, are still familiar.

What's more, the group said, *every* innovation carries with it the possibility (indeed, the probability) of unexpected, unforeseen consequences for society and the environment. Yet society does not, on principle, ban all innovation because it carries with it a certain level of risk.

In the end, one central objection to biotechnology remained. Biotechnology's opponents argued that technological innovations, risky or not, should be subject to some sort of democratic control. Industry should not have the right to sell anything that appears to be safe. If a product is unneeded, brings no compelling benefits to the public, and most people object to it, then people should have a legal way to block it. Herbicide-resistant crops, the opponents hardly needed to add, were not necessary, nor did they enjoy popular support.

This left opponents and proponents of biotechnology no closer to agreement, but, as van den Daele pointed out, it was not the same disagreement that had existed at the beginning. What began as an argument over the *risks* of biotechnology had been transformed over two years into an argument over the need for more democratic control over technological innovation.

"That situation was a strategic dilemma for the environmental groups," van den Daele says. "Because what we proposed at the end was this: There may be good reasons to resist genetic engineering, because one does not agree with it as a path for agriculture and society. But the idea of special risks is not a good argument. We should turn to the issues of democracy and who's going to decide how society develops.

"This is a very tricky problem, the democracy problem, because it involves the whole structure of capitalistic societies. But why not address it?"

On June 9, 1993, the day before van den Daele was scheduled to convene one last meeting to discuss his jury's final conclusions, nine environmental groups declared the entire process a failure and pulled out. The process, they declared, had become a farce. Several companies involved in the process, instead of waiting for the group's conclusions, had simply gone ahead with field trials of herbicide-resistant crops. In addition, they said, the process had become unduly burdensome. They found themselves drowning in paper and unable to match forces with the representatives of industry or the pro-biotechnology researchers. "Every few days, just a few days before the final conference, I received hundreds of pages in which van den Daele presented his conclusions," says Barbara Weber, one of the leading critics of biotechnology. "I'd have had to work through this whole thing. It just wasn't possible. I hadn't imagined this, that you can destroy participation by throwing paper on top of people!"

Van den Daele in his summery of the process discerned a different reason for the walkout. "Apparently it would have been difficult for them to declare explicitly that the conflict was not about risks but about social goals and political reforms, after they had committed themselves categorically to the rhetoric of risks and used it successfully in the mobilization of the public."

The full report from van den Daele's experiment, when it finally appeared, got a mixed reception. Many refused to accept van den Daele's conviction that this process, better than any other, had arrived at something approximating objective truth. Instead, they regarded van den Daele and the process that he set up as a captive of hidden ideological biases.

A few rejected not just van den Daele's conclusions but also the whole notion of objective truth. They argued that the search for objective truth about genetically engineered crops, using the tools of scientific inquiry, amounted to the pursuit of a mirage. "We [Germans] don't really believe in science," said one sociologist who followed the process closely. "We believe in economics and technology and politics." "Truth," then, will be determined by economic interest and ideology and will be different for each person.

Yet for others van den Daele's experiment was a profound event. One young ecologist named Detlef Bartsch arrived in van den Daele's circle as a confirmed critic of biotechnology. Two years earlier, he'd coauthored an essay entitled "How Biotechnology Brings Capitalism to Agriculture," a broadside aimed at the pesticide industry and its domination of agriculture, first with chemicals, then with genetic engineering. But as Bartsch got to know representatives from industry, he was tempted by the prospect of new knowledge. The German seed company KWS invited him to conduct ecological experiments in conjunction with some field trials of genetically engineered plants that the company was planning. Bartsch agreed after he secured government funding for the experiments.

"I was very keen to develop experiments that would show that there were lots of risks in this technology," Bartsch continues. But the more familiar the plants became, the less fearsome they seemed. His experiments convinced him that in many cases the risks are minimal. "There are, of course, environmental concerns. There is not a general answer for all crops," he says. "But I think that herbicide tolerance is not an environmental problem."

The debate in Germany over biotechnology became much less polarized and less emotionally charged after 1992. Van den Daele's "participatory technology assessment" certainly was not the main reason. Public concerns tend to ebb and flow like fashions. The impact of national unification overwhelmed German public attention in the mid-1990s, casting other issues into the shadows. Yet several participants in van den Daele's experiment give it substantial credit for altering the public debate. On van den Daele's "island," as he often described the process, genetic engineering was recast as a technology that was neither so promising nor so sinister as many people preferred to imagine.

# 9

# Seed Wars

"I can tell you the discussion of how we were going to make money in agricultural biotechnology went on into the 1990s," says Dick Mahoney, the longtime chief executive of Monsanto. "Nick Reding [who ran the agricultural business] and I would sit around and say, 'How the hell are we going to make any money off this stuff? The science is rolling along, but how are we going to make any money?'"

Monsanto's traditional business was straightforward. It manufactured an herbicide, then sold it directly to farmers. End of story. But how does one sell a farmer a gene? The gene comes encapsulated in a seed, and Monsanto wasn't in the seed business. It didn't employ scores of plant breeders patiently cross-pollinating and selecting new varieties of corn or soybean plants.

One man within Monsanto was convinced that he knew the answer to Mahoney's question. Robb Fraley, who'd arrived at Monsanto in 1981 as a driven, ambitious scientist, then became the co-inventor of Monsanto's first genetically transformed petunia plants, was elbowing his way up Monsanto's corporate ladder. In January 1992, just before his thirty-ninth birthday, he was named vice president for research in Monsanto's agricultural division. A few months later Fraley celebrated with a new house, a half-million-dollar piece of real estate more in line with his ambition.

Fraley was a warrior for the cause of biotechnology. He wore his scientific credentials like medals on his chest, giving credibility to his vision of the future. Biotechnology, he predicted, was destined to transform agriculture. Monsanto held in its hands the kind of opportunity that came along perhaps once in a generation. It had a chance to dominate an industry in the making, much as Microsoft with a small head start and a few strategic decisions had come to dominate the personal computer business.

Monsanto didn't need to sell seeds, Fraley argued. The company's genes were so valuable that seed companies would line up and pay large sums for the right to breed cotton plants containing the Bt gene or soybeans with Roundup resistance. Farmers in turn would pay extra—a *lot* extra—for those seeds. Monsanto would create genetically transformed cotton or soybean plants in its laboratories. It then would allow each seed company to take offspring from those plants and crossbreed them with the company's own varieties, transferring the gene gradually over the course of several generations to plants that farmers might grow in their fields.

Fraley seized on the analogy of the computer industry. A seed was hardware, like the electronic circuits of a computer; Monsanto's gene was the software that would turn it into a useful tool. Just as Microsoft licensed its Windows operating system to computer makers, which in turn sold the entire package to consumers, Monsanto could license its genes to a wide variety of seed companies. Those companies would breed the gene into many different varieties of plants and sell those seeds to farmers.

This was a seductive analogy in part because in the early 1990s it was becoming clear that Windows had put Microsoft in the driver's seat in the computer industry. To the surprise of many, software was turning out to be more valuable than hardware. People didn't care so much whether they got a computer from Dell or Gateway, but they *had* to have a computer that could run Windows. Similarly, said Fraley, farmers were going to demand Bt cotton or Roundup-resistant soybean plants no matter where they went shopping for seeds. Monsanto would be the Microsoft of agriculture.

Unfortunately, the analogy had one fundamental flaw. The seed business was nothing like the computer business, in both superficial and profound ways. It was fragmented among hundreds of companies, many of them mom-and-pop operations, few of them making significant profits. Like Brother Rabbit considering the Tar Baby, Monsanto's executives looked at the seed business and saw a backward, inert industry ready for the bracing shock of modern technology. Only dimly did they comprehend the complexities of creating seed or the depth of the business's anchoring in the immutable nature of biology itself.

Seeds are a paradox at the heart of agriculture. They are precious and irreplaceable, yet cheap. They exist in a twilight world somewhere between private property (like the farmer's tractor or the chemical herbicides he buys every year) and a public good (like sunlight and rain). The life they hold is the stuff of myth and metaphor. Companies that sell seed do not completely own it, because the seed, by nature, multiplies in the hands of the customer. Just as the Iroquois and Apache once considered it ridiculous and unnatural for individuals to own land, so farmers and lawmakers around the world have resisted laws that would convert a kernel of grain into intellectual property.

Take one of the most significant advances in the seed business, a variety of soybeans called Asgrow 3127. It emerged in the 1970s from the test plots of John Schillinger at the Asgrow seed company. Rarely is a new variety so clearly superior to all its rivals. It out-produced all other soybean varieties on the market, and gradually took over great sections of the Midwestern corn/soybean belt.

Asgrow reaped some benefits from its innovation, thanks to a 1970 law (the Plant Variety Protection Act) that made it illegal for competing companies simply to take samples of 3127 growing in farmers' fields and sell it themselves. But the law did not prevent rivals—most importantly, Pioneer Hi-Bred—from crossbreeding 3127 with their own varieties. "They copied it like crazy," says Schillinger. In just a few years, Pioneer and other companies started selling varieties very similar to 3127. Equally important, the law didn't prevent farmers from planting their fields full of 3127, saving perhaps one percent of the harvest, cleaning the grain, and planting it right back in the field as seed the following year. This seemed natural to farmers. After all, they said, we own our harvest. We sell it to the grain elevator. Why should we be prohibited from planting it back into our own fields? Yet this practice made every soybean farmer a competitor to Asgrow.

Seed companies couldn't, to use the lingo of business, "capture the value" that they created through plant breeding. It was a service business; seed companies mainly saved farmers the work of cleaning, storing, and testing seed. This was the nature of selling genes to farmers. But in Monsanto's vision this most traditional, slow-moving, and unprofitable of agricultural businesses would become a conduit for expensive new genes emerging from the laboratories of the world's biotechnology companies.

The question wouldn't go away: How are we ever going to make any money from this stuff?

By 1992 Dick Mahoney and others at Monsanto had run out of patience with their biotechnology project. The word came down to Fraley and his associates: Back up your theories with some commercial deals or shut down most of your program. Monsanto executive Paul Johanson remembers the marching orders: Monsanto's senior management "wanted a demonstration that there was value in this by the end of the year." There was only one company in the seed business that Dick Mahoney respected; one institution that could convince skeptics within Monsanto that their genes really were worth something: Pioneer Hi-Bred International of Des Moines, Iowa.

CORN IS a towering exception to the rules that generally govern the seed business, for one simple, eighty-year-old reason. In the 1920s, corn breeders discovered that, when they crossbred very different lines of corn, they sometimes saw a startling jump in the yield of the resulting "hybrid" plants. This created an opening for seed companies. With hybrids, farmers no longer produced exact copies of their seed. If farmers replanted grain from hybrid plants, they got a mixture of different, usually inferior, corn plants. So farmers chose instead to return to the seed seller every year for a fresh supply of hybrid seeds. For the first time, seed companies gained control over their products. Since they could charge more for better seed, they had good reason to hire plant breeders, who tried to come up with superior hybrids. Yields of corn rose steadily, as did prices for corn seed. Pioneer Hi-Bred grew to dominate this business. Some referred to the seed industry as "Snow White and the Seven Dwarves." Pioneer was Snow White.

Pioneer sold a billion dollars of corn seed each year. This accounted for more than 40 percent of the U.S. corn market and around 20 percent of all seed sales, of all kinds, in the United States. Pioneer also controlled about ten percent of the soybean seed market. Pioneer didn't make much, if any, money selling soybean seed. It was a service to corn farmers—Pioneer's real customers—who also happened to plant lots of soybeans.

But it was in soybeans, not corn, where Monsanto's new genes promised to have the greatest economic impact. So when Monsanto's executives traveled to Des Moines, Roundup-tolerant soybeans were at the top of their agenda.

In Monsanto's view, the value of Roundup tolerance could be calculated precisely. Soybean growers at that time were paying about twenty-five dollars for the herbicides that they sprayed on each acre of their crop. Roundup, by contrast, was cheap; an acre's worth could be bought for about ten dollars. (For years, Monsanto had pursued a spectacularly successful strategy of cutting prices for Roundup to boost sales.) So if you gave farmers an opportunity to spray Roundup on their soybean fields instead of existing chemicals, they'd jump at the chance. In fact, that opportunity would be worth up to a maximum of fifteen dollars an acre. They'd be willing to pay that much for Roundup-tolerant soybean seed.

Such numbers made jaws drop and ears ring in the seed industry. It was like telling the manager of a bread factory that if he just used this new, improved type of flour, people would pay twice as much for a loaf of bread. If these numbers were true, Roundup-tolerant soybean seeds might be *twice* as valuable as conventional soybeans, and since they shouldn't cost any more to produce than conventional seed, all of the extra money would be pure profit. Suppose the seed companies charged an extra ten dollars for soybeans with a Roundup tolerance gene. It would triple or quadruple their profit on a bag of seed—*if* they were allowed to keep the extra money. Needless to say, Monsanto's executives were not about to let the seed companies keep all of it. After all, their gene was the only thing that made the seed so much more valuable. They decided to demand approximately 75 percent of that extra money.

Monsanto wanted something else, seemingly unimportant, from Pioneer: the words *Roundup Ready* in thick black letters over curving stripes of light green and tan, printed on every bag of seed that contained Monsanto's new gene. That demand came from the new head of Monsanto's agricultural division, Robert Shapiro.

Shapiro, a slightly built, intense but soft-spoken lawyer from New York, had written his name into business history a decade earlier with a stroke of marketing genius. Shapiro loved to tell the story. He was negotiating with Coca-Cola, trying to sell the soft-drink maker a chemical sweetener called aspartame, for use in low-calorie soft drinks. Shapiro threw in an extra demand: Every bottle of Diet Coke that contained aspartame, he said, also had to show the trade name of aspartame—Nutrasweet—and Nutrasweet's trademark, a tiny swirl. Coke accepted. Shapiro built a marketing campaign around that trademark, convincing consumers that Nutrasweet (and no other company's version of the very same sweetener) was the key to losing weight. Nutrasweet became the symbol that every soft drink *had* to have on its low-calorie soft drinks.

Shapiro suddenly had more power. He could start charging Coke and Pepsi higher prices for his sweetener. They had always been in the driver's seat. Now Shapiro was. "To this day, the soft-drink industry curses the name Bob Shapiro," says one of Coke's former officials. The experience was the defining success of Shapiro's career, and he learned its lessons well.

"HERE'S HOW I see it: Shapiro's a smart guy. Very smart," growls Tom Urban, former chief executive of Pioneer Hi-Bred. "He made his mark with Nutrasweet. So he took that philosophy and he wanted to apply it to Roundup. He was trying to say that our brand, the genetic differences in our seed, weren't worth anything." In other words, farmers wouldn't care anymore about Pioneer's decades of plant breeding, creating superior varieties of soybeans or corn. Farmers would just look for Monsanto's new genes. Urban starts to get riled up just thinking about it. "He was trying to get himself into a position where, no matter what our variety was, if it didn't have Roundup Ready, you couldn't sell it. We were going to be dependent on him to sell our product! He was basically trying to take over the seed business by making the seed the vehicle for his product!"

Ideas and opinions strongly held and vividly worded erupt from Urban like windblown gusts of rain. For fourteen years he led Pioneer with stormy passion. "I'll be damned if this company is going to be run by lawyers and accountants!" he once yelled at the company's chief lawyer. For Urban, Pioneer wasn't just a company; it was a treasure that transcended profits, a mission handed down from father to son.

Pioneer is the legacy of a powerful, self-confident family, the Wallaces of Iowa. "Uncle Henry" was the family patriarch, a deeply religious man who founded a newspaper for Iowa farmers in the 1880s. When he died in 1916, Uncle Henry delivered one last sermon in his will: "There are possible temptations against which I must warn you. . . . The temptation to amass wealth for the sake of wealth, the temptation to gain position, political or social, for purely selfish purposes, comes naturally with prosperity. Avoid all this. Keep clean in speech, clear in mind, vigorous in body and God will bless you."

Listening to these words was twenty-seven-year-old Henry Agard Wallace, a precocious, awkward young man fascinated by economics, history, and the genetics of corn. He'd been introduced to plant breeding as a boy at the side of a family friend, George Washington Carver, the first African-American student to attend Iowa State University. In 1926, Wallace set up the Hi-Bred Corn Company, which later became Pioneer Hi-Bred.

Wallace's friends and their children would run Pioneer until the final years of the twentieth century. Wallace himself left Iowa in 1932 for Washington, D.C. He became Franklin Roosevelt's secretary of agriculture, then vice president, and eventually one of the most intriguing, idealistic, and controversial political figures in America. He fought on behalf of New Deal programs, proclaimed a "Century of the Common Man" (as opposed to Henry Luce's "American Century"), and ultimately broke with the Democratic Party to become the Progressive Party's candidate for president in 1948.

Tom Urban's father, Nelson Urban, was the first full-time employee Henry Wallace hired. "I grew up with the company," says Urban today. When "Tommy" graduated from Harvard Business

School, it was the only place he wanted to work. Pioneer turned him down, twice. Finally, the company sent him to work in a chicken hatchery in Minnesota. "I was the lowest-paid graduate from Harvard Business School in 1960," he recalls with satisfaction. In 1970 he got fired. "I was pretty mouthy," he says without evident remorse. "Had ideas about how things ought to be done. Torched a couple of guys." Some years later, the company gave him a second chance, and Tom Urban began his rise to the top of the company.

"In many ways, my father should have been a preacher," Tom Urban says. "He and Henry had a very highly developed sense of fair play and equity." In 1952, long before "mission statements" became popular in American companies, Nelson Urban and James Wallace (Henry's brother) wrote down what they considered the Pioneer philosophy. Called "The Long Look," it preached patience, honesty, fairness, and attention to the best interests of Pioneer's customer, the farmer. Tom Urban updated the document when he became CEO and made sure that every new employee got a copy. "It's up on our walls. We believe in it," he says. "Still do. It may sound Pollyannaish, but it's extremely important in the markets we're in, to get the farmers to trust you. There's a lot of barns out there with paint that runs and equipment that doesn't work. That's part of the culture."

In 1988, as Wall Street was gripped by a frenzy of leveraged buyouts, Tom Urban filled two pages of his company's annual report to shareholders with an unusual discourse on the role of businesses in society. Businesses must have a larger purpose than simply making money, he wrote; like all institutions in society, businesses embody ideas, traditions, and values that transcend the strengths and weaknesses of the people who lead them at any particular time. That larger purpose is critical to long-term success: "The profit motive alone is simply not enough to demand the loyalty of the breadth of talent and expertise needed to operate a successful business institution." He condemned buyouts and takeovers as "the financial world's exercise in 'post modernism'—blurring values, even celebrating 'valuelessness.'" Pioneer, he wrote, stood defiantly against this tide.

This was the self-image of Pioneer: guardian of small-town virtues, friend of the farmer, patient to a fault, honest and hardworking. Pioneer was also a ruthless competitor. It had deeper financial reserves, larger research programs, and a greater reservoir of experience in the business, by far, than any other seed company. The people running Pioneer in the early 1990s all had spent thirty years or more in the business; several of them traced their roots back to Henry Wallace's group of founders in the 1920s. "There's a certain noblesse oblige in Pioneer that goes all the way back to Henry Wallace," says Michael Roth, a Pioneer staff lawyer during the early 1990s, who now works for Monsanto. "I should add, Pioneer also believes that only it understands the seed business. And if anyone else thinks he understands the seed business, he probably has got it wrong."

"Monsanto didn't understand the seed business," says Tom Urban. "I'm sorry, they didn't understand the seed business."

WHEN PIONEER, king of seeds, confronted Monsanto, juggernaut of genes, it delivered some of the best theater in Des Moines. It was hard to imagine two more different corporate personalities. Monsanto was driven, frenetic; critics said it sometimes confused motion with progress. Pioneer was the ultimate patient company; it calmly sank money into research that it knew wouldn't produce results for a decade and tested products for longer than any of its competitors. Monsanto flaunted its success. Pioneer tried to hide it. The children of its founders drove respectable midsize cars, owned respectable midsize houses, and otherwise lived their lives as though in denial of their net worth, amounting to hundreds of millions of dollars. Monsanto came from the city; Pioneer from the country. Yet competitors of both companies universally described each of them as arrogant.

It was also a confrontation between the generations, in this case between generations of technology. Pioneer was the master of plant breeding, a technology perfected over the course of the twentieth century that requires nothing more than intelligence, sharp eyes, and a sharp knife. Corn breeders place bags over the tassels—the male genitalia—of each corn plant, to collect the pollen. The breeders then transfer that pollen to selected corn ears—the female genitalia—on the plants they have chosen as the female parent. They then take the offspring of this "cross," observe their genetic characteristics, and select those that seem most useful.

It is, in a sense, playing card tricks with nature. The cards are genes; each plant contains tens of thousands of them drawn from a deck of cards as vast as the genetic diversity of that species. With each cross-pollination, the breeder shuffles these cards together and draws a new hand, looking for the combinations of genes that will produce a more bountiful harvest. For plant breeders, it remained the most practical, elegant, and even sophisticated method for manipulating the genetic makeup of plants.

Plant breeders, particularly those at Pioneer, mocked the extravagant claims of genetic engineers. Their attitude resembled that of an aging revolutionary, convinced that true greatness lay in the past, unmatched by any accomplishment of the present. Yet their own technology, and their own company, had been born in a similar frenzy of enthusiasm. A former head of research at Pioneer, a dignified, austere man named Donald Duvick, is old enough to remember some of the pioneers of hybrid corn, including Henry Wallace. He described the spirit of the time: "They were motivated not by dreams of riches but by dreams of power—power to remold corn quickly and certainly into new and productive forms. The capacity to produce a handsome hybrid . . . produced a kind of disease—a continuing and nearly uncontrollable impulse to breed, test, and release new corn hybrids." Replace the word *hybrid* with *genetically engineered plants* and the description applies equally well to Monsanto's scientists.

The men in charge of biotechnology at Monsanto, possessed by their own "dreams of power," were convinced that the day of traditional plant breeding was passing; that Monsanto, with its new and superior science, had opened the door to an inevitable future.

Monsanto's Robert Shapiro painted a picture of that future for Tom Urban. Monsanto's gene for Roundup resistance, he said, would transform agriculture. Seed companies who offered new genes would prosper; those who did not would fail. The price of survival in the soybean business, he suggested, was the price of the Roundup Ready gene—millions of dollars in royalty payments.

Tom Urban remained unimpressed. He and his associates rolled out the speech that they had practiced on dozens of previous emissaries from biotech companies. People at Pioneer could practically recite it: "Congratulations! You've got a gene! Guess what? We've got fifty thousand genes! Our genes make a soybean plant grow tall, produce lots of beans, and fend off diseases; these are the genes that convince farmers to buy our varieties. Without our varieties, your gene isn't worth a thing. So who's bringing value to the table here? And who's going to make money selling herbicide to spray on those plants? You know what? You don't hold the keys to the market. We do! *You* ought to pay *us* for the right to put your gene in our varieties!"

Urban's broadside wasn't just showmanship. Pioneer's plant breeders were convinced, based on decades of experience, that single genes didn't matter; what mattered was the sum total of all the genes—a plant's "germ plasm." It was an earlier, fuzzier term for the genetic determinants of a plant, almost like "personality" or "genetic makeup." The breeders also felt personally offended that Monsanto would waltz into Des Moines and argue that one gene, by itself, should double the value of a seed.

Pioneer executives also didn't believe that a seed company could charge significantly more for a single new trait. They'd never been able jack up their prices when they introduced varieties that were resistant to diseases or more likely to stay upright in a storm. What's more, they said, they didn't *want* to.

One Monsanto negotiator described the Pioneer position as "a kind of socialism." Historically, for every four dollars in increased profits that a new corn variety produced, Pioneer raised seed prices by one dollar. The rest went into the farmer's pocket. The Monsanto approach, charging what the market would bear, struck them as immoral profiteering. "We're in the business of helping farmers," Pioneer executives insisted. (In fact, Tom Urban had once tried to raise prices more steeply on the theory that Pioneer was giving away value for free. Sales sagged and Pioneer quickly backtracked.)

"Sometimes we just stared at each other. It was like we were Martians. Didn't even speak the same language," recalls one Monsanto negotiator.

Yet behind their facade of bluster and bravado, Pioneer executives fretted. They knew how much farmers love to kill weeds, and they suspected that Roundup Ready soybeans might indeed turn out to be popular with farmers. They wanted the rights to Monsanto's genes; they just didn't want to pay much money for them.

Pioneer's negotiators had one crucial advantage; they were dealing with a divided company and one that was under deadline pressure. "The biotech people desperately wanted some cash, but then there were the Roundup people, who were practically ready to give the stuff away in order to sell more Roundup," says former Pioneer lawyer Mike Roth. So Tom Urban's followers played each side off against the other.

According to Roth, every time negotiations with the biotech division reached an impasse, executives from Pioneer had a private chat with someone in the division of Monsanto responsible for selling Roundup. The Pioneer people pointed out in amazement that Monsanto's negotiators were walking away from an opportunity to sell enough Roundup to cover millions of acres of soybeans. "Word would get back to the Roundup guys, and all of a sudden Monsanto would become more compliant," Roth says.

Late in 1992 Monsanto gave in. For a paltry one-time payment of half a million dollars, executives from St. Louis sold Pioneer the right to use Monsanto's Roundup resistance genes in Pioneer's soybean varieties forever. Pioneer did agree to print "Roundup Ready" on their bags of the seed. When it came to the financial value of a gene, though, the guardians of traditional values in agriculture in Des Moines had repulsed the prophets of a biotech revolution in St. Louis. The Roundup Ready gene had become a vehicle to sell more of Monsanto's chemicals, but little more.

Monsanto had one more gene in its arsenal: Bt, which turned corn into a deadly meal for the European corn borer. In this case, Monsanto could not, as it could with Roundup Ready soybeans, give the gene away and make money by selling an associated pesticide. The Bt gene *was* the pesticide, and Monsanto wanted to be paid for it.

Geert van Brandt, a Belgian who had worked for Monsanto in Europe, recalls an explicit order to sell rights to Bt, quickly. "Robb Fraley said: 'If you can't come up with the money in a hurry, then we'll find somebody else to do it for you.'"

The negotiations over Bt were, at least initially, similar to the Roundup Ready negotiations. Monsanto demanded lots of money, and Pioneer scoffed at Monsanto's grandiose estimations of the gene's value. Pioneer pointed out that corn borers aren't a problem for most farmers most of the time, so farmers would be unlikely to pay extra at the beginning of the year for a genetic trait that might turn out to be completely unnecessary. Some of Pioneer's old guard also simply could not stomach the idea that Monsanto's genetic engineers might have something useful to contribute to corn. Soybeans were one thing. Corn was something else entirely. It was the crop on which Pioneer had built its reputation, and executives were convinced that no outsider could even approach their deep understanding of this plant's genetic nature. For a time the negotiations broke off entirely.

Yet Pioneer couldn't afford to walk away from Bt. If the gene really did make a difference and Pioneer didn't have the right to use it, it was a threat to Pioneer's entire business. Every year, there was more substantial evidence that the gene really did work. During the spring and summer of 1993 the two sides came back to the table and hammered out a deal: Pioneer agreed to pay $28 million if Monsanto could deliver corn plants that killed corn borers, and another $10 million if those plants were commercially successful. Within Monsanto $38 million dollars from Pioneer was regarded as an important vote of confidence in biotechnology's prospects. And at the time, it seemed like a significant amount of money. Yet within a few years, it was obvious that Pioneer had paid only a fraction of what the Bt gene was worth.

ASKED ABOUT Monsanto's deals with Pioneer, Rob Horsch is silent for a long, long time. The cofounder of Monsanto's efforts to genetically engineer plants sighs. "This is a real sore subject," he says finally.

"I think basically our top management at the time wanted to see some real money, some evidence that other companies took this seriously and saw some value. They wanted that reassurance. But it bothered me enough that I'm willing to tell you I thought it was a mistake."

Horsch had argued vehemently that those commercial deals were premature. "If we had just waited and shown the full field efficacy of the crops, Pioneer would have come around, because it would have been in their economic interest. But that meant we would have had to hold the risk longer." In a phrase, Monsanto's top executives lost their nerve. That failure of nerve would poison relationships between the two companies for years to come. It also would lead to fateful decisions in an attempt to avoid such fiascoes in the future.

"There are people who still feel very upset about those deals," says another Monsanto scientist. "It was not the money. I think what hurt the most was the lack of confidence that people on our own team were showing in us. It showed that there were people [in Monsanto] who just didn't believe, despite all that we had done. That was the toughest part."

ONLY IN the South, in the crop that defined the Confederacy, did things go according to plan. When it came to cotton, Monsanto had a gene that simply was too valuable to ignore, and it found a far more motivated partner: Roger Malkin, chairman of the Delta and Pine Land Company in Scott, Mississippi.

Malkin is an incongruous figure, a gruff New Yorker who now lives in the smallest of towns—a company hamlet really—in the heart of the Mississippi Delta. For him, the seed business, at least initially, was simply an intriguing investment.

"We bought this business for nothing," he explains. Delta and Pine Land owned vast tracts of the Delta in addition to its seed business. In 1978 Malkin and a group of investors bought it for $44 million, then sold off the land for $40 million. With that, they owned one of the five largest cottonseed companies in the country along with the entire town of Scott.

"The company wasn't worth much more than that," says Malkin. "It wasn't making any money. It had made $80,000 profit the year before."

But Malkin was lucky. At the time, the cottonseed business was dominated by five family-owned companies, and within a decade most of those families either decided they were tired of the business or their companies went bankrupt. Malkin stepped into the void. By the mid-1990s, Delta Pine, as the company often is called, controlled 70 percent of the market in cottonseed.

A man rooted in agriculture and the seed business might have been content with that. But Malkin was a restless spirit and was intrigued by the prospects of biotechnology. He went on expeditions to the major companies working on gene-splicing. He signed a deal only with Monsanto.

"There were three companies that spent the same amount of money on agricultural biotechnology," he says. "DuPont, Novartis, and Monsanto. And Monsanto is the only company to make anything of it."

"The difference was all attitude," he says. "At Novartis there was no sense of urgency. If you went by their parking lot in Research Triangle Park [in Raleigh, North Carolina] on a Saturday, there were no cars in the parking lot. If you went to DuPont, those researchers all went home at 5:00 in the afternoon. At Monsanto there were always cars in the parking lot at 1:00 A.M. and on the weekends."

Monsanto's drive to succeed, he says, also had a destructive side, an impatience that churned through business plans and people alike. "Monsanto devours its own about every three years," he says. "They think they're better managers than they are. They're good at getting things done, but they don't get them done very smartly." Malkin's voice jumps to a higher pitch: "That's the hubris!"

Monsanto's Bt gene promised to transform Malkin's business. The numbers were even more dramatic than those for Roundup Ready soybeans. Cotton growers typically spent about eight dollars for enough seed to cover an acre of ground. But many of them spent more than a hundred dollars an acre fighting insects, with about half of that money devoted to battling the tobacco budworm and the cotton bollworm. If the Bt gene worked as promised, farmers wouldn't have to spray for those pests anymore. In theory, the gene was worth that savings in pesticide costs. And Roger Malkin would no longer just be in the seed business; he'd be in the insect control business, where people made much higher profits.

In April of 1993 Malkin and Monsanto's Milton Wilkins shook hands on a deal for Bt cotton. They agreed to charge an extra thirty-two dollars for an acre's worth of seed. "I think we decided to leave the grower 50 percent [of the gene's value], and we'd try to capture 50 percent," says Wilkins. Malkin agreed to return 70 per cent of that money to Monsanto. Yet the remainder, which his company pocketed, was a staggering increase over what he'd previously earned from a bag of seed.

If Delta and Pine's customers planted Bt cotton on a quarter of their land, for instance, Monsanto stood to earn an extra $55 million each year, and Malkin's company would pocket $23 million. It was the model for all future deals between Monsanto and seed companies.

MONSANTO'S DRIVE to become the Microsoft of agriculture, however, was not the only strategy in agricultural biotechnology. Calgene, Ciba-Geigy, and Mycogen decided to take over portions of the seed industry directly. Calgene bought a cottonseed company, Stoneville Pedigreed Seed, intending to use it as the vehicle to sell cotton plants that were resistant to an herbicide called Buctril. Ciba-Geigy and Mycogen each owned a corn seed company and intended to use those seed subsidiaries to bring their versions of Bt corn to the marketplace. Instead of following Microsoft's strategy of licensing new technology to any company that wanted it, these companies were trying to be, in a sense, the Apple Computer of agriculture. They wanted to build a better product—in this case a corn or a cotton plant—and use that superior product to take over increasing shares of the corn or cotton market.

Monsanto in fact employed a variant of this strategy for potatoes, a crop for which there isn't much of a commercial seed industry. One variety, called Russet Burbank, accounts for the vast majority of all potatoes grown in North America. (In fact this variety is practically sterile; it doesn't interbreed with other potatoes. All Russet Burbank potatoes are clones of each other, reproduced by taking pieces of a plant's tuber and replanting them.) Since there were few seed companies to which Monsanto could license its Bt gene, it decided to set up its own potato company, called NewLeaf.

The German company Hoechst, meanwhile, pursued exactly the opposite strategy in the marketing of its gene, which rendered plants resistant to the Hoechst herbicide Basta. (Basta was renamed Liberty when it entered the North American market in the mid-1990s, and by this time Hoechst had merged its agricultural operations with another company, changing its name to AgrEvo.) AgrEvo decided to give away its gene and make money simply from sales of its herbicide Liberty. It planned to set a high price for Liberty, much higher than what Monsanto charged for Roundup. (Monsanto couldn't raise prices for Roundup, mainly because the patents that covered this herbicide were expiring and other companies soon would be able to manufacture it and try to undercut Monsanto's prices.)

AgrEvo's approach made life easy for seed companies. In particular it sat well with Tom Urban and his fellow seed barons at Pioneer Hi-Bred. The German company wasn't demanding any money and it wasn't asking Pioneer to change the way it sold seed to farmers. It simply asked seed companies to label the seed "LibertyLink," so farmers would know they could spray Liberty on those fields to kill their weeds.

When AgrEvo's chairman, Gerhard Prante, came to Des Moines to visit, he and Tom Urban seemed to understand and trust each other far more than Urban and Monsanto's Robert Shapiro ever had. The two chief executives went off by themselves and wandered into a growing field of corn. Both seemed more comfortable there. Prante, it turned out, ran his own small farm on the side back in Germany. Quickly the two companies came to terms. Pioneer would take the corn that Günter Donn and his Hungarian collaborators had created and cross-breed it with Pioneer's best hybrids.

By 1994, Liberty-resistant corn, soybeans, and canola plants were moving toward the marketplace. So were Roundup-resistant soybeans, canola, and cotton, as well as Bt corn, cotton, and potatoes. While plant breeders labored to "backcross" these genes into the best varieties that they had in hand, regulators in Washington pored over data from safety tests.

Surprisingly, none of these products attracted a great deal of public attention. They were cast into the shadows, while another genetically engineered plant stole the spotlight. Monsanto, AgrEvo, and Ciba-Geigy were not destined to bring the first genetically engineered plant to the marketplace. Rushing past them, heedless of contrary advice, as impetuous and overconfident as a teenager, came a company possessed by the vision of a perfect tomato.

# 10

# The Tomato
# That Ate Calgene

Calgene could have been a tidy little research operation, and it might even have made money. It had a fine scientific reputation, and partners with deep pockets from Procter & Gamble (P&G) to Rhone-Poulenc, the French chemical giant. Its researchers could have continued probing the mysteries of DNA from the comfort of their small box of a building along Fifth Street in the well-scrubbed university town of Davis, California. But that wouldn't have been grand enough. "We wouldn't have been *Calgene*," says Vic Knauf, one of the company's first scientists. Calgene was supposed to be a force of revolutionary change within the most traditional and backward of industries. It intended to follow in the steps of Apple Computer or Genentech, companies that turned ideas into industries.

Calgene sometimes seemed like a playground masquerading as a company. Its laboratories churned with ribald humor, loud arguments, and, occasionally, startling discoveries. "We had a rule; anything the company's science board said was bullshit, we went ahead and worked on," says Dave Stalker, one of the company's more wild-eyed scientists. There were dreams of Calgene subsidiaries all over the world. Stalker liked the idea of one in Italy, named CalgenItalia. Luca Comai, perhaps the most creative of the lot, once flew to Lyon for a consultation with top executives from Rhone-Poulenc and spent the meeting drawing exquisitely scatological caricatures of their solemn

Gallic faces. Calgene's other representative at the meeting, blessed with a view of Comai's doodling pad, had to resort to frequent bathroom breaks to relieve her aching sides.

Driving things forward with restless energy and scant attention to inconvenient details was Roger Salquist, a charismatic former submarine commander in the U.S. Navy. Salquist yelled and cursed, but he also inspired. "You'd sit there and listen to him, and he'd convince you to take the hill, right?" says Andrew Baum, Calgene's first employee, who lasted until the bitter tumultuous end. "And sometimes the hill you were supposed take was full of machine guns, but he convinced you it was the right thing to do." Salquist had the same effect on investors. "He was so charismatic that people would just give him their money," says one Calgene scientist. "He could show you how we were going to replace entire industries with plants, and he could spin that story for investment bankers."

Salquist had a fine story to tell Wall Street. Calgene may have had the most productive group of scientists in the industry. They'd ventured fearlessly into the lair of the industry giant Monsanto and emerged with key patents on Monsanto's own specialty, Roundup-resistant plants. They'd discovered a gene that makes plants resistant to another herbicide, bromoxinil, and their scientific tour de force was the invention of ways to alter the oils that many plants store in their seeds. Canola plants, for instance, could be engineered to produce the kind of oil found in coconuts. (After P&G proved uninterested in pursuing the technology, Calgene's researchers divined the truth: P&G just wanted a weapon in its back pocket in case Ferdinand Marcos of the Philippines, who was organizing a coconut cartel, succeeded in his effort to jack up prices. The weapon hadn't been needed.)

But those were not the stories that made investors' mouths water or convinced them to reach for their checkbooks. The story that worked for Roger Salquist and for Calgene was of a discovery that would solve every vegetable shopper's pet peeve and turn Calgene into a jolly green gene giant. It was the story of red, ripe tomatoes in wintry Chicago.

"I DIDN'T know squat about tomatoes," says Dave Stalker. "But we were trying to get programs up and running, and I was reading this paper from 1978 about how these enzymes can do things in tomatoes, make them red and so on. So I said, 'This is pretty cool. How about we work on tomatoes?"

Stalker was Luca Comai's sidekick, one of Calgene's wild boys. He has a surfer's tan, and when he gets excited about an idea, which is often, his eyes tend to bulge out of their sockets. He stayed at Calgene, he says, "for the comedy."

Calgene's scientific advisors, as usual, were not impressed with Stalker's idea. As usual, this convinced Stalker to pursue it with special vigor, although he soon handed it off to another scientist, a Vietnam veteran with a penchant for black humor named Bill Hiatt.

Calgene's deal makers convinced the Campbell Soup Company to fund the research, and eventually a specific target came into view, an enzyme within tomatoes called polygalacturonase, known simply as PG. It seemed that PG broke down the solid structure within a tomato, making it soft. If scientists could somehow block production of PG, it might do two things, the Calgene scientists theorized. It might increase the amount of solid material in a tomato, which would make the tomato a better source of tomato paste. Or it might extend the shelf life of a ripe tomato.

Bill Hiatt worked on PG like a bulldog. He isolated the enzyme and worked out the sequence of the gene that produced it. But how to shut it down? "Why don't we turn it around?" suggested Comai. This was a technique that was known to work in bacteria. If you wanted to stop one gene from functioning, you could construct another gene from scratch with the first gene's sequence of DNA reversed. (The new, backwards gene was called an "antisense" gene.) The products of the two genes would stick to each other, gumming up the genetic works and preventing the first gene from doing its job. It was a bit like fashioning a piece of iron to match the gears of a huge, finely tuned machine, then dropping it into the spinning machinery, bringing the thing to a crashing halt.

Few seriously expected it to work. PG is an important gene, a big, powerful wheel turning within the cell. It wouldn't be easy to shut down. Bill Hiatt and his coworkers dropped their antisense gene into tomato plants, then ran tests to see if the amount of PG in the plants had changed. They were stunned. Production of PG had fallen off a cliff. "Boom! It worked," says Robert Goodman, who was head of research at Calgene at the time. "It worked so well that I couldn't believe that the antisense sequence was doing it."

When the tomatoes grew big enough to produce fruit, Dave Stalker took some home with him. "I put them on a shelf in my kitchen. They sat there for three weeks! Nothing happened to them!"

This was the picture that became Calgene's prime exhibit. It showed four tomatoes, two of them with the antisense gene and two without. All had been sitting on the shelf for three weeks. The two genetically engineered tomatoes looked almost perfect, their skin as clear and smooth as a child's. The two conventional tomatoes were wrinkled and shriveling.

Then there was the day researchers took a load of the genetically engineered tomatoes to Campbell's tomato processing plant in Dixon, California. They fired up the crusher, dumped in their load, and the tomato pulp from this more-solid tomato promptly clogged the filter that was designed to strain out stems, rocks, and tomato skin. Clearly the gene was working. This tomato was different. It was a "beaming day," recalls one Calgene researcher.

Al Stevens was in charge of research at the Campbell Soup Company at the time. Before taking that job, he'd spent a career breeding tomatoes at the University of California. "I was a traditionalist," Stevens says quietly as he rocks slowly back and forth on a chair in his living room. "But I got swept down that river, too. You see these effects, and it's just tremendously exciting."

Quickly, the marketing story took shape. It went something like this: This gene—Salquist christened it the Flavr Savr—would be the key to a whole new system for delivering tomatoes to grocery stores. It would keep tomatoes from going soft so quickly, so the tomatoes wouldn't have to be picked so early, when they're green and hard as rocks. They wouldn't need to be gassed with ethylene to turn them red; they'd be allowed to ripen on the vine. They'd taste like summertime, and the Flavr Savr gene would keep them looking red and luscious until they arrived in grocery stores all over America, even in the dead of winter.

"The tomato struck a nerve in a lot of people," says Dave Stalker. "It was great because it was so visual. You could commune with it. Roger communed with it almost too well, let me tell you."

Salquist became convinced that this was The Product. This would be the bet that paid for all the others, the home run that cleared the bases, the roaring money earner that would vault Calgene into that special place in the sun reserved for companies like Apple or Genentech, bold startups that made it. Calgene, he decided, could make this leap all on its own.

Some within Calgene wanted to start small, to learn the business by growing tomatoes in southern California and selling them just in Los Angeles and San Francisco. The idea was rejected. It was too small-minded.

At a meeting of Calgene's board sometime around 1991 a board member named Tom Churchwell stood up and called the Flavr Savr tomato the best business idea he'd ever seen. He even volunteered to run the business; his whole life, he said, he'd dreamed of doing something like this. The board was enthusiastic; several members had been thinking for some time that Calgene needed a more experienced hand to manage its growing ambitions. The board set the tomato business up as a separate business, called Calgene Fresh, with Tom Churchwell as chairperson and CEO.

Churchwell was everything that Salquist was not. His desk was always clean, his voice hushed with portentous pauses thrown in for effect. He was the same age as Salquist, but seemed older and more solid. He certainly was calmer. He'd been an executive at Monsanto's Nutrasweet division, so he presumably knew how a large business was run.

Salquist knew the Nutrasweet story—how Robert Shapiro, with Tom Churchwell by his side, placed the Nutrasweet symbol on every can of Diet Coke, and turned that sweetener into a name that millions of consumers look for when they buy low-calorie soft drinks. "It was the Nutrasweet strategy that, in a general way, I always thought we were trying to do with the tomato," Salquist says.

Salquist and Churchwell preached the message that Calgene Fresh could change the rules of the fresh produce business, just as Nutrasweet had changed the rules of the sweetener business. Tomatoes could be more than a generic commodity, they insisted. Calgene Fresh tomatoes would be different; they would become *the* tomatoes for the discerning consumer. Consumers would even shop at a particular grocery store solely because it sold Calgene's tomatoes. Good tomatoes, Calgene's executives were convinced, had that kind of power.

Churchwell brought with him the latest trends in management philosophy. Employees at Calgene Fresh would be "empowered" and imbued with a corporate vision. The company would be a close-knit team; everyone would learn to do everyone else's job. "It was this 'mission'; we were doing something nobody else had done, and it was very special," says Kenneth Moonie, a Calgene employee who never quite managed to get into the spirit of things. "I think [Churchwell] was more interested in having a religious, church-type thing rather than building a business."

The dangerous side of Churchwell's sense of mission was that it tolerated no dissent. Calgene had always been a place where people said what they thought, and "when people disagreed, it could get kind of exciting," says one longtime employee. But Churchwell regarded criticism as treason. John Callahan, Calgene's head of marketing, called it "Lord of the Flies management"; others referred to Churchwell's followers as the "Branch Davidians of Calgene." Says one of Churchwell's most bitter critics: "If you said the emperor had no clothes, it was because you just didn't have the vision to see the clothes."

Yet for a time, the emperor really did seem fully clothed. Research from grocery stores kept rolling in, and the business prospects looked better and better. To estimate future demand for the Flavr Savr, Calgene carried out experiments with conventional tomatoes that were specially selected for their taste and color. Their surveys showed that consumers would pay three times the going rate for top-of-the-line tomatoes and come back for more. "Suddenly, the numbers looked too good to be true," says John Callahan. "The finance guys are going nuts, and Churchwell is smirking and saying: 'And you guys thought we should just roll it out regionally!'"

The numbers that Churchwell paraded in front of Wall Street were, in fact, astounding. Calgene Fresh estimated that the Flavr

Savr tomatoes could take over a quarter of the entire $4 billion fresh tomato market, and nearly a third of that $1 billion would be profit.

BOB MEYER shakes his head about those meetings with Calgene. He's still a little angry after all these years. The Calgene people had come to him, after all. They'd recruited him, admired his tomato packing operation in King City, California, even fussed over his prize antique car, a 1930s-era Packard once owned by King Faisal of Saudi Arabia. Calgene had a gene that would make tomatoes taste better, they said. That was something Bob Meyer could understand. "If you ask people, what's the one vegetable you'd like to improve, it's the tomato," he says. "So that was a wonderful concept."

But then the parade of experts started. "I was talking to people who had MBAs and molecular biologists and genetic engineers, and there wasn't anybody who was very practical in the whole outfit," Meyer says. They talked about packaging and shipping and schedules. But they never seemed that interested in the actual nuts and bolts of *growing* the tomatoes.

"I remember Roger Salquist, the chairman of the board, and he was giving this big presentation, and he was saying, we're right where we want to be; we're down $175 million and we need another $25 million; we'll just go to the public and pick it up. And I thought, what the hell has this got to do with what we're trying to accomplish, producing a tomato?

"They were doing their genetic engineering; they were all Ph.D.'s. But put a molecular biologist out on a farm, and he'd starve to death. They had no concept of what agriculture was like. There was no one like myself. I'm the bottom of the bucket, you might say. I'm a dirt farmer. I'm the guy that puts the plant in and gets the fruit out and gets it shipped.

"They thought it was simple. You get a tomato plant and plant the damn thing. But you don't just get a seed and plant it. I work in the Salinas Valley, and that requires two different varieties as the weather changes; and the San Joaquin Valley, that requires two or three different varieties. At the southern end we have lots of sun; we need lots of leaves, and where we have rain we need a plant that doesn't have so many leaves, so the rain won't destroy it.

"They had no concept of how many varieties it would take. They said: 'So you mean we'll have to put this gene in more than one variety?' So I actually gave them a list of all the tomato varieties that I thought we should use, in the United States and Mexico. And it was a large list. They were . . . surprised. I was going to use another word. I'll be nice and say surprised.

"I had a hard time with them. After a while I just quit. They weren't really trying to develop a tomato. I think they had other motives."

ROGER SALQUIST did one thing brilliantly. He bushwhacked a path through the thicket of public opinion and government regulations, clearing the way for his tomato to enter the marketplace. Along the way, he fought against friend and foe of biotechnology alike. He beat off opponents of genetic engineering who called the Flavr Savr a "Frankenstein food" and tried to organize consumer boycotts of the product. He browbeat government officials into approving something that they weren't even sure they wanted to consider. Where some corporate executives avoid controversy, Salquist reveled in it; it was free publicity for Calgene, and it helped turn this tiny startup company from a college town in California into a symbol of the biotechnological frontier.

This was not what many of biotechnology's friends in Washington wanted. A succession of Republican administrations, determined not to lay new obstacles in the way of a promising new industry, had decreed that the products of biotechnology should face no special regulatory hurdles. They should slip into the marketplace unnoticed if possible. Government officials had a mantra: Regulate products, not the processes by which they are created. So in theory, if a genetically engineered tomato was still just a tomato, it didn't require any formal approval from government regulators.

It was supposed to be good for biotechnology companies, but Salquist considered it no good at all. Vice President Dan Quayle, who led a "Council on Competitiveness" that tried to block any new environmental regulation, sent Salquist into a rage: "The worst thing that ever happened to agricultural biotechnology was the Council on Competitiveness," he told the *New York Times*. "The industry has always said it wanted credible federal oversight; the American people want oversight."

Salquist wasn't just interested in the feelings of the American people; he thought that Calgene could use approval from the U.S. Food and Drug Administration as a "competitive weapon." "We didn't want to have schlocky companies come along and put genetically engineered products on the market without having done a certain amount of rigor," he says.

Whatever the reason, in 1991 Roger Salquist and a team of Calgene's scientists sent two requests to the FDA and sent out press releases to announce what they'd done. First, they asked the FDA to approve the very first gene ever engineered into plants, back in 1983—the gene that makes plant cells resistant to the antibiotic kanamycin—as a "food additive." Calgene was using this gene as a tool in the production of Flavr Savr tomatoes; it was the "marker" that allowed Calgene's scientists to select cells containing the Flavr Savr gene and regenerate those cells into complete tomato plants. Second, Calgene asked the FDA to issue an "advisory opinion" on whether tomatoes containing the Flavr Savr gene were safe to eat.

Those actions set off three years of intense publicity, opposition, and frantic attempts by government regulators to figure out exactly how to handle genetically engineered crops. It placed Calgene right where Salquist wanted it, in the spotlight of public attention. The red, ripe, presumably tasty tomato became the symbol of what biotechnology had to offer.

Jeremy Rifkin, already a balding veteran of the struggle against biotechnology, set up an organization called the Pure Food Campaign and declared war on the tomato. "I'm here to tell you this tomato will be dead on arrival. This tomato will go under. This tomato will find no market." He may not have been the inventor, but he was certainly a popularizer of the term *Frankenfoods*.

Rifkin didn't claim that the tomato itself was dangerous (although he argued that no one could prove it safe, either.) No, the real perils lay in the future, beyond a gate marked "Biotechnology." The tomato was the temptress opening that gate and beckoning an unwary public inside.

Yet the tone of most press coverage was more bemused and amazed than alarmed. Late in 1992 a reporter from London's *Daily Telegraph* took a Flavr Savr tomato home with him, placed it on a shelf in his kitchen, and contemplated it for a week or so. "It prompted disturbing thoughts of Faust and Mephistopheles, devilish pacts with immortality, of Frankenstein and monsters with bolts run through their necks." Yet a few paragraphs later, the reporter proclaimed the tomato "the cuddliest of Frankenfoods." He also seemed charmed by Salquist, who proudly showed off a newspaper cartoon depicting a "malevolent scientist hunched over a tray of human-eyed, sharp-toothed seedlings," rubbing his hands in pleasure as he says: "There is good news from the FDA, my little ones!"

Good news from the FDA, in fact, was a long time in coming. As months stretched into years, Salquist saw less and less humor in that cartoon. Calgene was already burning money. It signed contracts with tomato growers, set up a packinghouse in Chicago, and began selling conventional tomatoes in selected markets to learn how the business worked. Salquist promised investors that the Flavr Savr would be approved and in supermarkets by Christmas 1993, and Calgene planted a crop of Flavr Savr tomatoes, hoping that by the time they were ready for harvest they'd also be approved for sale. It didn't happen. Instead, FDA commissioner David Kessler announced that he'd appointed a special advisory committee (mostly composed of scientists, but also including a food critic from *Vogue*) to hold public hearings on Calgene's requests. Calgene had to plow under its entire harvest of genetically engineered tomatoes. Investors, who'd been assured by Salquist that FDA approval was practically assured, were shocked. "Our stock price dropped by 50 percent in one day," says Salquist. "It was completely out of the blue. I felt that I'd been stabbed in the back." He fired off a letter to the FDA expressing his "grave concern and total frustration" at the long delay.

When the hearings finally took place in April 1994, it became clear that this was Kessler's way of announcing that the FDA was ready to approve Calgene's requests. Over the course of three days, the FDA walked through the evidence the advisory committee needed to determine whether the kanamycin resistance gene, a standard tool of genetic engineering, was safe and whether the Flavr Savr tomato posed any more risk than any other tomato.

Answering the first question was the easier task; the FDA's scientists at least knew where to start. After all, evaluating food additives is one of the things they do for a living. It's simply a matter of isolating the chemical under consideration and testing every possible way in which it might affect human health.

Calgene had carried out experiments on the kanamycin resistance gene and the protein it produces. The company produced data showing that this protein is digested quickly in a person's stomach, broken down into short strings of amino acids having no biological function of their own. The protein did not appear capable of producing any allergic reactions. It was not toxic when fed to rats.

So far, so good. But for this particular food additive, there were several complicating factors. As a person ate Flavr Savr tomatoes, could the antibiotic resistance gene somehow migrate into bacteria living in that person's intestines? Could it create new forms of bacteria that were resistant to kanamycin?

Calgene produced some calculations: First, acids and enzymes in the human stomach chop the long strands of DNA into small bits, almost all of them shorter than the length of the kanamycin resistance gene. (Still, Calgene admitted, some tiny fraction of the DNA snippets would contain the intact gene). Second, no known microorganisms in the human gut are capable of incorporating the DNA they encounter (although some bacteria, found elsewhere, had demonstrated this ability). Third, even if it turned out that these bacteria were able to accept such a gene, this ability would not change the numbers of bacteria resistant to kanamycin. Calgene calculated that for every single bacterium that was rendered resistant to kanamycin through contact with the tomato gene, about three hundred thousand such bacteria would become resistant to the antibiotic through natural mutation. The FDA accepted this evidence and agreed that there was no additional risk to human health posed by the kanamycin resistance gene.

That decision left the question of the gene's potential effects on the environment. Here the FDA was out of its depth. The agency never had been required to evaluate the possibility, for instance, that a new variety of tomato might turn into a troublesome weed. But the agency's scientists moved ahead bravely. (In truth, most scientists would have been very surprised to observe any impact on the environment from adding an antibiotic resistance gene.) Calgene produced data on tomatoes, canola, and cotton plants that contained the kanamycin resistance gene. The plants behaved no differently from ordinary tomato, canola, and cotton plants. They didn't spread like weeds or affect other wildlife. The gene didn't make the plants toxic to insects or larger animals, and there seemed to be little risk of the gene migrating into large numbers of bacteria.

All in all, the new gene passed the FDA's normal tests for food additives with flying colors. The problem came with Salquist's second request, for a stamp of approval from the FDA on the genetically altered tomato itself. The FDA never had been asked to declare a tomato safe, and it wasn't sure it wanted to start. There was no obvious way to prove such a thing.

Simply put, no one could prove that a genetically engineered tomato was safe, because there existed no way to prove that any *traditional* food was safe. Tomatoes, potatoes, coffee, and all other traditional foods were simply *assumed* to be safe or at least safe enough, because humans had eaten them for a long time and survived. A tomato, like other foods, is a stew of chemicals, thousands of them, and the chemical makeup of different tomatoes from different fields can vary widely. What's more, the composition of many foods is constantly changing, as plant breeders introduce new varieties. One of the chemical constituents of a tomato, tomatine, is actually toxic if you ingest significant quantities of it; the FDA never would allow tomatine on the market as a food additive, but the food additive rules don't apply to traditional foods.

The nature of the problem became clear on the very first day of the FDA's hearings on the Calgene tomato, when Charles Rick, a living legend in the world of plant breeding, made his way to the front of the room. Rick had spent a lifetime wandering the mountains of Latin America, collecting both wild and cultivated varieties of tomato and its related species. He'd assembled the world's largest collection of tomato varieties, which he still tended from his office at the University of California–Davis. Rick was a man of no pretensions or apparent ambitions outside the world of science, and he'd made no concessions to the conventions of Washington. He wore his customary fisherman's hat and worn overalls and appeared not even to notice that he looked utterly out of place.

His presentation challenged almost every conventional notion of what a "normal" tomato might be. He showed slides of the ancestors of the backyard tomato: There were tomatoes of every shape and color, wild tomatoes with fruit too small to consider eating and others whose fruit was impossible to eat because it was poisonous. Out of this diversity, carefully tended, bred, and selected by peasants in Latin America and plant breeders in both Americas, had come the modern tomato. Calgene's new genes, he seemed to be saying, were insignificant; they were barely worth considering, compared to the transformation already wrought by human hands in decades and centuries past. And none of those previous changes had ever been regulated by the Food and Drug Administration.

Yet Salquist demanded that the FDA say *something* about Calgene's tomato—at a minimum, that Calgene's tomato was at least as safe to eat as any other tomato. So in the years following his initial request in 1991, the FDA was the scene of sometimes frustrating, sometimes comical debate over exactly how to evaluate the Calgene tomato. A few things seemed sensible to everyone. It made sense, for instance, to see if tomatoes with the Flavr Savr gene showed higher levels of tomatine (they didn't). It made sense to compare the chemical profile of Flavr Savr tomatoes with conventional tomatoes to see if there were any obvious differences (there weren't).

Some scientists at the FDA thought that Calgene should run experiments on rats, just in case something interesting happened to the rats fed Flavr Savr tomatoes. Others didn't see the point of such a trial, since no one really expected it to produce any significant results. For any consistent effect to show up in such an experiment, the animals would have to be fed large quantities of the substance— much more, per ounce of body weight, than a human would ever consume. And large quantities of highly acidic tomatoes aren't healthy for humans or rats, so the experiment was likely to produce lots of sick rats and little insight into whatever subtle differences might exist between conventional and Flavr Savr tomatoes.

The proponents of feeding studies prevailed, and Calgene paid an outside laboratory to conduct a series of three-month-long feeding studies. (The rats wouldn't eat raw tomatoes, so the tomato puree had to be squirted through tubes directly into the rats' stomachs.) In the first study, no rats showed any ill effects. In the second, disaster struck. Four of the twenty rats consuming genetically engineered tomato puree developed lesions in the lining of their stomachs. None of the rats on the conventional diet showed such symptoms. The third study produced confusion: Lesions showed up in the stomachs of rats eating both kinds of tomatoes.

Calgene and the FDA puzzled over these results for half a year. Calgene argued that the stomach injuries were a random phenomenon unrelated to the type of tomatoes the rats were consuming. The FDA scientists were inclined to agree, but insisted that Calgene needed to provide some evidence. "We have real data (however questionable) that raises a safety question and real data is necessary to resolve it," wrote one of the FDA's experts, somewhat plaintively.

In the end, the FDA was satisfied by the conclusions of an expert panel assembled by Calgene. Those experts decided that the damage to the rats' stomach lining was probably minor and temporary, and almost certainly wasn't due to the genetic alteration of the Calgene tomatoes.

On May 18, 1994, the FDA gave Calgene the green light to proceed with its Flavr Savr tomatoes. But it was careful not to declare that the Flavr Savr was safe; it reported only that, in the opinion of the FDA, Calgene's tomato was as safe as tomatoes already in the stores.

By that time, the decision was anticlimactic, which was just how Salquist wanted it. Reporters had been writing about the Calgene tomato for three years already; they were tired of the story. And several of biotechnology's most prominent critics didn't have any quarrel with Calgene or its tomato. Rebecca Goldburg, for instance, pointed out that Calgene had done more than the government had requested. There is no guarantee, she said, that companies developing future products would be equally responsible.

It was a guarded reference to the giant of agricultural biotechnology watching closely from its headquarters in St. Louis. At that moment, in fact, Monsanto was pursuing government approval for a long list of products: cotton, potato, and corn with the Bt gene, soybean and canola plants that were resistant to Roundup. But these had, as yet, garnered relatively little attention.

Salquist and his colleagues at Calgene took great pride, in fact, in doing things very differently from their big brother in St. Louis. Monsanto provided data to government regulators, in many cases, on the condition that it be kept confidential; Calgene released the results of every experiment. Monsanto worked quietly behind the scenes; Calgene publicized every move. Monsanto avoided controversy; Salquist practically courted it, on the theory that the more people talked about the Flavr Savr tomato before it was on the market, the less surprised and fearful they would be when it actually did show up in grocery stores. Salquist matched Rifkin quote for quote with equal amounts of humor and outrage.

Calgene had one other advantage, often overlooked. It was small. It fit the image, always popular in the United States, of the plucky innovator in a world of corporate giants. And it chose as its product the tomato, the most cuddly of Frankenfoods. Unfortunately for Calgene, the product's image did not match reality.

"I HATE agriculture," Churchwell said on occasion. He hated the sheer messiness of it and the fact that so much was beyond his control—the weather, the weeds, the fragile tomato plants, which responded neither to threats nor to offers of money.

What he loved, was new technology. At Calgene Fresh, there were dreams of a "War Wagon" in constant communication with harvesting crews, markets, and distribution centers; of trucks linked by satellite, reacting to shifting markets; of magic machines to tell you whether tomatoes tasted good as the fruit ran past on conveyor belts.

There were cellular telephones, lots of them, in a day when those phones were not cheap. "It was surreal," says Kenneth Moonie, who worked at Calgene Fresh's Chicago headquarters. "There were no expense controls. They'd hire these recent college graduates, give them a cell phone and a computer, and send them off to stores to talk to the produce guys. We had these people racking up fifteen-hundred-dollar cell phone bills talking to their friends."

Like a gun-toting European colonial power laying claim to distant, unfamiliar lands, Calgene marched into the tomato business carrying the banner of progress, singing a hymn to the transforming power of technology. "We're not just interested in making a million dollars here or a million dollars there," Roger Salquist said. "We're out to change one of the larger industries in the United States that has so far been immune to the progress of the late twentieth century."

ROGER SALQUIST insists that he always knew that Calgene would need to get the Flavr Savr gene into decent tomato varieties, and that tomato breeding was important. It just didn't seem as urgent as other things. "When you're up to your neck in alligators, sometimes you forget that your mission is to drain the swamp," he says. "I'd sit there and say, 'Here I am spending $7 million on molecular biology, and I'm supposed to spend another $3 million on plant breeding?' We just didn't have the resources to do that."

Perhaps the executives and scientists at Calgene assumed, without really being conscious of it, that since plant breeding was a century-old science, it must not be difficult or take very long. Perhaps they also were seduced by the rhetoric of genetic engineering. After all, if they could "splice" the Flavr Savr gene into any tomato plant, who needed plant breeders? Why couldn't they simply find a good variety, splice in the gene, and go plant it?

There were good reasons why not. Inserting new genes into plants was an unpredictable process. Every genetic transformation "event," as it's called, produced slightly different results, and only one out of ten genetically transformed plants—sometimes one out of a hundred—was usable. In some plants, the gene didn't work well or at all. In other cases, plants emerged weak, infertile, or with disfigured leaves. If those plants showed such obvious effects, many more probably had suffered damage in subtler ways: Perhaps they wouldn't hold up as well in hot weather or yield quite as many tomatoes. Those kinds of effects would only be discovered and weeded out through careful observation over several generations.

Not only that, every new transformation event that Calgene wanted to bring to market would require a separate review from regulators in Washington. Calgene would have to show exactly what genes had gone into the plant and how they functioned and prove that the plant's nutritional makeup hadn't been altered. Generating this data took many months and millions of dollars.

It made no sense to go through this process with every single tomato variety. It was far cheaper to pick one good genetically transformed tomato plant, get it approved, and move the Flavr Savr gene into other varieties through traditional methods of plant breeding. When this became clear to Calgene's executives, they finally hired some tomato breeders.

There was just one problem: Plant breeding takes time. When one plant breeder surveyed dozens of colleagues across the United States a few years ago asking which personal characteristics were most important for success in their field, the quality that ended up in first place was patience. Nature cannot be rushed, and it reveals its secrets slowly. A tomato plant will reproduce on its own schedule, not according to the whims of Wall Street.

Salquist, Churchwell, and the sharp young financial experts who were running Calgene Fresh weren't noted for patience. They weren't particularly interested in plant breeding, nor did they understand it. Not understanding it, they kept looking for shortcuts.

One of Calgene's tomato breeders, Cathy Thome, recalls a visit from one of Churchwell's troops. "I was trying to explain when the hybrids would be ready," says Thome. "He said, 'Can't you do it faster?' I said no. And he said, 'Come on! The sky's the limit! Don't worry about money! Can't you do it faster?' And I said, 'No! There are biological limits!' And he said, 'Come on! Think outside the box!'"

As a joke, Calgene's tomato breeders once suggested a list of names for their new varieties, a selection of the management-consultant lingo that rolled constantly off the tongues of Calgene Fresh executives: "Think Outside the Box" was on the list, along with "Synergy" and "Downsizing." "The marketing guys were thrilled," says one tomato breeder. "They thought it was great. They had no idea."

WHAT STICKS in Kenneth Moonie's mind and in Bill Hiatt's is the first truckload of tomatoes out of Mexico in January of 1994. It was late at night in the middle of a Chicago winter. Half a dozen Calgene executives waited for the truck in the freezing cold in a warehouse Calgene Fresh had built on Chicago's South Side. The truck rolled up. Moonie ran to the back of it, lifted up the door, and stopped in shock. Boxes were lying every which way. Tomatoes had fallen into crushed heaps.

Five highly paid executives started climbing over the pile, searching in desperation for intact fruit. Bill Hiatt remembers Kenneth Moonie's eyes, round as saucers. Moonie remembers shoveling tomatoes into a dumpster with a snow shovel and seeing one of the company's young vice presidents "sitting there with an Emery board or nail clippers or something, nervously clipping at his fingernails. I say, 'Can you believe this shit?' And he says, 'Think how much we're learning!'"

Final approval from the FDA was just a few months away. Calgene, with dreams of dominating the fresh produce business, still was learning how to pack a truck.

A FEW numbers begin to tell the story. Tomato growers generally collected two thousand boxes of tomatoes per acre from a typical field. Calgene, in its financial projections, assumed yields of fifteen hundred to eighteen hundred boxes to the acre and expected that 40 percent of those tomatoes would be big and beautiful enough to be sold in stores for high prices under the brand name "McGregor." As it turned out, Calgene's fields produced, at most, eight hundred boxes per acre; more often it was four hundred. Equally catastrophic, only 20 per cent of those tomatoes were of McGregor quality.

The tomato varieties that Calgene tried to grow, says one of the company's plant breeders, were "garbage." The harvest was poor in California, worse in Mexico, and horrible in Florida. In California the plants weren't leafy enough to protect the fruit from the hot sun. In Florida they were decimated by diseases. "There are so many things that can kill a plant, and it's all in the details," says one former Calgene plant breeder. Calgene, assuming that plant breeding was a low-tech, trivial matter, hadn't allowed time to work out those details.

Things got worse. Calgene tried to pick, sort, and ship tomatoes when they were red and ripe, which meant that they also were soft—Flavr Savr gene or no Flavr Savr gene. "The gene wouldn't take a soft fruit and make it harder," says Calgene's Bill Hiatt. "Good fruit would stay good longer. But if it had the crap beat out of it, the gene wouldn't do you any good." Tomatoes ended up split, crushed, and thrown into dumpsters. The company bought special padded processing lines, originally built for peaches, to handle the vine-ripened fruit. The equipment helped but cost a truckload of money.

Calgene's contract growers must have suspected that Calgene's plants would yield poorly. They'd insisted on guaranteed payments based on how many acres they grew rather than how much they produced. Unfortunately, this also took away any incentive to deliver the harvest. "We had places where 'pinhookers' [independent picking crews] were coming into our fields, with the approval of growers or some employees, and picking our fruit. They were stealing it," says Calgene executive Kenneth Moonie.

Moonie ended up managing Calgene's operations in Florida, where he got a crash course in the rougher side of the fresh produce business. The night his packing shed opened in Immokalee, Florida, a knife fight broke out between Mexican and Haitian workers. Later, truck drivers showed up drunk, and workers in the Chicago operation were caught dealing drugs.

Some at Calgene had wondered whether other companies in the fresh produce business might resort to sabotage and intimidation to defend their turf. But Mooney says Calgene faced no such problems from entrenched competitors. "They were too busy laughing at us. They'd never seen anything like it. They were used to packing sixteen hundred boxes an hour. We'd have just as many people, and we'd be packing twelve boxes."

By the end of 1994 Churchwell was out the door. With him went the cell phones, the "skunk works meetings," and high-flown dreams of transforming an entire industry. In came several veterans of the industry, men with twenty years' experience growing, shipping, and selling fresh produce.

Salquist told investors that it was just a matter of getting costs under control and boosting production of Flavr Savr tomatoes. Consumer demand, he pointed out, had never been a problem. "There's no question that the product has mass appeal," he said in December of 1995, still defiantly optimistic. "Wherever we've had it for sale, we've sold it for anywhere from two to five times the price of the garbage that's on the market masquerading as ripe tomatoes." The fruit was advertised in stores as genetically engineered, and some consumers bought it just for that reason; after all, it was new and improved. "The genetic engineering was almost a marketing gimmick," says one former Calgene employee.

Calgene shut down its operations in Florida. Kenneth Moonie moved to Mexico, and this time professionals were in charge. "We had a Mexican grower who, if you had a five-dollar problem, he had a five-dollar solution. Not a five-thousand-dollar solution," he says. Yields became more reliable, and consumer demand never flagged. But the profits, if there were any at all, were small.

"We failed again, but this time we failed for the right reasons," Moonie says. Those reasons represented Calgene's final bitter lesson. Its Flavr Savr gene, the discovery on which it had hung its entire business plan, its advertising, and its fund-raising on Wall Street, simply didn't make tomatoes noticeably better. Far more important than the new gene were the basics of the business: the varieties you grew and the way you handled the tomatoes, sorted them, and marketed them. The company would have done just as well—or just as badly—growing vine-ripened tomatoes that weren't genetically engineered.

In fact, one small company *did* transform the tomato business during the early 1990s. It did so, as if to throw one more insult at Calgene, with traditional plant breeding, the art and science that Calgene had disdained.

The company was called LSL, which stood for Long Shelf Life. Behind LSL stood Nahum Kedar, an Israeli plant breeder. Kedar had been a graduate student at Purdue University in the 1970s, where his faculty advisor had become intrigued with a peculiar mutant form of tomato that never seemed to become fully ripe. The particular gene that produced this trait was known as the *rin* gene, for "ripening in-hibitor".

During the 1980s, Kedar tried crossing these mutants with other tomato plants that produced rock-solid, extremely colorful fruit. He got back gorgeous red fruit that tasted more or less like tomatoes (although some disputed this claim, likening the taste to a brass doorknob). More importantly, at least for commercial growers, these tomatoes could last on the shelf for several weeks.

It was almost exactly what Calgene was claiming for the Flavr Savr—tomatoes that could be picked when they were red and ripe instead of green—except that in the case of LSL tomatoes, it really worked (although the taste was nowhere close to a backyard tomato.) What's more, LSL plants simply gushed forth fruit.

LSL varieties never really caught on in California, where the industry was wedded to its gassing chambers. But in Mexico the new varieties turned that country's vine-ripened tomato industry into a world beater.

"Historically the Mexican production was really bad," says Moonie. "They'd get twelve hundred boxes to the acre, and the quality was really bad. But when LSL tomatoes came in, the yields suddenly went up to thirty-five hundred to four thousand boxes an acre. These tomatoes were as hard as a rock, and they actually were better tasting than gas-green. So suddenly Mexican production just exploded."

LSL tomatoes sealed the Flavr Savr's coffin. They flooded the market, driving tomato prices into the ground. Those prices were crucial for Calgene, because only 20 percent of its tomatoes were big and beautiful enough to sell as high-priced McGregor fruit. The rest of Calgene's tomato harvest went on the market as standard tomatoes, at the worst prices in history.

"I WAS out of fund-raising gas, personally," says Roger Salquist, resignation creeping into his voice. "I'd done it too many times, and the company story was getting a little bit . . . spoiled. We finally concluded that we needed a major partner."

Monsanto had always been Calgene's greatest foe, the Goliath to their David. Many at Calgene were convinced that the feeling was mutual. "Monsanto wanted us to die. They hated us," says one longtime Calgene employee. "They thought they owned biotech. So when we got the first patent on glyphosate resistance, their reaction was like, 'Who the hell are these guys? They wear sandals, they're out in California, they swear a lot. Who are these guys?'"

Salquist himself had been known to shout that he would never, *never* accept Monsanto as a business partner. But as losses from the tomato business mounted and doors closed on Wall Street, Salquist decided that "sometimes your best enemy is your best partner."

"They, of everybody out there, understood agricultural biotechnology," says Salquist. In addition, Monsanto had just taken its own (equally ill-advised, as it turned out) step into the tomato business, in partnership with a large tomato grower in Florida called Gargiolo.

"I rolled the dice a little bit," says Salquist. "I said, 'Look! Gargiolo does $120 million a year in fresh tomatoes; they're the best guys in the business. They have their own breeding program. Let's put this in the Gargiolo operation. It's gotta work!'"

Monsanto wasn't actually much interested in Calgene's tomato business. Monsanto's executives had their eye on several other businesses that Calgene was just getting off the ground. Calgene had begun growing canola plants that produced a kind of oil that was used in detergents. It was small and unprofitable, but the technology looked promising, leading to various types of alterations in oilseeds of all kinds. Calgene had also launched a modestly successful but growing venture in cotton. It had bought a cottonseed company called Stoneville, which was selling varieties engineered to survive the herbicide bromoxinil. In addition Calgene was planning to splice a Bt gene into those varieties. It would have been a direct competitor to Monsanto's own Bt cotton, and Calgene was planning to undercut Monsanto's prices. "That was the hammer that drove the deal," says one former Calgene executive.

By July of 1995 the deal was in place. Monsanto bought 49.5 percent of Calgene and paid for it with a money-losing tomato venture—Gargiolo—plus $30 million in cash. Salquist now was in charge of an even bigger tomato company—except that he wasn't really in charge.

Any doubts about who really was running Calgene were erased within a few months. Salquist negotiated a deal with Pioneer Hi-Bred, the nation's largest seed company. Pioneer was willing to pay $18 million for a stake in Calgene's oils business and the right to use Calgene's oilseed genes in Pioneer's own seeds. Calgene considered it a very good deal. Salquist informed Hendrik Verfaillie, Monsanto's executive vice president, and Verfaillie, according to a former Calgene executive, said "Fine, go ahead. Make it happen."

Days later, Robb Fraley, warrior for the biotech cause, intervened. Fraley opposed giving away rights to any genes, at almost any price, especially to Pioneer, the archenemy. Those genes, he argued, were the basis of new crops that could be worth billions, and $18 million amounted to pocket change. Monsanto, he said, "would not let that deal happen," and it didn't.

After that, things went downhill quickly at Calgene. The Gargiolo business lost more money each month than Tom Churchwell's operation ever had, but Salquist didn't seem to care anymore. He'd lost control of Calgene, and he knew it. He was reduced to spitting obscenities at Monsanto's representatives in the boardroom. The ship was heading toward an iceberg with no captain on the deck.

Several of Calgene's top managers went to Monsanto's Hendrik Verfaillie with a set of urgent requests. Get rid of Jeff Gargiolo, who was running the disastrous tomato operation, they said. Replace Salquist with someone who knows Calgene but whom Monsanto trusts and pump in some more money. Monsanto did two of the three. It replaced Roger Salquist. It kept Jeff Gargiolo. And it bought the rest of Calgene, for another $200 million. Calgene's grand adventure was over.

# 11

# Tremors of Anticipation

Through the summer of 1995 in America's farm country there were voices in the wind, rumors of savior genes and miracle crops that weren't yet legal to plant.

A few genetically engineered plants already were in the fields, to be sure. In addition to Calgene's ill-fated tomato, Asgrow was selling seed for squash plants that were resistant to viruses, farmers in Georgia were growing Calgene's genetically engineered canola plants, producing oil suitable for use in soaps and detergents, and Monsanto had begun selling Bt potatoes. But these crops covered only a few thousand acres, and their commercial prospects were dim. They were mere ripples in the ocean; a tsunami was approaching.

America's dominant cottonseed company, the Delta and Pine Land Company, had covered thousands of acres in Arizona and Mississippi with Bt cotton, now bearing the trademark "Bollgard." This crop hadn't yet been approved for commercial sale, so the fields were under a kind of quarantine, separated from areas of conventional cotton. These cotton plants were being grown just for their seed; the harvest would generate enough cottonseed for a million acres. Delta Pine hoped to sell that much Bollgard cotton the following spring, after the government gave the crop its seal of approval.

Roger Malkin, the company's chief executive, had bet the survival of his company on this crop. He'd spent an extra $20 million, equal to his company's total profit that year, on a crash program to produce Bollgard seed. Malkin had good reason to expect approval for this crop from the Environmental Protection Agency. (Since the EPA regulated pesticides, it had jurisdiction over pesticidal genes that were inserted into plants.) But Malkin couldn't have predicted the natural disaster that converted his wager into gold.

In mid-July, a plague struck the cotton fields of northern Alabama and the hill country of northeastern Mississippi. Tobacco budworms infested the cotton fields. "It was the worst insect-related agricultural disaster we'd ever had in Alabama," says Ron Smith, the state's leading insect expert. Normally, cotton growers call in their air force—the airplanes that swoop back and forth across the fields spraying insecticide—when ten or twenty tiny white budworm eggs turn up on a random sample of one hundred cotton plants. In his test plots in July of 1995, Ron Smith counted more than seven hundred eggs per hundred plants. Even after showers of the insecticides, the caterpillars ate on. After fifteen years of spraying these chemicals, called synthetic pyrethroids, a resistant strain of budworms had appeared. The phone rang ceaselessly in Ron Smith's office and in his home. Farmers pleaded for answers, but Smith had none to give other than to plant some other crop the following year. "We thought it was the end of growing cotton in Alabama," he says.

Smith knew about the prospect of Bt cotton. He'd done some testing of the plants, and he knew that they killed the tobacco budworm, but he didn't tell his cotton growers about that new technology. He didn't want to promise something that might not be available. He didn't know about Delta and Pine Land's five thousand acres of Bt seed production in Arizona.

The Environmental Protection Agency gave its blessing late in October. An executive at Delta and Pine Land walked into the office of the company's CEO and said: "Get every bag of Bt seed you can. The demand for this is phenomenal."

The company had made a lucky mistake in its production calculations. The fields dedicated to producing seed had done better than expected; the company had harvested enough seed for almost two million acres of cotton. In the spring of 1996, Delta and Pine Land would sell every bag.

JOHN SCHILLINGER, head of research at the Asgrow seed company and the man who'd brokered the deal that made Roundup Ready soybeans possible, had made a similar wager. Schillinger had always believed that Roundup-tolerant crops would exert a magical hold on the imagination of farmers. "I knew how much farmers like to kill weeds and how much they like to do it in a way where they can go spray and then go off fishing in the summer," he says. During the summer of 1995 Schillinger set up a series of demonstration fields in specially designated farms across the Midwest. Thousands of farmers from miles around came to witness the plants' strange powers. "We'd actually let farmers run the sprayer," says Schillinger. "And then they could drive by on the way to the coffee shop and watch the fields. It was a fantastic show."

"They were just watching it at first," says Schillinger. "Then they couldn't believe it. And then they just wanted to buy it."

Finally they were able to buy it. As 1995 turned into 1996, farmers began ordering seed for the summer to come. Schillinger thought he'd been optimistic growing enough Roundup Ready seed to cover a million acres. Monsanto executives, always more inclined to look for the big score, thought he'd been too cautious. They were right. Schillinger sold every bag, and he could have sold many more.

EUPHORIA IN the halls of Monsanto's headquarters mixed with agony at the sight of potential profits going unclaimed. Monsanto's executives were haunted by memories of past deals. As part of the three-way deal to create Roundup Ready soybeans, Monsanto had promised John Schillinger's company free access to the Roundup Ready gene. Then, in a fit of impatience, Monsanto had sold Pioneer Hi-Bred International the rights to Roundup Ready soybeans and Bt corn. There wouldn't be any royalties coming from those seed companies.

In fact, there was an even more basic problem, casting doubt on the entire "Microsoft of agriculture" strategy. Most of the seed industry seemed incapable of charging farmers what Monsanto thought the genes were worth. Asgrow, for instance, planned to charge farmers only two or three dollars extra for each bag of Roundup Ready seed, and the company feared that even this margin might disappear in the years to come. It was the same old seed industry lament: too much competition and too little control over genes. This may have been Adam Smith's vision of capitalism, with the invisible hand of competition distributing benefits to consumers, but it was not Monsanto's.

The situation was better in cotton. Delta Pine controlled most of the market and was the only company with rights to Monsanto's Bt gene, so it faced fewer competitive pressures. But the fact remained, when Monsanto licensed its genes to seed companies, it turned over control of these treasures, in Monsanto's view, to weak-kneed enterprises with self-esteem problems. There had to be a better way, Monsanto's executives said to each other, a way for Monsanto to maintain control over these genes, to capture for itself more of their value.

The solution, as it finally took shape, was praised by some as a masterstroke of business strategy and condemned by others as a perfidious scheme to turn farmers into serfs. It emerged from conversations with executives at Delta and Pine Land. "We felt that the sticker shock [of Bt cotton] would be staggering," says Delta Pine's Roger Malkin. "If we simply went from 30 dollars a bag to 120 dollars a bag, the farmers would get mad at us. So we got the idea of the farmer paying for the insecticidal portion separately." Farmers would pay the same price they always had for the seed and pay a separate fee—32 dollars an acre—for the Bt gene.

Lights flashed in the heads of executives in St. Louis; bells rang. Perhaps farmers could pay a separate "technology fee" to Monsanto, in effect buying the new genes in a separate transaction from the seed purchase. Indeed, perhaps Monsanto could *license* its patented genes directly to each farmer! The arrangement would make Monsanto the sole supplier of these genes to every farmer, allowing Monsanto to set and maintain a standard price for its genes. Even more important, Monsanto could use that license to enforce a ban on farmers using part of their Roundup Ready harvest as seed for the following year.

This became the standard arrangement between Monsanto and seed companies. When farmers arrived at a seed dealer to buy some Roundup Ready soybeans, they ended up concluding two separate transactions. They bought the seed from the dealer just as they always had. But now they also signed a technology agreement: the license that governed their use of the Roundup Ready gene contained in that seed. Monsanto set the price for that license (first $5, then $6.50 per acre of soybeans). And the license banned the replanting of any part of the harvest containing those patented genes.

It was the most significant attempt to turn biology into a product since the advent of hybrid corn in the 1930s. Monsanto's licenses asserted its control over a gene and, by extension, over the seeds and plants that contained it. That control continued even after the farmer bought the seed, planted it in the ground, and harvested the offspring. But most Monsanto executives, rooted as they were in the business of selling agricultural chemicals, regarded it merely as a sensible modernizing step. "To me, it was all just logical," says one former Monsanto official. "We were about to double or triple the net income of seed companies, so they ought to be happy."

For the new scheme to work properly, Monsanto had to convince several seed companies to give up the rights to Monsanto's genes, which they had acquired in negotiations several years earlier. Delta and Pine Land, the cottonseed company, signed on quickly. The company's CEO, Roger Malkin, wasn't wedded to the seed industry's traditions, and he saw some advantages to the new scheme. For one thing, it took seed companies out of the line of fire. If farmers were angry about the price or the performance of genetically altered crops, they had Monsanto to fight, not Delta and Pine Land. For another, Delta Pine needed Monsanto's muscle if it was going to keep farmers from replanting seed from their own harvest, especially since seed was about to become far more expensive. This hadn't been a problem in prime cotton lands of the Deep South, but on the Texas high plains "brown-bagging" was common.

John Schillinger at Asgrow was caught between temptation and fear. On the one hand, Monsanto offered his company "a sweetheart deal." If Asgrow agreed to give up its royalty-free rights to Monsanto's genes, the St. Louis company would charge higher prices for Roundup Ready seed and return most of the "technology fee" to Asgrow. Monsanto would also take on the unpleasant job of enforcing the ban on seed saving.

But Schillinger and his colleagues worried about the competitive threat posed by Pioneer. "We kept saying, yeah, we'll sign this, and we'll be out there with all these big prices and tech fees. If Pioneer offers seed without all of that, we're really up a creek!"

Monsanto's negotiators tried to allay Schillinger's fears, promising that Pioneer would see the benefits of this arrangement as well. One episode in particular sticks in the craw of several Asgrow negotiators. They remember a Monsanto executive, a native of France, waving a letter in the air. On it were the green loops of Pioneer's corporate logo. As one Asgrow executive remembers it, the Monsanto negotiator said, "As soon as we finish here, we're getting on a plane to Des Moines. And Pioneer has told us, as soon as Asgrow signs, they'll sign." In fact, Monsanto had received no such assurances from Pioneer. (Another Monsanto negotiator says his French colleague didn't intend to mislead. Perhaps language difficulties subverted accurate communication; also, the Frenchman was "a hopeless optimist.")

Schillinger signed. And Monsanto's negotiators did get on a plane for Des Moines. When they got there, Pioneer's executives told them, as one Monsanto official recalled later, "You must be kidding. Go away."

"They came and said, 'We need to redo this soybean thing,'" recalls Tom Urban, Pioneer's former chief executive. "And we kept saying, 'Why?' And they'd say, 'Well, it isn't fair.' And I said, 'Excuse me?'" Urban cocks his head and feigns confusion. "I don't understand what you mean here."

The deal that Urban already had in hand was looking better and better every year. Monsanto was intent on driving up the price of Roundup Ready soybeans and prohibiting farmers from replanting part of their harvest. If they succeeded in doing so, Pioneer could (and later did) match those prices and quietly insist on similar terms for its Roundup Ready soybeans, without taking much of the heat or surrendering any of the profits.

When farmers visited their local Asgrow or Delta and Pine Land dealer during the spring of 1996 and saw Monsanto's technology agreement for the first time, many were shocked, suspicious, and resentful. Farmers typically don't like lawyers, they don't like signing things, and they don't like threats. They didn't react well to sentences like these:

In the event that the Grower saves, supplies, sells, or acquires seed for replant in violation of this Agreement and license restriction, in addition to other remedies available to the technology provider(s), the Grower agrees that damages will include a claim for liquidated damages which will be based on 120 times the applicable Technology Fee. THIS AGREEMENT IS GOVERNED BY THE LAWS OF THE STATE OF MISSOURI AND THE UNITED STATES. THE PARTIES CONSENT TO THE EXCLUSIVE JURISDICTION OF THE U.S. DISTRICT COURT FOR THE EASTERN DISTRICT OF MISSOURI, EASTERN DIVISION, AND THE CIRCUIT COURT OF THE COUNTY OF ST. LOUIS, STATE OF MISSOURI, FOR ALL DISPUTES ARISING UNDER THIS AGREEMENT.

"WE KNEW that farmers' first reaction was going to be, 'This is unconstitutional!'" says Robert Shapiro, who took over as Monsanto's chief executive in 1995. "If you had to characterize farmers with one word, it's that they are independent. Their whole history has been one of fighting big institutions—banks, the railroads, the government. And the idea that some corporation was going to come and tell them what to do—we knew what the reaction was going to be.

"But we also knew, from conversations with people you might call leading-edge farmers—the people we felt represented the future of agriculture—that they could understand our position: We put a lot of money into this stuff. We gotta get paid for it. If *you* can keep replanting seed, we can't get paid for it, which means we can't invest in it, which means that it's not going to exist! They understood that."

In the end, most farmers went along. They signed, grumbled, and joined the new agricultural order. They'd seen farming change in lots of unsettling ways during their lifetimes. This was just one more thing that most of them figured they'd have to accept.

GENETIC ENGINEERING, in any company's hands, was bound to shock the agricultural system. Genetically engineered crops rattled assumptions and challenged established ways of doing things. Seeds suddenly took sales away from chemicals. Genes became property. Soybeans were no longer simply soybeans; they included genetic traits that aroused public protests and required government approval in distant lands.

"I can remember a meeting of the corn-breeding association where we talked about Bt corn," says Mike Roth, a lawyer who worked first for Pioneer, then Monsanto. "And the breeders were saying, 'Well when can we have this material to use in our breeding programs?'" These breeders thought of the Bt gene as just one more genetic trait to be shared within the breeding community, perhaps in ten years emerging in varieties that might be sold to farmers. "I said, 'Look, this is going to hit the market on such and such a day, and you guys are barely going to see it. It's going to be like signing your name on a cannonball as it goes by,'" Roth says. "The plant breeders just had no conception of how fast it was going to move."

None of these changes was easily digested. But a company other than Monsanto might not have insisted on challenging the status quo in agriculture so directly. Indeed, several companies had declined to challenge the status quo or at least opted to move slowly, testing public reaction cautiously. Ciba-Geigy (later Novartis) had rejected the notion of selling seeds that were resistant to the company's own herbicides. The Swiss company also had decided not to work with crops, like soybeans, whose seeds farmers could save; there was no promise of adequate profits. "So you can see that Monsanto did all the things that the Swiss bosses in my company decided not to do," says Mary-Dell Chilton, the pioneer of genetic engineering who led Ciba-Geigy's research on biotechnology for ten years.

But Monsanto had long been a company with a chip on its shoulder, headstrong and dismissive of outside critics. This corporate personality had its roots in the company's phenomenal success against all conventional wisdom with Roundup. In the 1970s, recalls one veteran of the European chemical industry, Monsanto was "scorned and jeered within the industry" for its single-minded promotion of this herbicide while other companies developed a broad spectrum of different agricultural chemicals, each one suited to a particular niche. But Monsanto's strategy triumphed. "Their triumph fed an arrogance and disregard for the outside world."

The triumph of Roundup also fed an appetite for blockbuster products. "It's the culture. They're a home run company," says John Howard, who dealt frequently with Monsanto while he was at Pioneer Hi-Bred. "If it's not a billion-dollar product, they don't want to hear about it." For biotechnology to survive within this culture, it had to be sold, and sold hard, as a billion-dollar business.

By the mid-1990s there was just enough hard evidence that these dreams might come true to fill the halls of Monsanto's headquarters with the intoxicating whiff of vindication. After so many years of doubt, the company's executives displayed a bravado they might not have dared exhibit in normal times.

Robb Fraley and his band of visionaries had been right; Pioneer and the traditional seed companies had been wrong. Farmers *didn't* care so much about the seed varieties. They were asking for Monsanto's genes: Roundup Ready soybeans and Bollgard cotton. Competitors, meanwhile, if they still survived, had nothing comparably exciting in the works. Agrigenetics, the original pioneer of agricultural biotechnology, had long since disappeared. Calgene was fading from the scene. So was Agracetus. Hoechst, with its LibertyLink gene, was still years away from the commercial marketplace. Ciba-Geigy did have a Bt gene in corn and was preparing to bring it to market in 1996, but only in a limited fashion. Monsanto alone stood triumphant; its genes were driving the decisions of farmers, and changing the face of agriculture.

Moreover, a new chief executive reigned in St. Louis, a man disdainful of traditions of all sorts. Robert Shapiro was an unconventional CEO, at least for Monsanto. This quick-witted, cerebral man had little time for backslapping, glad-handing, and country club camaraderie. When he became the company's chief executive, he ditched his suits in favor of oddly mismatched sweaters and flannel shirts.

Richard Mahoney, his predecessor in the job, once described Shapiro as having "the soul of a visionary and the heart of an accountant." Mahoney probably meant it as a compliment, but the statement also pointed out Shapiro's greatest weakness. Visions and an accountant's numbers are both abstractions, divorced from a human world filled with messy details. Shapiro sometimes acted as though he'd prefer to live in a world of ideas rather than real people.

Shapiro preached a new era of "rapid, discontinuous change" that would render obsolete the structures and strategies of the traditional corporation. He engaged in long philosophical monologues at retreats that went on for days, sounding more like a guru-in-chief than a chief executive. He preached inclusion, openness, flexibility, and the importance of every individual. "We're great people," he said concluding an emotional speech to an assembly of Monsanto employees. "We can't even begin to imagine our full potential together. Let's go do it."

There were skeptics within the company but others who drank up the Shapiro gospel. At a "global forum" that Shapiro organized in March 1995, a Monsanto employee took the name tag that was hanging around her neck and draped it on Shapiro's "as a sign of her commitment and loyalty," according to *Monsanto Magazine*. Others imitated the gesture, and by the end of the evening Shapiro had scores of the name tags hanging from his neck.

For Shapiro, the perceived lessons of the past often were worse than useless; they were dangerous traps or signposts to long-vanished destinations. "Bob fundamentally does not believe in institutional knowledge," says one former Monsanto executive. "He thinks it gets in the way."

Monsanto's success would depend on "ceaseless creativity, profound creativity, radical creativity, and relentless speed," Shapiro told his subordinates. In the rush of accelerating world change, "getting it right the first time" was no longer a real option. "Don't wait for perfection. Don't wait for complete information," Shapiro said. "Make decisions, then make corrections."

EVEN BEFORE he ascended to the CEO's chair at Monsanto, Robert Shapiro had been wooing Pioneer Hi-bred, singing a seductive song of world domination. And hell hath no fury like a suitor scorned.

"Shapiro has this messianic sense about him," says Tom Urban, Pioneer's former CEO. "If he said it once, he said it three or four times: Put us together and we'll rule the world. We're going to own the industry. Almost those exact words. We can be a juggernaut. Invincible."

Urban wasn't interested. "We had no interest in being bought. We felt no cultural affinity with Monsanto. None," he says. He also didn't have to fear a hostile takeover. A dominant share of Pioneer still was held by the children of the company's founders. They stood firmly behind Tom Urban, and a decade earlier they'd agreed to erect legal barricades that made it nearly impossible for outsiders to take over control of the company.

Instead of a dramatic merger, Pioneer suggested a modest collaboration. "We'd say, 'Let's do a project. Start small, learn to work together, build trust,'" says Urban. "And he'd say, 'No, we have to do a deal right now, and if we put these companies together we'll own the world.'"

"I think Shapiro felt that ultimately he could get us," Urban says. "I think that not getting us was extremely frustrating to him and forced him to do a lot of things that he didn't want to do." The rift between these two men and between these two companies soon descended into open warfare.

THE DISPUTE had begun, in a concrete sense, with the two fateful deals of the early 1990s, when Pioneer had walked away with the keys to Monsanto's kingdom—permanent rights to the Bt gene in corn and the Roundup Ready gene in soybeans. Pioneer had paid less than $40 million for those genes. By 1995, it was becoming clear that those genes might soon translate into profits for Pioneer of more than $100 million per year. Shapiro wanted some of that money, and Urban flatly refused to hand it over.

As the relationship deteriorated, Monsanto went looking for a different partner in the corn business, one that would allow Monsanto to battle Pioneer on its own turf. In April 1995 Shapiro met in Chicago with Bruce Bickner, the head of DeKalb Genetics in DeKalb, Illinois. DeKalb had been Pioneer's arch rival for most of the century. It too had been a family-run business and a pioneer in the development of hybrid corn. As recently as the early 1970s DeKalb and Pioneer had held equal shares of the corn market. The last twenty years, though, had been disastrous for DeKalb. The company's breeding program had fallen behind Pioneer's, and members of the founding Roberts family had taken to feuding. DeKalb's share of the corn market fell by half, while Pioneer's swelled to more than 40 percent.

Yet DeKalb still was a name that farmers recognized, and Monsanto believed that it could once again become powerful enough to challenge Pioneer. In addition, DeKalb had several patent applications pending, based on scientific accomplishments of 1989 and 1990, when researchers at DeKalb (and a company that DeKalb later acquired) created the first fertile transgenic corn plants. Those applications, DeKalb believed, eventually might yield patents that declared DeKalb the inventor of all genetically transformed corn. That declaration would give DeKalb a lever of dominance over the entire industry. It might be able to demand royalties from any other company selling genetically engineered corn or even stop such sales altogether. For Monsanto this was both a threatening and an enticing prospect.

Shapiro and Bickner met frequently through the summer of 1995, discussing, as a filing with the Securities and Exchange Commission later put it, "potential opportunities for collaboration." The negotiations became intense by the end of 1995. On January 16, 1996, DeKalb's board met to consider Monsanto's offer. That same day the U.S. Patent Office announced that it had granted DeKalb a patent covering genetically engineered corn containing a Bt gene.

On January 31 the deal was done. Monsanto paid $177 million for a substantial chunk of DeKalb (10 percent of DeKalb's stock that came with voting rights, plus 43 percent of the company's nonvoting stock). Robb Fraley joined DeKalb's board. Fraley, on behalf of Monsanto, also signed a series of agreements in which the two companies agreed to share their genetic knowledge, techniques, and custom-designed genes. DeKalb granted Monsanto rights to its patents and the right to sublicense these patents to other seed companies, with one significant exception: Pioneer Hi-Bred International.

Shapiro made one last approach to Pioneer. "They called us up," says Tom Urban. "They said, 'Look, don't be upset by this. We've written this contract in such a way that if you decide to join us, we can dump the DeKalb deal.'" Once again, Pioneer's executives rejected Monsanto's overtures.

Three months later, DeKalb swung its hammer. It sued Pioneer (and several other seed companies) for patent infringement. More patents were issued to DeKalb in the following months. After each patent appeared, DeKalb filed a new lawsuit accusing competitors of infringing the latest patent. (The lawsuits had no immediate impact on Pioneer's sales. The suits finally went to trial in spring 2001, but a jury in Rockford, Illinois, could not agree on a verdict. A mistrial was declared.)

Observers of the industry offer two theories to explain DeKalb's lawsuits. According to the first theory, DeKalb's major stockholders, mainly members of the founding Roberts family, hoped to pump up the company's stock price so they could sell their share of the company for a higher price.

The second theory takes a more conspiratorial view of events. In this view DeKalb was merely Monsanto's pawn in a campaign to bring Pioneer to its knees and force the Des Moines company to pay Monsanto full value for its Bt and Roundup Ready genes.

"It was clear to us that Monsanto was holding DeKalb as a hammer right over Pioneer's head," says Roderick Stacey. Stacey is an Englishman and a veteran of the seed business. In 1995 and early 1996 he had a front-row view of the mounting enmity between the two companies. Stacey was the second in command at Calgene, trying to arrange the terms of his company's final sale to Monsanto. He faced across the negotiating table some of the Monsanto executives, such as Robb Fraley, who simultaneously were arranging the partnership with DeKalb. He also had good friends at Pioneer, whom he'd known for twenty-five years.

"It had a lot to do with, with . . . well, you can't really use another word than *arrogant,*" Stacey says. "It came from disbelief that Pioneer didn't want to do a deal and didn't see that they *had* to do a deal with Monsanto. So Monsanto saw them as closed-minded, small-minded, Midwestern, parochial, all those things."

Fraley, for instance, really thought that Monsanto's genes, linked to DeKalb's seeds, could quickly overwhelm Pioneer, Stacy says. "The feeling was Pioneer had nothing. Sure, they had the best germ plasm, but the technology would just revolutionize everything, so that Pioneer would be out of business in a matter of years."

"An awful lot of bad blood was created in the course of those conversations," Stacey continues. "A lot of things were said and at senior levels—right at the tops of those companies. Monsanto made it clear to Pioneer that if they didn't do a deal, they were going to be out of this technology.

"A lot of that was just vindictiveness, I think. And Monsanto didn't need to do it, because they had terrific technology."

Soon after the lawsuits were filed, Robb Fraley talked by telephone with an executive at Pioneer, a rising star in the company named Rick McConnell. McConnell recounted the conversation later during an appearance in court, under questioning from his lawyer.

"I asked Robb what we needed to do about the situation with the DeKalb patent."

"And what did Mr. Fraley say?"

"He said, 'I hope you have enough chips.'"

MONSANTO WAS playing another game of poker at this time, on a different continent, with billions of dollars worth of international trade at stake. If it hadn't been for rules instructing David Erickson how to "destruct" his test plots of soybeans, Erickson might never have realized that the game was underway or how high the stakes were.

Erickson is a big-time corn and soybean farmer in western Illinois. He's also a past president of the American Soybean Association. In the summer of 1995 his farm was the site of several test plots filled with Asgrow's new Roundup Ready soybeans.

Such field tests are standard. But Erickson had never seen anything like the rules governing these particular trials. Late in the summer, but before the plants produced beans that hardened into viable seed, Erickson was instructed to mow down that crop, chop it up, and plow it back into the dark Illinois soil. Under penalty of law, the genes in that crop were not supposed to escape into the environment or into the nation's food supply.

Within a few months the USDA rescinded those regulations. American farmers now were free to plant Roundup Ready soybeans, harvest them, and ship them off to their local grain elevators. But, Dave Erickson wondered, *what then?* Half the American soybean harvest is exported. What would happen when those beans arrived in Europe? What if European laws treated Roundup Ready genes like biological threats, as the U.S. had just a few months earlier?

Erickson called several fellow leaders of the soybean association. Together, they asked for information from the U.S. Department of Agriculture, the U.S. Trade Representative's office, and Monsanto. What they heard was disquieting if not downright alarming. In the spring of 1996, as farmers in Iowa and Minnesota enthusiastically bought Roundup Ready soybean seed, neither the European Union nor Japan had yet agreed to import the harvest. Officials from Monsanto and from the U.S. government seemed confident that the crops would, in fact, be approved by harvest time. But, if this didn't happen, Erickson could imagine a nightmarish scenario. If a small percentage of Roundup Ready soybeans ended up "contaminating" the mighty river of grain that flows out of the American heartland every fall, foreign markets could conceivably ban imports of the entire American soybean harvest. Asgrow—and Monsanto—were putting the livelihood of American farmers at risk, and almost no one seemed to realize it.

"We weren't convinced that Monsanto had done an adequate job of explaining the product and the circumstances surrounding it," Erickson says dryly. He drove several hours south to St. Louis and joined others from the soybean association in a series of meetings at Monsanto's headquarters. The farmers demanded that Monsanto at least send letters to all soybean growers explaining that these soybeans, unlike any soybeans they had ever grown, required approval from regulators in America's foreign markets, and there was a risk the new soybeans might *not* be approved. Monsanto agreed to send out such letters, but they had little effect. Few farmers appeared to take the threat seriously; it was too foreign, literally, to their experience in agriculture.

Meanwhile, another power in American agriculture glowered resentfully toward St. Louis. Archer Daniels Midland (ADM), the country's largest processor of grain, based in Decatur, Illinois, had built its entire business on the standardization of grain crops. Corn and soybeans flowed through ADM's grain elevators and processing plants in rivers. As far as ADM was concerned, anything that disrupted that river, whether it be excessive moisture, dirt, or government regulations, was an evil to be barred from ADM's smoothly functioning factories. If Roundup Ready soybeans couldn't be shipped to Europe or Japan, ADM considered them a contaminant, a destructive force all the more insidious because the beans looked, tasted, and behaved exactly like any other part of the holy river of grain.

"ADM was giving us a hard time," recalls John Schillinger, Asgrow's head of research, Monsanto's ally, and Roundup Ready soybeans' chief backer. "Monsanto really camped out in their offices." But the giant grain processor refused all entreaties. It informed its largest suppliers that Roundup Ready soybeans were unwelcome at ADM's grain elevators until both Europe and Japan had approved them. Seed dealers working in ADM's home territory of central Illinois found that they couldn't get rid of Roundup Ready seed. Asgrow trucked the seed out to Iowa where it sold like fresh apple dumplings at a fair. But that didn't resolve the lingering worries about the fate of that year's soybean harvest.

"We were all incredibly nervous," says Denise Bertrand, Monsanto's former manager for Roundup-resistant crops. "In the end, all of us—Monsanto, the seed people, the grain handlers—just held hands and said, 'We'll figure this out at harvest time if we have to.'" If they had to, they were prepared to set up a separate grain handling system for the Roundup Ready harvest: separate elevators, trains, barges, and processing plants, all engaged in a complicated, expensive, and perhaps even futile attempt to keep a million acres worth of soybeans from leaking into international trade.

"We never made that public," Bertrand continues. "It would have taken the pressure off the Europeans."

THE AVENUE de Tervuren, leading south and west from the heart of Brussels, is wide and grand but fails, in a typically Belgian way, to make much of an impression. Scattered along it are a collection of classic nineteenth-century structures, interrupted by postwar blocks of glass and steel. The buildings face each other across an avenue so wide, with its lanes of motorized traffic divided by green parkland

and ribbons of streetcar tracks, that the two sides of the street seem to have little relationship to each other.

On the northern side of the avenue, at number 277, occupying an imposing six-story structure of glass and steel built into the side of a small hill, lies the European headquarters of Monsanto. Here the company's team of biotech advocates gathered during 1995, hoping to coax, cajole, and prod the bureaucrats of Brussels into opening the continent's markets to Roundup-resistant soybeans.

Steve Rogers was among them. The lanky, genial pioneer of Monsanto's experiment in genetic engineering remembered well his earlier time in Europe, five years before. He remembered the intense hostility he'd encountered from environmental activists in Germany and the polite disinterest exhibited by political leaders. Rogers imagined that things would have changed during the intervening years. They certainly had in the United States, thanks to Calgene's tomato and Monsanto's rush to market.

Rogers soon discovered that the same was not true of Europe. "Very little had happened," he says. "Field-testing was going on but not much more. It wasn't five years later, not like it was in the U.S."

Monsanto first had to request approval from one of the European Union's member states. The company chose the United Kingdom, which along with France was considered the government most supportive of biotechnology. On May 3, 1995, the British government concluded that Roundup Ready soybeans were safe and that foods containing them did not require special labels. The British forwarded a "dossier" on the matter to Brussels. Now it was up to the member countries of the European Union to study the dossier and vote on Monsanto's application.

The process looked on paper as if it should take six months from start to finish—meaning approval would be granted a full year before the first major harvest of Roundup Ready soybeans in the United States. Specialists on biotechnology within the executive branch of Europe's government, the European Commission in Brussels, had crafted these rules back in 1990. They intended the process to be a purely scientific one, driven by data, but it became clear very quickly that European officials responsible for approving this product had concerns that went far beyond scientific data.

"It was a surprise to us," admits one longtime civil servant in Brussels who oversaw the process from its beginning. "Among member states, there was an uneasiness and uncertainty about what to do." Governments raised new issues. Denmark, Austria, and Sweden wanted products derived from the new soybeans to be labeled. Austrian and Danish officials wanted to examine the environmental and health effects of increased use of Roundup on soybeans. The discussion dragged on; some governments seemed to prefer unending discussion to the prospect of any vote. The commissioner in charge of the process, a Danish official named Ritt Bjerregaard, reflecting the broadly antibiotech attitudes of her home government in Copenhagen, seemed unwilling to draw the protracted debate to a close.

Fall gave way to winter, and winter to spring. In the American Midwest Asgrow began selling Roundup Ready seeds to farmers, and in Brussels Monsanto's executives became increasingly agitated. They did what they could to turn up the heat.

To this day, European officials speak guardedly and obliquely about the Monsanto lobbying campaign in the spring of 1996. Monsanto's chief executive, Robert Shapiro, a liberal Democrat, had good friends in the Clinton administration, and coincidentally or not, the most intense pressure on the European Commission apparently came from the U.S. government. The U.S. Special Trade Representative, a hot-tempered lawyer named Mickey Kantor, held stormy meetings with European officials in which he accused them of setting up illegal trade barriers against Roundup Ready soybeans. (Kantor, after leaving the government, joined the Monsanto board.) Some in Brussels say that pressure came from the "highest levels" of the United States government. Others insist that there was no undue pressure at all.

The matter finally came to a vote in mid-March 1996. The exact tally of votes has never been released, but a "qualified majority"— governments representing at least 70 percent of Europe's citizens— did vote in Monsanto's favor. The decision was announced two weeks later, on April 3. The path to Europe's ports was clear. Japan, where approval had never really been in doubt, gave its approval within a few months.

At a public meeting almost a year later, Robert Shapiro was asked about the effort to secure European approval for Roundup Ready soybeans. "We played chicken with the Europeans," he replied. "And we won."

IN THE early summer of 1996, a few months after Roundup Ready soybeans were approved in Europe, but before the American harvest had begun, Robert Shapiro and his second-in-command at Monsanto entertained a visitor from England. The visitor, Simon Best, was the energetic, opinionated young director of biotech projects at the British company Zeneca. The three men met for lunch at a club in downtown St. Louis.

Best was worried and a bit angry. He was convinced that Monsanto was gambling with the future of biotechnology in Europe, risking a virulent consumer backlash that, if it came, wouldn't just affect Monsanto. Best feared it would sweep aside everything he'd accomplished during the previous three years while introducing England to its first genetically engineered food.

The food in question, the focus of Simon Best's passion, was a variant of Calgene's Flavr Savr tomato. While Calgene had tried to sell fresh tomatoes, Zeneca pursued the market in processed tomatoes. The hope was, by switching off a gene that made tomatoes go soft, processing plants could more efficiently turn crushed tomatoes into thick puree. The plants could boil crushed tomatoes at lower temperatures, preserving the natural tomato taste while still turning out the kind of thick tomato ketchup that consumers prefer.

During his campaign on behalf of genetically altered tomato paste, Simon Best had worked arm-in-arm with Roger Salquist from Calgene. He'd also adopted the Salquist strategy of inciting as much press coverage as possible, well before the product ever went on the market. (Salquist and Best became brothers in arms but only after they resolved a nasty fight between their companies over patent rights to genetically altered tomatoes. Relations reached a low point when Salquist called Best a "Bozo from Britain" while speaking to reporters.)

"We got food safety approval [in Britain] nine months in advance of when the product could be shipped and launched," says Best. "So we named a date six months in advance. We said: 'You will be able to go into a supermarket in February of 1996 and buy this.' There was a huge uproar. But then it was all over. By the time the product hit, it was all over."

Even before that announcement, Best and his colleagues at Zeneca Plant Sciences had spent an enormous amount of time cultivating British journalists and lining up partners in the food business. They'd already decided that this tomato paste would be packaged in special cans and labeled as the product of "genetically altered tomatoes," even though such labels weren't required. Two large supermarket chains, Sainsbury and Safeway, agreed to carry the product and promote it. They even turned genetic engineering into a marketing gimmick, advertising the launch of the tomato paste as "a world-first opportunity to taste the future."

The Zeneca tomato paste was in fact purely an experiment in marketing. The tomatoes were grown during a single summer in California and processed using conventional methods, then packaged and flown to Europe. As a consequence, the genetically engineered paste actually cost more to produce than conventional tomato paste and tasted exactly the same. Yet Zeneca and its partners decided to charge less than the going rate for it. They were willing to take a financial loss just to find out if the British public would buy a genetically engineered product.

The answer turned out to be an unequivocal "yes." Through the summer of 1996 Zeneca's red cans of tomato paste, proudly labeled "genetically altered," outsold all competitors.

"You needed to give the consumer a choice," says Best. "Once they had that choice, eaten it for a couple of years, found that there was no big deal, I think that the whole thing would have gone away."

But Best didn't have the luxury of a couple of years. Hard on the heels of his tomato paste came Monsanto's flood of Roundup Ready soybeans. Unlike Zeneca's tomatoes, Roundup Ready soybeans were supposed to be exactly the same as any other soybeans, no better and no worse. No one saw the need to keep them separate from other soybeans or sell them separately. (Indeed, any effort to do so would have been very costly and negated any incentive a farmer might have had to plant them.) And unlike Zeneca, Monsanto had done almost nothing to explain to European consumers or food sellers what these products were, why they were harmless, or even that they were on their way. Monsanto's executives had concentrated their efforts almost exclusively on government officials and regulators. Once Roundup Ready soybeans were approved, the company seemed to assume that the job was done.

"We're sitting there in 1996, and Monsanto is doing *nothing*. And we're starting to tell them, loudly, that they are heading for a disaster," says Best.

Over lunch in St. Louis, Best tried to convince Robert Shapiro to change course quickly and radically. "I said, 'Look, you're severely underestimating the situation in Europe. If you don't either label or start a communications program now, the food chain isn't going to back you up. And there's going to be a major consumer reaction. We haven't had enough time yet to get over the labeling issue. If you just ship these things in as a surprise, it's going to be a huge disaster.'"

As Best recalls the conversation, Shapiro was unperturbed. "We think you're wrong," he told Best. "Our people in Europe say that this is an exaggeration. We've talked to all the right government people in all the countries of Europe. You're creating a problem that isn't there."

Many Monsanto executives, in fact, were convinced that European companies such as Zeneca had their own self-interested reasons for predicting a consumer backlash. Monsanto believed it was merely a tactic to slow Monsanto's biotechnology express down a bit and give European companies time to catch up.

Simon Best, for his part, thought Monsanto was behaving like a "uniquely arrogant company." "At no point did they actually listen to the people who knew, . . . the food companies," he says.

For years, in fact, large food companies had been carrying out consumer surveys and conducting focus groups, trying to figure out who consumers trusted most when it came to genetically altered food. Already in the early 1990s they had uncovered some intriguing differences between American and European consumers. On both sides of the Atlantic, consumers considered private companies the least trustworthy. But there was a stark difference between Europe and the United States in their evaluation of government regulators and environmentalist advocacy groups. European consumers ranked government agencies near the bottom, just a bit above private companies, but judged environmentalist groups such as Greenpeace as most trustworthy. In the United States, consumers considered environmentalists less trustworthy than family doctors, dietitians, and government agencies.

A government stamp of approval, in other words, didn't count for much with European consumers. And in the spring of 1996, just as Monsanto was getting that stamp of approval, it became almost worthless.

On March 20, 1996, five short days after Europe voted to accept Roundup Ready soybeans, British Prime Minister John Major announced to an incredulous, tumultuous House of Commons that at least ten people had died from a human form of "mad cow disease," and the victims appeared to have gotten the disease by eating British beef. Major and his cabinet continued to insist, haplessly, that beef from British livestock was "safe in the common usage of the term," but consumers took matters into their own hands. Across Europe consumers stopped buying British beef. English farmers were forced to slaughter livestock by the tens of thousands. Every beef-eating member of the British public awoke to the same secret fear: *Is it already eating holes in my brain?*

Intrepid journalists from the British magazine *New Scientist* took a quick survey at a cafe down the street from their London offices. All the customers had chosen nonbeef dishes to eat, not because they were convinced that beef was dangerous, but because they simply didn't know. As long as they didn't know, why should they take the risk? It took almost two years for Shapiro and his fellow Monsanto executives to realize it, but from that moment the burden of proof, when it came to the safety of Europe's food, had firmly settled on the shoulders of the biotechnology industry.

# 12

## Summers of Triumph, Summers of Discord

Frank Mitchener, Jr., amateur historian, former president of the National Cotton Council, and prominent citizen of Tallahatchie County, Mississippi, works from an office that is built like a chapel or an art gallery. The wooden beams of the ceiling vault upward. The walls are white except for one, made of glass, which overlooks the green banks of a quiet stream called the Cassidy Bayou.

Drop a stick into that stream, and it will travel through countless detours a hundred miles southwest to meet the Mississippi River at the city of Vicksburg. Its route will traverse the heart of the Mississippi Delta, which is not a delta at all, strictly speaking, but a floodplain that stretches from Memphis in the north to Vicksburg in the south, from the levees along the Mississippi's banks in the west to the edge of Mississippi's "hill country" in the east. It is a land of legend, a birthplace of Faulknerian visions and the Blues, home to inexhaustibly rich soil, pervasive poverty, racial atrocities, and proud, aristocratic gentility.

Historian James Cobb called it "the most Southern place on earth" in 1985 and discovered only later, as he immersed himself in the area's history, that the Delta represented not so much the Old South as the New. At the time of the Civil War the Delta was a land of forests and swamps, shunned by most as a breeding ground for disease. Only later, with the arrival of railroads and the federally financed levees along the Mississippi and its tributaries, did the Delta become the domain of "planter aristocrats." But Cobb realized that this new elite was no traditional aristocracy, concerned more with social tradition than the aggressive pursuit of profit. The post–Civil War cotton growers of the Delta organized their plantations according to modern principles of industrial management, adopted new technology, and lobbied successfully for federal aid.

They were in every sense the ancestors of Frank Mitchener, Jr. Mitchener owns or manages somewhere between five and ten thousand acres of Delta farmland from the serene comfort of his office. Seventy years ago such an operation would have entailed supervising an army of tenant farmers or sharecroppers. Landowners in the Delta generally employed about five tenant families, each with a team of mules, for every hundred acres of cotton.

Today the tenant farmers are gone. The wooden shacks where those families used to live have vanished from the landscape but certainly not from the memories of Mitchener and others of his generation. According to the standard telling of this story, technology swept aside the sharecroppers. The mechanical harvester and chemical herbicides, it is said, eliminated the need for human hands to hoe the weeds or pick the cotton. In reality, technology was not so much the driving force as a useful tool in the service of other forces that pulled and pushed tenant farmers out of Mississippi. The process began with New Deal programs that benefited landowners at the expense of sharecroppers. It accelerated when World War II sent young men overseas, creating overnight a shortage of labor in cotton country. Jobs and the promise of a better life beckoned in northern and western cities. Later, Mississippi's political elite responded to the civil rights movement with a campaign to drive black people out of the state. These historical tides drove demand for the mechanical harvester and not the other way around.

Frank Mitchener is now not so much a supervisor of people as a manager of technology. Like a general gathering his forces, he marshals seeds, equipment, and chemicals in an annual campaign to transform soil, sun, and rain into truckloads of cotton fiber.

The most insidious of Mitchener's foes are the insects: the tobacco budworm and the tarnished plant bug, aphids and weevils. Twice a week during the cotton-growing season, Mitchener hires an expert to inspect his fields for insects. At the first sign of infestation, Mitchener calls in the airborne cavalry. The small airplanes fly low across the fields, then bank high in the sky, turn, dive, and come in again to paint another insect-killing stripe across Mitchener's land.

Twenty years ago Mitchener had faced disaster at the hands of the tobacco budworm. The insecticides he'd been using stopped working. The insects had developed resistance to them. "We could not control worms in 1975 and 1976," he says. "We had terrible harvests those two years." But new chemicals, so-called synthetic pyrethroids, arrived and saved the day. "They were magic," Mitchener says.

In the mid-1990s Mitchener saw the cycle of history repeating. This time the synthetic pyrethroids were losing their power. Every year, Mitchener had to spray more often, eating away more of his profits. In the mid-1990s he spent as much as $140 an acre to fight off insects, and half of that was spent battling the tobacco budworm.

And once again, technology promised an answer. This time it was a gene from *Bacillus thuringiensis,* a product of nature and of Monsanto's laboratories. It made cotton plants themselves poisonous to the tobacco budworm.

When Monsanto arrived in the Mississippi Delta, it managed to offend as well as impress. The Delta's cotton growers are a proud lot. They are the elite of their society; many are on friendly terms with U.S. senators and representatives. Yet they found themselves on the receiving end of edicts from Monsanto. The company informed cotton growers that, if they wanted to get their hands on Bt cotton, they needed to attend meetings where Monsanto would reveal to them the mysteries of its revolutionary technology. Some cotton growers walked out of those meetings vowing never to buy a Monsanto gene. "They sold it as if we had no choice. That we simply had to buy their product to survive," says one cotton grower.

Monsanto's representatives (and Delta and Pine Land) also oversold their product. Some of them told cotton farmers that with Bt cotton they'd never have to spray for caterpillars again. As it turned out, this was true for the insect that cotton growers feared most, the tobacco budworm, but it was not true for the cotton bollworm.

During 1996 and 1997 cotton growers in some parts of Texas watched in horror as cotton bollworms decimated their fields of Bt cotton. Many of the growers filed lawsuits against Monsanto alleging false advertising.

Yet many others, including Frank Mitchener, swallowed their pride, made a few mental calculations, and signed up to plant the new crop. Ever since 1996, the first year Bt cotton was available, Mitchener has planted it on 96 percent of his cotton fields.

Mitchener also watched the arrival of Roundup Ready cotton, which proved very popular, and Calgene's BXN cotton, resistant to the herbicide Buctril. He listened to Monsanto's scientists promise other, even more powerful genes, and he became a believer in the potential of biotechnology. "This may be bigger than the mechanical harvester," he says. He pauses. "It *may* be."

The very first year that Bt cotton was sold commercially, cotton farmers in Alabama planted it on 75 percent of their acres, even though the gene was only available in cotton varieties that were suited for the longer growing seasons of Mississippi or Louisiana. Bt was their lifeline; the previous year, tobacco budworms had almost wiped out their cotton crop. In the cotton heartland of Georgia, Mississippi, and eastern Arkansas, Bt cotton accounted for more than a third of the crop in 1996. Two years later, it covered 60 percent of those areas.

Bt cotton didn't just clobber the tobacco budworm; it also delivered a staggering blow to the companies that sell insecticides to cotton farmers, and the crop dusters who spray those chemicals on fields. Before 1996 Frank Mitchener was spending up to $140 per acre fighting insects. After 1996 he spent on average $90 an acre, and a third of that was the "technology fee" he paid for the right to use Monsanto's Bt gene. Statistics on the frequency of insecticide spraying tell an even more dramatic story. In 1995, cotton farmers in the Mississippi Delta sprayed their fields 4.5 times on average to control the tobacco budworm and the cotton bollworm. A year later, the average had dropped to 2.5, and farmers who planted Bt cotton sprayed even less. In the hill country of Mississippi and in Alabama the drop was astonishing: Farmers sprayed an average of 8 times for the budworm and bollworm in 1995, and only 1.5 times in 1996.

A WORLD away in Des Moines, Iowa, Pioneer Hi-Bred, supplier of seed for almost half the corn planted in the United States, jumped hurriedly and belatedly onto the biotech bandwagon. Field trials of Bt corn had produced unequivocal results: These plants killed one of corn's prime enemies, worms called European corn borers. John Howard, the company's most vocal internal advocate for biotechnology, remembers a member of the company's old guard, a plant breeder who'd risen to the rank of vice president, turning into a "babbling little kid" as he saw the difference that this one gene made. "He never really understood it until he saw it in the field. And he couldn't believe that it was real," says Howard.

Some time later, Pioneer's second in command, a hulking giant of a man named Charles Johnson, called Howard into his office. "This Bt corn—I know you've been yelling at us about it," Johnson said, as Howard recalls the conversation. "I hope you understand that to you this was very real. But to us [in Pioneer's senior management] it was a very abstract thought. We really couldn't appreciate it until it was in front of our face."

Field trials also proved something else, something that entomologists had long suspected: The European corn borer had been silently harvesting up to 7 percent of the Midwestern corn crop and as much as 20 percent of some fields. Farmers east of Iowa didn't generally spray their corn fields for corn borers; it wasn't considered a major pest. But in field trials conducted by university researchers during the summer of 1996, Bt corn produced a significantly more bountiful harvest than conventional corn, because it repelled corn borers. In 1997, which saw some of the highest infestations of corn borer on record, the effect was unmistakable.

Two of Pioneer's competitors, Ciba Seeds and Northrup King, rushed to market with Bt corn in 1996 and 1997 and shocked Pioneer with their success. (Ciba Seeds was using its own Bt gene; Northrup King had licensed a Bt gene from Monsanto.) Pioneer's executives were amazed to see farmers paying premium prices for what

Pioneer considered second-rate hybrids, just because that seed contained a Bt gene. Ciba and Northrup King could have sold more, in fact, if they'd produced larger and more diverse stocks of seed.

It was a direct challenge to the sustaining beliefs of Pioneer's plant breeders: that single genes didn't make a difference; that genetic engineering could supplement, but could never replace, traditional plant breeding. Pioneer's sales force, though, was drooling with anticipation. *If farmers will pay $30 extra for a Bt hybrid from Ciba Seeds,* the salespeople rejoiced, *think what we can charge!*

Pioneer kicked its formidable machinery for the production of seeds into overdrive. It finished crossbreeding the Bt gene into its most popular varieties, multiplied its stocks of seed through three growing seasons in Hawaii, then shipped those seeds to South America for one more growing season. While North American farmers waited out their winter, Pioneer harvested a bumper crop of Bt corn seed in the southern hemisphere's summer and rushed those seeds back to customers in Iowa, Illinois, and Indiana. In the spring of 1998 Pioneer began selling huge volumes of genetically engineered seed. That year the amount of land planted with Bt corn more than doubled, from 6 million to 15.6 million acres, accounting for almost a quarter of all the corn grown in the United States. The corn seed was sold by many different companies: DeKalb, Novartis (which merged the operations of Ciba Seeds and Northrup King), Pioneer, and many smaller independent seed companies. But more than 90 percent of those Bt genes came from Monsanto's laboratories.

MAC EHRHARDT knows his customers and neighbors, the farmers around the town of Albert Lea in southern Minnesota. His whole life he's watched them amble into the Ehrhardt family business, the Albert Lea Seed House, exchange observations on the weather with his father, and walk out with bags of seed for native grasses or hairy vetch, or the staples of agriculture in this part of the world, corn and soybeans. Like their Scandinavian ancestors, they believe in sobriety, responsibility, and self-discipline. On Sunday they go to church, and on Monday, when they return to their fields, they tend straight rows of flourishing crops that express the earth's proper moral order in their neatness and freedom from all contamination.

Colonies of water hemp or cocklebur in a Minnesota soybean field don't merely consume a bit of the field's potential harvest or impose a small financial penalty when the farmer brings a truckload of "dirty" soybeans to the grain elevator. They are evidence of a moral lapse, an occasion of public scandal and private gossip.

When Roundup Ready soybeans appeared on the scene, they allowed farmers to abolish weeds from their soybean fields with a single spraying, or perhaps two, of Roundup. It was like cheap grace, a blanket absolution.

"Roundup Ready soybeans made bad farmers into good farmers," says Mac Ehrhardt. "It was just a phenomenon, and I don't know if I'll ever see anything like it again. Farmers were just crazy to get Roundup Ready soybeans. They bought every bag. They didn't care about varieties or disease resistance or anything else."

Seed companies rushed Roundup Ready seed onto the market, in some cases before they had bred the Roundup resistance gene into varieties that suited their particular weather conditions or that resisted common diseases. "There were some real dogs released during those first years," says Walter Fehr, a soybean breeder at Iowa State University. "Even calling them dogs is a compliment." And still farmers bought them.

In Albert Lea the Ehrhardts wondered if their small, family-run business could survive. The Ehrhardts didn't have a license from Monsanto to sell Roundup Ready varieties, nor did they have any reasonable prospect of getting one. "Our first reaction was fear, that we were going to be shut out of the market, that only the big seed companies would have access to this stuff," Ehrhardt says.

Ehrhardt is no particular friend of biotechnology or companies like Monsanto that have pushed the technology into the marketplace. He's a liberal Democrat and an environmentalist. "I basically don't think that biotechnology is a good idea," he says. "I think there's a law of unintended consequences with technology, whether it's nuclear power or biotechnology." But business survival tolerates few such qualms. Ehrhardt banded together with twenty other small Minnesota seed dealers to form a joint venture called North Star Genetics. They hoped that the new company would be substantial enough to earn them a license for Roundup Ready soybeans.

Late in 1996, on behalf of North Star Genetics, Ehrhardt called Monsanto's regional representative and arranged a meeting. "I got all dressed up in a suit and tie. I was really nervous," he says. They met at a Perkin's Restaurant beside Interstate 35, in Owatonna, Minnesota. "Monsanto's rep showed up all supercasual, just slumming it with the boys in Owatonna," Ehrhardt recalls. "And he turned out to be a really sharp, calm, impressive guy. Here I am meeting with the Evil Empire, and the guy said—I still remember this, it really made an impression—'We really need to get away from using all these chemicals.'"

Monsanto agreed to license its genes to North Star Genetics. ("I still think it's because the Monsanto rep goes deer hunting with one of our guys," Ehrhardt says.) And Ehrhardt signed up with Monsanto's "Value Club," which is designed to lock seed companies into selling seeds with Monsanto's genes and no one else's.

"They send you this fifty-page document that nobody reads," says Ehrhardt. Under the terms of this "incentivized" contract, Ehrhardt is rewarded for selling more genetically engineered seed. He also agrees to limit his sales of genetically engineered seed purchased from any other company and to make sure farmers who buy seed containing Monsanto's genes have signed the Monsanto technology agreement.

It's not a task Ehrhardt enjoys. Every time a farmer wants to buy some bags of Roundup Ready soybeans, Ehrhardt has to ask the farmer if he's brought along his Monsanto card, which is how Monsanto keeps track of its customers. If the farmer doesn't have one, Ehrhardt has to spend ten minutes explaining the terms under which Monsanto licenses its genes to farmers. "A lot of time, I end up with resentful farmers."

And yet, he says, "I admire the company in a weird way." Monsanto was the only company with the audacity to introduce biotechnology so boldly and successfully into the seed business. And it's been a financial boon even for small seed companies like Ehrhardt's. The Albert Lea Seed House, like all members of Monsanto's Value Club, gets to keep a quarter of the technology fee that farmers pay. Its share, currently $1.50 for each bag of Roundup Ready soybeans, far exceeds its profit margin on a bag of conventional seed.

So Mac Ehrhardt added a small trickle to what became a flood of Roundup Ready soybeans entering the market. In 1996, their first year on the market, these soybeans covered one million acres. The next year, it was nine million acres. In 1998, the total grew to twenty-five million acres, a third of all soybean acres, and still seed companies were having difficulty keeping up with demand. Argentina, meanwhile, took to the new varieties at an even more breathtaking pace; by 1998 Roundup Ready soybeans blanketed more than ten million acres and accounted for half of the South American country's harvest. According to some, it was the most rapid and enthusiastic adoption of a technical innovation in the history of agriculture.

For every acre planted with Roundup Ready soybeans in the United States, Monsanto earned about fifteen dollars, one-third from the sale of seed and two-thirds from the sale of Roundup. Monsanto was taking those revenues—hundreds of millions of dollars—straight out of the hides of chemical companies that previously had dominated herbicide sales to soybean farmers. Those companies, including American Cyanamid and DuPont, hadn't really believed that Roundup Ready soybeans would work as advertised. Executives in those companies felt as if they'd been sucker punched.

MANY AGRICULTURAL experts, especially those who'd done careful financial analyses of the benefits and costs of the new genetically engineered crops, were stunned at how quickly farmers accepted them. Evaluated strictly according to considerations of profit and loss, there often wasn't a compelling case for these crops, despite Monsanto's claims. Bt corn, for instance, brought clear benefits only one year out of four in most parts of the corn belt; the rest of the time, there weren't enough corn borers to justify the extra cost of the seed. When Roundup Ready soybeans came on the market, companies that sold competing herbicides cut their prices drastically, to the point where farmers spraying Roundup on their soybean fields often weren't saving any money. (And especially in the first years, Roundup Ready soybeans sometimes yielded poorly because the gene hadn't yet been bred into some of the best varieties.) Even Bt cotton often wasn't worth the extra cost of the seed, especially in years when tobacco budworms failed to surface in large numbers.

For many of Monsanto's critics, from environmentalists to business competitors, these studies were evidence that Monsanto was hoodwinking or strong-arming farmers into buying products they didn't really need. Monsanto's salesmen had in fact made promises that the new genes weren't able to keep: Bollgard cotton was not, as sometimes claimed, impervious to infestation by the cotton bollworm, and some farmers found it necessary to spray Roundup twice on their soybean fields rather than once.

Yet farmers learned quickly to discount such claims, and still the new crops grew in popularity. American farmers, it seemed, were as susceptible to the charms of new technology as the rest of their countrymen. (I write the word *men* intentionally; it is largely a male phenomenon.) Roundup Ready was new, and "new" in North American culture means better.

There was also another factor, probably even more important. Both Roundup resistance and Bt were simple solutions to common problems. "If an easy tactic comes along, that's what farmers will do," says Kevin Steffey, an entomologist at the University of Illinois who spends most of his time working with farmers, advising them on the best methods for controlling insects. "Along came this technology where the only thing they had to do was plant the seed." This is what technology long has offered: a quick and easy way to solve at least a few of life's problems. So genetic engineering took its place of honor in the tradition of technical innovation, right beside vacuum cleaners, washing machines, paper handkerchiefs, and yellow post-it notes.

WITH NEW technology came new rules for agriculture, edicts that some farmers found disorienting and aggravating.

Never before, for instance, had farmers been ordered to exercise restraint in their war against insects. But when cotton growers purchased Bt cotton seed, they had to sign agreements that they would set aside at least 4 percent of their land as a "refuge" for their enemies, the tobacco budworm and the cotton bollworm. Cotton growers promised that they would neither plant Bt cotton in that refuge nor spray insecticides on it. (As an alternative farmers could maintain a much larger refuge that could be sprayed.) Corn farmers, for their part, were asked to set aside refuges equal to 5 percent of their corn acres.

These refuges were the result of a campaign waged by scientists who believed that, without restrictions, new strains of insects would soon emerge that were resistant to Bt. But the refuges were also a compromise. Biotech companies, which wanted to sell as much genetically engineered seed as possible, pushed for small refuges. Many scientists believed that much larger refuges were necessary to preserve Bt as a useful tool; because once Bt failed, this gift of God would be gone forever.

The strategy for preserving Bt had been worked out in the course of years of research. It was called the "high-dose/refuge" strategy, and it required two things. First, cotton or corn plants had to produce megadoses of Bt toxin, enough to kill practically all the tobacco budworms or corn borers that attempted to feed on these plants. Otherwise, insects that were at least a little bit resistant to Bt would survive, mate with each other, and produce offspring with a double helping of resistance genes. Each successive generation would further concentrate these genes, rapidly producing a strain of insects totally resistant to Bt. (For a similar reason patients suffering from a bacterial infection are advised to take antibiotics for many days, even after the infection seems to have subsided; it is the medical equivalent of the "high-dose" strategy.)

Yet the high dose by itself might not be enough. The scientists had to assume that somewhere among billions of insects a few individuals existed with genetic mutations that rendered them resistant even to a high dose of Bt. It was crucial that these insects not mate with each other but rather with normal insects that were susceptible to Bt. This was the point of refuges: to serve as breeding grounds for normal insects that could mate with any survivors from the killing fields of Bt crops.

Some scientists wanted refuges equal in size to the fields of Bt crops. Monsanto and other companies protested that under such onerous conditions no farmer would want to buy Bt seed, and the environmental benefits of these crops, Bt cotton in particular, would go unrealized. This led to the compromise of 1995, which provided for refuges in cotton that were as small as 3 percent.

Until the crops actually were in the fields the issue always had seemed purely theoretical. The runaway success of Bt cotton and corn made it very real.

The battle was joined first in corn. In 1997 a collection of academic researchers from the entire corn belt issued a report that was unprecedented in its political bravado. Refuges of non-Bt corn should cover at least 20 percent of a farmer's cornfields, they argued. Refuges that were sprayed with insecticide should be twice that large.

The most important company in agricultural biotechnology decided to dig in its heels and fight. "Monsanto looked at the recommendations and said, 'We can't live with that,'" says Scott McFarland, a young lawyer who was working for Pioneer at the time. Monsanto calculated that if farmers were required to establish refuges on such a large scale many would decide not to spend the extra money for Bt corn. The requirement would derail the Bt boom.

Monsanto turned to farmers, represented by the National Corn Growers Association, which also had its headquarters in St. Louis. Monsanto's executives convinced the leadership of the NCGA that large refuges were a threat to farmers' free use of Bt. The NCGA in turn hired Scott McFarland to lead their campaign against the entomologists and their proposals.

McFarland was a former Indiana farm boy who looked like he was more at home in the big city; a trim, energetic, stylishly dressed lawyer who was barely out of his twenties. Before he went to law school, he'd worked briefly "beating the Bt bandwagon" as a sales representative for Ciba Seeds in Illinois.

Matters came to a head on September 25, 1998, when all sides in the controversy met in Kansas City. The academic researchers were joined by representatives from the biotech companies and corn growers, including McFarland. The day before, McFarland had sent out a press release warning that "the EPA is on a course toward restricting insect-protected crops to the point that they will no longer be practical for farmers to use."

The press release and McFarland's opening speech to the assembled researchers did not go over well. The researchers were put off by McFarland's youth, his polished confidence, and his subtle hints that the wishes of corn growers carried more weight among government officials than the recommendations of scientists. They also were irritated by Monsanto's all-out efforts to keep refuges small. To some at the meeting it was a sign that the company didn't want to understand the risk that these crops might destroy Bt's usefulness, or that Monsanto simply didn't care.

Later that day, an agricultural economist from the University of Minnesota presented some figures estimating the economic cost to farmers of planting either too much refuge or too little. According to his figures the added cost of planting a larger refuge, measured in lower yields, was almost inconsequential, yet the benefits of preserving Bt's viability were huge. According to one computer model, there was almost a 50 percent probability that corn borers would develop resistance within a short period if farmers planted refuges covering only 10 percent of their cornfields. If the refuges were increased to 20 percent the probability of resistance dropped to less than 1 percent.

"It was a significant presentation," admits McFarland. Corn growers who attended the meeting began to reconsider their position. So did Monsanto. Within a few months the corn growers, the seed companies, and the researchers agreed on a compromise: Farmers would plant refuges amounting to 20 percent of their corn acres.

The same battle over refuges among cotton farmers in the South became, if anything, even more intense. For one thing, the cost of leaving a cotton field unprotected against insects is incomparably higher than is the case with corn, so growers felt even less inclined to compromise and plant larger refuges. In addition, cotton growers in many parts of the South are politically powerful and used to getting their way.

Entomologists and cotton growers generally have been allies in the war on cotton's pests. In the fall of 1999, however, that alliance came apart. Entomologists from the USDA and leading universities across the cotton belt issued a challenge to federal regulations that governed Bt refuges in cotton. Refuges that occupied only 4 percent of a grower's land were too small, they asserted. The researchers demanded refuges equal to 10 percent of a grower's land and 30 percent if the refuges were sprayed with insecticide. What's more, said the report, those refuges had to be placed right inside the fields of Bt cotton (because the whole point of the refuge is to encourage insects from the two areas to mate with each other.)

Some cotton growers regarded the report as an act of betrayal and organized to fight it. Entomologists who dared to defend their report too vigorously and publicly sometimes felt the impact of growers' wrath and political power. The scientists learned to speak cautiously and anonymously.

"The problem is, we're asking cotton growers to produce insects. They are not interested in growing insects. They want to destroy insects," said one. "We're in kind of a pickle. Some growers think that we're being too rigid. And Monsanto lines up with the growers."

But the entomologist also says he won't give in. There is too much at stake. If Bt remains effective, it opens new vistas in cotton growing. If cotton growers spray less, they preserve their secret allies, spiders, wasps, and lady beetles that feed on cotton's pests and thus reduce the need for chemical pesticides even further. And for those few harmful insects that still create problems, there are non-chemical antidotes such as simply clearing away weeds where those pests like to breed. As the entomologist describes these possibilities, his eyes light up. "In my lifetime, I will see the day when we won't have to spray cotton for insects!" he says. "It is a real possibility."

But if insects develop resistance to Bt, the entomologists can flush such dreams. "The growers don't understand. We may not have another chance. If we don't do something to prevent or delay resistance, it's going to be gone before we even get started," says one. "We can't sit around and wait."

After the scientists submitted their recommendations, economic and ideological interests mobilized for and against them. Monsanto and cotton growers, who wanted to make their profits from untrammeled use of this new technology, lined up against biotechnology's longtime opponents. Environmentalists accused the biotech industry of shortsighted, reckless pursuit of profits. Monsanto's spokesmen, for their part, accused environmentalists of defending the status quo in cotton farming and blocking a new technology that promises to reduce the use of harmful chemicals. As of this writing, the dispute awaits a final resolution.

Watching carefully is Frank Mitchener, Jr., one of the most influential cotton growers in Mississippi, who'd prefer to plant as much Bt cotton as possible. He doesn't see why he should have to plant large refuges of non-Bt cotton. "I have neighbors who are my refuge," he says. Nor is he perturbed by the thought that Bt cotton might stop working just as synthetic pyrethroids did a few years ago. "Let's assume that we've got fifteen years," he says. "I know that Monsanto has another gene on the way." Mitchener has adopted a modern faith: Science will always deliver an answer.

THE NEW seeds brought with them other unsettling decrees that reflected the commercial forces driving them forward. Roger Peters, a farmer and seed dealer in Ottawa County, Ohio, carried a copy of these rules to his simple wooden barn one day. Inside that barn stood a contraption straight out of the late nineteenth century, defying the possibilities of the twenty-first. It was a seed cleaner, essential equipment for farmers who wanted to save seeds from their soybean or wheat harvest and replant them the following year. Next to the seed cleaner, right by the doorway, Rogers nailed the new rules to the wall.

"IMPORTANT INFORMATION FOR INDIVIDUALS SAVING SEED AND REPLANTING" was the title. Further down: "Seed from Roundup Ready soybeans cannot be replanted. It is protected under U.S. patents 4,535,060; 4,940,835; 5,633,435 and 5,530,196. A grower who asks to have Roundup Ready seed cleaned is putting the seed cleaner and himself at risk."

The penalties, if a farmer was caught violating these rules, were draconian. When farmers bought Roundup Ready soybeans, they signed a contract promising not to replant any part of their harvest. Under the terms of that contract, if they were caught doing so Monsanto could demand nearly eight hundred dollars for each acre planted, plus legal fees, plus the right to inspect the farmer's business records for three years.

Roger Peters hated to put up that sign. He considered it an attack on his way of life. "We've always cleaned seed in the Peters family," the old man says hoarsely. "My son presently, myself in the past, my father, my grandfather, even my great-grandfather."

Peter beckons to his son Dan, a taciturn, bearded man in his thirties. Dan flips one switch, then another. Belts hum, fans roar, and hidden screens rattle and shake. Dan pulls on the gate of a nearby grain wagon, and a small river of soybeans pours into the cleaner.

Soybeans are like small marbles, brown and hard. They grow in pods hanging from knee-high bushes. When the leaves turn yellow and drop off, it's time to call in the combine. This self-propelled machine roars through the field, ingesting the plants, stripping off the pods, ripping them open, and disgorging the hulls. What's left are the beans themselves along with bits of hull, plant stems, and bits of dirt. These soybeans are fine for taking to the grain elevator, but any farmer who wanted to plant them as seed would want to run them through the seed cleaner.

The machine's racket fills the barn. Small pieces of soybean and other debris come bouncing out of several small chutes in the side of the machine. The elder Peters points to them, leans close, and shouts in my ear: "The small seeds, weed seeds, and cracked seeds come out of this one. Pods, stems, pieces of dirt are rejected here. There's a fan that blows through the seed; any part of the hull and light material gets rejected at that stage."

The Peters men, father and son, clean seed for themselves and many of their neighbors. Anywhere from 50 to 150 farmers each year drop off soybeans or wheat and pay a dollar for each bag of cleaned seed they get back. "It's the cheapest way a farmer can seed his own acres," Peters declares with conviction. Farmers do have to take one precaution—sending samples off to a state-run laboratory for testing to make sure the seed will germinate. But once that's done, field tests show little difference in yield between "certified" seed from a commercial seed company and home-produced, "bin run" seed.

"If somebody pulls up and says, 'Clean these beans,' we have no idea what we're cleaning, no we don't," says Dan Peters.

I ask if they ever wonder whether those beans really are Roundup Ready varieties.

"It's crossed my mind, but they'd sure never tell you that they were," says Dan, looking sideways at his father, his mouth twisting into the slightest hint of a smile.

What's it feel like, having to worry about this sort of thing?

"Feels like you're living in Russia!" the elder Peters interjects. "You can't talk to your neighbor. Everyone is secretive. What's unfair is, if we clean somebody's seed and it contains the Roundup gene, we and they are liable to pay the penalties. If somebody lies to me, I would be liable."

Under what law?

"It's Monsanto's rules!" snorts Roger Peters.

HUGH GRANT, copresident of Monsanto's agriculture business, makes no apologies for his company's rules. He speaks softly in a Scottish brogue so thick it's almost a caricature of itself. "We are interested in protecting our intellectual property, and we make no apologies for that. In the absence of that, you sell seed once, and the investment goes away. It's as hard as that.

"There's a gene in there that's the property of Monsanto, and it's illegal for a farmer to take that gene and create it in a second crop. It's necessary from the point of view of return on investment, and it's against the law. It's an illegal act."

Monsanto repeated that message in advertisements that ran on radio stations across the Midwest beginning in 1997. The company provided a toll-free telephone number for farmers to call if they suspected any of their neighbors of replanting Roundup Ready seed. Monsanto also mailed out instructions for people interested in reporting "seed piracy":

> Dial 1-800-ROUNDUP; tell the rep that you want to report some potential seed law violations or other information. It is important to use "land lines" rather than cellular phones due to the number of people who scan cellular calls. You may call the information in anonymously but please leave your name and number if possible for any needed follow up.

Through 1999 the company received fifteen hundred such tips and investigated some five hundred. It threatened legal proceedings against sixty-five farmers. Almost all of them agreed to pay fines rather than defend themselves in court.

Jim Wiebe (not his real name), who grows wheat and soybeans on his farm in Kansas, has a brother who's replanting Roundup Ready soybeans. Not that his brother told him outright. "It's just some things I heard," says Wiebe with a smile. "I think I'll say something to him just to let him know that I know."

His brother has always been a bit more successful and a bit more reckless. "He sort of feels like he can get away with things. That nobody can stop him." Jim Wiebe hasn't tried to stop his brother. He doesn't pick fights, and he's certainly not a snitch.

One farmer in western Canada decided to stand and fight. The farmer, Percy Schmeiser, is an adventuresome and combative man. By 1998 he'd climbed Mount Kilimanjaro in Kenya and tried three times to scale Mount Everest. He'd served as mayor of the small Saskatchewan town of Bruno, and was a member of Saskatchewan's legislature.

Schmeiser's fields contained Roundup Ready canola in 1998; he and Monsanto agree on that point. They also agree that Schmeiser never bought Roundup Ready canola seed from Monsanto and never signed the company's standard technology use agreement. So how did Monsanto's gene end up in Schmeiser's fields? And if Schmeiser never signed Monsanto's papers, did the company have the right to demand that he pay for using its gene? These questions became the crux of a celebrated battle that played out in the news media and in a Canadian court.

According to Schmeiser, the Roundup Ready gene arrived in his fields by accident. Roundup Ready canola must have blown off passing trucks, he insisted, or perhaps pollen drifted in from neighboring fields. Schmeiser added that, as an experiment, he'd sprayed Roundup on about three acres of one field, to see how much of his field might have become tolerant to Roundup through such "contamination." About sixty percent of the plants survived, he said. This created a plot of nearly pure Roundup Ready canola. He happened to harvest that section of the field first and saved mostly that part of the harvest as seed for the following year, although it was mixed with other seed as well. According to Schmeiser, this was how his fields in 1998 came to contain mostly Roundup Ready canola. But he also claimed that he didn't take advantage of this trait; he continued to rely on other herbicides to control weeds.

Schmeiser's story contained a number of problems. Monsanto produced receipts showing that the farmer had purchased a substantial volume of Roundup herbicide in 1998, enough to spray a thousand acres of canola. Schmeiser's fields, according to Monsanto's tests, were planted with 90 percent pure Roundup Ready canola seed. Such a concentration of Roundup-tolerant plants could not have emerged simply through cross-pollination or through seeds blowing off a passing truck. (When Monsanto's representatives collected these samples, they provided a portion to Schmeiser, and the samples that were in Schmeiser's possession later proved to be only of 60 percent purity. This discrepancy was never resolved.) Finally, before planting his seed in 1998, Schmeiser had taken it to a local seed processing plant to be treated with chemicals. The company had kept a sample, and the sample didn't appear to have come directly from the harvesting machinery, as Schmeiser claimed. The seed appeared to have been cleaned; it lacked the usual bits of plant stems and dirt. Monsanto's executives believed, but couldn't prove, that Schmeiser had obtained his Roundup Ready seed from a neighbor.

On March 29, 2001, a judge in Saskatoon issued a peculiar decision. The decision stated, on the one hand, that wind-borne pollen and canola seeds from passing trucks almost certainly were not the source of Percy Schmeiser's Roundup Ready canola crop. But the judge then argued that it didn't really matter where Schmeiser had gotten his seed or even whether he had taken advantage of Monsanto's gene by spraying Roundup on his crop. All that mattered was the simple fact that Schmeiser had knowingly grown Roundup Ready canola without paying Monsanto for the right to use its intellectual property. In so doing, the judge ruled, Schmeiser had infringed Monsanto's patents.

Biotechnology's opponents were outraged. In their view, this meant that farmers might have to pay Monsanto for genes that simply blew into their fields. The case became a touchstone for anti-Monsanto passions, and the decision was widely reviled. Nothing else, according to one Monsanto official, produced as much hate mail directed at the company.

To hear Monsanto's Robb Fraley tell it, most farmers are in favor of the company's crackdown on seed saving. "If you think about it, it puts the farmer who's playing by the rules at a real disadvantage," he says. "Privately, in small grower groups—and I've been around many of them—the discussion goes like this: 'We may not like technology fees; we may not like the fact that the price of the seed has gone up, but we think we're getting fair value, and we know what we're getting into when we buy that seed. Once we've made that decision, please protect us. If our neighbor is using the products illegally, give us a level playing field.'"

The way Fraley sees it, the ban on saving seed simply makes the seed for Roundup Ready soybeans equivalent to hybrid corn. In both cases farmers know when they buy the seed that replanting it is not a practical option. They buy it anyway.

Yet there is a difference: The creators of hybrid seed exploited the possibilities and the limits of biology. This is something farmers instinctively know and understand. The biological limits of a corn kernel are the boundaries of a farmer's life. A farmer in a pinch could always replant hybrid seed; there still would be a harvest the next year, though reduced in size.

Monsanto, by contrast, set legal limits on biology. Roundup Ready seeds from a farmer's harvest will grow just fine; they just aren't *allowed* to. This is something that farmers have greater difficulty accepting.

ROGER PETERS sits in his kitchen now at a plain, Formica-topped table. Smoking cigarettes one after the other, he retrieves a big envelope filled with sheaves of legal-size paper. He pulls out a document that represents the latest round in the battle over saving seed, the text of a proposed state law that's just been introduced into the Ohio state legislature. "This really has me riled up," he confesses.

"A BILL," it begins, "to create a system of registration for persons who clean or condition self-pollinated seeds." (Soybeans and wheat are examples of self-pollinated seeds, unlike corn, which can be pollinated by any corn plant nearby.) On page 8 the document gets to the point. If this law is adopted, Peters will have to keep records of who brings in seed for cleaning, how much, and which variety. He will be required to keep samples of the seed for at least eighteen months afterward. State agricultural officials will have the right to inspect these records and test these samples. If the records and seed samples reveal that Peters helped violate patent laws or the Plant Variety Protection Act, he will be liable for damages.

Peters sees the hand of Monsanto at work. "Now they want the Ohio Department of Agriculture to do their policing for them!" he says.

I'm skeptical. The workings of politics rarely have such simple explanations, I think. A few weeks later I call the office of state representative Joe Haines, who's listed as one of the bill's two cosponsors, and speak with the staff member who's responsible for agriculture issues. She says that Representative Haines received a flood of protest from the state's soybean farmers. He no longer supports the bill as it is currently written. "We wrote it the way Monsanto wanted us to," she says.

"Who at Monsanto?"

"I have the name somewhere." She rummages in her desk. "Here's a card; Travis Brown." Brown is director of Monsanto's office of legislative affairs in St. Louis.

Such were the conversations, repeated a thousand times across American farm country during the late 1990s, that cemented Monsanto's reputation. The reputation Monsanto acquired was that of a hard-driving, uncompromising company bent on changing the rules of the game—and the face of farming.

# 13

# Power Plays

"**M**onsanto's corporate culture in the mid-1990s was like the culture of the Communist Party in Russia from about 1917 to 1925," says one now-embittered former Monsanto executive. Those were the years when Lenin led the party, before Stalin's purges, when the party faithful still believed in the idealistic rhetoric of revolutionary freedom and equality. "There were all these great statements about how Monsanto was going to be a new company with new ideals—empowerment of the individual, and there were going to be no favorites."

Robert Shapiro infused the company with visions of a coming global apocalypse with Monsanto playing a messianic role, offering the world the technology and skills necessary to avert a looming environmental catastrophe. "The system is unsustainable," Shapiro asserted during a videotaped retreat with leading Monsanto executives in 1997. On this point, he said, there could be no dissent. "Whenever people start to deny this," Shapiro paused and waved his hand impatiently, "it's almost a sign of bad faith." Shapiro set up a new unit within the company to look for business opportunities in solving the coming crisis. "This world will not go quietly toward extinction," he said. "The world is going to be prepared to pay people who can help it survive."

Several rungs down the corporate ladder from Shapiro stood the guarded, calculating figure of Robb Fraley. Shapiro and Fraley developed a kind of symbiosis, says another former Monsanto executive.

"Shapiro wanted to be famous and to do something great. He wanted to be wowed." Fraley was happy to oblige. He was so convinced of the world-changing potential of biotechnology, "he felt you could claim anything, and it would only turn out better anyway," says the former Monsanto executive. "But we created such a wonderful story in order to get the money, that no one could possibly deliver on it. And then you were stuck with all the hyperbole, which became dogma within the company. It was almost to the point where you couldn't challenge it."

To stretch the Bolshevik analogy, if Shapiro was the charismatic leader of the revolution, "Robb Fraley was Monsanto's Lavrentii Beria" (the head of the Soviet secret police under Stalin), says the former Monsanto executive. "He's a really smart guy, but absolutely merciless."

ROBERT FRALEY, surveying the landscape of agriculture in 1997, might have thought of himself as Moses standing on a mountaintop overlooking the Promised Land, ripe for conquest. This had been his dream back in 1981 when he'd caught up with Ernie Jaworski in a Boston airport and convinced the Monsanto scientist that he, a mere postdoctoral researcher, was the man to solve the problem of inserting genes into plants.

The plants now in farmers' fields were the vanguard, but merely the vanguard, of a coming revolution. There would be more Roundup-resistant crops: Roundup Ready corn, canola, sugar beets, potatoes, wheat, and rice—all of them were on their way. Soon the globe would be blanketed with crops tolerant to Roundup. Additional pesticidal genes similar to the genes from *Bacillus thuringiensis* were in the pipeline. One would make corn impervious to the corn rootworm, a far more serious pest than the European corn borer. Another would make cotton poisonous to the dreaded boll weevil. These products alone could earn Monsanto *billions* of dollars in annual revenue.

But Fraley kept reminding people to look beyond such genes. There's a limit to the value of genes that simply help farmers grow the same old commodities, he said. They're limited by the value of those crops. But think of genes that actually make the harvest more

valuable! What if plants could be engineered to produce new products: oils, nutrients, or even pharmaceuticals for which consumers
would pay high prices? He assured his listeners with calm conviction
that this was the inevitable shape of the future. It was reality already
in the laboratory. Scientists had created soybeans and canola that
contained healthier oils. They'd raised the starch content of potatoes
so that fries absorbed less fat. They'd also begun turning plants into
drug factories. Foreign genes inserted into the cells of a plant were
capable of churning out therapeutic proteins that were as precious as
gold.

There was almost no limit to this business, he said. All the trends
of genetic discovery were accelerating, doubling every few years just
like the speed and capacity of computer chips. So imagine standing
in the quiet orange groves of Santa Clara County before there was
an Intel, an Apple, or a Netscape—before America was online. That
was where Monsanto stood, at the dawn of a world-changing industry. There were fortunes waiting to be claimed.

And Monsanto could own it all, Fraley believed, if the company
stayed the course. It had assembled all the pieces required to dominate this business. It had the cash, the technology, the patents, and
the sales networks. Indeed Monsanto *deserved* to claim the fortunes
of biotechnology. It had poured money into agricultural biotechnology in good times and bad. Through the early and mid-1980s it had
led the way with its science, methodically pushing back the boundaries of the possible. Now ten years later that work was paying divi-
dends in the form of patents over tools of genetic engineering that
Monsanto could wield as weapons against potential competitors,
Monsanto, more boldly than any competitor, had marched into
the marketplace with genetically engineered crops, and farmers
had responded.

The situation now was fundamentally different from the early
1990s, when Monsanto had lost its nerve and signed those humiliat-
ing deals with Pioneer Hi-Bred. Monsanto's genes had proven their
value, and seed companies were competing for the right to deliver
those genes to farmers. Indeed it now was time to move beyond the
licensing of genes to seed companies. Seeds were about to become
valuable enough to warrant Monsanto's buying part of that business

as well. It might be expensive. But it was necessary, Fraley thought. He was going to make sure Monsanto didn't lose its nerve again.

Monsanto's first foray into the seed business had produced a partnership with DeKalb but not direct control. Now it was ready to take a bolder step. The first target was Asgrow, Monsanto's partner in developing Roundup Ready soybeans, a seed company with a long and proud history in vegetables and more recently in soybeans.

Asgrow had a new owner, a strong-willed, flamboyant Mexican named Alfonso Romo of Monterey. Romo had made his fortune in the tobacco business but was in the process of assembling a new empire in seeds. Romo was mainly interested in Asgrow's vast collection of vegetable seeds, and Monsanto's executives thought he might be willing to sell the soybean and corn part of the business.

Romo wanted something from Monsanto as well. Asgrow's researchers had created squash that were engineered to resist certain viruses. But the foreign gene that produced this resistance was activated by a crucial fragment of DNA, the 35S promoter that Monsanto's researchers had isolated and patented in the early 1980s.

Robert Shapiro flew to Monterey, Mexico, to meet Romo. The two men, both of them relative newcomers to agriculture, both of them given to grand gestures and oversized ambitions, hit it off. Within a few months, in late September 1996, Shapiro and Romo had a deal. Romo's seed company, called Seminis, got to use the 35S promoter (and several other key pieces of genetic engineering technology that Monsanto owned). Shapiro agreed to pay $240 million for Asgrow's corn and soybean seed business.

The acquisition of Asgrow accomplished something else, something with enormous implications for any company hoping to introduce new genetic traits into agriculture. By acquiring Asgrow, Monsanto torpedoed the plans for a competing technology promoted by the German company AgrEvo.

The Germans too had considered Asgrow their partner. Together the companies had created soybeans that tolerated an herbicide called Liberty (known in Europe as Basta). These "LibertyLink" varieties were almost ready to go on the market. LibertyLink soybeans were, on paper at least, formidable competitors to Roundup Ready plants; they promised similar benefits. And in contrast to Roundup Ready soybeans, a farmer wasn't required to sign any special contracts when buying them or pay an extra technology fee. (Liberty, however, was a more expensive herbicide than Roundup, and most farmers had never used it before, so Monsanto was convinced that farmers would prefer Roundup Ready products.) Still, no matter which type of seed a farmer wanted, Asgrow was happy to sell it, as long as Asgrow remained an independent company. "Until Monsanto bought us, we were really in the driver's seat," says John Schillinger, who became president of Asgrow in 1996. "We'd really have been rocking and rolling."

Monsanto's purchase of the seed company put a stop to such ideas. Monsanto wasn't going to promote a competitor's herbicide. Monsanto ended Asgrow's collaboration with the German company. LibertyLink soybeans were stranded at least temporarily, without a seed company to breed AgrEvo's gene into soybean varieties that farmers could plant.

AgrEvo tried to recruit other seed companies as partners, but Monsanto with its head start blocked the German company at every turn. If any seed company wanted rights to Monsanto's Roundup Ready gene—and all of them did—it had to agree that at least 90 percent of any herbicide-tolerant soybeans it sold would contain Monsanto's genes. Those agreements locked AgrEvo's LibertyLink soybeans out of most of the market. (In the year 2000, after Monsanto's practices came under greater scrutiny by government regulators, Monsanto dropped its minimum share of sales to 70 percent.)

In part AgrEvo had only itself to blame for its predicament. To some the company had confirmed every stereotype of the lumbering, bureaucratic European corporation. It was "the most frustrating company I ever worked with, in terms of getting things going," recalls Asgrow's John Schillinger. Initially Schillinger had to prod the German company into working with soybeans at all, and his European partners, in stark contrast to Monsanto, never seemed to expect much from their new product. "Maybe 10 percent of the market, six million acres, was all that they thought they could do," says Schillinger. Because of this caution AgrEvo risked ending up with nothing at all.

If a company that sold computer software or cars or jewelry found itself in the German company's position with supermarkets refusing to sell its wares, it might simply open a new store to compete with the existing ones or sell its merchandise over the Internet. But it's not so simple with seeds. Superior varieties of soybean (or of any crop) are built on many years of painstaking breeding, creating what's often called "elite germ plasm"—good combinations of genes. It wasn't a sales network that AgrEvo lacked; it was access to elite germ plasm.

Monsanto's acquisition of Asgrow, and its restrictive contracts with many other smaller seed companies, forced people to radically revise their estimates of what germ plasm was worth. It appeared that elite germ plasm was just as rare and difficult to create from scratch as new and valuable genes. Seed companies never had earned substantial profits. But it suddenly became clear to many in the industry that they had become very valuable indeed. Control over seed companies meant access to billion-dollar markets. "Germ plasm," said one veteran industry observer, "is king."

Monsanto's campaign to own seed companies had begun in optimism, with the conviction that seed companies were necessary to turn scientific discoveries more rapidly into valuable products. It soon was driven as well by a fear of being locked out of the market; a fear that other companies might do to Monsanto what Monsanto had done to them.

RIGHT UP to the time when he put his family's seed company on the auction block, Ron Holden maintained that he had no interest in selling out. Holden's Foundation Seeds was the partner and the guardian of the nation's small, local corn seed companies, he said. He wasn't going to put their fates in the hands of some multinational company concerned only with the bottom line.

Until the 1960s the nation's mom-and-pop seed companies had relied on breeding programs at agricultural universities, which regularly distributed, free of charge, new corn hybrids. But those publicly funded breeding programs gradually fell behind the efforts of Pioneer and DeKalb and closed down. Ron Holden stepped into the gap. Holden's maintained a small but well-run breeding program that delivered new "inbred" lines that became the parents of hybrid seed sold by family-owned seed distributors all over the country. The smallest companies often relied exclusively on Holden's for their seed stock; larger enterprises such as Golden Harvest or Doebler's or even DeKalb used parental lines from Holden's to supplement their own breeding programs. Only Pioneer refused to use any material from Holden's.

When one added it all up, corn lines from Holden's were the immediate ancestors of 40 percent of all the corn grown in the United States. Biotech companies soon realized that Holden's was a gateway for genes, and on the other side of that gate lay tens of millions of acres of corn. By turns biotech executives made their pilgrimages down Interstate 80 across rolling Iowa farm land to the sleepily prosperous town of Williamsburg, Iowa, to see Ron Holden.

DuPont came offering genes for improved oil content. The executive board of AgrEvo flew in from Germany promoting the gene that made corn plants tolerant to the AgrEvo herbicide Liberty. Monsanto came offering Bt genes (which worked well) and genes for tolerance to Roundup (which did not work well in corn).

Ron Holden signed deals with one and all. Monsanto proved to be the most difficult partner.

Executives in St. Louis didn't like the idea of Ron Holden delivering Monsanto's genes to hundreds of small ragamuffin seed operations across the country. For one thing, Monsanto didn't want to endanger its own reputation by entrusting its genes to companies that might not deliver pure batches of seed to their customers. What's more, Monsanto didn't really see any economic benefit in helping the smallest of these companies survive. In Monsanto's view the seed industry needed some consolidation. Fewer seed companies meant less competition and more of a chance for seed companies to raise their prices.

But Ron Holden dug in his heels. His company's whole reason for existence was to help the small seed companies, he said, and he wasn't willing to let Monsanto pick and choose among them. "We made it a condition of our cooperation that we make their genes available to everybody on equal terms," says one top executive at Holden's. In response, as Ron Holden later put it, Monsanto "flushed" Holden's, canceled their cooperation, and forced corn breeders at Holden's to destroy all the plants that contained Monsanto's genes.

A year or two later Monsanto reconsidered, and the two companies started cooperating again. Monsanto also put out the word they were interested in buying Holden's outright. In 1996 bankers from Goldman, Sachs finally convinced Ron Holden that it really was time to cash in the family legacy.

Remembering Monsanto's previous attempts to drop some of his smallest customers, Ron Holden took several steps to prevent any eventual buyer from changing his company's practices too dramatically. The buyer was required to treat all of Holden's customers equally, at least for several years. All of Holden's agreements to produce such traits as Liberty-tolerant corn or DuPont's high-oil corn were to remain intact.

But while Holden was preparing to sell his company, he got a message from DeKalb's lawyers. DeKalb announced that it was in possession of a newly issued patent that made DeKalb, not the German company AgrEvo, the inventor of Liberty-tolerant corn. DeKalb demanded that Holden's or its customers pay a royalty of twelve dollars for every bag of LibertyLink corn that they sold.

It was an assault on the partnership between Holden's and the German company AgrEvo. "Nobody is going to convince me that it wasn't at the direction of Monsanto. It clearly was," says one bitter AgrEvo executive. After all, Monsanto was one of DeKalb's major shareholders at this point, and Robb Fraley sat on DeKalb's board. The AgrEvo executive thinks it went something like this: "Monsanto went to Ron Holden and said: 'Take a license to these DeKalb patents and force your customers to do so as well. If you don't, we might have to litigate against you, Ron Holden; and, Ron, that's not going to be pretty. It might blow the whole thing up.' And of course, Ron just wanted to get his billion dollars and go home."

Ron Holden did agree to DeKalb's terms. LibertyLink corn from Holden's thus became more expensive. This severely restricted sales. First in soybeans, then in corn, AgrEvo's gene for Liberty tolerance had been forced to the sidelines.

As bidders lined up to make their offers, such episodes were fresh in their minds. Each company realized that, if it lost the bidding, it might be locked out of a large part of the North American corn seed market. Each made what it considered a highly generous offer. But none came even close to Monsanto's bid. "It was clear that Monsanto was ready to pay anything," says Roderick Stacey, who now runs a consulting group called Verdant Partners and worked with one of the unsuccessful bidders. "Whatever any company was willing to offer or consider, Monsanto was willing to go considerably above that. They just were not going to take the risk that they were not going to get it."

In January 1997 Monsanto announced an agreement to purchase Holden's and the company that distributed the seed company's products for a cool billion dollars. The annual profits of Holden's had never been made public, but they probably didn't exceed a few million dollars. Overnight, Ron Holden became a very rich man.

THE HOLDEN'S purchase set off gold rush fever for germ plasm. Events cascaded out of control. The landscape of American agriculture seemed to crack and shift, sliding this way and that in response to tectonic forces of remorseless, overwhelming power.

The share price of the Delta and Pine Land Company of Mississippi, which owned some 70 percent of the American market for cottonseed, soared. The shareholders anticipated a merger. They *demanded* a merger, and they owned the company, after all. Roger Malkin, Delta and Pine Land's chairman, lost control of the company he had acquired with farsighted ease a decade and a half earlier.

In northern Illinois the Roberts family, owners of DeKalb, decided that if ever there was a time to sell off the family heirloom, this was it.

Both companies started entertaining offers in 1997 and early 1998, feeding an acquisitive fever in the world of agricultural biotechnology. Executives from Basel and Frankfurt shuttled to New York and back. So did representatives from DuPont in Wilmington. All were scrambling to find secure footing on terrain that Monsanto seemed intent on overturning.

Financial calculations led to discussions of legal rights and possible antitrust concerns. Seeds, those small packages of life, symbols of resurrection and hope, had completed their transformation into economic matter. Germ plasm was king, even in the sterile haunts of Wall Street.

Both deals saw the light of day on May 11, 1998, and Monsanto had the privilege of announcing them both. Robert Shapiro's company revealed that it would pay $2.3 billion dollars for DeKalb and another $1.8 billion for Delta and Pine Land. Once again, according to some involved in the process, no other bidder even came close to Monsanto's offers.

Three weeks later Shapiro dropped another bombshell. Monsanto had agreed to merge with a much larger company, American Home Products, Inc. Monsanto, he explained to stunned employees in St. Louis, was too small. It needed a bigger partner to carry out its dreams and, in particular, to compete in the global pharmaceutical business. Monsanto would be the junior partner in the new merged company when it came to pharmaceuticals. In agriculture it would be the dominant partner.

Finally in July of 1998 Monsanto bought Plant Breeding International, a leading seed company in Great Britain, for half a billion dollars, and three months later Shapiro announced that he would pay $1.4 billion for the international seed businesses of Cargill, operating in Asia, Africa, Europe, and Central and South America.

The grand, $8-billion buying spree was finished. Monsanto was now the world's second-largest seed company, smaller only than Pioneer. Monsanto's reach and influence over the business, however, were much greater than a simple accounting of its seed sales would indicate. Through Holden's Foundation Seeds, Monsanto supplied germ plasm to almost half of the North American market in corn. It dominated most of the soybean market that it did not own through contracts with seed companies that were anxious to sell Roundup Ready seed. It also had established a foothold in seed markets around the globe from Brazil to Indonesia.

In the midst of this mad rush of deal making, Robb Fraley found time to make a personal move. In the beginning of 1998 he and his wife Laura and their two children moved into their new custom-built home, a palace with three fireplaces and six bathrooms hidden at the far end of a long cul-de-sac deep in a wooded suburb of St.

Louis. It was the perfect home for a man who relished wealth, power, and the relative safety of the shadows. It was also a statement of this Midwestern farm boy's quintessentially American, Gatsby-like image of success.

THIS WAS the culmination of Monsanto's twenty-year foray into biotechnology. All the scientific curiosity, the exhilaration of discovery and creation, all the personal ambitions, the dreams of doing good in the world, and the overwrought promises of boundless financial reward—all had come down to this fateful roll of the dice, a stupendous bet that small strands of DNA transferred into plants were the foundations of economic empire. It was a riverboat gambler's wager, more fraught with risk than Robert Shapiro or Robb Fraley were able to comprehend. With every billion-dollar deal, Monsanto's empire became larger, more intimidating, yet more vulnerable.

For one thing, Shapiro and Fraley had saddled their company with a crushing burden of debt. They believed, and were able to persuade Wall Street, that the potential rewards of biotechnology were worth almost any short-term burden. But investors are a notoriously impatient lot, and the clock was ticking on their expectations. Any delay in delivering on Shapiro's promises risked ruining Monsanto's name on Wall Street and even its survival as an independent company.

But this at least was a familiar sort of risk and the kind of thing that corporate executives consider regularly. Another danger was more difficult to calculate: Monsanto's acquisitions, aimed at securing access to the genetic lifeblood of agriculture, made the company the target of increasingly hostile and emotional attacks.

Fraley certainly had an inkling of the danger. He was riveted in the fall of 1997 by the federal government's antitrust accusations against Microsoft. Philip Angell, who became Monsanto's director of public affairs at that time, recalls that his first conversation with Fraley featured a discussion of the "Microsoft scenario" and the danger of similar attacks against Monsanto. "The idea was we, like Microsoft, are on the cutting edge of technology," Angell says recalling Fraley's concern. "If we accumulate these [seed company] assets, we risk getting government attention."

Some of Monsanto's tactics, in fact, were uncomfortably close to practices that the government's lawyers considered illegal when Microsoft employed them. Microsoft, for example, required computer makers who licensed the Windows operating system also to license other Microsoft products and to avoid competing products. Similarly, if a seed company wanted to sell Roundup Ready soybeans, Monsanto required it to renounce any competing products, such as LibertyLink genes furnished by AgrEvo. Both were examples of tying one product to another, and Monsanto's competitors did complain about them to government regulators.

Yet the government's antitrust lawyers should not have been Fraley's major worry. For all its efforts to control seed markets, Monsanto couldn't easily be labeled a monopoly. After spending a fortune, Monsanto's total sales of seed were significantly less that Pioneer Hi-Bred's. Its genetically engineered seeds, even those licensed and sold by independent seed companies, still accounted for only a fraction of the total seed market. Government regulators raised serious questions only about Monsanto's proposed purchase of the Delta and Pine Land Company, which controlled 70 percent of the American market in cottonseed.

The real danger lay elsewhere, and Monsanto's leaders seemed oblivious to it. In their drive to capture the economic fruits of agricultural biotechnology, they had given concrete, full-blown expression to the most fearsome visions of biotechnology's opponents. Twenty years earlier Jeremy Rifkin had prophesied the emergence of companies driven to mold life itself into the most profitable form. Activists opposed to the expansion of the Plant Variety Protection Act in 1980 had predicted the rise of genetic monopolists who would assert control of the earth's genetic resources. And environmentalists of all stripes had long bemoaned the industrialization of agriculture, the disappearance of family-scale farming, and the increasing power of large agrichemical enterprises. Monsanto, chemical giant turned seed mogul, had become the incarnation of such fears.

"We were following Monsanto's moves very closely," says Tony Juniper from the British environmentalist group Friends of the Earth, who led that organization's fight against genetically engineered food. "It meant that food production was slipping into the hands of a few multinational corporations. We saw that as a grave threat and obviously mobilized public opinion to fight that threat."

The grander Monsanto's vision became, the more ominous the company appeared, at least to those who were already inclined to question the company's motives. There was the fiasco, for instance, of the water business. "Try this word: *water,*" Bob Shapiro said once during a large gathering of Monsanto employees. Shapiro was in full guru mode, expounding on the environmental crisis descending upon the world and the opportunity to make money helping the world survive. "Take a look at the trends [in water consumption]. My guess is that there will be a market created involving water," he said.

Monsanto did in fact look into buying water supply businesses in several Third World countries, and the result was a public relations fiasco. Tony Juniper in London saw it as the true measure of Monsanto's fiendish ambition. "It revealed the extent to which it was a conscious strategy to seize control of food production," he says. "It was the final bit of the jigsaw puzzle. They own the chemicals; they own the intellectual property inside the seeds; they own the marketing; in some cases they own the land through contracts with farmers; they own the water. That leaves the fresh air for them to purchase, I guess."

Until the summer of 1998, agricultural biotechnology had been, for most people, an abstract concept or a disembodied technology. Even Monsanto had remained relatively unknown. It was merely a manipulator and seller of genes. Its sudden emergence as an agricultural power gave biotechnology a face, a name, and an often unpleasant corporate personality. For the committed opponents of biotechnology the villain had emerged from hiding, and its appetites spanned the globe.

# 14

# Backlash

Judging by appearances, one might mistake Benedikt Härlin for a junior executive at a multinational corporation. He's clean shaven with hair neatly trimmed. On this day he even wears a suit albeit a rumpled one. He has the slightly doughy face of someone who's spent a bit too much time recently in hotels and airplanes and the wry smile of a man who's survived countless intrigues with his sense of humor intact. He distributes pithy quotes to the international media in his native German and nearly flawless English, never deviating from the arguments that are most helpful to his cause.

Härlin is in fact an employee of the international environmentalist organization Greenpeace. He coordinates its campaign against genetic engineering. His political roots reach back to a far more tumultuous time and place, to the *Häuserkampf*—the battle of the houses—which rocked West Berlin's neighborhood of Kreuzberg during the early 1980s. At that time, Kreuzberg was a realm of protest within a city that was itself dislodged from reality, an island floating in the middle of a resurgent Cold War, home to hordes of disaffected German youth who moved there to find adventure or escape military service. Scores of them, including Härlin, occupied Kreuzberg's abandoned tenement houses almost in the shadow of the Berlin wall. They declared the houses liberated zones, sprayed the walls with slogans of class warfare, and dared the police to dislodge them by force. "I was ready to riot in the streets to defend the houses," says Härlin. Along the shadowy fringes of this *Szene* lurked the Revolutionary Cells, an underground anarchist group, although some people wondered if the group really existed at all.

"Benny" Härlin joined a collective that published the magazine *radikal*, a "newspaper for uncontrolled movements." It published, among other things, declarations from the Revolutionary Cells and helped mobilize protests that turned violent on the occasion of Ronald Reagan's visit to Berlin in November 1982. The police responded by raiding the magazine's offices, where they found assorted manifestos from the Revolutionary Cells. Prosecutors decided that this was sufficient evidence to charge the magazine's leaders with aiding and inciting terrorist acts.

They arrested Härlin in June 1983 and confined him in a maximum-security cell. The case became a national sensation. During the trial Härlin proclaimed the importance of free speech and the fundamental right of any citizen to express unpopular, even repugnant, political views. It was a useful argument. Yet deep in his heart, Härlin says, he didn't really believe it. "I kept thinking, if this had been a fascist, telling people to kill Jews, I'd be saying, 'Lock the guy up!'" he says. "I think there are limits to free speech." The judge didn't believe it either. He convicted Härlin and sentenced the young "terrorist" to thirty months in prison.

Then came the break of Benny Härlin's life. The newly ascendant Green Party of Germany agreed to place him on its list of candidates for the European Parliament. When the votes were counted in May 1984, the twenty-seven-year-old Härlin acquired a new job as a European lawmaker and with it immunity from criminal prosecution. Härlin left Berlin behind along with much of his Marxism.

He encountered the cause that would come to dominate his life during a visit to Washington, D.C. He stayed a few nights with American allies of the Green Party who shared a house near DuPont Circle. One of them, a soft-spoken environmental activist named Linda Bullard, filled Härlin's ears with news of a strange and powerful new science. She suggested that Härlin come meet her boss. It turned out to be Jeremy Rifkin, biotechnology's original prophet of doom.

Rifkin gave the young German visitor his speech about genetic engineering. Härlin was amazed, he says, "that I'd never heard of it before!"

Härlin returned to Europe and became the most vocal member of the European Parliament regarding issues of biotechnology. He led efforts to ban at least temporarily any releases of genetically modified organisms into the European environment, but the proposals failed to pass.

In 1990 Härlin left the European Parliament and returned to Germany. He fought successfully to have his earlier conviction overturned and went to work for Greenpeace, where he campaigned against toxic pollution. But when Roundup Ready soybeans and Bt corn were approved for import into Europe in 1996, Härlin became fixated once again on biotechnology. Genetically engineered foods were about to become a standard part of Europe's food supply, and Härlin was itching for a fight against them.

Many within Greenpeace were skeptical. At the time the organization was overextended and short of funds. The international headquarters in Amsterdam was trying to cut down on its campaigns, not start new ones. Härlin pressed his case. "Genetic engineering will be the dominant technology in many different areas that we work on, whether it's global warming, deforestation, or pesticides," he argued. Here was a chance to stop a technology and an industry before it was well established, before it caused an environmental catastrophe, rather than afterwards.

*And this is a battle we can win*, Härlin thought. He'd learned in the years since his firebrand days in Berlin that capitalists were seldom united, and that the free market could be a friend as well as a foe. In this case, he suspected, the forces of the free market were on his side. It didn't necessarily matter whether genetically engineered food was safe to eat; more important was the fact that European consumers simply didn't want to buy it.

Monsanto and the farmers growing Roundup Ready soybeans had placed themselves and the entire food chain in an excruciatingly vulnerable position. (Härlin did not really understand just how vulnerable their position was.) Grain handlers couldn't avoid mixing these new soybeans in with the rest of the American soybean harvest; the hassle and expense of trying to keep all Roundup Ready soybeans separate would have driven every farmer back to conventional soybeans. Yet the products of soybeans—oil, protein, and lecithin, an

emulsifier—are ubiquitous in processed foods. Genetically engineered soybean products were going to end up in most of the
prepackaged soups and chocolate and baby food that European consumers bought every day. If consumers objected with enough vigor,
their response would reverberate like a toppling line of dominoes all
the way back to the fields of Iowa.

European buyers of food, Härlin argued, held in their hands the
power to shape an industry. Härlin just needed to convince them
that genetically altered foods *were* different and that eating them involved risks, however murky and ill-defined, that they shouldn't be
forced to take.

Härlin carried the day within Greenpeace. The organization's
leaders put him in charge of a new campaign against genetic engineering. In the fall of 1996, when the first ships bearing that year's
soybean harvest arrived in the German port of Hamburg, they
were met by a small flotilla of rubber dinghies from Greenpeace.
The activists swarmed the ships, prevented them temporarily from
docking, and unfurled banners calling for a ban on the import of
genetically engineered food. It was an attempt to grab the public's
attention.

Bare skin, the activists learned, worked even better. In December
of 1996, during a World Food Summit in Rome, activists printed
themselves fake press passes and infiltrated a press conference with
the U.S. Secretary of Agriculture, Dan Glickman. "We just wanted
to put genetics on the map, really," says Zoe Elford, one of the
stunt's organizers. At a signal the protesters stood up and stripped
off all their clothes, revealing naked bodies painted with antibiotech
slogans. "Glickman didn't know where to look," Elford says. "Apparently it's stuck with him. He's made references to that action at
various conferences he's been at."

Yet across most of Europe few people seemed to care. Even in Germany, Denmark, and the Netherlands, formerly the strongholds of
opposition to biotechnology, Greenpeace wasn't able to stir up much
public reaction. "Environmental topics were dead in Germany," recalls Härlin. The Green Party was more interested in forming a rul-
ing coalition than fighting vague threats posed by novel foods. It
seemed as if the country had moved on to other issues.

The German food industry, meanwhile, was intent on avoiding any controversy. Most companies quietly eliminated soy protein from their products just to spare themselves any unwelcome publicity. (Soy oil, which is used much more widely, presented no difficulties; all the protein or DNA which would have identified it as genetically modified was refined away before it arrived on supermarket shelves.) In the Netherlands, meanwhile, asterisks appeared beside certain ingredients listed on food labels, directing readers to the following note: "Made with the help of modern biotechnology." Yet few Dutch consumers seemed to mind. There was even less reaction to the south in Italy, Spain, and France.

Härlin had hoped to compel the food industry to supply European consumers with traditional rather than genetically modified grain. But he'd miscalculated the ability and the willingness of grain traders to separate Roundup Ready from conventional soybeans. Most of them simply refused even to attempt such a thing. Härlin suspected a deal behind closed doors to force the world to take America's genetically engineered grain. He also was stunned by the surging popularity of Roundup Ready soybeans. He'd expected that perhaps a tenth of the American soybean harvest would be genetically engineered, not a third or even half. It seemed that Europe and Greenpeace were about to be overwhelmed by a technological tide. Monsanto appeared to be winning its game of "chicken" with the European consumer.

SOON AFTER the first shiploads of Roundup Ready soybeans arrived in foreign ports Toby Moffatt, the head of Monsanto's office in Washington, took a long trip to Europe. He met, among other people, Benny Härlin and came back worried about growing public opposition. "He thought we were in a lot of trouble," says Linda Fisher, who worked with Moffatt at the time. "But Bob Shapiro's reaction was, the battle was over and we'd won."

Shapiro was convinced that any storm of controversy would blow over. It was a lesson he'd drawn from Monsanto's experience with its first product of biotechnology, bovine growth hormone, which dairy farmers could inject into cows causing them to produce more milk. That product had provoked passionate controversy among activists and consumer groups, but most ordinary consumers didn't seem to care.

*And that was milk, the most emotion-laden of all foods. If they didn't care about milk, how could they care about soybeans?* The lesson, Shapiro says, was clear: "There were a relatively few groups that were going to be generally opposed to biotechnology. They would have good media coverage, at least until the story got boring, but in the end it was not the kind of subject that the public was going to get excited about."

Moffatt and Fisher were not convinced. Both had spent years of their lives in and around environmental campaigns. "You develop a sense for the power of people who are committed," Fisher says. "I tried to explain it this way: These are people who, when they wake up in the morning, the only thing they are going to do that day is stop biotechnology."

Kate Fish, Monsanto's director of public policy, who'd led an environmentalist alliance in St. Louis before she went to work for the company, also tried to convince Shapiro that the company needed to respond to the concerns of critics. "I went round and round with Bob [Shapiro] on this," she says. "But when the market is responding so positively to the vision, to the prospects, and the stock market is skyrocketing, it's very hard for people to hear negative things."

"We had two companies," Linda Fisher continues: "the people who felt you had to deal with the opposition and the people who felt it would just go away. Plus, you had a very St. Louis attitude that Europe didn't really matter."

Robb Fraley led the "Europe doesn't matter" faction. The apostle of genetic engineering was driving Monsanto's biotechnology train at full throttle, gearing up to introduce yet another genetically engineered crop, a Roundup Ready version of corn. The United States approved Roundup Ready corn in the fall of 1997, but prospects for approval in Europe were uncertain. The campaign against genetically engineered food had caused some European governments to drag their feet, and raise additional questions. Fraley was undeterred. U.S. farmers started planting Roundup Ready corn seed in the spring of 1998. Another game of chicken had begun with the Europeans.

FROM THE outside, the British appeared to be the Europeans who were most comfortable with biotechnology. Genetic engineering, after all, was based in large part on the scientific discoveries of British scientists. Britain's biotechnology industry was by far the largest in Europe. And British officials, like those from the United States, regularly called for biotechnology regulations that were based solely on scientific data rather than on moral judgments regarding genetically altered food or the companies that created it.

But under this surface, outside the confident confines of government bureaucracies and university laboratories, another current flowed. It was emotional, anxious, and distrustful.

Robin Grove-White went looking for this current in the fall of 1996. Grove-White is a political scientist and an environmentalist. He directs the Centre for the Study of Environmental Change at Lancaster University in northern England. He also chaired the board of Greenpeace's affiliate in the United Kingdom. In November and December of 1996, soon after genetically modified soybeans began arriving in Europe, he and several of his fellow social scientists assembled nine different groups of British citizens for intensive discussions of genetically engineered food. Their study was funded by the food company Unilever and by several environmentalist organizations.

The groups were carefully selected to represent different slices of the British public. The researchers gave each group a label. There were Working Women, Non-Working Mothers, Church Goers, Green Consumers, Risk Takers, and School Girls. From North London to Lancashire they seemed anxious but fatalistic about the consequences of altering the genetic makeup of food.

> It's like an interference with nature. Although they may say that it will be better, how do you know it is going to be better, because you don't know what they've done to it, do you? So I'd be very untrusting of it really. . . . I mean anything to do with genetics is frightening, isn't it?
> (Non-working mother in Lancashire)
> I think it should be left alone. I don't think we should mess with nature. Nature was designed for specific reasons. We mess about with it, we've no right. . . . I don't know, you can mess about too much, can't you?

(North London working father)
They're messing with food; the next thing is going to be human beings.
(Lancashire churchgoer)
It's that sensation of being completely out of control. You're sat there on top of it and you don't know where you're going, what's happening, it's going so fast, and you don't know what's going to happen.
(North London working mother)

On the one hand, many scoffed bitterly when "government regulators" (played by actors to control the information provided to each group) asserted that there was "no scientific evidence" that the products could cause harm in humans. The shock of mad cow disease was fresh in their minds, and many felt betrayed by the British government's handling of it.

I think he's just trying to cover up a scam that's going on. . . . The minute they tell you not to worry about something, you worry."
(North London working mother)
That's what they said about BSE [mad cow disease]. "There's no scientific evidence."
(Lancashire working woman)

On the other hand, when other actors, representing environmentalists, raised concerns about genetic engineering, these citizens were comforted that someone seemed to be "on our side."

Grove-White noted an apparent paradox. Consumers regarded themselves as powerless. They were resigned to buying genetically altered food that they found unpleasant and even threatening. As a social scientist he found the results intriguing. As a leader of Greenpeace he found them promising. In Britain at least, there was a vast reservoir of public unease about genetically engineered food dammed up behind a consensus of political and academic elites who dismissed popular concerns. If that dam ever cracked, it could unleash enormous forces.

IN MONSANTO'S offices in Washington, D.C., Philip Angell was constructing a similar portrait of the British mind from public opinion polls he'd commissioned in Europe. Angell was Monsanto's head of "corporate communications." He thought of himself as one of the world's good guys, fighting corruption and dishonesty wherever he encountered it. He'd spent many years working for William Ruckelshaus, a moderate Republican who'd first attained fame during the Watergate scandal, when Ruckelshaus resigned, rather than carry out Nixon's order to fire the Watergate special prosecutor, Archibald Cox. Ruckelshaus and Angell had brought stability to the Environmental Protection Agency in the mid-1980s, cleaning up after some scandalous behavior on the part of Ronald Reagan's first appointees to run the agency. Then Angell had followed Ruckelshaus to Browning-Ferris Industries, where they'd battled the New York mob while bringing honest competition to Gotham's trash-hauling business. Loquacious, enthusiastic, a red handkerchief perpetually hanging out of his back pocket, Angell was ready to fight for biotechnology, which he believed was a tool of human progress.

As Angell pored over the results of the European polls in the later summer and fall of 1997, several results stood out. Europeans, still caught up in the trauma of mad cow disease, didn't trust official statements about the safety of genetically engineered food. This was not surprising. But Angell hadn't expected the differences that turned up among major European countries when it came to general attitudes toward technology.

"The British tended to be the sad sacks of Europe," Angell recalls. "They didn't generally see science or technology as providing a better future. The French did. The Germans did. The United States clearly did. But the British just generally had a dour view of what the world was going to look like." In Monsanto's surveys 55 percent of the British felt that "progress causes as many problems as it solves"; in the other countries, this was a sentiment shared only by a minority.

Angell concluded that Monsanto faced potential problems in Europe, especially in Britain. "What you detected was that people weren't comfortable with the biotechnology, and that it might affect buying habits," he says. He proposed that Monsanto do something to improve biotechnology's image in Europe.

What Angell regards as cultural pessimism, of course, Britain's defenders consider sophisticated realism. "People in Britain are not

Luddite," declares Colin Tudge, a prolific British science writer. "We know what technology is; we were the first to get the railroads running, et cetera, et cetera, but we don't like technology stuffed down our throats. We don't look at technology through rose-colored spectacles. We don't think all technology is good, we don't think all technology leads to progress, and we don't think all progress is good!"

Indeed, Tudge notes, "insofar that there's a vision of what England is all about, it's a rural vision, a rustic vision, and it's an eighteenth-century vision." No nation in Europe harbors such a cult of the countryside. "Rambling" through farmland and bird-watching are British national pastimes. (Tudge himself, bearded and generally dressed as though he's ready for a walk in the country, cultivates a bit of rustic life in the midst of London; he maintains a colony of chickens in back of his house, to the aggravation of his neighbors.)

In fact by mid-1997 the campaign against genetically engineered food was already gaining ground in Britain. The leading association of British organic farmers, the Soil Association, had joined the battle. So had Friends of the Earth and dozens of smaller environmentalist organizations. Activists passed out leaflets to shoppers at supermarkets, wrote letters to newspapers, and debated the issue at small public meetings all over the country. Everywhere, they accused Monsanto of sneaking genetically engineered food into the supermarkets without giving consumers any choice in the matter. They also questioned the food's safety. "After BSE, you'd think the food industry would know better than to slip 'hidden' ingredients down people's throats," announced Friends of the Earth in its first press release on the subject in April 1997.

Zoe Elford, the young activist who'd helped pull off the "naked action" in Rome, spent much of 1997 at grocery stores, talking to shoppers. At first, they had no idea what she was talking about, she says. "But within six or eight months you'd go back to the supermarket, and the reaction was, 'Oh yes, I've heard about this. I've heard of Monsanto. I can't believe what they're doing, it's outrageous, blah blah blah blah.' They realized it was driven by profit, and there was this yuck factor, an instinctual reaction that I don't want my food messed about with—this kind of 'enough already' thing. Genetic engineering was kind of a final straw, really."

Through the fall of 1997 and the early spring of 1998 Monsanto executives met repeatedly in St. Louis, Chicago, London, and Brussels, drawing up a plan of action for Europe. They hired two of the hottest, hippest advertising agencies in the United Kingdom and France and asked them to draw up ad campaigns.

The meetings were not filled with panic. The antibiotech campaign in Europe remained an annoying distraction, not a serious problem. Monsanto's top executives were in fact preoccupied with bigger things. They were in the middle of their multibillion-dollar campaign to build a seed empire.

In February 1998 Robert Shapiro and several of his top executives flew to London. They approved plans for a British ad campaign. Monsanto's executives also tried to enlist the support of European biotech companies, including Novartis, Zeneca, and AgrEvo. "We wanted to avoid making it a Monsanto issue," says Angell. "We wanted other companies to join us. We said, 'Work with us. We'll change the campaign and make it something you're comfortable with.'"

One can imagine the response among executives in Frankfurt, Basel, and London: *Lend you the use of our good name? While you spend billions to lock us out of the American seed market? After you ignored our warnings about opposition to biotechnology in Europe? You pulled out every trick in the book to dominate and control this industry. Well, you can defend it!* Several of these very companies were fighting Monsanto in court over disputed patents and contracts. Some even thought of themselves as members of a tacit alliance whose common foe was the company in St. Louis. As one observer of the industry put it: "Monsanto has been such a bulldog; people are trying to figure out how to emasculate the bulldog." In the end, Monsanto went ahead alone with its public relations efforts.

If Monsanto's ads had run immediately after Shapiro approved the campaign in February of 1998, they might have seemed unremarkable or even inoffensive. But the months dragged on; Monsanto dithered, trying out slightly different versions of the ads on test audiences. And "the ground shifted underneath us," Angell says. As England's gray winter gave way to spring, the opposition suddenly seemed more intense, more hostile, and more threatening to Monsanto's interests.

In March one supermarket chain broke ranks with the rest of the industry. Malcolm Walker, chairman of the supermarket chain Iceland's, announced that he was determined to find a way to eliminate all "Frankenstein foods" from his shelves. He sent executives to Brazil looking for areas where he could secure soybeans that weren't genetically engineered. Walker's announcement shattered the aura of inevitability that had accompanied genetically engineered food. Perhaps supermarkets and consumers *did* have a choice. He was taking this step, Walker said, because it was the right thing to do. Other food retailers watched Iceland's stores nervously, looking for any hints that it was also the more profitable thing to do.

As the days grew warmer and farmers prepared the ground for planting, the "Guy Watson affair" erupted. It was the first of what Patrick Holden, chairman of Britain's largest organic farmers' group, the Soil Association, referred to as "acts of God; windfall events which hugely altered the attention that the media gave to the issue."

In reality, it was an act of Patrick Holden. Holden is an enormously articulate man with silver hair, a lean, tanned face, and piercing, unsmiling brown eyes. In the early 1970s, when Holden was barely out of his teens, he spent a year living near San Francisco and discovered the Californian counterculture in all its glory. It was one of the "defining influences" of his life, Holden says. "I became interested in new models for communities, for rural development, and for agriculture."

During the 1990s the Soil Association had moved from an "openminded" stance on genetic engineering to fierce opposition. There were many reasons for this position, Holden says. They included fears of environmental disruption and worries about the safety of food but also objections to biotechnology's scientific "arrogance" and lack of respect for nature. Skeptical observers of the organization perceived another, more self-interested reason. Organic producers stood to gain if they could convince consumers that conventional foods were tainted and possibly dangerous. Whatever the reason, the Soil Association began the biggest campaign in its half-century of existence, and the Guy Watson affair became its central event.

Watson owned a large organic farm near the town of Totnes in the southwestern corner of England. Totnes, says one of Watson's employees, is "a thriving community of artists, alternative therapists, greens, and even new age travelers. If a fervent anti-GMO campaign was going to start anywhere in the UK, it would have to be in Totnes."

In April of 1998 one of the citizens of Totnes, reading the legal notices in the local paper, came across a notification that a seed company was planning a field trial of genetically engineered LibertyLink corn nearby. The test crop would be planted right across a small river from Guy Watson's farm.

At this point the Soil Association got into the act. It declared that "genetic contamination" from the LibertyLink corn might endanger Guy Watson's status as an organic grower. If windblown pollen from the genetically engineered corn appeared likely to fertilize his sweet corn plants, the letter stated, "we reserve the right to withdraw certification from the crop." Guy Watson, backed by the Soil Association, went to court trying to block the field trial of genetically engineered corn, which he claimed was a grave threat to his livelihood.

Various environmental groups issued statements of outrage. "FRANKENSTEIN FOODS THREATEN ORGANIC FARMER," trumpeted the press release from Friends of the Earth. Patrick Holden told journalists that "there could be no future for organic farming unless genetically engineered crop testing is brought under control and commercial planting prevented."

Most media coverage echoed Holden's fears. Few journalists paused to ask how the presence of genetically engineered pollen in a farmer's field might render it nonorganic or why the Soil Association claimed that it would. If windblown grains of pollen had fertilized a few strands of silk on the ears of Guy Watson's organic sweet corn, foreign genes would have ended up in the small embryo deep within those kernels of corn. But no genetically altered offspring would have grown from those kernels, since Watson didn't replant seed from his own harvest. Nor would the presence of this pollen have altered Guy Watson's organic farming methods in the least.

"I always thought it was a bit of a bogus argument," admits Watson, looking back on those days of controversy and fame. "But I suppose you can't get into these fights and stay squeaky clean." The possibility of cross-pollination was a "tool," he says; the leaders of the Soil Association "were quite keen to use the situation, and I was willing to be used."

But no matter. The idea that genetically engineered plants would "contaminate" the countryside through windblown pollen seemed, instinctively, to make sense. It became the central metaphor for environmental dangers posed by genetically engineered crops. And one night, before the LibertyLink corn near Guy Watson's farm sprouted tassels bearing pollen, activists went into those test plots and ripped out the genetically engineered plants. (It was among the first such "decontamination" efforts. Some were carried out in secret, others as open acts of civil disobedience. A year later art imitated life. The entire British nation listened in rapt attention as Tommy Archer, a main character in the BBC's wildly popular radio drama "The Archers," went on trial for destroying genetically engineered crops near his family's organic farm. The jury declared him not guilty.)

Events began to tumble over each other. On May 11, a few days after Guy Watson's troubles grabbed the attention of the British public, Robert Shapiro announced his plans to buy DeKalb and the leading cottonseed company, Delta and Pine Land, for a total of $4 billion.

The mainstream press in the United States and in Europe barely noticed the deals. For committed activists, though, it was a different matter entirely. They were transfixed by this evidence of Monsanto's expansive ambitions. Some began calling the company "the Monster."

And soon after the deals were announced, news arrived of another development, a symbol of everything the activists considered repugnant and evil about biotechnology, and especially about Monsanto.

"LET'S CALL it the Terminator!" The words burst from Pat Roy Mooney's mouth as he stood in a pay phone on the streets of Victoria, along Canada's Pacific coast. Mooney was the executive director of the Rural Advancement Foundation International, (RAFI) an organization dedicated to fighting corporate control over the world's seeds. On the other end of the line was Hope Shand, the group's director of research.

It was the first week of March 1998. Shand had come across an intriguing item in the *Wall Street Journal* in a column on notable new patents. According to the story, researchers from the USDA and the Delta and Pine Land Company had invented a way to stop plants from producing seeds that were capable of germination. (This was several months before Monsanto announced that it intended to buy Delta and Pine Land.) A press release from the USDA explained that this invention might open new markets for genetically engineered crops, particularly when it came to crops in which farmers typically saved their own seed and planted it the following seasons. In plain words it was a tool to enforce commercial control over seeds, which is what Shand and Mooney had been fighting for twenty years.

Mooney and Shand founded RAFI in the late 1970s, convinced, as Mooney put it, "that the great neglected issue in agriculture was the control of seeds." They believed that seeds were the common heritage of humanity; that no company had the moral right to own them. Mooney was a brash, self-taught high-school dropout who also happened to be legally blind. He cultivated a gift for the catchy phrase and gunslinger rhetoric. Shand, her soft voice registering equal portions pathos and moral outrage, stayed behind the scenes, gathering information useful to their cause.

Shand called Melvin Oliver, the scientist listed as the primary inventor of the new seed control technique, who worked at the USDA's research center in Lubbock, Texas. Oliver, a talkative Australian, was happy to explain his invention. It was composed of a whole series of genes, several of which acted as genetic "switches." Until these switches were tripped, the seeds would develop normally; the genes were arranged in such a way that they were "repressed," a bit like a mouse trap that's cocked, just waiting to snap shut. Before seeds were sold to the farmer, they'd be soaked in an antibiotic called tetracycline. This would flip the first switch, in turn releasing others, and the trap would snap shut. The plant would grow normally and produce seeds, but those seeds would never germinate.

Finally Shand called her comrade-in-arms, Pat Mooney in western Canada. As Mooney listened to Shand's description of the patent an image flashed through his mind and the name that would forever hang around the invention like a curse.

On March 11 Shand had issued her first broadside against "Terminator technology," calling it "a global threat to farmers, biodiversity, and food security." "If the Terminator technology is widely utilized," she wrote, "it will give the multinational seed and agrochemical industry an unprecedented and extremely dangerous capacity to control the world's food supply."

Yet for two months the Terminator remained an esoteric topic of interest only to a few. This tool in the hands of the USDA and an obscure cotton seed company in Mississippi just didn't seem terribly threatening. That changed when Monsanto announced that it would buy Delta and Pine Land.

Hope Shand read news of the impending merger on an airplane as she left a UN-sponsored conference on biodiversity in Bratislava, Slovakia. From the next airport she called her colleagues who remained at the conference. "I can't believe that I'm reading this in black and white," she told them.

"It's now or never," RAFI declared in its next press release. "This is a technology that deliberately sterilizes farmers' fields, . . . that is now in the hands of a giant, aggressive multinational company with more than enough resources to follow through on the plan." RAFI reminded everyone who would listen that Monsanto already had banned the replanting of its seeds in North America, using such tools as patents, contracts, and the threat of lawsuits. The Terminator would accomplish the same goal in parts of the world that were beyond the reach of the company's legal arsenal. It was a tool, in short, to enforce "bioserfdom."

Now the world was listening. As RAFI spread the news among delegates at the biodiversity conference, delegates from a series of Third World countries stood up and condemned the Terminator.

More significantly and astonishingly, fear of Terminator technology caught fire on the Internet. The issue possessed a hard-to-define quality—some mixture of conspiracy, novelty, and apocalypticism—that thrived within the limitless, yet claustrophobic atmosphere of the online world. People who'd never cared about agriculture before, who'd never seen a cotton plant or a soybean, started forwarding RAFI's press releases to friends and authoring outraged commentaries of their own.

Before most journalists from the mainstream media even noticed the controversy, the online version of the Terminator grew into something larger than life. Millions "knew" that Monsanto was on the verge of forcing poor farmers in the Third World to plant crops that would produce sterile seeds.

In fact, Monsanto never did acquire control of the Terminator patent. (Its attempt to acquire Delta and Pine Land was rejected more than a year later by antitrust regulators.) And as of this writing in spring 2001 the Terminator gene still has not "terminated" a single plant, even in the laboratory. Pieces of the Terminator exist in various plants, but Melvin Oliver and his colleagues at the USDA research center in Lubbock still have not assembled a working collection of their genetic switches.

The Terminator, as it existed in the public debate, was not really a technology at all. It was a symbol, and it crystallized a long-standing conflict between those who considered the genetic makeup of a plant a kind of private property and those who considered it a gift of nature freely available to all. Ultimately, the conflict was over the morality of capitalism as it transformed international agriculture into its own image.

This was not a simple debate. One could in fact make reasonable arguments on the Terminator's behalf. Harry Collins, the research director at Delta and Pine Land Company, tried in his earnest and ponderous way to persuade the world that the Terminator was no threat to anyone, that no farmer would be forced to plant Terminator-type seeds, just as no farmer was forced to plant Roundup Ready soybeans. Quite the opposite, he argued: Terminator would lead to *more* choices for farmers. Just as the advent of hybrid corn had enticed private companies into the breeding of that crop, so the Terminator would accomplish something similar for many others. Farmers finally would see superior versions of crops that private seed companies had ignored. Collins's claims were drowned in a torrent of scorn and outrage.

MONSANTO'S ADVERTISING campaign marched into this cauldron like a witless, hopelessly naive tourist. The first ads ran during the first week in June 1998. A few days later, on June 8, the campaign was struck by a bolt from on high, from His Royal Highness the Prince of Wales. Prince Charles declared in Britain's leading conservative newspaper, the *Daily Telegraph,* that "this kind of genetic modification takes mankind into realms that belong to God, and to God alone." The heir to the British throne declared such crops unnecessary, incompatible with agriculture that "proceeds in harmony with nature," and possibly dangerous. Even if scientists had found no evidence of danger from genetically modified crops, there might still lurk unforeseen consequences either to the environment or to human health, he wrote. "I personally have no wish to eat anything produced by genetic modification, nor do I knowingly offer this sort of produce to my family or guests."

Charles, for all his marital troubles and personal eccentricity, remained the prince. Leftist opponents of biotechnology might scorn him, but his words, not theirs, were capable of reaching the eyes and minds of middle- and working-class consumers from Sussex to Scotland. The prince's broadside and the flood of media attention given to it obliterated Monsanto's efforts to win sympathy for genetically modified crops. "It had a huge impact," says Philip Angell, Monsanto's former head of public relations. "It changed the coverage of the debate and the profile of the issue almost forever. And it blew away the low profile approach of our advertising."

Monsanto's ads, filling full pages in leading newspapers, were notably understated in form and, in most cases, in their language. ("FOOD BIOTECHNOLOGY IS A MATTER OF OPINIONS. MONSANTO BELIEVES YOU SHOULD HEAR ALL OF THEM.") Some were simple blocks of text; the rest were adorned only with a single small photo of a strawberry, a tomato, or a field. Each ad also gave the phone number and Internet address of a prominent organization opposing biotechnology, suggesting that readers should contact it to "hear all sides of the debate."

Still, the ads managed to infuriate. What enraged opponents more than anything was the assertion that Monsanto's venture into genetically engineered crops was a humanitarian and moral one. ("WORRYING ABOUT STARVING FUTURE GENERATIONS WON'T FEED THEM. FOOD BIOTECHNOLOGY WILL.") The ads reflected the conviction of Shapiro's inner circle that Monsanto's genetically engineered crops weren't just acceptable; they were *good*. They could reduce the use of toxic chemicals, improve the taste of tomatoes, and feed a growing world population. Monsanto's technology and indeed Monsanto itself was a force for progress toward a better, healthier, more sustainable world. "People almost felt that they were involved in a noble mission," says Kate Fish, Monsanto's director of public policy.

To British activists who'd been spending their evenings reading about Monsanto's new seed empire and about the Terminator, this claim to the moral high ground seemed absurd and deceitful. Nothing destroys the possibility of civil conversation and compromise more quickly than the feeling that one is being lied to.

Activists responded in kind. They retrieved a selection of tales from the archive of genetic engineering, assembled them into a portrait of technology run amok, and with the enthusiastic participation of large sections of the British news media spread them liberally across the public consciousness.

There was, for instance, the tale of the allergy-inducing soybeans. In the early 1990s researchers at Pioneer Hi-Bred had stumbled upon what seemed, at first glance, like a good idea. They could improve the nutrient makeup of soybeans by adding a new protein that was rich in certain amino acids the soybean lacked. The gene for this new protein came from the Brazil nut. The research was still several years from commercial application when independent scientists pointed out to Pioneer that the Brazil nut is one of the most common causes of food allergies and that there was a chance this Brazil nut gene would cause allergies. (The FDA had drawn up a plan to review all transgenic food to prevent exactly such transfers.) Pioneer commissioned a test at the University of Nebraska, and, sure enough, blood serum collected from people who were allergic to Brazil nuts also reacted to the new soybeans. Pioneer killed the project.

In the retelling, the story lost some of these details and carried a more threatening message. Opponents sometimes suggested that Pioneer discovered the soybean's hazards only by chance; others who heard the story became convinced that the soybeans actually ended up on the market and killed some people. Yet behind these false impressions lurked a real risk. Scientists could test for allergy to the

Brazil nut because this allergy is well-known. When genetic engineers import genes that have never before been eaten in large quantities by humans—genes from obscure bacteria, for instance—scientists can't know for certain whether the genes will set off allergies. They can only check to see whether the products of the new gene fit the typical profile of an allergy-causing protein. Still, up to now, Pioneer's Brazil nut experiment is the only known example of an allergen transferred through genetic engineering.

Then there was the deadly story of L-tryptophan, a food supplement sold in health food stores. In 1989 a Japanese company called Showa Denko tried to boost its production of L-tryptophan by using microbes that had been genetically engineered. At the same time, the company changed its manufacturing process and reduced the amount of filtering it used to clean out impurities. Shortly thereafter Showa Denko's food supplements started poisoning large numbers of consumers in the United States. Thousands got sick, and at least two dozen people died.

The exact cause of the sickness remains something of a mystery. Scientists at the FDA decided that it probably was caused by a contaminant called EBT which was present in tiny quantities in those particular batches of L-tryptophan. But because Showa Denko had destroyed its stocks of genetically altered bacteria, no one would ever know for sure whether these bacteria were to blame or whether it was simply inadequate filtration in Showa Denko's factories.

Genetic engineering probably wasn't the cause, since a few cases of L-tryptophan poisoning had occurred even before genetically engineered bacteria were employed. Indeed, if the tryptophan case showed anything, it was the dangers residing in food supplements that often are sold in health food stores, not genetically engineered foods. Showa Denko's L-tryptophan, since it was considered "natural," had not been subjected to safety reviews. Roundup Ready soybeans, on the other hand, *had* been. Yet the mystery became fertile ground for speculation and fear. And at least one national television broadcast drew an exact parallel with genetically engineered food. As this broadcast put it: "The L-tryptophan tragedy suggests there may be hidden dangers in genetic modification. A tiny proportion of the population took it, but hundreds fell ill. Now, millions of us eat GM ingredients and their by-products every day. So have the regulators learnt any lessons?"

There was much talk of "superweeds" which might emerge as herbicide-tolerant crops transferred their novel genes to wild, weedy relatives. Others worried that antibiotic resistance genes present in genetically modified corn might migrate into bacteria that live in the human gut, making patients immune to medical treatment. Several opponents of genetic engineering warned that the powerful genetic engine used to drive Monsanto's novel genes, the 35S promoter, might recombine with other genes in plants or even in the human body, suddenly sending genes into overdrive and disrupting the cell's normal function. (Most scientists considered such scenarios farfetched and the risks minuscule. They pointed out in addition that people already consume many copies of the 35S promoter whenever they eat cauliflower, cabbage, or broccoli. Why should one worry about completely hypothetical and undemonstrated risks, they asked, when people engage in real and quantifiable risks every day while eating everything from hamburgers to celery?)

Finally, there was the disturbing appearance of an elderly, Hungarian-born scientist named Arpad Pusztai on the television news magazine *World in Action* on August 10, 1998. Pusztai reported that he'd been feeding genetically modified potatoes to rats in his laboratory at a government-sponsored research establishment called the Rowett Institute. These rats, he said, grew more slowly and suffered from a weakened immune system compared with rats fed conventional potatoes. The presenter of the broadcast then asked the obvious question: "If genetically altered foods can affect *rats* in this way, could they possibly have long term effects on *humans* too?" For the rest of the broadcast, the *World in Action* team pursued a variety of Monsanto officials, asking insistently, "what long-term studies have been carried out on feeding genetically modified soya to mammals?" They received a variety of unsatisfactory answers. A Monsanto press spokesman refused to be interviewed on the subject. Another company official was filmed saying, "Well, we don't—we don't do long-term animal tests on any new variety."

The exact details of Pusztai's experiments were not revealed during the broadcast and remained the subject of controversy for many months afterward. (Pusztai's employer, the Rowett Institute, covered itself in disgrace by its handling of the controversy, first praising Pusztai, then condemning him, then, through sheer confusion, putting out wholly inaccurate information about the experiment.) Outside scientists assigned to review his work, first for the British Royal Society and later for the journal *The Lancet*, found themselves frustrated by a confusing welter of data. And most of them came to the conclusion that, whatever caused the ill effects that Pusztai observed in his colonies of rats, it probably was not, as Pusztai suggested, the process of genetic engineering.

Pusztai might instead have observed the effects of starvation rations on young rats. Potatoes don't contain enough protein to sustain a healthy, growing rat. Pusztai's rat colonies were being systematically malnourished. This circumstance should have produced equivalent effects on each group, but the colonies of rats were so small (six in each group) that, if just a couple of them reacted strongly to this stressful diet and those rats were assigned to one group, it would be enough to produce a damning result.

In addition, the two groups of rats might not have been eating equivalent diets at all. The genetically engineered potatoes that Pusztai used in most of his experiments contained 20 percent less protein than the potatoes from which they'd been derived. (Such effects, discovered at the dawn of genetic engineering, are relatively common though not well understood. Most of these effects seem to arise because the process of growing a plant from an individual cell in a petri dish causes genetic mutations of various sorts.) Pusztai's genetically engineered potatoes thus were not "substantially equivalent" to conventional potatoes and would not have been approved for commercial sale. Pusztai compensated by adding additional protein to the diet of rats eating these potatoes. But there may well have been other differences that went unrecognized. Pusztai never provided any information, for instance, on whether the potato diets contained identical amounts of natural poisons, called glycoalcoloids, that are found in potatoes.

What's more, Pusztai's conclusions conflicted with the results of more credible studies. Four years earlier, Dutch researchers had fed rats large quantities of powdered tomatoes, some of which were engineered to contain the Bt gene. For three months researchers had fed their rats as much powdered tomato as the rats could eat without falling victim to potassium poisoning. The Dutch researchers used twice as many rats as Pusztai; they accounted carefully for the chemical makeup of their tomatoes. In the end they saw no differences between the two colonies of rats.

But such details, in the end, were unimportant. So were the details involved in understanding superweeds or allergies or L-tryptophan. Scientists could try to refute every one of the charges made against genetically modified food; indeed they thought they had done so, years earlier. They could point out endlessly that, if a weed acquired a gene for Roundup resistance, it would be a "superweed" only as long as the farmer kept spraying Roundup. They could argue, for instance, that long-term feeding studies sometimes *could not* sensibly be used to examine genetically engineered foods; you simply ended up "discovering" that rats aren't happy on a steady diet of potatoes, genetically engineered or not.

But for every danger that scientists dismissed, for every fear that they considered unfounded, an anxious public had one more question: What about the dangers that you haven't even imagined yet? What about the unforeseen risks? *What about mad cow disease, which the experts didn't think could possibly infect humans?* And to these questions the defenders of genetically engineered crops had no real response except to sputter that no one could possibly make any decisions based purely on the possibility of something not yet known.

The whole debate, in fact, turned on the possibility of unknown dangers. When scientists said, as they often did, that they saw "no evidence" that genetically engineered food posed special dangers, their critics were fond of quoting an old saying: The absence of evidence is not evidence of absence. But what, then, *did* the absence of evidence mean? For many it merely showed the limits of human knowledge and the inability of science to identify dangers that might remain hidden in the shadows.

As public opinion settled ever more firmly into an attitude of hostility toward biotechnology and disbelief of assurances provided by science, many British scientists involved in the controversy felt enraged, helpless, and betrayed by their own culture. "This stuff is straight out of the Dark Ages," glowered one of them darkly.

The professional opponents of genetically engineered food—sophisticated activists like Benny Härlin or Tony Juniper of Friends of the Earth—never claimed exactly that Roundup Ready soybeans and Bt corn were dangerous to eat. They had begun this campaign because they perceived risks to the environment, not directly to human health. But they also believed that biotechnology companies, reckless and impatient in their drive for quick profits, could not be trusted. Nor could governments be trusted to look out for the public's interests. In the United States or Europe centrist politicians like Tony Blair and Bill Clinton were in thrall to technology and beholden to private interests. Moreover, the activists believed, the scientific establishment couldn't be trusted to render an honest judgment, not when science itself was under attack. One had only to witness the bumbling and panicked response of leading British scientists to media reports of Arpad Pusztai's experiments. Pusztai was suspended from his job, and the Royal Society's investigation of his case looked suspiciously like a premeditated effort to discredit a well-meaning scientist.

Where there was no trust, there could be only suspicion and fear. If fears of tainted food turned out to be the weapon that brought down a profit-mad industry, many felt, so be it.

HARVEST TIME arrived in the fall of 1998, and behind closed doors the secretive men who manage America's grain trade struggled to deal with yet another crisis precipitated by biotechnology. The complications that had been narrowly averted in 1996 were becoming reality. For the first time, combines roaring through Midwestern fields were harvesting grain—Roundup Ready corn—that was not yet approved for export to Europe. It mixed inevitably with the rest of the harvest as grain flowed through combines, grain bins, rail cars, and barges. Yet it could not end up in ships bound for Europe. European officials were threatening to send back any ships found to be carrying traces of such "unapproved varieties." The collision between American producers and European consumers had arrived, yet almost no one spoke openly about it. Few farmers even knew what was going on.

Two circumstances permitted a quiet solution. First, Europe did not require a large amount of imported grain. It normally imported 2 percent of the U.S. grain harvest, worth about $200 million. Second, European regulations on genetically engineered plants covered only imports of whole grain, not processed products created from them such as corn meal or corn gluten. (Corn gluten is used primarily in animal feed.) International grain handlers quietly organized a solution to the problem. They shifted the routes of their cargo ships so that no grain from the United States ended up in Europe. Europe's imports came from South America instead. Yet corn gluten from American processing plants, millions of tons of it, continued to flow across the Atlantic to feed Europe's chickens and hogs.

# 15

# The Wheels Come Off

In the middle of October 1998 Monsanto executives gathered in Brussels to review their battered and bloodied European strategy. Philip Angell flew in from Washington, D.C. Hugh Grant, the Scotsman who'd recently been named copresident of Monsanto's agricultural division, came from St. Louis.

It was not a pleasant meeting. Polls in Britain showed support for genetically engineered crops falling through the floor, despite—or perhaps because of—Monsanto's continuing advertising. The uproar in Britain, meanwhile, was breathing life into antibiotechnology forces elsewhere in Europe. The French government had flipped sides completely. Once Europe's most popular site for field trials of genetically engineered crops, it now was leading a voting bloc in Brussels which refused to approve any new products of genetic engineering. This pirouette was due not to a sudden swell of public opposition but rather to the calculations of coalition government. France's Green Party was a junior partner in the government and controlled the nation's environment ministry.

Yet Philip Angell refused to abandon the fight. He recommended that Monsanto simply stick with what it had been doing and continue its advertising. Hugh Grant erupted in disbelief, "You can't be serious!" Most others agreed. The advertising, Angell says, "was universally reviled."

They were still meeting on October 13, when shocking news arrived. The proposed merger of Monsanto and American Home

Products, the keystone of Shapiro's strategy for the future, had been called off. AHP, creator of such household names as Robitussin, Advil, and Chap Stick, was twice as large as Monsanto, and its deep pockets were supposed to put a stable financial foundation under Monsanto's riskier ventures, like agricultural biotechnology. But the plan to join forces could not survive ugly power struggles between rival executives in the two companies. With the merger in shreds Shapiro's spell over Wall Street was broken. In an instant Monsanto's stock lost a quarter of its value and dropped further in the days that followed. The wheels had come off the Monsanto biotechnology express.

"Shapiro has never been the same since the day the AHP merger fell through. I think he was undone by that," says one former Monsanto executive. The week after the stock price collapsed, Monsanto's largest shareholder, the Janus Fund, ordered Shapiro to fly to the fund's headquarters in Denver and explain himself. "No CEO likes to go through that experience answering to shareholders, especially shareholders who are really angry, who have lost a lot of money—particularly Shapiro, who has a fairly high view of himself," says the executive.

Further humiliation followed in a matter of days. As Shapiro finished a speech at the Fairmont Hotel in San Francisco and walked off the stage, a protester hurled a vegan tofu-cream pie that caught the slightly built CEO full in the face. "I talked to Shapiro the next day," says Philip Angell. "He was somewhat jovial and dismissive of it, but he said something that was kind of telling. He said, 'You know, when you think of all the trouble they went to, they could have at least killed me.' I'm not sure that at the end of the day he didn't come to the conclusion that *'they could have killed me!'* I think it rent a hole in his sense that he could drift through this world as CEO of Monsanto, and that he was not at risk."

On Wall Street, too, Monsanto's image reversed. Monsanto was no longer the daring pioneer of agricultural biotechnology, a company with shining prospects for further growth. Instead, it was an overstretched company that desperately needed a larger partner.

The obvious partner was DuPont, a company with substantial financial resources and its own ambitions in agricultural biotechnol-

ogy. DuPont's executives years earlier had decided that they were going to work on so-called "output traits": genetic alterations that
made crops more valuable as they left the farm, such as extra-
healthy soybeans and corn. It seemed a perfect complement to Monsanto's "input traits," such as herbicide tolerance, which helped
farmers produce crops more efficiently.

There was one hitch. DuPont had begun courting Monsanto's
nemesis, the proud and fiercely independent seed company Pioneer
Hi-Bred International. With Pioneer's permission DuPont had purchased 20 percent of Pioneer's stock, and the two companies had begun a variety of joint research projects. Pioneer's executives insisted
that they intended to remain independent, but many considered the
arrangement a sort of engagement with marriage to follow. If Shapiro
wanted to woo DuPont, he would have to cut in on this dance.

Documents on file at the Securities and Exchange Commission reveal in the dry language of an official disclosure to investors the effects of Monsanto's flirtation. On January 4, 1999, the CEO of
DuPont, Charles Holliday, met with Charles Johnson, the CEO of
Pioneer. At this meeting, "Mr. Holliday ... mentioned that DuPont
had engaged in discussions with Monsanto regarding a possible
business combination of Monsanto and DuPont." Holliday told
Johnson that he was mentioning this because he felt it was something that the Pioneer CEO might want to know. Indeed. ("By the
way, dear, that fetching Mr. Shapiro next door said he'd like to
marry me tomorrow! Isn't that sweet?") Pioneer's Charles Johnson,
according to the SEC document, "responded that he needed more
time to think through the potential issues."

Two days later, the two chief executives met again. Johnson suggested to his partner from DuPont that their alliance surely would be
"negatively affected" if DuPont joined forces with Monsanto. The
"spirit of cooperation" undoubtedly would be lost, he said.

This was severe understatement. Pioneer and Monsanto were, at
that moment, at war. Monsanto's corn seed company, DeKalb, had
started the battle with lawsuits alleging patent infringement. Pioneer,
in a rage, was fighting back on several fronts. Pioneer had filed its
own lawsuits accusing DeKalb of stealing Pioneer's most prized lines
of corn. Pioneer executives had taken to calling up government an-

titrust officials and journalists, spreading the word about Monsanto's ruthless behavior toward farmers who violated Monsanto's ban on the saving and replanting of seed. Across the Midwestern farm belt, Pioneer dealers were systematically undercutting their rival's prices for soybean seed, carving away at Monsanto's most profitable crop, Roundup Ready soybeans. "Pioneer had a million bags of seed sitting in warehouses," says Glen Donald, an executive at the time with the German company AgrEvo. Those bags were ammunition for a price-cutting battle. It was a "bloodletting," Donald says.

Pioneer was willing to do almost anything to prevent DuPont from walking to the altar with its enemy—even renounce tradition, identity, and pride. Charles Johnson, according to the dry account of events submitted to the SEC, "suggested the possibility that, before combining with Monsanto, DuPont first acquire the remaining interest in Pioneer not owned by DuPont." Johnson knew, of course, that DuPont could not do both. It didn't have the money to buy both companies, and the government's antitrust authorities wouldn't have allowed it. If DuPont acquired Pioneer there would be no deal with Monsanto.

With Johnson's words, Pioneer Hi-Bred, the legacy of Henry Wallace and the pride of Des Moines, had capitulated to the tide of events. The company that subscribed to the "Long Look" would not survive the twentieth century. The last—in many ways the only— true power in the seed business could no longer go its independent way. It had fought off St. Louis, only to fall into the clutches of Wilmington.

"YOU HAVE to understand, Monsanto blew the business apart," says Tom Urban, Pioneer's retired chief executive. For a decade, Urban had spurned every attempt by outsiders to buy his (and his father's) company. But by 1998, he says, the company had no real choice. Biotechnology and Monsanto had pushed the Des Moines company to the edge of a cliff. Pioneer couldn't manage to cooperate with Monsanto, but it didn't have the resources by itself to compete with Monsanto either.

"Our research budget was going from $50 million to $75 million to $100 million to $200 million a year," Urban says. "We simply could not pass that on. We felt that it was better to be part of a company that has a pharmaceutical division, that has deeper pockets for research. And Monsanto caused all that. They went out and changed the industry. By paying huge amounts of money [to acquire seed companies]. They went out and paid six or seven billion dollars for no earnings."

But hadn't Wall Street come to the conclusion that Monsanto's strategy and its decisions to acquire a seed empire were ill-advised? Monsanto's stock price had been hammered, its reputation battered. Couldn't everyone just return to the comfortable patterns of the past and let seed companies earn their modest profits without big industrial partners?

"No!" Urban retorts. "Once you pissed in the soup, you pissed in the soup!"

Urban's thoughts turned often to the memory of another conversation with Monsanto executives twenty years earlier. In the mid-1970s, before genetic engineering of plants became possible, Pioneer and Monsanto had begun a research collaboration.

One day in the late 1970s Monsanto's two top executives flew into Des Moines in their corporate jet. "They walked in and said, 'Now we need to write a commercial contract,'" Urban says. Such a contract would have settled the companies' shares of revenue from any eventual commercial products. "So I said, 'On what basis are we going to write this commercial contract? We don't know where this is going! We don't have anything. You don't have anything!' And they said, 'Well, if we don't, we'll have to terminate.' So we broke apart."

Urban drove the two Monsanto executives, Jack Hanley and Nick Reding, to the Des Moines airport and watched as they walked to their airplane. One thing sticks vividly in his memory: Hanley reaching out and putting his arm around Reding. "Don't know what it meant," he says. "It was a really interesting gesture."

"In my opinion, if they'd been really smart they'd have stayed right with us, wooed us, worked with us, and when the time came, who knows, maybe they'd have bought us," Urban says. "If they'd had the patience to work with us the plant biotech world might look very different today."

Yet Urban's own combative attitude also played a part in determining the course of events. Turn the clock back to 1992–1993, when Tom Urban scoffed at the value of Roundup Ready soybeans or Bt corn, and Monsanto, anxious for a deal, sold those genes for a mere $38 million. Those deals, Monsanto's frustration with them, and Pioneer's refusal to give up a good deal produced constant conflict. Unable to cooperate, the two companies tried to compete on the other's home field: Pioneer started pouring money into biotechnology, and Monsanto bought seed companies. The effort weakened them both to the point where neither company could survive as a freestanding, independent enterprise.

ON MARCH 15, 1999, DuPont announced that it was buying the 80 percent of Pioneer that it did not already own, spending a total of $9.4 billion for the seed company. (The transaction was concluded six months later.) DuPont's hefty bet on biotechnology thus matched Monsanto's own. DuPont's executives, focused on their prize in the Midwest, didn't spend much time looking over their shoulders at Europe, but they probably should have. The dam of official and scientific consensus that had stood firm so long against the swell of public sentiment finally was cracking, and the ensuing flood would reach even the shores of North America.

# 16

# The Deluge

As the wrenching year of 1998 gave way to 1999, the men at the helm of Monsanto allowed themselves to hope that they'd weathered the storm. For several months, no significant new revelations had roiled British attitudes. Tony Blair, defying the polls, had held his ground, refusing to satisfy opponents who demanded a moratorium on approvals of any new genetically engineered crops. Few foresaw the cataclysm that lay in wait.

Yet in hindsight the events that transpired during the spring of 1999 were almost predictable. The popular will could not be frustrated forever, not with tens of millions of British men and women convinced that genetically engineered crops were a menace. Those sentiments were a pent-up force waiting to be harnessed. For William Hague, leader of Britain's conservative opposition, they represented potential votes and power. For John Ingham, environmental writer at the *Daily Express*, they meant banner headlines, juicy exposés, and newsstand sales. Tom Clayton of Marks and Spencer, an upscale food and clothing store, sensed shifts in consumer attitudes that could unbalance a balance sheet.

Late in the afternoon on February 4, Hague rose from his front-row seat in the House of Commons and fixed Tony Blair with a critical gaze. "Why," he demanded of his adversary, "hasn't the government accepted the advice of English Nature [a government agency promoting habitat conservation] and delayed for at least three years the commercial release of genetically engineered crops until more research is done?" Hague's query carried a dose of revenge. Two years earlier, Tony Blair had stood in Hague's spot and berated a conservative prime minister for failing to protect the British public from mad cow disease.

As if at a signal, three major newspapers launched campaigns against genetically modified food the following week. They included two mass-circulation tabloids, the *Daily Mail* and the *Express*, which are the newspapers read most regularly by women, Britain's primary shoppers for food. The headlines screamed of "MUTANT CROPS," "ASTONISHING DECEIT OF GM FOOD GIANT" and "TERRIFYING TAMPERING." In the *Daily Mail:* "GM FOODS ARE PLAYING GAMES WITH NATURE: If cancer is the only side-effect we will be lucky." And in the *Express:* "LIKE IT OR NOT, you and your family have been turned into guinea pigs for untested GM foods." When Blair declared that he ate genetically modified food and thought nothing of it, *The Mirror* splashed outrage across its front page: "THE PRIME MONSTER; FURY AS BLAIR SAYS: I EAT FRANKENSTEIN FOOD AND IT'S SAFE."

"Papers launch campaigns all the time," says John Ingham, the short, ruddy-faced redhead who wrote many of the stories in the *Express*. "Most of the time they don't catch the public's imagination, and they keel over after two weeks." This campaign, though, struck a chord. "We got more letters on this than virtually every other issue." So the stories kept on coming. As Ingham sees it, he was helping to expose hidden dangers. "You have to remember that these foods were being brought in very quietly and secretly," he says. "A lot of the stories we've written have really upset the biotech industry. I don't set out to upset people, but I stand by everything I've written, because they've all been based on the facts."

"They went on a circulation war," says an executive from one British food chain. "They just outshouted each other. They kept finding another angle; any little bit of research was just massive headlines."

I mentioned that I'd just come from a meeting with John Ingham of the *Express*. "What did Mr. Ingham say?" the man demanded.

"Did he tell you it was for the good of the country that he was doing it? Like shit. He was selling newspapers." He paused, then shrugged. "Fine! We sell food."

"It just escalated," says Tom Clayton, the chief technical officer at Marks and Spencer, "the noise, the pitch, the tenacity, the ferocity of the whole thing." Clayton was used to complaints, but not like this. At the peak of the uproar, Marks and Spencer was getting eight hundred questions a week from customers who were worried about the presence of genetically modified ingredients in the store's food. "We could just see the graph going up and up. It became the single biggest issue," Clayton says.

Marks and Spencer had no desire to be cannon fodder for the cause of biotechnology. "It was no benefit to the consumer. All they could see was large multinational companies having benefits, or farmers in distant countries like the United States," says Clayton. "The consumer was telling us that this was happening too fast without their involvement, and they just wanted to blow the whistle and have, in your terms, a time out." On March 15, the chain announced that it would eliminate genetically modified soybean and corn ingredients from its shelves. Within weeks, every other leading British supermarket chain did the same, followed by major European food processors such as Nestle and Unilever.

The task of eliminating genetically modified ingredients was daunting but not insurmountable, Clayton says. When feasible, the chain simply changed its recipes to eliminate corn or soy products. "We took lecithin [an emulsifier derived from soybeans] out of soups and stocks and bouillons and replaced it with egg. When soy oil was just a small ingredient, then we simply replaced it with any other vegetable oil." In some cases, they couldn't change the recipe. Nothing can replace lecithin in the production of chocolate, for instance. But Clayton managed to find sources of soybean and corn products that were guaranteed to be free of novel genes.

Consumer power had overrun government regulation. The British government retreated in disarray. Blair announced that the government would approve no new genetically modified crops for three years. During that time it would conduct a series of "farm-scale trials" of genetically modified crops to study all the ecological dangers posed by these crops. (Friends of the Earth immediately denounced the trials as "a cover for creeping commercial development of GM crops." Greenpeace and several undercover groups, taking matters into their own hands, began plotting to destroy these test plots.)

In Brussels the process for evaluating and approving genetically engineered crops fell apart completely. It had been stuck in place for some time, trapped by chronic differences between the European Commission—the centralized bureaucracy in Brussels—and the elected governments of the European Union's various member states.

The Commission is the executive branch of pan-European government. Its various "directorates-general" are the European equivalents of the U.S. Department of Commerce, Department of Agriculture, Environmental Protection Agency, and Food and Drug Administration. In the case of genetically engineered crops, the Commission, relying on advice from scientists drawn from across Europe, generally recommended approval; after 1997, national governments almost always refused to follow these recommendations. When such disagreements occurred, the rules of European governance dictated an odd solution, intended to strengthen the institutions of European unity by giving them great power. The commission's recommendations went into effect unless *every single member state* voted against them. Thus, a series of genetically engineered crops were approved during 1998 over the opposition of a majority of Europe's governments. In one case, a crop was approved despite a 14–1 vote against it.

This situation made no one happy. Environmentalists were outraged and accused the European Commission of undemocratic behavior. Officials at the Commission, for their part, complained that member countries were cynically taking the easy way out, forcing civil servants in Brussels to make decisions that were necessary but politically unpopular. "Biotechnology is something that everybody wants to avoid," said one official at the Commission with evident anger and disgust. "So the member countries just sit there and do nothing. They let the Commission do the dirty work. It stinks!"

Early in 1999, the Commission refused to play that game anymore. It approved new rules that gave it less power; henceforth, no recommendation would be enacted unless a majority of Europe's member states voted in favor of it. In effect, the Commission shoved responsibility for approving genetically engineered foods back into the hands of member governments. Forced to declare their position, twelve of the fifteen members of the European Union announced that they would not approve any more genetically engineered crops until there were full procedures for "labeling and traceability" of genetically modified crops and products derived from them.

The European opponents of genetically engineered crops had triumphed. No new products from the laboratories of Monsanto, Novartis, or AgrEvo were welcome on European shores. Even old ones declared safe years earlier were shunned by consumers. Europe had become a fortress against the expansion of genetic engineering, standing defiantly in the path of Monsanto's plans to introduce a steady new stream of genetically engineered crops and to sell them in every market across the globe.

PHILIP ANGELL, Monsanto's man on the front lines of public opinion, faced hostility wherever he turned. Every morning at 4:00 A.M., he rolled out of bed in his Maryland home and called Monsanto's office in Brussels for a report on the latest indignities that Monsanto had suffered in Europe. Later, when he arrived at his office in Washington, D.C., he had to fend off barbed queries from Monsanto executives in St. Louis who could not comprehend the disaster unfolding on foreign shores and demanded that Angell do his job and put an end to such nonsense.

"There is a strong part of the Monsanto culture which I think is enviable," Angell says. "It's the unfailing belief in the power and validity of science. The people at Monsanto believe that they do the best science, that they go the extra mile. But it is not an attitude that lends itself to a lot of tolerance for nonscientific reactions."

Many executives at Monsanto simply dismissed the fears of genetically engineered foods as ignorant and silly. They couldn't understand why the press and even government officials would pay any attention to such fears. As Monsanto's image and commercial prospects in Europe continued to plummet, disbelief gave way to frustration, and then to anger. The anger, aimed at foes far away, settled on friends nearby, including Philip Angell. By March, eighteen months after he took over as Monsanto's public voice, Angell knew that it was time to find another job.

The executive in St. Louis who refused most adamantly to offer any concessions to biotechnology's opponents was Robb Fraley, who had risen to become copresident of Monsanto's agriculture business. Fraley interpreted the challenge in starkly economic terms. "The vast majority of opposition is commercially driven," he said with resolute assurance. The commercial interests, as he saw them, were threefold: activist groups used the issue to raise money and get attention; marketers of high-priced organic food hoped to gain market share by spreading doubt about the safety of lower-cost conventional food; and European competitors and governments had begun an "orchestrated effort" to block technology that gave American companies and farmers a competitive advantage. Fraley did not appear any more offended by this than he would have been by Monsanto's own competitive strategies. All's fair, his expression implied, in the love and war of business.

Fraley and his allies, including Mickey Kantor, a Monsanto board member who'd served until 1996 as the Clinton administration's chief trade negotiator, tried to go on the offensive. They accused European governments of illegal trade barriers and urged the U.S. government to threaten retaliation.

Others within Monsanto considered Fraley's cynical, take-no-prisoners attitude both wrongheaded and self-destructive. "A lot of people care deeply about agricultural biotech, and they're afraid that in Robb Fraley's hand it could be wrecked," said one. Or as another executive put it, "Fraley is the heart of the problem. He *is* the problem. I've never met a person who felt, as much as he does, that he knows everything about everything. He is by far the strongest personality within the senior leadership. And because he's so powerful, the government affairs people toe his line."

THE UNITED States still seemed untouched by European worries about biotechnology. Across the corn and soybean belt of the United States, the spring of 1999 was notable mainly for being hot and dry. Farmers got their seeds into the ground early that year. More of them carried Monsanto's genes than ever before. Across the Midwestern states, Roundup Ready soybeans covered 57 percent of the land planted in that crop, up from 42 percent the year before. A third of all corn acres contained a Bt gene or genes making corn resistant either to Roundup or Liberty. Genetic engineering to these farmers remained irresistible. Why, after all, should they resist it?

It was inevitable, given the laws of supply and demand, that the battle over biotechnology would trace the path of trade routes back to the corn and soybean fields of North and South America, source of the world's genetically engineered grain and of Monsanto's wealth. It was inevitable, for instance, that someone like Timothy Ramey, a financial analyst in the New York office of Deutsche Bank, would wander into a meeting of food companies and discover that much of the food industry no longer wanted any part of the vaunted genetic revolution in agriculture.

Ramey went to such a meeting in mid-May 1999. He arrived believing, like most Wall Street analysts, that the campaign against genetic engineering was noisy but relatively unimportant—that everyone was buying the new products and that there was no turning back. He was stunned to hear a representative from Nestle, the world's largest food company, describe her company's plans to use only ingredients derived from traditional varieties of soybeans and corn. "Don't expect *us* to take a bullet for *your* GMO products," she said. (*GMO*, the acronym for "genetically modified organism", was the term favored in Europe. As European opposition grew, Americans came to use it as well.)

Ramey went back to the office to write a new report. "Perhaps we don't fully realize it, but genetically modified organisms have just crossed the line," he wrote. "Thirty days ago, the investment community accorded only positive attributes, such as innovation, productivity, and progress, to GMO corn and soybeans. . . . We predict that GMOs . . . will now be perceived as a pariah, . . . and we would broadly recommend a sale of the seed sector." Ramey predicted that falling demand for GMOs would work its way backward through the supply chain. Farmers would get lower prices for the genetically engineered portion of their harvest, and they no longer would pay extra for genetically engineered seed. In fact, they might pay less. "That would be an earnings nightmare for Pioneer Hi-Bred and, we would guess, for Monsanto as well." Ramey added a final kicker in the title: "GMOs Are Dead."

Ramey's report hit the street on May 21, just in time to catch a wave of public interest. Two days earlier, on May 19, the furor surrounding genetically engineered crops had finally and definitively leaped the Atlantic and erupted in the United States.

This eruption, or at least the catalyst for it, was not part of any strategy crafted with care by opponents of genetically engineering. It was a simple science experiment. A young assistant professor of entomology at Cornell University named John Losey had been quietly dusting leaves of the milkweed plant with pollen from Bt corn, then feeding these leaves to caterpillars. Losey hadn't picked just any caterpillars; he was experimenting with larvae of the resplendent Monarch butterfly. Activists from Greenpeace or the Union of Concerned Scientists could not have crafted anything more perfect for their cause than Losey's short article which appeared in the scientific journal *Nature* on May 19: "Transgenic Pollen Harms Monarch Larvae."

Losey reported that nearly half his caterpillars died when they were fed milkweed leaves covered with Bt pollen. By contrast, there were no casualties among caterpillars feeding on leaves dusted with pollen from conventional corn. "These results have potentially profound implications for the conservation of monarch butterflies," Losey wrote. Monarch larvae eat only milkweed leaves, and in the summer milkweed coexists with fields of corn across vast stretches of the northern United States and southern Canada. Many larvae might be exposed to pollen from Bt corn plants. Genetically engineered corn, Losey suggested, might be killing off one of America's favorite insects.

The study, as Losey took pains to explain in interviews with the media, didn't prove anything by itself. His results came from laboratory experiments, under artificial conditions. He didn't know how prevalent milkweed plants really were in cornfields or whether caterpillars, if given a chance to roam, would avoid leaves covered with pollen that would kill them. Yet no journalist could possibly ignore this study. It was the sort of dramatic result, visually arresting and easily communicated, that science rarely delivers. What's more, it

represented a classic, even mythic, story about the unintended consequences of technological hubris. The weekly meeting of the science
desk at National Public Radio was typical.

"So what do we have in *Nature* this week?"

At the far end of the table, a grinning reporter waves a press release in the air: "Bt corn kills Monarch butterflies!"

Stories ran in newspapers from coast to coast and on national television. The *New York Times* put a picture of the Monarch on its
front page and called it the "Bambi of the insect world." On National Public Radio the butterfly was "the Elvis of insects," referring
to the butterfly's gaudy garb. It was a story that grabbed the public's
attention and fixed in many minds an impression of risk and danger
linked to genetically engineered crops.

Critics of biotechnology, seizing a priceless opportunity, pounded
home the point: *Nobody knew this! What other surprises will genetic engineering spring on us?* As a group of environmentalists put
it in a letter to the Environmental Protection Agency: "*One cannot
help but wonder what other, perhaps less obvious, environmental
impacts of genetically engineered crops have been missed by the
EPA*" (italics in the original).

More than anything, John Losey's paper unlocked a door.
Through that door marched an entire cast of characters, all the issues that had been raised during the previous decade of debate over
genetically engineered crops: Gene flow and "superweeds"; corporate domination of agriculture, patents on genes, and the Terminator; and the risks of the unnatural and the unknowable in the genetic
makeup of plants.

JOHN LOSEY didn't set out to bring down genetic engineering, although, like most young entomologists, he's no great fan of pesticides, including pesticidal plants like Bt corn. Even "pests," after all,
play a role in thriving ecosystems, and most modern entomologists
feel, deep down, that efforts to eradicate them are sure to backfire.

Losey mainly wanted to keep his job. His three immediate prede-
cessors in the entomology department at Cornell all had been denied
tenure, forcing them to leave the university. Losey himself will be
"up for tenure" in 2004. Like any young scientist, he needed to raise

money for his research and publish his results in the most prestigious journals possible, or perish.

He believed—indeed, he needed to believe—that his experiments were so important that they should appear in *Science* or *Nature*, the two journals that represent the pinnacle of scientific recognition. Many, probably most, of his colleagues disagreed. They found the results of his work unsurprising. *Of course Monarch caterpillars die if you force them to eat Bt pollen*, they protested. *But how much pollen would they really be exposed to in the real world, and how much would they choose to consume? Answer that, and we might be interested!*

"You don't have a story here," said Anthony Shelton, a senior colleague of Losey's at Cornell. But Losey persevered. He submitted the paper to *Science*, which rejected it. Next, Losey tried *Nature*, which is headquartered in London. Even cloistered editors at scientific journals are shaped by their surroundings, and *Nature*'s editors were surrounded at that moment by a raging furor about genetically engineered crops. They were more inclined to see the significance of Losey's work and accepted it, in abbreviated form, for publication.

Losey's triumph came accompanied by great peril. He got a call from a scientist at Monsanto, then one from Novartis. The companies that had pioneered the Bt corn business wished to visit him to discuss the *Nature* paper.

The meeting took all day. In the morning, Losey and his two coauthors, both relatively junior members of the Cornell research staff, presented their work. In the afternoon, Losey met privately for three hours with Novartis's emissary, Jeff Stein.

"I expressed my professional concerns to John," says Stein. He reiterated the same criticisms that Losey had heard from colleagues, including Anthony Shelton. Losey's caterpillars didn't really have a choice; they had been forced to eat Bt pollen or starve, whereas caterpillars in the wild might crawl to different parts of a milkweed plant, such as lower leaves that were somewhat shielded from pollen. Stein "took great issue" with Losey's proclamation of potential widespread harm to Monarchs, considering that Losey's paper contained no evidence on the actual exposure of monarch larvae in the field. Stein urged Losey to consider the potential damage that his paper might cause. Europe was already in flames over genetic engineering, he reminded Losey. The Monarch had a cultlike following; it was perhaps the most charismatic insect on the continent. A paper that predicted its doom at the hands of genetic engineering could be "a trigger" to a similar reaction in the United States.

The Novartis representative also suggested that Losey might be endangering his own career. "I asked him who he was trying to reach with this paper—his scientific peers or the media?" Losey's peers, Stein suggested, would be unimpressed by this paper and would hold him responsible for any ensuing public outcry.

In the aftermath of the paper's publication, Losey did come under vicious attack rooted partly in professional disagreements and partly in personal rivalry. Scientists who'd been studying caterpillars when John Losey was still in diapers resented the sudden fame of this lowly assistant professor as well as the implication that they'd ignored obvious dangers posed by Bt corn. "We've had to clean up your mess," said one scientist to Losey as both shared a podium at an annual meeting of the American Entomological Society.

Anthony Shelton, Losey's more senior colleague at Cornell, penned a commentary comparing Losey's study to the character Rumor, who appears in one of William Shakespeare's plays "stuffing the ears of men with false reports." When it was suggested to Shelton that the fame Losey acquired through his study might still, in the long run, be good for his career, Shelton paused before replying. "We'll just have to see," he said with a threatening undertone.

Losey sometimes sounded frightened and sometimes defiant in the midst of the controversy he'd started. He promised to follow the advice of his colleagues and "stick to the science." He agreed that his study raised questions that could only be answered by scientists observing Monarch larvae in actual corn fields. But when a coalition of biotech companies began passing out millions of dollars to a group of academic researchers, funding such studies, Losey refused to participate, questioning the credibility of studies funded by industry.

The ensuing frenzy of research into the fate of Monarch larvae and the battles over interpretation of that research gradually devolved into farce, but few of those involved could appreciate the humor of it all. They were all too busy stabbing each other in the back or managing the media's coverage of scientific experiments.

Within weeks of Losey's article, entomologists swarmed into corn-fields across North America, setting out their insect traps, counting grains of pollen on milkweed leaves, and observing the life cycle of Monarch larvae. Some of what they saw vindicated the concerns of Losey's article. Pollen from Bt corn could, in fact, kill Monarch larvae. But the scientists also found that larvae wouldn't normally encounter a lethal dose of pollen except on milkweed plants that were within three feet of a Bt cornfield. They also discovered that not all Bt corn affected caterpillars in the same way. One type of Bt gene, known as Event 176 and contained in corn from Novartis, produced a much larger toxic dose in its pollen than other Bt corn. Fortunately for Monarchs, Event 176 only accounted for a small and shrinking share (about 2 percent in 2000) of the corn crop. (According to the data from one researcher, Monarch larvae actually grew *better* in the presence of low to moderate amounts of pollen from the most common type of Bt corn. The pollen apparently was a good source of protein.)

Executives at Monsanto, in particular, fell over each other in efforts to publicize these results. In November 1999, when the researchers planned a quiet meeting near Chicago to share their preliminary data, the industry's public relations officials organized a conference call with reporters the day before the conference. During the meeting, the Biotechnology Industry Organization issued a press release declaring "no harm to monarch butterflies" from Bt corn. Environmentalists were apoplectic.

Many months later, the opponents of biotechnology paid the industry back in kind. A group of entomologists at Iowa State University published results of an experiment in which larvae were placed on milkweed leaves that had been collected from plants near Bt corn fields. Roughly 20 percent of the larvae died. The study claimed to be the "first evidence" that Monarch larvae die when exposed to Bt corn under field conditions.

In fact, some of the evidence was misleading. For the experiment in which 20 percent of Monarch larvae died, the scientists had employed pollen from corn plants containing Novartis's Bt gene, Event 176, containing 40 to 50 times as much Bt toxin as pollen from other, more prevalent, types of Bt corn. This result thus drastically overstated the potential effect of the nation's Bt corn crop.

The study was published in a journal that reporters rarely would read, but environmental groups immediately began faxing it to as many journalists as possible. It received wide coverage in the media, comparable to the attention the industry-sponsored conference on the Monarch attracted in Chicago, reaffirming in the public's mind the idea that genetic engineering was indeed a threat to one of America's most beloved wild creatures.

The dust finally started to clear in the fall of 2001, more than two years after Losey's original paper, when a large group of scientists finally published half a dozen carefully vetted reports. The threat posed by Bt corn to the Monarch butterfly, they concluded, was "negligible."

INSPIRED BY successes on foreign shores and catalyzed by an accident of science, tired remnants of the American movement against genetic engineering stirred into life. The issue was hot. Foundations opened their checkbooks. Long-dormant networks buzzed with activity. In July, dozens of activists gathered in Bolinas, California, to discuss what they might do. Marc Lappe, a longtime critic of agribusiness, recalls the gathering's "spiritual" atmosphere, infused with concern over the fate of the planet's genetic heritage. A second, smaller meeting with activists from around the world, including Greenpeace's Benny Härlin, took place a few months later at a camp in the Adirondack Mountains. People emerged from those meetings with renewed energy, direction, and in some cases funding for a fresh wave of protest against genetic engineering in agriculture.

A series of full-page ads in major newspapers across the country set the tone and laid out the major themes of the campaign. The first, bearing the headline "WHO PLAYS GOD IN THE 21ST CENTURY?" proclaimed the "gravest moral, social, and ecological crises in history." Another—"UNLABELED, UNTESTED ... AND YOU'RE EATING IT"—announced that "in secret, genetically engineered foods are showing up on American grocery shelves. A third—"GENETIC ROULETTE"—decried the "grave risk of destructive—

and irreversible—genetic pollution," accompanied by a portrait of the Monarch butterfly.

Just as in Europe, the motivations of the campaign's core activists differed markedly from their most visible public arguments. Lappe, who drafted the "Pacific Declaration" that emerged from the Bolinas Meeting, was stirred into action in large part by Monsanto's control over the genetic resources of agriculture through its growing power in the seed industry. Others wanted to halt violations of "the genetic integrity of natural species," as the Pacific Declaration put it, or assert democratic control over biotechnology, wresting it from the profit-seeking hands of private companies.

But the most politically savvy of the activists understood that their campaign would rise and fall not on *their* fears, but on the moods and passions of the American public. So, like any company introducing a new product, they rolled out the tools of market research, including focus groups and polls. The answer was clear, says Christina Desser, who coordinated an "affinity group" on biotechnology for a large group of environmental funders. "Human health and personal safety. That's what really seems to move people."

Those questions became the campaign's centerpiece, emblazoned, for example, across envelopes sent out by Friends of the Earth: "HOW SAFE IS THE FOOD YOU EAT? (The answer is inside—and it may startle you!)." In the enclosed letter, the group's president wrote, with underlined emphasis, that *"If deadly toxins that kill butterflies are being introduced into our food supply, what effect are these toxins having on your and your family? . . . The scary answer is that no one really knows."*

The campaign took off with remarkable speed. Within a certain part of the American political spectrum, among those who bought organic food and voted for Ralph Nader, opposition to genetic engineering already existed; it merely had to be kicked into motion to become a political force. City councils took up resolutions banning genetically engineered foods from school lunch programs. Major food companies faced shareholder initiatives opposing any participation in genetic engineering. Lawmakers in the U.S. Congress and in more than a dozen states considered proposals either to restrict the use of genetically engineered food or at least to label all foods containing such ingredients. And the issue rode a new wave of political activism on college campuses, aimed at fighting free trade and corporate power worldwide. When these "antiglobalization" protesters shut down a meeting of the World Trade Organization in Seattle in December 1999, opponents of genetic engineering took their place beside marching steelworkers, religious activists demanding cancellation of poor countries' debt, and defenders of tropical forests.

For scientist activists like Rebecca Goldburg and Margaret Mellon (from the Environmental Defense Fund and the Union of Concerned Scientists, respectively), the moment of triumph was mixed with self-doubt. They had carried the banner of the antibiotech movement for over a decade. Here, finally, was the long-sought social movement in opposition to biotechnology, yet the movement had also passed them by. Within the campaign, Goldburg, Mellon, and their ilk were sometimes dismissed as "wonkish," elitist, and ineffectual. The day of the campaigners had arrived, and, like most campaigns, this one was filled with lurid, half-true accusations and broad-brush depictions of evil on the opposing side.

Margaret Mellon, her long hair turning gray, confessed that recent events had been an education. "The Europeans taught us that you can mobilize people without a shred of evidence [regarding actual harm to human health], just based on this precautionary idea," she mused one day in her office. She also wondered quietly whether she had a duty, as a scientist, to distance herself publicly from some of the campaign's more egregious fear mongering.

Rebecca Goldburg found herself questioning her "science-based" approach. "I've become radicalized to some degree," she said, and persuaded that facts were not as compelling as she'd hoped. Companies like Monsanto and Novartis didn't rely so much on science as on the tools of politics: money, political connections, and public relations. Recent history showed that environmentalists had to do the same. "Most of the gains that the environmental community has experienced recently have come from the fairly radical work of Greenpeace in Europe."

Robert Colwell, an ecologist who'd been among the most prominent scientists demanding regulation of transgenic crops in the mid-

1980s, stopped to peruse antibiotech brochures that were tacked up on a bulletin board in his local organic food store in Connecticut. Reading them, Colwell felt a little "weird." He was happy to see opposition to genetically engineered crops, "but I'd kind of like it to be for the right reasons."

For a time, the campaign swept from victory to victory. Titans of the food industry renounced the use of genetically engineered ingredients. All it took, in some cases, was a press conference at which activists displayed the results of laboratory tests showing the presence of exotic DNA in some packaged food bearing the company's hallowed brand. Heinz and Gerber promised not to use genetically engineered ingredients in their baby food. Frito-Lay told its corn suppliers not to grow Bt corn. Japanese brewers, including Sapporo and Kirin, renounced the use of genetically engineered grain.

Commercial prospects for two minor genetically engineered crops—Monsanto's Bt potatoes and Novartis's Bt sweet corn—crashed and burned. These were not crops from which Monsanto or Novartis expected large commercial returns; they occupy hundreds of thousands, not millions, of acres, and Monsanto had discovered that the potato seed business, in particular, is complicated and financially unrewarding. Yet these crops, along with cotton, offered the most convincing environmental benefits of all genetically engineered crops. The Bt gene in both cases eliminated substantial spraying of insecticides. Sweet corn, for example, covers only one percent of America's corn acres, yet it accounts for 70 percent of all insecticides that farmers spray on those fields. Commercial growers of sweet corn normally spray their fields with insecticides five or six times during a growing season. Bt sweet corn, by contrast, requires only one spraying. Moreover, because sweet corn is harvested before the insect larvae are mature, insects are unlikely to develop resistance.

This was of little concern to food companies. Leading producers of french fries, such as McDonald's and McCain's, announced that they no longer would accept shipments of Bt potatoes, effectively killing the business. Many sweet corn growers, meanwhile, decided that they simply could not take the risk that consumers would refuse to eat genetically modified corn-on-the-cob. They canceled their orders of Bt seed and went back to spraying.

And on the radical fringe of the movement, under cover of darkness, bands of activists cut through fences, broke locks, and crept into university and corporate research stations in San Diego, Berkeley, and Davis, California, as well as other sites in Michigan, Minnesota, and Maine. Such direct action had become a standard feature of every strong movement against genetic engineering of plants. It had occurred in Germany and the Netherlands during the early 1990s, and again in Britain in 1998 and 1999. Fields were hard to protect, and the act of ripping plants out of the ground in order to rid the earth of these "unnatural" organisms carried a powerful symbolism.

Some of these actions certainly hurt the movement more than they helped. When the Earth Liberation Front set fire to the office of Catherine Ives in Michigan State University's Agriculture Hall on New Year's eve of 1999, it introduced the news media to Ives, a passionate and articulate defender of agricultural biotechnology. Since many of the attacks were aimed at university research, they converted some academic scientists, previously skeptical observers of the battle, into probiotechnology partisans. But the actions also served to publicize the issue and intensify the tension and drama surrounding it.

MOST OMINOUS from Monsanto's point of view were signs that the forces of the market, like a shifting tide, were turning against genetically engineered crops. The signals came first in the form of ambiguously worded announcements from the nation's leading processor of grain, Archer Daniels Midland.

ADM, along with a few other large grain-handling firms, dominates the worldwide trade in soybeans and corn. These companies preside over the flood of grain that flows out of America's heartland every year, directing some of that flood directly to foreign markets while processing a portion of it into everything from engine fuel to food ingredients.

The waves of grain follow well-worn stream beds, from farm to local grain elevators that buy the harvest, store it in bins, and ship it by rail car to processing plants or to the tall concrete silos of grain terminals along the Great Lakes or the Mississippi River. Barges carry more than a thousand tons of grain apiece down the Mississippi to the Gulf of Mexico. Forty such barges carry enough to fill the largest ocean-going vessels bound for such foreign destinations as the port of Rotterdam in the Netherlands.

The grain is bought and sold in distant markets, unseen by buyer and seller alike. The system works with astounding efficiency because all the grain is treated as a single commodity. Buyers and sellers alike assume that every ton of soybeans is like every other, each one containing a standard package of starch, oil, and protein.

When consumers in Europe began rejecting specific bits of DNA in some of that grain, they challenged the "commodity system," throwing the grain traders, including ADM, into disarray. The traders had two choices, neither of them very attractive. They could try to set up a separate, small, and expensive river of grain that contained no objectionable bits of genetically altered DNA to satisfy European consumers. Or they could try to maintain the great, unified river of grain and drive genetically engineered crops from the market. In practice the grain traders and processors tried to do a bit of both.

Corn shoots were barely emerging from the ground in Illinois and Iowa when ADM announced that, when harvest time came, it would not accept some types of genetically engineered corn at its elevators. These were the varieties containing genes that the Europeans had refused to approve, principally Roundup Ready varieties of corn. These varieties didn't account for a large portion of the corn crop, but ADM's announcement still was an enormous shock. Confusion filled the coffee shops of the Midwest. Never before had consumers in distant lands cared what sort of seeds an American farmer planted.

Farmers would have been even more confused and angry had they known that ADM's announcement would turn out to be largely a charade devoid of any real consequences. When harvest time came, no one actually would check at elevators to see if a farmer's corn crop contained these "unapproved varieties," because none of that grain was headed toward Europe anyway. U.S. exports of unprocessed corn to Europe had halted a year earlier, when the first of these unapproved varieties came on the market. ADM was "posturing" for the benefit of its European customers, says Kimball Nill at the American Soybean Association. "It didn't cost them anything, and they could say to the Europeans: 'Look, we're on your side. We're *trying* to supply GMO-free grain.'" There is a more charitable interpretation. ADM may have been preparing for the possibility that Europe would suddenly broaden its regulations to cover not just raw corn but also processed products like corn starch and corn gluten. (Huge quantities of corn gluten derived from Roundup Ready corn, for instance, continued to flow to Europe for use in animal feed.) Such a step, however, never occurred.

In late August, as harvest time approached, ADM sent another, more powerful shock through American farming communities. "Some of our customers are requesting and making their purchases based upon the genetic origin of the crops used to manufacture their products," the company wrote in a letter to many of its grain suppliers. "We encourage you as our supplier to segregate non-genetically enhanced crops to preserve their identity."

Within days, word of this letter spread to farmers, turning their confusion into stomach-churning fear. In plain speech, ADM had confirmed the predictions of Deutsche Bank's analysts. ADM's customers didn't want genetically engineered crops; as a consequence, this part of the harvest probably would bring a lower price. It was every farmer's nightmare: a harvest that couldn't be sold for a decent price, or at all. But the crops were in the ground. There was nothing to be done except wait and worry.

Harvest arrived, and for almost all farmers the worries evaporated. When trucks rolled into almost every Midwestern grain elevator, no one bothered to ask the driver if he was hauling Roundup Ready soybeans or Bt corn. Elevator operators simply stuck in a probe, as they always had, and checked the load's grain size, moisture, and contamination with weeds and dirt. Barges of soybeans and corn continued flowing down the Mississippi to the great ocean terminals on the Gulf of Mexico.

"But you know, some elevators actually fell for it!" says the American Soybean Association's Kimball Nill. A few elevators took ADM at its word. Anticipating hot demand and rising prices for non–genetically modified (or "non-GM") soybeans or corn, they tried diligently to keep such grain separate from the genetically engineered varieties. But they couldn't do it perfectly. The truckloads of non-GM soybeans that farmers brought in often had a few Roundup Ready beans as well and often more than a few. So these elevators ended up with bins full of soybeans that were merely 90 percent free of genetic engineering. Nobody, it turned out, was willing to pay extra for *that*. The Europeans wanted their beans completely free of foreign DNA.

As the operators of these grain elevators waited for a buyer, they sometimes called Kimball Nill, looking for advice. "They sounded sadder and sadder and sadder," says Nill. "Eventually they sold those soybeans just as standard Number 2 beans. It cost them tens of thousands of dollars in time and effort. And you know what it cost ADM? Not a dime."

The great GM scare of 1999 turned out to be far less significant than advertised, and few knew the reasons why. It was a confounding riddle: If the entire European continent, the largest single market in the world, was eating only non–genetically engineered food, why didn't American farmers notice any shift in demand for their products?

PART OF the answer to this riddle lies in the Red River Valley along the border of Minnesota and North Dakota. This is about as far north as you can go and still grow soybeans in North America. Farmers here grow varieties that have been bred to produce beans quickly, before the first killing frosts of early autumn. When Roundup Ready soybeans first came on the market in 1996, seed companies hadn't yet bred the Roundup Ready gene into such varieties. So for a year or two soybeans in the Red River Valley were practically untouched by genetic engineering.

That caught the attention of a Norwegian grain processor named Denofa. Already in 1996 several Scandinavian countries had passed laws requiring food retailers to label any food containing genetically modified ingredients, so food companies in these countries were looking for supplies of grain that were free of any artificially inserted genes.

A few smaller grain handlers, such as Cenex/Harvest States in Minnesota, saw an opportunity for profits, linking GM-free fields of the Red River Valley with GM-free stores of Scandinavia. Rail cars hauled the grain from country elevators to a terminal in Duluth, at the western end of Lake Superior, where it was poured into the cargo holds of ships that were small enough to navigate inland waterways yet large enough to handle the open ocean. These vessels steamed through the Great Lakes, squeezed through the Welland Canal, which bypasses Niagara Falls, and continued down the St. Lawrence River and across the Atlantic to Denofa's soybean-crushing plants in Norway.

Denofa paid extra for their GM-free beans, but in the first years, farmers in the Red River Valley didn't see any of that money. Later, when Roundup Ready soybeans did go on sale in the Red River valley, Cenex/Harvest States offered to pay an extra ten cents per bushel to farmers who agreed to plant only conventional soybeans and haul their harvest to special GM-free elevators.

So in the spring of 1999, when Tom Clayton from the British food chain Marks and Spencer began the search for ingredients that weren't genetically engineered, he quickly stumbled onto Denofa's stream of GM-free soybean products. He and his fellow food retailers discovered similar opportunities in Brazil, where Roundup Ready soybeans weren't yet legal to plant. "There's [non-GM] channels everywhere. We found them quite readily and easily," says Clayton.

They did discover to their dismay that some of these channels weren't quite as pure as promised. Even after stores went GM-free, tests conducted by environmental groups turned up persistent traces of genetic engineering. The problem began at the source with contamination of seeds. Keeping particular varieties separate in the seed production process had never before been of crucial importance; it wasn't considered a problem if 2 or 3 percent of the seeds in a bag were of some variety other than the one on the label. Corn was a particular problem because ears of conventional corn in one field could easily be fertilized by pollen from genetically engineered plants across the road. Even in the case of soybeans, industry insiders say that shiploads from Brazil certified as GM-free sometimes turned out not to be. Thousands of farmers in southern Brazil had begun planting genetically engineered soybeans that were purchased on the black market from neighboring Argentina.

In the United States, the search for GM-free soybeans produced one particularly ironic result: A joint venture between ADM and DuPont began selling a variety of soybeans that had been altered in the laboratory in such a way that it could withstand sprays of one of DuPont's herbicides, called Synchrony. But these soybeans were not considered "genetically modified," because no new gene had been imported from another organism. Instead, genes had been altered *within* the plant by soaking hundreds of thousands of soybeans in chemicals that induced random genetic mutations. A few of those random mutations, it turned out, resulted in a plant that could tolerate DuPont's herbicide. So consumers who wished to avoid the Roundup Ready gene were supplied with another type of herbicide-tolerant soybean instead. DuPont turned the herbicide tolerance trait into a selling point. These soybeans, the company argued, were guaranteed to be free of contamination from genetically modified varieties, because all Roundup Ready soybeans growing in a farmer's field would be killed when the field was sprayed with Synchrony. DuPont sold large quantities of these soybeans to Japan, where a booming market for GM-free tofu emerged during 1999.

These streams of GM-free soy products were modest in size, but they turned out to be adequate to satisfy demand in Europe, Japan, and a few other countries. Herein lay the second answer to the great GM riddle of 1999: It didn't take all that much to satisfy the portion of the market that cared, because the bulk of the soybean and corn harvest never did go into food for humans; it fed animals. Consumer protests in Europe blocked a small part of the market, while vast quantities of genetically engineered soy meal and corn gluten continued to flow to pig and chicken farms across the continent.

During the fall of 1999 the European arm of Greenpeace turned its weapons toward this market as well. "TAKE THE GM OUT OF ANIMAL FEED," it proclaimed on posters and bumper stickers. Activists boarded and blocked cargo ships en route to European harbors and chained themselves to the gates of a Cargill plant in Spain. Greenpeace, along with other anti-GM campaigners, called on consumers to contact food retailers and demand that these stores sell only meat and eggs from animals fed a GM-free diet. As Benny Härlin put it: "Since we are against the release of GMOs, it is important to put pressure—market pressure—on their use as animal feed."

This time, however, it was harder to get the public's attention. Some food retailers promised to sell meat and eggs from animals that were fed no genetically engineered ingredients; others decided to ignore the protests. European consumers didn't seem highly motivated by Greenpeace's ultimate goal of eliminating the threat that GMOs might pose to agricultural areas of the United States. Most seemed content to let the Americans face the risks of their own genetically engineered crops.

THE ANTI-GMO movement began to lose its most powerful motivation and organizing tool in the fall of 1999. Monsanto, the face of the enemy, no longer seemed quite so fearsome and all-powerful; indeed, it appeared wounded, floundering, and sometimes even apologetic.

Investors who once outbid each other for the right to jump aboard Monsanto's biotech bandwagon now turned up their noses and walked away. Amid a rousing bull market on Wall Street, Monsanto's stock stagnated. Financial analysts pointed out that Monsanto's pharmaceutical business alone would justify the company's stock price, meaning that investors were willing to pay nothing at all for Monsanto's entire agricultural business, including seeds and Roundup. Several of them urged Robert Shapiro to break up his "life sciences" company, separating its attractive pharmaceutical business from its now-disreputable agricultural ventures. Shapiro continued searching for a new partner.

Monsanto's executives abandoned, for the time being, dreams of further conquest. Instead they focused simply on limiting further damage. Several of them decided to hoist a white flag and try to arrange a cease-fire with the company's most implacable critics.

They decided to pry the Terminator gene, that public relations albatross, off the company's neck, announcing that Monsanto would make no commercial use of it. And several of the company's top executives traveled to Europe for meetings with such opponents as the British Soil Association, Friends of the Earth, and Greenpeace. The meeting with the Soil Association took place on September 9, 1999, in a small room at the elegant Grosvenor House Hotel in London. Hendrik Verfaillie, the mild-mannered Belgian who was Shapiro's second-in-command, told Patrick Holden of the Soil Association that "Monsanto was in trouble and had come to recognize that its faith in the ultimate sustainability and benefits to mankind of their technology was not shared universally." (This is according to notes of the meeting recorded by another leader of the Soil Association.) Verfaillie said that "they had been humbled by this experience, and the purpose of their mission was to find how they had got it wrong so that they could start to put things right."

As Holden explained in detail the reasons why the Soil Association had campaigned so vigorously against GM foods, the Monsanto representatives were "visibly affected," Holden said. "The impression I got was that they were deeply disturbed by what we said. You could see that the ideas were resonating with them personally as human beings." Holden recalls one of the visitors from St. Louis saying that she had always believed that Monsanto's genetically engineered crops were a contribution to sustainable agriculture, and that this was the first time she'd heard that argument challenged. "You could see it was a serious moment for them," Holden said.

The campaign of conciliation reached its high point in October when Robert Shapiro himself addressed a Greenpeace conference in London. Initially Monsanto executives had treated Greenpeace's invitation as a joke. One executive sent out an April Fool's e-mail announcing that Shapiro would accept the invitation. A senior vice president of the company saw a glimmer of genius in the joke, and Shapiro's acceptance was soon winging its way back to London. The wisdom of this decision came under repeated, agonizing debate within Monsanto, but no one could think of a face-saving way to back out. In the end, Shapiro appeared via video link rather than in person.

In his speech, Shapiro, too, admitted mistakes: Monsanto was so convinced of its technology's value that it had "forgotten to listen," said the Monsanto CEO, and it had regarded those with opposing points of view as "wrong or at best misguided." Monsanto still believed in the technology, but the company now was ready to listen to its critics, Shapiro said.

Peter Melchett, the leader of Greenpeace's British organization, listened to Shapiro's speech and was relieved. Shapiro hadn't announced anything earthshaking, so Melchett didn't need to revise his prepared response. That response showed no mercy toward Monsanto's newly repentant CEO. "You behave not as a company bringing life and hope but as bullies trying to force your products on us. You sue those who oppose you and try and injunct them and anyone they've been in contact with, suppressing dissent," said Melchett. Greenpeace would be glad to cooperate with Monsanto, Melchett said, but only if the company agreed to stop producing GM crops and pesticides and the patenting of living things.

Shapiro's physical appearance and body language on that day left a more vivid impression than his words. The Monsanto CEO hadn't been feeling well. On the giant screen in front of the Greenpeace gathering he appeared wan and uncomfortable or, as Melchett put it later, "suitably depressed." Shapiro's best line of the day even got a sympathetic laugh from the audience: "If I'm a bully," he remarked plaintively, "I don't feel like a very successful bully."

A few months later, Monsanto abandoned the attempt to acquire a dominant position in the cotton business, withdrawing its offer to buy the Delta and Pine Land Company. Monsanto blamed federal antitrust regulators for imposing onerous conditions on the sale. Government officials had demanded, for instance, that Monsanto give competing cottonseed companies rights to some of its patents, which Monsanto was loathe to do. Others suspected that Monsanto simply decided to back out of the deal and used antitrust obstacles as a convenient excuse. This at any rate was Delta and Pine Land's view. The cottonseed company sued Monsanto for breach of contract and demanded damages of at least $1 billion. Monsanto's seed empire, once so imposing, was shrinking and squabbling.

Finally, just a few days before Christmas 1999, Shapiro succeeded in negotiating his exit from the stage. The Monsanto CEO announced that he'd finally found Monsanto's long-sought partner: Pharmacia, originally a Swedish company, now based in New Jersey. The combined company would simply be called Pharmacia, and when the merger was complete, Robert Shapiro would retire. Yet Monsanto, in another form, would live on. Pharmacia planned to turn Monsanto's agricultural businesses into an autonomous company, based in St. Louis with its own board of directors, in which Pharmacia would be the majority shareholder. (The partial spin-off was carried out in October 2000.) Some speculated that this was merely a preliminary step toward selling it outright to another company.

The day after the merger plans were announced, employees in Monsanto's St. Louis headquarters crowded into the building's cafeteria for a meeting with Shapiro's second-in-command, Hendrik Verfaillie. "We simply have to be bigger," Verfaillie told them. He said he was excited by the combined company's prospects. But he also admitted that the merger was the end of Shapiro's vision of a "life sciences" company. "I have a mix of feelings. There is a fair amount of sadness," he admitted. "I followed Bob, and I was willing to break my back to get Bob's vision to happen—the vision of food, health, and hope. I really would have liked to pursue it, but doing it on our own would have been too risky."

Monsanto the world-devouring giant had shrunk into the chastened subsidiary of a company dominated by, of all people, Swedes. The proud, presumptuous words "Food—Health—Hope" vanished from its corporate signature. And the debate over biotechnology started to become, once again, an argument over technology and economics, not a crusade against the personality and ambitions of one overweening American company.

# 17

## Global Claims

**A** visitor from another planet eavesdropping on defenders of genetic engineering during the summer of 2000 might have come to the conclusion that it was a technology developed mainly to feed the world's poor and malnourished.

The claim that biotechnology *could* do so became a battle cry, an assertion of the virtue and necessity of technological progress. Raymond Rodriguez, founder of a small biotech company called Applied Phytologics in Davis, California, called his critics "political narcissists," placing their personal aesthetic wishes ahead of the planet's needs. "We're talking about the food security of the world," he said. "When people talk about crimes against humanity—wouldn't it be a crime if political narcissism delayed things to the point where there were major food shortages in the Third World?"

The extraterrestrial visitor might even have become convinced that the most successful genetically engineered plant on Planet Earth was not Roundup Ready soybeans or Bt corn but a curiously yellow-tinted strain of rice, a grain created in the hope that it might save lives.

"Golden rice," as it came to be called, contained genes imported from daffodil plants and from various bacteria. The genes produced beta-carotene, the substance that makes carrots orange and supplies the body with vitamin A. The plants were a German-Swiss coproduction. Peter Beyer at the University of Freiburg had isolated the genes, and Ingo Potrykus at the Swiss Institute of Technology in Zurich had inserted them into rice plants. Funding for the venture came from the Rockefeller Foundation. (Various European governments contributed large amounts as well.)

The Rockefeller Foundation supported the venture, despite doubts about its chances for success, because of its potential in the battle against vitamin A deficiency, a scourge of the developing world. Across much of Asia, people rely heavily on a few staple grains—above all, rice—for nourishment. Such crops contain little beta-carotene. As a result, millions of pregnant women suffer hemorrhages, millions of children die or suffer impairment in their mental and physical development, and hundreds of thousands go blind. If Potrykus and his collaborators could convert rice into a source of vitamin A, thought officials at the Rockefeller Foundation, it could benefit vast numbers of people. This transformation would be simpler and more feasible, they thought, than persuading people to grow and eat different crops.

Potrykus spent most of the 1990s trying to blast Beyer's assembly of genes into rice, with only partial success. In 1998 a Chinese researcher in Potrykus's laboratory, Xudong Ye, took over, bringing fresh energy and a new scientific approach. Triumph followed early the following year: the first grains of yellow rice. The researchers submitted their work to the journal *Nature*, which summarily rejected it. Potrykus later wrote darkly that "we got the impression that *Nature* was more interested in cases which would rather question instead of support the value of genetic engineering technology."

Instead, Potrykus's triumph was introduced at a press conference during an international botanical congress in St. Louis in August of 1999. There was little public reaction. Supporters of genetic engineering then lobbied for publication of the research in the other leading scientific journal, *Science,* where it appeared early the following year. By that time, the political situation, especially in the United States, had changed. Genetically engineered food was under full-throated assault, and defenders of biotechnology seized upon this innovation as if it were a rope thrown to drowning sailors.

"Golden rice" became the poster child for the potential of genetic engineering. It graced the cover of *Time* and the pages of major newspapers. No major speech in favor of biotechnology failed to mention it.

It was more symbol, in fact, than practical reality. (In this respect "golden rice" mirrored the "Terminator" gene.) The first grains of golden rice produced barely enough vitamin A to make a difference in anyone's health. Years of testing lay ahead to resolve all the potential safety issues. In addition, no one could be certain that rice consumers really would consent to eat the odd-colored grain, especially if people came to regard it as food for poor people. (Yellow-grained corn, for instance, is considered unfit for human consumption in much of the world. People would get more vitamin A by eating it, but no one seriously suggests this as a solution to the problem.) Yet "golden rice," as a symbol, carried a potent message: *If you stop genetic engineering, you're taking better food away from people who need it.*

The Rockefeller Foundation's Gary Toenniessen, no particular friend of the biotechnology industry, found the whole saga slightly humorous. He'd sponsored Potrykus's work because no private company had showed any interest in rice. Now those companies were leading his cheering section. "To some extent, we're being used," Toenniessen mused. "On the other hand, I think that there's a great chance that it'll be a product with a significant impact for good."

THE FATE of the world's poorest farmers certainly did not weigh heavily on the minds of Monsanto's executives as they dove into biotechnology during the 1980s. Outsiders brought those concerns to the company's front door. Three names stand out: Gary Toenniessen, Luis Herrera-Estrella, and Clive James.

Toenniessen, from his office at the Rockefeller Foundation, monitored the origins of biotechnology during the 1980s. The Rockefeller Foundation had a long history of concern with global agriculture. It had been among the sponsors of the so-called "Green Revolution"— the breeding of new, short-stemmed, highly productive varieties of rice and wheat which spread across much of Asia during the 1960s and 1970s. Toenniessen wondered if advances in biotechnology might precipitate yet another revolution and another surge in food production. In the early 1980s he visited leading laboratories in academia and industry and came to a disturbing conclusion: Almost none of the researchers were studying rice, the plant on which the world's poor depend most. Toenniessen saw a gulf opening between the capabilities of private biotechnology companies, on the one side, and the needs of the world's population, on the other.

Luis Herrera-Estrella had a foot on both sides of that divide. As a researcher at the University of Ghent, in Belgium, he'd been among the pioneers in the genetic manipulation of plants. Many of his colleagues in Ghent had gone to work for Europe's most successful private venture in agricultural biotechnology, Plant Genetic Systems, which was located nearby, and several had attained great riches. Herrera-Estrella considered joining them but instead decided to return to his homeland of Mexico to work in a government-funded agricultural research institution. "I felt that, whatever I can do in plant biotechnology, it is better that I do it in Mexico. I've never regretted my decision," he says.

Clive James, meanwhile, was the former deputy director of the International Center for the Improvement of Wheat and Maize (CIM-MYT) in Mexico, one of the birthplaces of the Green Revolution. A native of Wales, with a Welshman's loquacity, he could hold forth for almost any length of time on the subject of Third World agriculture, then digress with equal enthusiasm into the subject of fine wines. No one was better at raising money for hot new ideas, and no idea in international agriculture was newer and hotter in the late 1980s than biotechnology.

Each of these men—the philanthropist, the scientist, and the deal maker—tried in his own way to bring the expensive, delicate, privately owned tools of biotechnology within the reach of those who could never, by themselves, have paid for them.

Toenniessen, with the substantial resources of the Rockefeller Foundation behind him, tried to build a public counterweight to private companies. In 1984, just a year after scientists in St. Louis and Ghent created the first transgenic plants, the foundation began pouring millions of dollars into a research program that ran parallel to efforts by private companies. While Monsanto and its competitors focused their research on corn, soybeans, and cotton, the Rockefeller Foundation paid researchers, most of them at universities, to explore the genetic nature of rice. The foundation also helped finance small research programs at several international research centers that are devoted to improving crops grown by "resource-poor" farmers. The best-known of these centers are CIMMYT and the International Rice Research Institute (IRRI) in the Philippines.

Clive James, meanwhile, felt that it made little sense to compete with the corporate world; its resources dwarfed those of the international agricultural research institutes as well as the efforts of university researchers. James decided to try enlisting companies as allies instead, persuading them to donate their tools and expertise to researchers working on crops grown by the poor.

James says he faced overwhelming skepticism. "Most people said, 'Well, when you deal with the private sector, there will be lots of positive reaction, but when you really get down to the bottom line—are they really prepared to donate the technology?—there will be excuses and it won't happen.' So we said, 'There's no point in arguing about it. It's a testable hypothesis.'" James set about looking for a project that would match the desires of a developing country with the capabilities of the biotech industry.

In 1990 James visited Gary Toenniessen at the Rockefeller Foundation and came away with the promise of funding for such a project. ("Clive is a good salesman," Toenniessen chuckles. "Whenever he comes here, I joke with the receptionist that she should lock up the safe and throw away the combination.") Toenniessen also suggested that James get in touch with Luis Herrera-Estrella, who by this time had returned to Mexico.

Herrera-Estrella proposed the perfect project: Virus-resistant potatoes. Viruses were a major problem for potato growers in Mexico, especially small farmers who couldn't afford to buy seed potatoes that were grown in special disease-free areas. It was a problem that genetic engineering could solve; a piece of the virus inserted into potato plants could act as a "vaccine" against the disease.

Herrera-Estrella pointed out that it would be a simple matter to ensure that their project would never take any sales away from Monsanto. The Mexican researchers could apply the technique only to traditional varieties of potatoes grown by small-scale subsistence farmers. Unlike corn or wheat, potatoes don't lend themselves easily to crossbreeding, so there was little risk that someone could transfer

Monsanto's gene illicitly into varieties grown by larger, commercial farmers. Those could remain a potential market for Monsanto if the company chose to pursue it. (Monsanto, in fact, hadn't bothered to make any commercial use of virus resistance. The potential commercial returns it offered were meager.)

In 1990, Luis Herrera-Estrella and Clive James flew to Monsanto's headquarters in St. Louis. They met with the godfather of plant biotechnology himself, Ernie Jaworski, who was enthusiastic about the project.

"Having talked to Luis, I just felt that we've got a lot of technology here, and it would be nice to share that with people and places that don't have a lot of wealth and technology," says Jaworski. There was another "subliminal" consideration, he says. As part of the project, the Rockefeller Foundation would fund efforts to set up regulatory institutions in Mexico to handle genetically engineered crops. The potato might thus smooth a path for other, more commercially valuable products emerging from Monsanto's laboratories.

Herrera-Estrella doesn't doubt Jaworski's humanitarian instincts. "Ernie was always very supportive," says the Mexican scientist. "Even before this, he came several times to our institute and wanted us to do some contract work for Monsanto, more to support us than to support Monsanto." But equally important for Monsanto, he says, was the project's public relations value. "The interest of Monsanto was, they were always claiming that genetic engineering would help solve the food problems of the world. This was a very good opportunity for them to show that this technology could indeed help a developing country."

Indeed, the project was so appealing that Jaworski decided to create another one. While visiting Washington, D.C., he called an official at the U.S. Agency for International Development (USAID), then walked over to the agency's headquarters and presented his idea. Virus resistance, he said, might also be useful in Africa. Monsanto would be willing to donate its expertise and technology if USAID could fund the rest of the project. Within a year, with money from USAID, a Kenyan scientist named Florence Wambugu arrived at Monsanto for two years of training. (Jaworski persuaded Monsanto to come up with the additional financial support necessary for

Wambugu to bring along her three children.) The Kenyan scientist began working on virus-resistant cassava plants, but cassava, a yam-like plant that's a staple crop in much of Africa, proved difficult to regenerate from genetically transformed cells. The focus of the project then shifted to sweet potatoes.

Wambugu rapidly became Africa's leading expert on genetically engineered crops. Monsanto's public relations department, meanwhile, regularly featured her in brochures and videos promoting the benefits of such crops.

JAWORSKI DROPPED both projects in the lap of Rob Horsch. "Ernie came to me and said, 'I want to do this; make it happen,' says Horsch. The apostle of biotechnology, whose hands had coaxed full-grown plants out of a few genetically altered cells in petri dishes, had not, to that point, exhibited great interest in the problems of tropical countries. Joel Cohen, the USAID official responsible for the cassava project, wondered at first whether he really could count on the Monsanto scientist to stick with it. "I said, 'Look, Rob, you're not going to get promoted for this," says Cohen.

Cohen turned out to be wrong, both about Horsch's commitment to these projects and about their potential to boost Horsch's career. Horsch became engrossed in them; they seemed to fulfill a latent desire to do something worthwhile with his expertise. "My grandfather was a Mennonite," Horsch says, trying to explain his motives. "It's part of the tradition; you want to be useful."

Horsch became one of Monsanto's most knowledgeable people not just on biotechnology but on farming practices and environmental problems across the globe. As fate would have it, that expertise meshed perfectly with the passions of Robert Shapiro, who took over as chief executive of Monsanto in 1995.

Soon after Shapiro was named CEO, he authorized a small conference for selected Monsanto employees in Aspen, Colorado, on global trends and their environmental sustainability. Only twenty-five people were invited, among them Rob Horsch. Horsch listened, transfixed, as speaker after speaker painted a picture of a world racing toward environmental catastrophe, its population consuming energy, soil, water, and the genetic diversity of species at an ever increasing rate. Horsch calls it a "transforming experience; a real turning point."

During one day of the conference, Shapiro and two other top Monsanto executives took a trip to the Rocky Mountain Institute, a nearby organization headed by Amory Lovins, one of the planet's most visionary environmentalists. They came back, says another Monsanto executive, "with stars in their eyes."

Shapiro challenged every Monsanto employee to turn the vision of a more sustainable world into a business opportunity and to look for ways in which Monsanto could use its expertise to tackle the world's most pressing problems. Rob Horsch accepted the challenge. He looked to the technologies that he knew best: genes that could render plants resistant to insects, diseases, or the herbicide Roundup. Many would criticize this choice later; if all you have is a hammer, they pointed out, the entire world looks like a nail. But to Horsch it seemed like a reasonable place to start. After all, why not begin with what's possible? Step-by-step he built a case for genetically engineered plants as a tool to promote more sustainable agricultural practices around the world.

The argument was based on concrete observations. There is, for instance, no better method for distributing new technology to the poor than through seeds. New seeds do not require a large up-front investment, at least nothing comparable to the construction of irrigation systems or the purchase of equipment. A new gene, inserted into seeds, works exactly the same way on small farms and large, owned by rich and poor alike. Seeds can be, to use an expression beloved by economists, "scale-neutral." Through the miracle of biological reproduction, a new variety of seeds can spread from farmer to farmer with little outside intervention.

Second, new genes can substitute for expensive chemicals and protect crops against disease and insects. Bt crops had shown this, most dramatically in the case of cotton.

Third, and perhaps most important for Monsanto's business prospects, was the serendipitous marriage of Roundup and soil conservation. Around the world, soil erosion is a huge problem, and much of it is caused by plowing up the soil in preparation for planting. Farmers could do a better job of preserving topsoil, particularly in hilly or dry, windswept areas, if they planted their seeds instead directly into the stubble left from the previous season's crop. Herbicides, Roundup in particular, make it much easier for farmers to carry out such "no till" practices. Farmers normally kill off the existing weeds first, then go ahead and plant their crops. The benefits would be multiplied if farmers could plant Roundup Ready crops. This would allow them to continue spraying Roundup after their crops emerge from the ground, instead of hoeing or spraying more dangerous chemicals, such as the highly toxic paraquat.

Those were the bare facts. But in Robert Shapiro's mind, such facts merely laid the groundwork for much grander conclusions. When Shapiro looked at biotechnology and sustainability, he didn't just see seeds and their concrete effects. He saw historical trends, paradigm shifts, and the shape of the future. "We have entered a remarkable and very rich moment in an agricultural history that is ten thousand years old," Shapiro told one interviewer.

"Everywhere," Shapiro said, "information" was replacing "stuff." Just as electrons pulsing through computer networks were displacing entire industries based on paper, roads, and buildings, the Bt gene—information stored as DNA—had replaced chunks of an industry based on heavy, physical insecticides. And that was only the start, the "equivalent of Intel's four-bit microprocessor in 1971—very useful but no more than the tip of the tip of the iceberg."

Information in the form of biotechnology offered an escape from environmental perils. More food, with a better balance of nutrients, might be grown on *less and less* land. Forests might replace farmland rather than the other way around. Topsoil could be replenished instead of vanishing forever into the depths of the world's oceans. "If we grow by using more stuff, I'm afraid we'd better look for another planet," Shapiro wrote in 1998. "The substitution of information for stuff is essential to sustainability."

The world, in Shapiro's view, needed Monsanto, and Monsanto had the opportunity—even the responsibility—to go where the needs were greatest. Existing programs, including the experiments with virus-resistant potatoes in Mexico and Kenya, were repackaged as elements of a strategy for a more sustainable style of agriculture. Employees of Monsanto's sustainability division soon were visiting the corn and sorghum fields of small farmers in Mexico, Indonesia, Kenya, Senegal, and Ghana. They promoted "conservation tillage," Roundup, and hybrid corn seeds.

Shapiro became enamored of "microcredit," an approach pioneered by the Grameen Bank of Bangladesh. It involves giving small loans to people—especially women—who want to start small home-scale enterprises, who could never get the attention of conventional banks.

The Grameen Bank's founder convened a "microcredit summit" in Washington, D.C., early in 1997, and Shapiro was invited to speak.

"I was on the plane trying to come up with some remarks," Shapiro recalls. "I was trying to answer the question of why a corporation would be interested in this. The real reason is, we are people. People in corporations are, astonishingly enough, human beings with souls and hearts and minds. And what I thought on the airplane and what I said in the talk was, poverty is our common ancestor. You don't have to go back very far in my family and, I suspect, your family, before you come to people who didn't know where their next meal was coming from. That's been the nature of human existence on this planet. Some of us are lucky to have broken out of that."

Shapiro admitted that he didn't know how helping people to break out of poverty would work as a business venture. "It's difficult, in the short term, figuring out how I am going to make money dealing with people who don't have money," he said at one point. "But in practice, the development of agriculture at a village level is something that could make an enormous amount of business sense over time."

MANY OF Monsanto's employees were inspired by Shapiro's words. Many outside the company considered his ideas an unsurpassed provocation.

These critics—among them church-based international aid organizations and independent advocates for the rights of the poor—were, from the start, inclined to distrust Monsanto's intentions. In their view, Western corporations enter the Third World in order to exploit and dominate, and the poor will better their lives by resisting such behemoths, not by buying their products. And nothing exposed the reality of Monsanto's ambitions so clearly, in their eyes, as the Terminator gene. As the Rural Advancement Foundation International put it: "The seed-sterilizing technology threatens to eliminate the age-old right of farmers to save seed from their harvest and it jeopardizes the food security of 1.4 billion people—resource poor farmers in the South—who depend on farm-saved seed." It was inconceivable to these groups that the Terminator might be used to offer farmers something new or that farmers might choose such new seeds over their traditional varieties. In this view of the world, the Terminator could have only one purpose: to capture and enslave.

In India's southern state of Karnataka, the estimable Professor Nanjundaswamy and his Karnataka State Farmers Association, veterans of previous battles against foreign companies, mobilized for action. Nanjundaswamy has called the executives of multinational seed companies "murderers" and proclaimed a "blitzkrieg" to drive them from India's shores. His followers once ransacked the offices of Cargill's headquarters in India. In person, this elderly lawyer and member of the Karnataka state legislature is composed and soft-spoken. He wears a green shawl, the mantle of the Gandhian movement for self-reliance. "We consider seed freedom to be the key to the nation," he says. "That's why we are opposing the multinational corporations."

In November 1998 Nanjundaswamy learned that Monsanto was conducting field trials of Bt cotton in India in collaboration with India's largest private seed company. He issued a call to action, distributed by e-mail around the world:

> On Saturday the 28th of November, at midday, thousands of farmers will occupy and burn down the three fields in front of the cameras, in an open, announced action of civil disobedience. These actions will start a campaign of direct action by farmers against biotechnology, called Operation 'Cremation Monsanto.' . . . The campaign will run under the following slogans:

STOP GENETIC ENGINEERING
NO PATENTS ON LIFE
CREMATE MONSANTO
BURY THE WORLD TRADE ORGANIZATION

Professor Nanjundaswamy's farmers did, on the appointed day, destroy one field, although they were unable to locate two others.

In neighboring Bangladesh, the controversy doomed the most auspicious product of Robert Shapiro's interest in "microcredit," a collaboration between Monsanto and the Grameen Bank. Just a few months earlier, Shapiro and the founder of the microcredit movement, Muhammad Yunus, had unveiled plans for a "Grameen Monsanto Center for Environment-Friendly Technologies." Shapiro had promised $150,000 to help fund the center. Some of the money would have gone to provide low-interest loans to farmers who could use the money to purchase, among other things, seeds and herbicides sold by Monsanto. The partnership did not, however, envision the sale of genetically engineered seeds.

Monsanto's foes were outraged that the Grameen Bank would link its name to Monsanto's, giving the company greater credibility. According to RAFI, Yunus came under "intense international pressure" to cancel the deal, and within a month he did. In South Asia Monsanto had acquired such a bad name that it couldn't even give money away.

THERE'S A hall-of-mirrors quality to the passionate arguments that rage around the question of genetic engineering's impact on the farmers in the poorest parts of the world. Everywhere one turns, one confronts brilliant, oversized images: Monsanto as hero and villain; biotechnology, the creator and destroyer. Yet behind those reflected images, little is real.

Step behind the mirrors, and one encounters, as just one example, life in the highlands of Mexico. It's the life of Bruno de la Luz, a farmer in the village of Concepcion de los Baños, a man whom Monsanto has targeted as a potential customer for the company's improved commercial seed.

I arrive at Bruno de la Luz's house on a sunny day in September. The farmer arranges chairs for everyone on the concrete floor. His wife ducks in and out of the room, handing around glasses of Coke.

De la Luz is a dignified man. He sits calm and erect, his weathered face impassive as I pose my questions. A copy of the Bible, in Spanish, rests on the table behind him. The farmer's native tongue is

Mazahua; his ancestors lived in this area long before the Spanish conquerors arrived. Next door to this room, he keeps a box filled with Mazahua-Spanish dictionaries, which he shows off proudly to visitors.

He grows only corn on his twelve acres of land, he tells me. Until this year, he'd grown only *criollos,* native varieties of corn, as do most small farmers in this area. He doesn't need to buy seed for *criollos;* he simply picks the best-looking ears of corn from his own harvest and uses them as seed for the following year's crop, as his ancestors have done for thousands of years. This region, in fact, is the birthplace of the modern corn plant, a precious and enduring cultural legacy that Mexico has passed on to the world. For the Aztecs, corn was a gift from the great god Quetzalcoatl, intertwined with the origin of human life itself. But for Bruno de la Luz, better corn now comes from the breeding programs of Monsanto's seed companies, formerly known as Asgrow, DeKalb, and Cargill.

This year, for the first time, Monsanto's representatives persuaded him to plant commercial hybrid seeds. The hybrids cover two-thirds of his fields, *criollos* the other third. These are not genetically engineered hybrids, but someday, if Mexico's government allows it, they might be.

De la Luz has no objections, in principle, to buying seed from private companies rather than replanting part of his harvest. It's true that the seeds are expensive, he says, but naturally, if you want a larger harvest, you have to invest more. And in Mexico, as in most parts of the world, seed from private companies has a better reputation than what farmers can get from government-run suppliers. In Mexico, for instance, the government's seed distribution venture is called PRONASE. According to one oft-repeated joke, if one asks a Mexican farmer why he doesn't buy seed from PRONASE, the farmer offers the rhyming reply, *"No nace"* ("Doesn't germinate").

This year at least, the investment in hybrids paid off. De la Luz says that Monsanto's hybrids produced twice as large a harvest as his native varieties. Next year he expects to plant even more.

Still, he says, he'll never get rid of his *criollos* completely. They're reliable. They are ready to harvest within four months, which is the most important thing in this area ten thousand feet above sea level, where the growing season is short and the weather is erratic. The commercial seed companies haven't yet come up with a hybrid offering a comparably short growing season. Monsanto's hybrids must stay in the fields almost three weeks longer, into September and October as the weather turns increasingly perilous. At any time, a hard frost can destroy the entire crop. Other farmers have mentioned other reasons for sticking with traditional varieties. Some maintain, for instance, that tortillas made from commercial hybrids don't taste as good.

My questions are finished. I thank the farmer and close my notebook, ready to leave. But Bruno de la Luz has his own agenda. "I have some questions as well," he announces, turning toward Guillermo Alafita and Olga Haas, two representatives from Monsanto's office in Mexico City, who've accompanied me on this visit.

Alafita and Haas are Mexican, but they come from a different world. Both are college educated, their faces unlined by wind and sun, their clothes neatly pressed. Cellular telephones hang from their belts. They are young, just starting their professional careers, earnest and idealistic. Guillermo studied agronomy, he says, because his country's greatest social problems are found in its agricultural areas. Both went to work for Monsanto only about a year ago. They wear identical uniforms, brown shirts printed with the words "*Campos Unidos; La Siembra de Nuevas Esperanzas*" (United Fields; Sowing New Hope). It is the slogan of a Monsanto initiative that mystifies Bruno de la Luz.

The Mexican farmer has listed his questions in a notebook so as not to forget any. He is polite but insistent. Why is Monsanto handing out what appear to be gifts? The company has employed two dozen people to travel among small farmers in certain regions of Mexico, offering advice on the best mix of fertilizers and arranging loans to farmers so that they can buy fertilizer and seeds that promise larger harvests. Monsanto's employees have interceded on farmers' behalf with insurance companies, persuading the companies to pay, as promised, when weather has damaged the farmers' crops. Monsanto has even attempted to arrange more reliable markets for corn grown by farmers in remote areas of Chiapas, Mexico's southernmost state, so that these farmers can be assured of a fair price for their harvest.

Bruno de la Luz can understand why the government might offer such services. But not Monsanto. "Is this a private enterprise or a nonprofit or what?" he asks.

Guillermo Alafita leans forward in his chair to reply, as though to bridge the space across ten feet of concrete floor that separates him from the farmer. Monsanto believes that it can help itself by helping the small farmers of Mexico, he says.

Alafita doesn't bother with the statistics that are the foundation of this argument, though he knows them by heart. Even though Monsanto's seed companies dominate the hybrid seed business in Mexico, they reach only the largest, most prosperous farmers. There remains a vast untapped market because *criollos*, grown from a farmer's own harvested seed, account for 80 percent of all the corn grown in the country. These lands are fragmented among two million small farms. Bruno de la Luz's landholdings at twelve acres are much larger than most. *Campos Unidos* is Monsanto's attempt to break into this market.

Some farmers are signing up. "I've already talked with about ten other farmers, and they are motivated, they want change," says Bruno de la Luz . In this community, he says, "we have about eight hundred *ejidatiarios* (small-scale farmers who work on land that was confiscated long ago from huge *haciendas*); I think there are about three hundred who are looking for alternatives. We want to be able to produce better crops and have a market for our crops."

Those words are music to the ears of Monsanto executives. Their hopes are built on the notion that Mexico need not be any different from Iowa; that farmers, no matter where they live, *will* spend money for seeds that promise a better crop. All Monsanto has to do is deliver a product that fulfills that promise.

Yet as Guillermo Alafita leaves and climbs into his truck, ready to visit another farmer, he can't escape nagging doubts about the future of *Campos Unidos*. His doubts aren't about the program's value to farmers; Alafita is convinced he's doing some good. The problem is that *Campos Unidos* loses money, and Monsanto isn't a charity.

*Campos Unidos* is a labor-intensive, and thus expensive, operation. It employs two dozen Monsanto employees. Even though they've reached several thousand Mexican farmers, those farmers account for just 1 percent of Monsanto's sales of hybrid seed in Mexico. It may simply not be worth the effort. Most of Mexico's small farmers continue to plant *criollos,* even though they know commercial hybrids are available, and Guillermo Alafita has spent enough time with them to understand some of the reasons why.

In some cases, Monsanto doesn't have a product that matches what the farmers want—a hybrid that matures within the short growing season of the Mexican highlands, for instance. In addition, Monsanto's calculations of risk and benefit seem foreign to many of the farmers. Some will never qualify for credit; they lack any recognizable assets that could serve as collateral, and without loans they can't afford to buy hybrid seeds or herbicides. Others don't want to spend money on better seed, taking on financial risks to boost production of corn, for perfectly rational reasons. The more money they sink into their land, the more they stand to lose should bad weather come along and destroy the crop. Farmers who participate in the *Campos Unidos* program are supposed to sign up for crop insurance to cover this risk, but Alafita has seen how reluctantly the insurance companies pay out money to poor farmers.

The smallest of these farmers, in fact, are not farmers in the North American sense. They are simply poor residents of rural villages. Growing corn is not an occupation; it is the most practical, life-giving thing to do with a small plot of land, but no new seed—not even the most wondrous genetically engineered product of Monsanto's laboratories—will make possible a different, more prosperous life. For that the people look elsewhere. In droves they are leaving their villages, migrating toward the vast metropolis of Mexico City or across the inviting international border that lies to the north. Most of the farmers whom Guillermo Alafita meets are growing old. Their children have little interest in tilling the soil, and Alafita cannot blame them.

Is MONSANTO turning Mexico's farmers into serfs? Hardly. The country's farmers buy $70 million worth of Monsanto seed each year for their own good reasons. But those farmers are a minority. Will the company's hybrids—and in the future, its genetically engineered seed—reach the *majority* of Mexico's farmers? Probably not.

This is the essential ambivalence that afflicts any honest discussion of biotechnology and its potential for agriculture in developing countries. On the one hand, as Monsanto's executives never tire of pointing out, there *are* markets for privately controlled commercial seed in the world's poorest countries. In Kenya, Indonesia, El Salvador, and Vietnam, hybrids *are* popular among small farmers. "They buy new seed corn every year, and they're making a living on one acre," says Monsanto's Hugh Grant, speaking of Indonesian farmers. "And the reason why they're choosing hybrid seed is it produces a better crop." If genetically engineered hybrids promised an even better crop in the future, these farmers would presumably spend the money required to buy those seeds.

Monsanto's executives also point to the rapid spread of Bt cotton in China. A joint venture between Monsanto and Delta and Pine Land has been selling Bt cotton in China for several years now through regional Chinese seed companies. The Chinese government, meanwhile, has been selling its own version of Bt cotton developed by the Chinese Academy of Agricultural Sciences. The seeds cost much more than what Chinese farmers are used to paying; they cost, in fact, more than what American farmers pay for Bt cotton seed. Yet genetically engineered cotton now covers practically all the cotton acres in some provinces.

On the other hand, these are special cases. Chinese cotton farmers had already been spending significant amounts of money on pesticides, and they could see that the pesticides were becoming less and less effective. Bt cotton didn't require them to spend more money and take on more financial risk; it just shifted their spending from pesticides to seeds.

In addition, in both hybrid corn and cotton there are special advantages to buying new seed each year rather than saving part of the harvest and replanting it. This opens the door to commercial seed companies. No similar commercial venture can be easily imagined in rice or wheat, to say nothing of potatoes, cassava, chickpeas, or any of the other staple crops on which so many of the world's inhabitants rely for survival.

The conclusion remains: The vast majority of the world's farmers lie beyond the limits of a commercially viable seed trade. They will not or cannot for the foreseeable future spend enough on seeds to make them a profitable market for biotech companies like Monsanto. As a result, those companies will have very little impact on the poorest farmers in the developing world, either for good or ill. If biotechnology offers any benefits at all for such farmers, those benefits will have to emerge from nonprofit institutions or from the relatively ill-equipped facilities of publicly funded laboratories in the developing countries.

"THEY WERE going to do it all!" says David Hoisington, speaking of Monsanto with an expansive wave of his arm. The tone of his voice expresses another thought: *What were they thinking!?*

A slice of the planet's genetic diversity is visible outside Hoisington's window, stretching across wide, flat fields. These are the breeding plots of CIMMYT, the International Center for the Improvement of Maize and Wheat, located an hour's drive east of Mexico City. The plots are unlike any farmer's field; they are covered with a meticulously weeded, carefully arranged patchwork of different strains of corn and wheat. The different varieties are drawn from the resources of CIMMYT's "germ plasm bank," a climate-controlled storehouse containing 145,000 jars filled with samples of corn and wheat, many of them traditional "landraces" that have long since disappeared from agricultural fields. In CIMMYT's test plots, breeders carefully supervise the natural recombination of these genetic packages, shuffling genes like cards and watching for the emergence of a superior hand. Paper bags cover many ears of corn and heads of wheat. Breeders have pollinated these plants by hand, and they don't want any further pollen, drifting on the wind, to confuse things.

Agricultural researchers from all over the world take the products of this breeding effort, try them out under local conditions, and distribute the best seeds to farmers. The process has worked admirably in wheat, less successfully in corn. Corn plants are such promiscuous cross-pollinators that genetic packages, carefully assembled in breeding plots, rapidly disintegrate within a few generations when grown in farmers' fields. Yet across vast areas of the world, especially in the tropics and in mountainous highlands, farmers harvest grain that is descended from plants first created in these breeding plots. Arrayed in front of CIMMYT's main building are the center's greatest hits: lines of wheat plants, each with a small white identification sign. "Sonalika," states one: "The most widely adopted Green Revolution variety; sown on more than 12 million hectares [29 million acres] in the past and still grown today." On another sign: "Yaqui 50. The first major tall variety with durable stem rust resistance bred by Dr. Borlaug and his Mexican colleagues and released in NW Mexico in 1950." "Dr. Borlaug" refers to Norman Borlaug, an American plant breeder at CIMMYT who won the Nobel Peace Prize in 1970 for his efforts. Borlaug, possessed of legendary stubbornness and strength of will, still maintains an office at CIMMYT.

Hoisington is in charge of CIMMYT's biotechnology research. In effect, he's supposed to find a way to use this new technology for the benefit of a billion or so wheat and corn growers around the world.

His staff, numbering two dozen scientists and technicians, doesn't have a prayer of competing directly with companies like Monsanto, Novartis, or Pioneer. Hoisington can only bite his lip with envy when he visits the laboratories of these giants, filled with million-dollar pieces of equipment.

But Hoisington would love to get his hands on some of the results of their work. He's interested in Bt genes, for instance. The Bt toxin kills a worm called the stem borer, which regularly devastates corn crops in parts of Africa. Other genes have the potential to make wheat and corn better able to withstand drought or the predations of a devastating weed called *striga*, which covers parts of Africa. He might even be interested in Roundup resistance, Hoisington says. Roundup might be a good way to get rid of *striga*, particularly in combination with Roundup-resistant corn. "We're looking at it, discussing it."

Starting in the early 1990s, Hoisington made the rounds of biotech companies and universities "in the North," asking for permission to use their intellectual property. What he wanted essentially was a global version of Monsanto's agreements to donate technology for potatoes in Mexico or cassava in Kenya. Monsanto, Novartis, and Pioneer, he argued, were never going to make their money selling genetically engineered seeds to poor farmers in Africa or Asia.

So why not split the market? Let the companies sell seed to commercial farmers, while CIMMYT and its partners delivered these genes to poor farmers for free.

In many cases, Hoisington really didn't need to ask permission at all. If he could have laid hands on the genes he wanted, he could have used them with impunity. Most of these tools were patented only in North America, Europe, Japan, and Australia. Those patents didn't prevent Hoisington and his staff from using them in Mexico, Africa, and most of Asia. But Hoisington was reluctant to take such a confrontational approach. For one thing, he said, some developing countries, including Mexico, were moving toward patenting as well. More importantly, CIMMYT's work would certainly suffer if private companies concluded that it couldn't be trusted.

It took time, but eventually most companies were willing to provide what Hoisington wanted, at least for research purposes. Novartis provided its Bt gene. Other companies, including Pioneer, set up joint research projects with CIMMYT, agreeing to share rights to the results. If any of this research leads to a plant that's worth planting in farmers' fields, Hoisington is confident that CIMMYT will be able to distribute those seeds free of charge, as it has always done. "All of our agreements have clauses that allow us either to provide these materials directly to our partners at no cost or at least to 'negotiate in good faith'—that's the catch legal phrase—how we would provide it."

Only Monsanto refused consistently to accept these terms. Some blamed the company's intransigence on its tradition of driving the toughest of bargains. But it was also a perverse consequence of Shapiro's messianic vision and his belief that business opportunities lurked in the most remote villages of Bangladesh. It was as if Shapiro was saying, *No, Mr. Hoisington, we don't think the world really needs CIMMYT anymore. We'll handle the world's problems ourselves, thank you very much.*

Hoisington occasionally asked the St. Louis company to provide access to one or another piece of technology. Monsanto's legal department always sent Hoisington a draft "Material Transfer Agreement" to sign. "The agreements read, in my mind, as if we were basically working for them, as a technology provider to the Third

World," Hoisington says. If CIMMYT used Monsanto's property to create a new product, for instance, Monsanto would earn royalties on the sale of those products. "In some ways, they felt that we were just another seed company," Hoisington says. "They could license the technology to us, and we would provide it on a royalty-bearing basis to partners in developing countries."

"They felt that they could control the partnership, and CIMMYT was more an outlet for their technology. That's why we just said, 'Fine. We can't deal with that. We don't work for anyone. We work for the world.'"

Then came the European revolt and the ensuing deflation of Monsanto's ambitions. Hoisington noticed a new flexibility in the St. Louis company's attitudes and greater willingness to donate expertise and tools. The reasons, Hoisington says, went beyond a simple desire to appear philanthropic or to demonstrate biotechnology's social benefits. Monsanto's leaders were more willing to recognize their own limits, step aside, and let the CIMMYT do what Monsanto never would. "It provides us a window of opportunity," Hoisington says, "to say, 'Look, you guys tried. You succeeded some. You failed some. We're still plodding along, and we still have some credibility. We do have a role to play. We tried to tell you that all along.'"

# 18

# Perched on a Precipice

At the dawn of the new millennium, the battle over biotechnology settled into a kind of trench warfare—bitterly contested, expensive, and wearying, with many casualties but little movement in either direction. The opposing sides in the genetic modification (GM) debate became intimate enemies, each familiar with every argument and tactic wielded by the other. Thrust and parry, attack and counterattack, claim and refutation matched each other in newspaper columns, Web sites, and public meetings on several continents. Each side became convinced of corrupt, dishonest motives among its opponents. On an Internet discussion group dominated by probiotech scientists, much vitriol was aimed at the organic food industry, which allegedly was fueling the anti-GM campaign in order to sell organic food at inflated prices to gullible consumers. Opponents of genetic engineering, meanwhile, often regarded those taking the opposite view as dupes or agents of the biotech industry.

Each side searched desperately for winning arguments and tactics, levers that might tilt history in its direction. Each took comfort in the support of relentless and impersonal forces at work under the surface like opposing tides. The supporters of biotechnology waited for time and inevitable scientific advances to heal their wounds. A few more years, they believed, and the storm would pass. The opponents of biotechnology, for their part, found their most powerful ally in the world of commodity markets, which persistently worked to rid themselves of inconvenient, disruptive "contaminants."

TWICE, MONSANTO had marched ahead with new products that weren't approved in America's export markets, courting chaos in the world's grain markets. Twice, it had escaped with only minor damage. In 1996 Europe had approved Roundup Ready soybeans in time for harvest. In 1998 the world's grain traders simply had adapted to Europe's refusal to accept Roundup Ready corn and routed American corn away from European ports. But when, in 1999, the giant European company Aventis took a similarly cavalier attitude toward government regulation and began selling farmers a product that was not yet approved for human consumption, it provoked a global debacle: the Starlink affair.

Aventis had just arrived on the scene as a union of the German company AgrEvo and the French company Rhone-Poulenc. It had developed its own version of Bt corn, which it called Starlink. And Starlink had a problem. Most versions of the Bt protein, when placed in an acidic solution that simulated the human stomach, were promptly broken down into small, innocuous chunks of amino acids. This was a test devised by Monsanto to prove that new genes and the proteins they produced were incapable of causing allergic reaction in humans. But the Starlink protein didn't pass this test. It just sat there for more than an hour. This didn't prove that Starlink *would* cause allergies, but the possibility couldn't be ruled out.

The Environmental Protection Agency finally came up with an interim solution, one that agency officials would come to rue. In May 1998 the EPA approved sales of Starlink corn as long as the harvest was used only for cattle feed and not for human consumption. AgrEvo dutifully promised to abide by these conditions, and Starlink went on the market.

In fact (as everyone involved should have realized) traces of Starlink genes were bound to end up in human food. Farmers had no financial incentive to handle their Starlink corn with special care, nor did most of them see any particular reason to. Even if they had taken special measures to ensure that these fields were fed only to cattle, Starlink genes were destined to drift across neighboring fields anyway in the form of windblown pollen.

This unavoidable drift didn't mean that these genes actually posed a threat to anyone's health. Even if the suspicious protein was capable of causing allergic reactions, it almost certainly would not do so, because it would be present in such vanishingly small concentrations in human food.

Still, rules are rules. Any trace of Starlink would be an illegal contaminant in food. And modern tests made it possible to detect Starlink's specific sequence of DNA with excruciating precision. Aventis had set a trap for itself.

The trap snapped shut in July 2000. Larry Bohlen, who was leading a campaign against genetically engineered foods for Friends of the Earth in the United States, knew that Starlink was in the fields, and he suspected from conversations with farmers that no one was keeping careful track of it. Bohlen went to his local supermarket, a Safeway in Silver Spring, Maryland, and filled a grocery cart with dozens of items that contained corn: muffin mixes, breakfast cereals, corn chips, corn meal, an enchilada TV dinner, and taco shells. He sent them to Genetic ID, a testing laboratory in Iowa run by another prominent opponent of genetically engineered foods.

Almost two dozen of the packages he bought turned out to contain Starlink DNA, including taco shells manufactured by Kraft and served in Taco Bell restaurants. On September 18, Bohlen and his partners in the Genetically Engineered Food Alert unveiled the results to a crowd of reporters.

*Unfit for human consumption! It's in your tacos! And the government never knew!* The revelation was like a charge of dynamite in a mountainside snow pack. It unleashed an avalanche of disruption in the American grain-handling system, starting at the supermarket and ending up at the farm. Starlink corn amounted to less than 1 percent of the American grain harvest, yet traces of it showed up everywhere that people looked. Manufacturers pulled offending packages off store shelves. According to one estimate, half the grain elevators in Iowa held traces of Starlink. Corn processors such as Archer Daniels Midland began testing the contents of every train car before allowing it to unload. Waves of amber grain were diverted to feed lots, costing elevators and shippers millions of dollars. Then Starlink turned up in shipments to foreign ports, including those of America's most important export market, Japan. The U.S. government rushed a delegation urgently to Tokyo, hoping to contain the damage.

One jaw of the trap in which Aventis found itself was purely of its own making, shaped by commercial impatience, a casual attitude toward the letter of the law, and the conviction that a few stray genes couldn't possibly become a serious problem. The other jaw was a sudden and ferocious need on the part of food makers and the government to reassure the public that food was indeed free of dangerous new substances.

Ironically, in dealing with Starlink American companies and the U.S. government adopted a standard of absolute purity, one which they previously had scorned as unscientific and unworkable when employed by Europeans. When Europe had insisted on the right to reject any shipment of grain if the smallest particle of DNA from an unapproved crop turned up in that shipment, American representatives had heaped ridicule on the European position. European regulations, they pointed out, allowed grain shipments to contain small traces of rat feces, dismembered insects, animal hair, dirt, and toxic pesticides. *Rat feces?* they scoffed. *But not one shred of Roundup Ready corn?*

Yet when the American government, in its turn, needed to assure the public that food was safe, it also applied a standard of absolute purity. Starlink was "unapproved for human consumption," period. It was an irrational standard, but it was one that people understood.

SURPRISINGLY, STARLINK had little impact on American public attitudes toward biotechnology, at least as measured by polls. It had a huge impact, however, on the attitudes and practices of grain handlers and food processors. These are the people and companies, in fact, who hold the future of genetically engineered crops in their hands. Giant food companies such as Archer Daniels Midland, Nestle, and Philip Morris, have tolerated these crops but warily. Genetic engineering has brought them no benefits, only complications. It has disrupted the fundamental assumption of their operations, that all soybeans and corn are created equal and can be treated as identical. Their headaches will intensify as more countries, including Japan and Australia, introduce mandatory labeling of genetically engineered ingredients in food. European officials say they will go further and require labels on any food containing ingredients—such as soybean oil—that are *derived* from genetically engineered crops, even if all the genetically modified protein or DNA has long since been removed in the refining process.

"We don't have a dog in this fight," said one food industry executive. "I believe personally that biotechnology is a powerful tool to improve the human condition. So I believe it's important to preserve it as a tool. But the paramount issue for us is to maintain our relationship with the consumer. And if I have a label that says 'contains GM ingredients,' many consumers will reject it out of hand."

At what point will the food giants decide that genetically engineered crops are more trouble than they are worth? These companies are not natural allies of Greenpeace. If they move, they will not issue inflammatory press releases or send people into the streets with banners. But their verdicts will be decisive. They are vastly larger and more powerful than Monsanto, or the agricultural businesses of Aventis or DuPont. Food companies could, if they put their minds to the task, crush the current products of the agricultural biotechnology industry, leaving behind only fading memories of past hubris.

For this reason, the most ominous consequence of the Starlink fiasco for Monsanto was the establishment of procedures to detect the forbidden gene and divert train cars containing Starlink grain to cattle feedlots where it was sold at a discount. If the food industry chose, it could do the same for other versions of Bt corn or even Roundup Ready soybeans. At that point, farmers would get the message immediately, and sales of genetically engineered seeds would plummet.

THE BACKERS of biotechnology, meanwhile, continue to look to that distant horizon where new scientific breakthroughs beckon. They strain to catch a glimpse of the genetically engineered plant that will reawaken the public's faith in the saving grace of technology, one that promises dramatic benefits directly to the consumer. It could be, for instance, a soybean with oil that will make people live longer (or at least lower their cholesterol). Such products would solve many problems at once. Farmers would have an economic interest in keeping this part of the harvest strictly separate, because it would command a higher price. Products that contained them would be labeled, because the label would be a selling point, and any potential risk they might harbor would be balanced by a promised benefit.

Skeptics scoff at such dreams. The promised benefits of a genetic alteration would have to be huge, they say, to pay for all the special handling that such a product would require and still make money. But those who keep the flame of technological enthusiasm burning are adamant: It will be just a matter of time, they say, before that breakthrough product comes along and all will be well again in their world—because science always marches forward.

Indeed, in these early days of the twenty-first century, science isn't just marching. It's racing forward, shredding the veils that have hidden the genetic secrets of life from human gaze.

# 19

# Infinite Horizons

*September, 2000*

"I feel like I'm back in graduate school again," says Steve Rogers with a grin. The cocreator of Monsanto's first genetically engineered plants stands in front of an imposing brick edifice that stretches along a combination of street and park in Cambridge, Massachusetts. It is the home of Cereon, a wholly owned subsidiary of Monsanto devoted to unlocking the secrets of plant DNA.

Of Monsanto's biotech apostles, Rogers was always the one with the purest attachment to science. Twenty years ago, he was the company's premier "gene jockey," cutting and splicing the bits of DNA that would end up in Monsanto's first genetically transformed plants. For reasons he cannot remember ("I couldn't have volunteered for it!") he took a detour into the public sphere in the mid-1980s. He met with government officials on two continents, making the case for regulatory approvals and debated biotechnology's opponents from Berkeley to Oxford. He happened to be living in Europe during the biotech backlash of the late 1990s. It seemed to leave him more perplexed than angry, as though he couldn't locate the missing piece of data that would allow him to decode the phenomenon.

At the end of 1999 Rogers came home, back to the United States from Europe and back to the world of science at Cereon. He became copresident of the company.

1999 felt like 1980 all over again. Science had opened up new frontiers, as the advent of genetic transformation in plants had done twenty years earlier. As before, Rogers felt the pulse-quickening atmosphere of discovery and the tension of scientific competition. Once again, nervous and hopeful venture capital flowed into new startup ventures: Mendel Biotechnology, Paradigm Genetics, Ceres, CropDesign, Large-Scale Biology. Land-rush fever gripped the field of agricultural biotechnology. Grand estates of intellectual property were up for grabs.

THINK OF the genes in any particular organism as the inhabitants of a small city numbering in the tens of thousands. One can look down at the town, as if from a jetliner, and see that it is alive: Smoke pours from its factories, lights blink, traffic races through its streets. Yet the citizens of these cities until the late 1990s were almost completely hidden from view.

Only their work was visible. One could observe, for instance, that caterpillars, upon eating certain strains of *Bacillus thuringiensis,* died. One could work backward from this visible phenomenon, seeking its cause. Scientists isolated the bacteria's lethal protein, and from the structure of this protein they deduced a piece of its identity: the sequence of links in a short chain of DNA, only a fragment of the whole gene. That fragment was like a name tag. They could shout that name out into the darkness, and the gene, if it was present, was forced to reveal itself.

It was called "reverse genetics," working from the visible to the invisible. It produced every genetically engineered plant currently on the market, including the Flavr Savr tomato, crops that employ Bt, and others that are tolerant to Roundup.

It had been impractical in the 1980s to think of moving "forward", as nature does, from cause to visible effect. The starting point for such a quest, the DNA that contained the code for every gene, was beyond the grasp of science.

To be sure, scientists had built devices for decoding DNA. By the early 1980s they were able to decode snippets of DNA a few hundred links, or "base pairs," long. It was like reading one sentence from one book taken from a library that filled a room. The chromosomes of every human included some four *billion* base pairs; the strands of DNA in corn were four times longer still. Deciphering the entire genetic code, or genome, of such organisms, using the standard tools of the day, would have occupied every scientist on the face of the planet for several lifetimes.

Yet the human imagination wasn't limited by the tools at hand, especially not in the intellectual hot springs of Stanford, Caltech, Cold Springs Harbor, Oxford, and Cambridge. If the wizards of Silicon Valley could increase the switching speed of electronic circuits a million times, why not the sequencing of DNA? "There wasn't any equipment that would allow you to do it," says Virginia Walbot, a professor at Stanford University. "But around here people were asking, 'What would it take to do that? Let's invent it.'"

Invent it they did, in a prodigious eruption of human creativity. The decoding of raw DNA was transformed from a tedious, messy undertaking into a task for smoothly humming machines, each generation twice as efficient as the one before. Others dreamed of shortcuts. Craig Ventor, a balding ex-surfer and Vietnam veteran turned biochemist at the National Institutes of Health, realized that he could capture a kind of name tag for each gene if he monitored the cell's own machinery for "expressing" genes and turning them into proteins. In the early 1990s Ventor turned his laboratory into a veritable factory for these "expressed sequence tags," or ESTs, churning out hundreds of new ones each week. These ESTs meant nothing by themselves, but like name tags scattered across a table, each one signified the existence of a real gene with a real function. Almost overnight, the community of biologists had thousands of new names to call out; fish hooks on which to pull in new genes from the uncharted depths. They could begin to start where nature starts, with the genetic code—the genome—of each organism.

The *human* genome, luring venture capitalists and government officials alike with its siren song of self-knowledge, brought forth the cash that fueled genomics. But anything that worked with human DNA worked equally well with the DNA of any other organism. In the plant world, scientists first turned their new machines loose on their favorite research subject, a small mustard plant called *Arabidopsis thaliana*. Other genome projects soon got underway covering corn, rice, wheat, and tomatoes. Scientist began to assemble rosters of genes, the vast majority of which had no known function.

They were like huge galleries of anonymous faces—the inhabitants of those still-mysterious cities.

As the first rush of genes came into view in the late 1990s, even jaded veterans of the laboratory stopped breathing for a moment. *Similar faces were turning up in the gallery of each genome.* They could have predicted this, of course. Darwin, a hundred years earlier, had arranged organisms into family trees based on visible characteristics. The invisible realm revealed the same phenomenon in even more dramatic fashion. Each of these individual genomes, it became clear, whether taken from a virus, bacterium, animal, or plant, belonged to a common family, the single, unified, genome of life on earth. By tracing changes in this genome from organism to organism biologists could trace the paths of evolution across a family tree that encompassed all living organisms.

Scientists might also take evolution into their own hands. (Although most shied away from the idea of doing so in humans.) They might create alternate forms of crucial genes by introducing random changes in the gene's sequence of base pairs, just as natural mutation does, but a million times faster. They might bring back genes which that organism's ancestors had abandoned millions of years earlier or import genes from other living organisms.

Moving genes from one species to another was no longer novel by this time. Truly new, however, was the sheer volume of genes that were becoming available. The data, streams of letters denoting the identity of individual links in the DNA chain, gushed forth in a quantity that overwhelmed human intelligence. They spilled across pages of scientific journals, comprehensible only with the aid of powerful computers programmed to recognize patterns in the accumulating information. The genome was simultaneously a fount of knowledge and nonsense. A few companies decided that this field, now called genomics, was destined to become a fount of profits as well.

MONSANTO JUMPED into genomics with both feet in 1997.

"At that time, we were being asked to look for new areas of business, growth initiatives," recalls David Fischhoff, a round-faced, cerebral scientist who is copresident of Cereon with Steve Rogers.

"The idea was, things were changing, and we had to look toward the future. The company was clearly looking for new things."

Roundup Ready soybeans and Bt corn were just hitting the fields. Those crops promised profits as far as the eye could see.

"So we were sitting there saying, 'We can do this!'" Fischhoff says. "The marketplace says it's valuable. And yet, we need more genes. Genomics looks like a way to get more genes."

The rush into genomics, in agriculture as well as pharmaceuticals, was also a kind of land rush. Companies like Human Genome Sciences were busily filing patent applications covering every potentially useful genetic sequence they discovered. Pioneer Hi-Bred had already signed a deal with Human Genome Sciences under which HGS promised to deliver tens of thousands of "identity tags" for corn genes. Just as it was while buying the seed companies, Monsanto was gripped by a fear that competitors might lock up all the best assets to be found in the genomes of major crops (or, indeed, gripped by the hope that Monsanto itself might lock them up.)

In one respect, though, 1999 was utterly unlike 1980. Unlike Monsanto's first venture into genetic engineering of plants, genomics could not be done on the cheap.

When Steve Rogers went to work at Monsanto in 1980, the entire biotechnology staff of the company could sit around a small table. Even when Monsanto dominated the field of plant biotechnology a few years later, the staff who worked in that field numbered only a few dozen. A few *hundred* people work at Cereon. Monsanto employs an equal number back in St. Louis. In addition, the company pays millions of dollars for access to research conducted by other small genomics ventures. On top of all that, Cereon leans—literally—on another company with much greater expertise in the new science. Cereon fills two floors of its building on Sydney Street. The remaining three floors, along with the entire building next door, are the home of Millennium Pharmaceuticals, which is busy mining the human genome on behalf of several large pharmaceutical companies. Monsanto paid Millennium $100 million for access to the company's accumulated expertise. Monsanto will pay another $100 million if the collaboration produces plenty of ideas for potential products. All together, Monsanto is likely to spend a billion dollars on genomics research before it sees a single product.

And what might those products be? Cereon has embarked on a search for a few crucial genes, the few individuals in this gallery of faces who wield real power, who can change the life of a town in dramatic ways.

It is, in part, a door-to-door search. Researchers can shut down particular genes, or "overexpress" them, shifting the genes into overdrive. Then they watch the plants that result. Any changes are clues to the function of those particular genes.

The key, says Fischhoff, is to carry out this search on a systematic, factorylike scale, gathering information on thousands of genes at once from several different plants as well as microbes and humans. Only then will the pieces of data start to fit together like an enormous jigsaw puzzle. Gradually through the sheer accumulation of data a complete picture of community life in each town may emerge. The picture may reveal a few genes (Fischhoff hopes for hundreds) that are "key leverage points" in the life of the organism. Those genes, if altered, suppressed, or transferred to plants that don't currently posses them, may produce crops with stunning new qualities, some of which can't even be imagined today.

Rogers and Fischhoff aren't saying what they've found so far, if anything. But almost every week, scientific publications provide a taste of future possibilities.

Most of these new plants exist only in laboratories or in test plots. They are like the creations of avant-garde fashion designers, assembled to promote creative expression and expand the boundaries of the possible rather than to serve any immediate practical purpose. The innovations swish down the runway; appreciative scientists murmur and applaud each new tour de force of human creativity: plants with higher levels of nutrients, such as iron, thiamin, vitamin A, or vitamin E; others that secrete citric acid from their roots, canceling out the toxic effects of aluminum in the soil; soybeans that contain healthier forms of fatty acids or oils useful in industrial processes.

More frequent than the creation of new genetically altered plants are discoveries of genes that seem important, although the path from gene to improved plant remains uncharted: a gene, for instance, that appears to make plants tolerant to freezing temperatures and another that tells the plant to start flowering and thus to produce fruit. Through control of this latter gene, scientist might induce plants to bear fruit more quickly, which is crucial for farmers in northern latitudes.

Or consider the genes responsible for photosynthesis, which allows plants to thrive on sunlight and carbon dioxide in the air around them. It's the basis of all plant and animal life on the face of the planet, but all plants do not carry out photosynthesis in the same way. Corn, as it happens, possesses far more efficient photosynthetic machinery than most other plants, including rice or wheat. A few of the genes responsible for corn's remarkable photosynthesis machine are known; others, probably the majority, remain undiscovered. Scientists at Washington State University, Nagoya University in Japan, and Japan's National Institute of Agrobiological Resources transferred the pieces of this machine that are known—three genes—from corn into rice. According to the scientists, the genetically altered rice plants produced almost a third more grain than equivalent conventional plants. The scientists believe that even greater increases will be possible if they can get their hands on more of the genes that make corn so efficient and can transfer those genes into rice. If such dreams prove real, it means that the planet's largest food crop could yield dramatically larger harvests simply through more efficient use of air and sunlight.

*And yet . . .*

The world has heard such dreams and optimism before. Genomics represents, without doubt, an explosion of knowledge regarding the workings of biology. But knowledge, particularly in agriculture, doesn't always translate into products, much less profits.

Agricultural biotechnology has been, so far, a massive pyramid scheme financed by hopes of great wealth down the road. Few, if any, companies that invested heavily in biotechnology for agriculture have recovered that investment through sales of a genetically engineered product. Monsanto may have, but one could see that success as a fluke. Their most profitable biotech crop—Roundup Ready soybeans—rode to success on the back of a hugely popular herbi-

cide. Most people who made money in this field—the financiers behind Plant Genetic Systems, for instance, or the owners of DeKalb—
did so by selling their stakes in this dream at a good price when the
next wave of speculative money came rolling along. A few others—
most prominently, Pioneer Hi-Bred—made money for a time selling
genes developed by other companies and acquired at fire-sale prices.
In the light of that history, one has to ask: Could genomics simply be
the doubling of a bad commercial bet?

IF ANYONE has the right to be skeptical about the promises of genomics, it's John Bedbrook. No one has been more devoted to agricultural biotechnology, and no one has suffered more at the hands of
this cruel mistress than the balding, avuncular New Zealander with
smile-creased eyes.

Bedbrook is one of the field's true pioneers. In the early 1980s, he
was director of research for a company called Advanced Genetic
Systems (AGS). The company achieved a dubious kind of fame when
it tried to carry out field trials of a genetically engineered organism,
in this case a strain of bacteria that was supposed to prevent ice
from forming on the surface of strawberries. For five years, from
1982 until 1987, the proposal bounced between federal regulators
(who generally saw no danger) and various courts (which ordered
the regulators to reconsider.) When AGS employees finally got to
spray their bacteria on an acre of strawberries in 1987, they were
dressed up in full moon-suit regalia and surrounded by dozens of
photographers. The biotech industry has blamed those pictures ever
since for cementing an image of danger in the public's mind.

AGS ran out of money, and in 1988 it merged with a company
called DNA Plant Technologies, or DNAP. Bedbrook became the
merged company's vice president for research. DNAP was pushing
genetically altered products that weren't considered controversial.
Instead of splicing genes from one organism into another, the company induced random mutations in plants. A few of the mutants
emerged with new desirable traits.

DNAP had created some carrots that stayed fresh longer, making
them ideal as prepackaged snacks. (This was before the popularity of
packaged "baby carrots.") The company marketed them as VegiSnax,

and they sold well. In the early 1990s McDonald's even carried DNAP's product.

"Compared to your average carrot, it was phenomenal," says Bedbrook. "People loved it." DNAP's scientists felt justly proud; their genetic tinkering had created a better carrot. "We were convinced that people loved it because of the taste and the convenience," recalls Bedbrook. "And then these baby hulled carrots came out, and we discovered what the driver really was. It was the convenience." Not only were the competing baby carrots just as convenient, they were cheaper. They blew DNAP's VegiSnax into oblivion.

"People did prefer the taste of VegiSnax, but . . ." Bedbrook reflects for a second. "It just doesn't matter that much to people. A carrot's a carrot! And I'm not sure I'm going to pay a premium for a bloody orange carrot. At the end of the day, it's a great idea that just really doesn't matter."

DNAP and Bedbrook tried again. They created the Endless Summer tomato, a direct competitor to Calgene's Flavr Savr. Like the Flavr Savr, this tomato stayed firm longer because a ripening gene was turned off. And DNAP learned the same expensive lesson that Calgene had. Technology that seemed to work wonders in the safe confines of a laboratory didn't make much of a difference at all when it encountered the harsh rough-and-tumble reality of fresh tomato production.

"You're producing products outside, for God's sake!" says Bedbrook. "The wind blows, the rain falls, the sun shines! All of these tomatoes aren't perfect little animals. It's a crappy business! End of story. It's a crappy business!"

This is the lesson Bedbrook finally learned from two decades of misadventures in biotechnology: Agriculture, for all its charm, is a hostile place for subtle technological improvements. Compare agriculture with pharmaceuticals; any new drug that improves a patient's health, no matter how slight the effect, can be worth billions. In agriculture, a new gene has to have the effect of a sledgehammer or no one will notice.

So did Bedbrook give up? No. He joined a new biotech company, one that owns a technique for creating sledgehammer genes out of toothpicks.

The company is called Maxygen, and its technology is called DNAShuffling. Essentially it is a technique for creating a better version of a gene that already exists.

Turn the DNA shufflers of Maxygen loose on a gene, and they will create a dizzying number of variants of that gene through a random shuffling of links in the chain of DNA. Then they check to see if any of the variants performs better than the original. The process mimics plant breeding, which shuffles the genes of an entire plant. (Maxygen, in fact, calls the process "molecular breeding.") It is also a bit like natural selection, but unlike evolution it runs at industrial speeds. According to Bedbrook, it yields astonishing results.

"The most studied enzyme on the planet is an enzyme used in laundry detergents," he says. For twenty years, companies have studied this enzyme trying to improve its performance. They've probed its structure with X-rays and created computer models of it.

The Danish company Novo Nordisk asked Maxygen to take a look at the gene that produces this enzyme. In a matter of weeks, Bedbrook says, DNA shuffling produced an enzyme that was far superior not just in one respect but in every important way. The scale of the improvement was "unheard of," Bedbrook says. For the first time, genetic engineers can truly mold genes to carry out particular functions, just as chemical engineers tinker with the characteristics of chemicals.

DNAShuffling would have been the perfect tool for Monsanto, in fact, when Robb Fraley's scientific crew was searching the world for a perfect Roundup resistance gene. They knew that Roundup kills plants by binding to a particular target, a crucial enzyme within the cell. The gene that creates Roundup's target exists in practically all plants and bacteria, but it comes in slightly different forms. Monsanto's scientists went searching for an alternate form of this target enzyme, one that could slip free of Roundup's grasp. Eventually, such a target enzyme turned up in a rare strain of bacteria. That search took nearly a decade. Had Maxygen's technique been available, Monsanto might have had its Roundup Ready gene in hand within a few weeks.

There are hundreds of genetically engineered plants that never made it to market because the imported gene didn't work quite well enough, Bedbrook says. In the past, genetic engineers didn't have much choice; they had to use what nature gave them. Now Maxygen can improve those genes, cheaply and dramatically.

Best of all, John Bedbrook can stay in the controlled environment of the laboratory. His job is simply to fashion superior genes. Let other people in other companies introduce those genes into agriculture. (Maxygen has set up partnerships with Pioneer Hi-Bred and with Advanta, a European seed and agricultural chemical company.) Let *them* deal with cranky farmers, muddy roads, drought, windstorms, unreliable machinery, and depressing commodity prices. Genomics looks much better if you stay close to the genome.

It's the lesson that economists often tell about the California Gold Rush. Few of those who flocked to California, feverish for the sight of gold, ended up wealthy. The people who really made money, *lots* of money, were those who made and sold the gold-crazed forty-niners their shovels, blankets, tents, and guns. Bedbrook has stepped out of the muck of the Gold Rush; now, he's selling Gold Rush tools.

"WHAT DOES genomics lead to? Ha! Ha! That's the question, isn't it?" chortles John Howard, founder of a biotech company called Prodigene, in College Station, Texas. "It leads to a very fashionable statement that investors get really hot about, and a lot of money. If you want to go beyond that, it's harder."

Howard checks his mirth and scrambles back to sober ground. "As a benefit to society, it's great. But how will you make money in it? How will you make money *in plants* with it?"

Howard, like Bedbrook, believes he knows an answer. It's different from Bedbrook's answer, but similar in one way: It involves taking the *agriculture* out of agricultural biotechnology. Howard wants to turn plants into pharmaceutical factories.

This is not a new idea. It goes back at least to the late 1970s, when the founders of the biotechnology industry first realized that they could splice new genes into bacteria. Brilliant minds raced ahead and conceived of microbes containing human genes, churning out valuable proteins that are normally produced in the human body—insulin, for example. They spliced the gene for insulin into bacteria, and presto! the bacteria began producing human insulin. Each microbe created only a small amount of this protein, to be sure, but in the right conditions bacteria multiply at an astonishing rate. In a fermentation tank one insulin-producing microbe can turn into billions, all of them busily churning out insulin. Run the contents of that tank through a chemical strainer, and you've got thousands of dollars worth of insulin ready to sell.

This is how the first wave of successful biotechnology companies, including Genentech and Amgen, made their money. Today more than a dozen pharmaceuticals, including almost all insulin, are produced in fermentation tanks containing genetically engineered microbes. Most drugs are not simple proteins and can't be created this way, but a significant number are. They include many vaccines, promising new cancer treatments called monoclonal antibodies, and hormones.

If bacteria can be drug factories, Howard asked, why not plants? Splice those genes into a corn plant, and it, too, would manufacture valuable proteins. What's more, plants are able to create some proteins that are beyond the capacity of a microbe's biological machinery. Plants also could make vastly larger quantities than microbes; that should translate into lower costs. And you wouldn't need to build special fermentation facilities; just sign up a few farmers to grow these special plants, then ship those plants to special processing facilities that can extract the valuable proteins. Howard even wondered whether plants might become factories for lower-value proteins, such as enzymes that are used in industrial processes.

In the early 1980s, he proposed the idea to senior executives at Stauffer Chemical, "and everybody laughed at it pretty hard," he recalls. More than a decade later, after spending most of the intervening years at Pioneer Hi-Bred, Howard decided to pursue the idea in earnest. In 1996 he set up Prodigene.

Howard wasn't alone. Within a few years, Prodigene had half a dozen competitors, all trying to do roughly the same thing. Most were small startup companies, although Monsanto had entered the business as well. Some of the commercial ventures chose tobacco plants as their protein factories; others, including Prodigene, concentrated on grains. Most began by attempting to manufacture pharmaceuticals that already were on the market, trying to see if proteins produced in plants were identical to those manufactured in other ways. (They turned out, in some cases, not to be. A plant cell's machinery for the production of proteins is different from that of a microbe or of a human, and identical genes sometimes produce proteins with altered shapes and functions. The reasons for this are still under investigation.)

In other cases, the idea did work. In various corners of the United States, Canada, and western Europe, green, leafy pharmaceutical factories are sprouting from the ground. The cells of these plants contain antibodies that are intended to fight cancer, vaccines that protect pigs from an intestinal virus, drugs that break up blood clots, and enzymes that industry uses. One nonprofit group, the Boyce Thompson Institute for Plant Research at Cornell University, even began trying to engineer banana plants so that they would contain vaccines against the most common causes of childhood diarrhea. If successful, children eating these bananas would become immune to ailments that currently kill some three million infants each year, mostly in developing countries.

"Pharming," as it's called, remains a speculative venture. None of these companies has yet demonstrated that they can, as they promise, drastically cut the cost of making pharmaceuticals on a large scale. Nor have drug companies made up their minds whether they really *want* their high-tech, billion-dollar molecules growing in fields, even if it would mean cheaper production.

Yet this may be the surest route by which transgenic plants can escape the economic limits of agriculture. These are plants, to be sure; but they are not *commodities.* They aren't John Bedbrook's "bloody orange carrots" or Number 2 soybeans, which anybody can grow anywhere in the world driving prices down to a level where only the most efficient producers can survive. If the products of these plants eventually enter the market, the plants themselves will be surrounded with carefully constructed legal walls, built of patents and contracts. Prodigene will produce only as much as customers demand, and *it* will set the price of its products, not the commodity markets of Chicago.

The most enthusiastic backers of pharming sometimes talk as though this will be a boon for farmers as well, giving them opportunities to grow vastly more profitable crops. This is mostly empty rhetoric. Farmers won't own this harvest; they simply will grow it. Pharming companies likely will pay farmers just enough to convince them to grow the crop, not a penny more. Farmers will take it and be grateful, but there won't be many of them. To take one example, the largest manufacturing facilities for monoclonal antibodies in the world are said to produce about thirty thousand liters of such products each year in their fermentation tanks. It will take only about five hundred acres, one small Midwestern farm, to produce a similar amount in corn. Pharming, in other words, may rescue transgenic plants from the limits of agriculture, but in so doing, it will leave agriculture behind.

# Epilogue: The Story

*Are genetically engineered foods safe to eat? Do they harm the earth's environment?*

These questions, which dominate all current discussions of genetically engineered foods, masquerade as simple questions of fact. In truth, they are nothing of the sort, which is one reason why I've avoided, until now, directly addressing them. The questions are important, of course. But the really intriguing thing about these questions is the attitudes people bring to them that confound attempts to provide a satisfactory answer.

Take for example the question about the safety of genetically engineered food. If it were a question of fact, the answer would be straightforward. One can create genetically engineered plants that would be harmful to eat. Yet there is no credible evidence that genetically engineered foods currently on the market pose any greater risk to consumers than conventional food. The genetic alterations have introduced no substances that are known to be toxic to humans, nor have they increased the levels of toxic substances that already are present in those foods. On the face of it, these genetic alterations should be of no concern at all, compared to many other things that North Americans and Europeans already eat, from high levels of fats and sugar to small amounts of toxins from both natural and industrial sources.

Yet for vast numbers of consumers, that comparison isn't enough. They demand stronger proof that these foods are safe. In fact, they demand stronger assurances of safety than they do for many other foods or nutritional supplements. The truly interesting question is, *why?*

The question of possible environmental harm is similar. Genetically engineered crops can affect ecosystems. Some Monarch butterfly larvae have perished as a result of consuming milkweed leaves dusted with pollen from Bt corn. One could imagine other effects on the environment. Yet on balance the genetically engineered crops currently on the market probably have produced a net *benefit* to the environment rather than harm. I won't argue that the benefit is huge. It's not. Indeed, when one considers the enormous impact of conventional agriculture on the environment, the additional impact of genetic engineering, for good *or* ill, is tiny and hardly worth mentioning.

Why, then, do so many people regard genetically engineered crops as threatening apparitions in the countryside? By the same token, why do enthusiasts of biotechnology proclaim that genetic engineering represents a "revolution" in agriculture, and why do they sometimes talk as though this technology represents the last best hope for feeding the world's expanding population? These, too, are fascinating questions. The answers, I'm convinced, are not matters of fact and argument. They are embedded in stories.

I am a storyteller by profession and with conviction. Stories stay with us longer than any collection of miscellaneous facts and help us make some sense of the world.

When I began working on this book, I imagined that storytellers got a special exemption from being drafted into the war over genetically engineered plants. I thought I could stroll unimpeded between the bristling barricades, and I tried to persuade everyone I met that I posed no threat to anyone: *I just want to tell this story.*

They still didn't trust me. Below the surface of almost every conversation, evident in opaque expressions, in hesitations and vague answers, lurked uncertainty: *Friend or foe?*

Later, as I struggled to carve a narrative out of masses of information, I decided that the people I'd been interviewing had been right all along. Storytellers are not onlookers in this battle; we are, if anything, its grand strategists. The dispute over genetic engineering involves facts, to be sure. But its parties disagree far more passionately over the *story*. They quarrel over the nature of the characters, over the plot, and over the editing. They also feud over the unknowable: the ending.

AMONG THE anecdotes that occupy our minds a few are embedded so deeply that they shape the way we perceive the world. Those stories—sometimes we call them myths—create cavities within our brains shaped to accept any similar narratives. Facts and experiences stick with us—they "strike a chord," to use a common phrase—if they slip into these preformed contours. And as it happens, the tale of genetically engineered plants fits some of the most cherished narrative spaces that our minds possess.

It is, for instance, a tale of progress, of discovery and creativity solving problems and expanding the boundaries of human possibility. It follows outlines carved out by the Wright Brothers, Alexander Graham Bell, and Jonas Salk with his vaccine for polio. It's Gregor Mendel, planting peas in the garden of his monastery more than a century ago and discovering the patterns of human inheritance. These stories form part of the professional ideology of scientists, each of whom dreams of finding his or her role in this grand tale. And it is a powerful myth the shapes many people's understanding of genetically engineered food. (When I interviewed people recently at Cereon, Monsanto's genomics subsidiary, we met in a small room with a revealing name: the Copernicus Room.)

One particular version of this story holds sway over business executives and investors looking for the Next Big Thing. It's the saga of technology that destroys old businesses and builds new ones, creating enormous wealth along the way. At the moment, it's the story of personal computers or the Internet. In an earlier era, it was the telegraph, the automobile, or plastics. Sano Shimoda, the first financial analyst to recognize the potential of agricultural biotechnology, put his hopes into words: "It's like—and this may sound crazy—if you got plunked down fifty years ago in the orchards of Sunnyvale and Palo Alto." Those communities now are at the heart of Silicon Valley, in the midst of what may still be the greatest surge of empire building, in a financial sense, that the world has yet witnessed.

Then there are the stories that emerge from political ideology. They turn events of the world into endless loops as history repeats itself, and each plot unfolds again and again. There is, for example, the agrarian populist story: Corporate giants and city slickers exploit honest vulnerable farmers. Or the leftist one: Profit-mad companies lay claim to the earth's genetic heritage, subvert the government's halfhearted attempts at regulation, and rush into the marketplace with new products before anyone can fully comprehend the consequences. Mirroring this tale is the free-market conservative version: Opponents of capitalism resort to fear mongering in an effort to undermine private enterprise in agriculture.

A countervailing myth flows like an undertow beneath the triumphal story of progress, undermining it. It's the story of unpredictable, threatening technology unleashed upon an unsuspecting world through human folly like Pandora opening her box: Rachel Carson's account of DDT in *Silent Spring;* nuclear power and Chernobyl. In the words of a passionate opponent of biotechnology in New Zealand: "Today, the smug status of genetic engineering eerily recalls that period in the early 1960s when nuclear reactors were 'commercialized' on the basis of enthusiasts' claims of understanding and control. . . . Alongside airy dismissals of the dangers, the promised benefits are wildly exaggerated. . . . "

Several layers deeper, almost buried in our collective unconscious, lie other stories, ancient ones from the Middle Eastern cradle of Western civilization, warning against the temptation to overstep humanity's rightful bounds. In the Garden of Eden, the serpent tempts Eve: You *can* eat the fruit of this tree. *You will be like God.* Just a few pages further on, God contemplates humanity's attempts to build a tower that will reach to heaven and confounds its hubris in a confusion of languages. Centuries later, Mary Shelley repeats the warning in her story of Dr. Frankenstein and his fateful, doomed monster. Echoes of these tales resound in the antibiotechnology proclamation of Charles, Prince of Wales, from the summer of 1998: "[T]his kind of genetic modification takes mankind into realms that belong to God, and to God alone."

It's pointless to argue over which one of these versions of the agricultural biotechnology story is true. They all hold some truth. They all are, in the same measure, false in that they aren't really about agricultural biotechnology at all. They are literally preconceptions. They allow us to recognize important things about the world, but they also blind us to reality when that reality doesn't fit such preset patterns.

I've tried in this book to liberate agricultural biotechnology from the seductive clutches of myth, to give it its own space in our mental world, carved exactly to fit. I've tried to turn it from an epic into simply a story—the kind of tale one tells about a slightly crazy uncle with all his quirks and contradictions. The contours of this story aren't always smooth and clean, but it isn't merely a random collection of information. If one follows it closely, there are themes and patterns and a few useful lessons.

HERE'S THE first lesson: Agriculture is different. Those differences— from pharmaceuticals or chemicals or any factory-made product— are destined to annoy and frustrate the grandest ambitions of genetic engineers.

In 1981 a visionary entrepreneur named David Padwa went to see George Soros, the noted financier. Those were the days of the first biotech boom on Wall Street. Monsanto had just hired Rogers, Fraley, and Horsch. David Padwa was promising, with a new venture called Agrigenetics, to transform agriculture through genetic engineering. He tried to persuade Soros to invest in the company. When Padwa was done with his pitch, Soros said: "I'm not going to give you the money, for two reasons. I don't like businesses where you only get to sell your product once a year. And I don't like businesses in which anything you could possibly do will be overwhelmed by the effects of the weather."

When Padwa, twenty years older and wiser, told me this story, he chuckled: "Two very good reasons!" Agrigenetics ran out of money in the late 1980s.

The fresh produce business, messy, low-tech, and recalcitrant, deflated the dreams of Calgene and its Flavr Savr tomato. I treasure the image of a Calgene executive confronting one of the company's tomato breeders, insisting that she find a way to transcend biology and make plants grow and reproduce faster. ("Money is no object! . . . Think outside the box!") In the end, Calgene's genetically transformed tomatoes turned out to be no more desirable, or valuable, than any other tomato.

Then Monsanto arrived on the scene with a few genes that really did make a difference. This company also collided with agriculture, but in a different way. For Monsanto to realize its dream of becoming the Microsoft of agriculture (beware of those seductive epics!), agriculture would have to change. Specifically, the seed business had to become a real business with real control over its products. Monsanto embarked on a campaign to redefine the nature of seed, to make it a product like a car or a barrel of chemicals rather than a free good provided by nature. Monsanto rolled out its legal arsenal of contracts and patents, all aimed at capturing the value that the company's executives and shareholders felt was rightfully theirs. Eventually, Monsanto became convinced that the only way it would earn what it truly deserved from the seed business was to own large chunks of it outright.

Similar acquisitions of chemical companies, or fast food chains, pass with little public controversy. But seeds are different. They symbolize the bounty of the earth and the mystery of life. Monsanto's attempts to assert control over them as products became match, fuel, and flame for the campaign against genetic engineering.

There's a moral to these stories, one that applies to all of agricultural biotechnology. Agriculture, even more than most human endeavors, demands a healthy dose of the old-fashioned virtues of modesty and patience. It requires modesty in one's promises regarding the potential of new technology and patience in one's expectations for public acceptance and financial returns.

Modesty and patience are out of fashion in an era when businesses operate around the clock without regard either to natural cycles of the sun or cultural patterns of work and Sabbath. But agriculture, ancient and resilient, operates according to its own rhythms. Biology sets some limits. Culture sets others. Human attitudes toward the land, toward plants, and toward food do not change at the crescendo pace set by computer software and the Internet.

It's true that private investors and corporate executives, who, after all, pour most of the money into this technology, aren't noted for modesty and patience. Monsanto's scientists faced a demand in the early 1990s that the company finally see a return on the company's biotechnology investment, or the program would be shut down. Calgene's survival as a company depended on overhyped promises to investors about the size of the potential market and the speed at which the tomato could conquer that market. Yet hype and haste proved self-defeating. If people—whether scientists or investors—can't afford to be patient and modest in their handling of this technology, they shouldn't be handling it in the first place.

THE TALE of agricultural biotechnology is one of new wine in old wineskins, of new technology emerging within a traditional industry unwilling to change its practices. It is a story of double standards, as the public demanded strict assurances from genetic engineering while taking a relatively laissez-faire approach to traditional agriculture. Indeed, if the standards governing genetic engineering were applied to the rest of agriculture, much food production would have been banned long ago.

Forget chemical factories and toxic waste dumps. The single most environmentally destructive human activity on the planet is agriculture. Clearing and plowing land in order to grow crops (even following organic methods) amounts to an ecological disaster visited annually upon most of our planet's surface.

Nor are the products of traditional agriculture uniformly safe to eat. Food from some plants, such as peanuts, causes allergic reactions among hundreds of thousands of people. Other grains, including wheat and corn, contain small amounts of extremely toxic and carcinogenic compounds that result from certain plant diseases. Yet the public, for the most part, smiles indulgently. As the hapless George Banks says of fox hunting in *Mary Poppins:* "Well, I don't mind *that* so much. It's tradition!"

Except for the use of technology invented since World War II—primarily pesticides—agriculture is largely unregulated. Farmers can plant what they want on their land. They can plow right up to the edges of creeks, causing soil erosion; they can overdose their land with fertilizer or agricultural chemicals, placing nearby streams or ground water at risk. They can plant the same crops year after year, depleting the soil of nutrients and risking infestations of destructive pests or epidemics of plant disease. Farmers *shouldn't* do any of this; it's not in their economic self-interest, and most don't. But none of it is illegal.

Plant breeders, for their part, are free to introduce genes into crops from almost any possible source without worrying about any reactions either from government regulators or consumers. Some years ago a plant breeder located wild relatives of the soybean in Australia that appeared to be immune to one of the major pests afflicting soybeans in the United States, a worm called the cyst nematode. He took pollen from these plants, fertilized conventional soybeans, and managed to recover fertile offspring of this union that also were immune to the pest. The trait was then bred into standard soybean varieties, ready for planting by any American farmer. These varieties were products of the laboratory, not of nature. No one in this case even knew what genes made the plant immune to the cyst nematode, or why. No one needed to know. They were subject to no regulatory review.

Nor were so-called STS soybeans, which can tolerate sprays of an herbicide called Synchrony. These plants were created by soaking soybeans in chemicals, inducing random mutations in soybean DNA. One of the mutants proved to be resistant to this particular herbicide. Because the mutation was created *within* the cell and not spliced in from an outside source, it faced no government review.

Then genetic engineering arrived. It was new and high-tech and emerged from within the heavily regulated chemical and pharmaceutical industries. By promising to overcome all limits of nature, it awakened deep suspicions and fears. Not surprisingly, biotechnology ran into a wholly different set of standards and expectations.

A few people imagined that the old standards might apply also to biotechnology. In the mid-1980s, conservative opponents of regulation within Ronald Reagan's administration tried to argue that genetic engineering of plants should be regulated more or less the way plant breeding is—that is, hardly at all. They ultimately were shouted down, although they succeeded in draping the reality of regulation within the garb of "voluntary consultations." Most farsighted company executives realized, in fact, that they needed some form of regulation. They could not by themselves convince the public that this technology was safe. If genetically engineered crops were to earn the public's confidence, they required a stamp of approval from public institutions with untarnished credibility.

As a result, genetically engineered plants are examined for evidence that they might pass on genes to wild relatives or that they might be different in their chemical makeup from conventional crops. Farmers planting insect-resistant Bt corn are required to plant "refuges" of corn susceptible to insects to preserve the effectiveness of this new gene. Farmers planting insect-resistant strains of wheat or corn produced by conventional breeding are subject to no such regulations. The makers of Roundup Ready soybeans had to submit evidence that these beans were safe to eat; the makers of STS soybeans did not, even though both forms of herbicide resistance are created by altering the form of a gene that exists naturally within the plant.

My favorite example of the double standard was the view, voiced by the British government's environmental advisors, that Roundup Ready crops should be banned or restricted because they allow farmers to eliminate weeds more efficiently from their fields, thereby potentially harming wild birds that relied on the seeds of these weeds for food. The danger was not exactly a result of genetic engineering; vigorous hoeing can, and does, eliminate weeds as well. Indeed, cultivation of the countryside, with traditional methods, certainly had had dramatic effects on the bird population of the United Kingdom. But when had government agencies ever stepped in to make sure that farmers grew a requisite number of weeds?

Most people pretend to believe in logical consistency, and few will admit to endorsing this double standard. Opponents of biotechnology largely deny that it exists. Genetically engineered crops, they insist, are inherently more risky, so it's proper to subject them to greater scrutiny. The supporters of biotechnology, meanwhile, speak constantly and with great irritation about the higher standards applied to genetically engineered crops. It would be more logical (and therefore more *correct,* they believe) to apply the same standard across all crops.

But *which* standard? Consider the unspeakable: That all of agriculture deserves the same scrutiny applied to genetically engineered crops. Perhaps, when plant breeders create STS soybeans or a variety of wheat that resists the predations of the Hessian fly, they shouldn't be allowed immediately to start selling such seeds to farmers. Perhaps they should be required to find out which genes produce this trait and whether these varieties might cause any unwanted effects either to the ecosystem or to human health.

If farmers are required to limit their plantings of Bt corn or cotton for the good of the ecosystem (as indeed they should be), why not go further? Why not compel (or induce through cash incentives) farmers to do other things that would produce substantial environmental benefits, such as allow some of their land to revert to grasslands and woods?

Plant breeders and most farmers will be outraged at such suggestions. They will point out that the burden of such initiatives will fall most heavily on the smallest seed companies and on farmers already teetering on the edge of financial oblivion. Others will point out that efforts to subsidize better (but less efficient) agricultural practices might be incompatible with free trade in agricultural products. (For years, the United States has been using free trade as a battering ram to beat down the European Community's agricultural subsidies.)

That's all true. Those are good reasons for proceeding cautiously and patiently, alert to the social and economic consequences of our actions. But they aren't reasons for turning a blind eye toward the environmental effects of traditional agriculture.

The double standard exists, in fact, not because of special risks that genetically engineered crops present to health or the environment, but because of two concerns that transcend any calculation of risk.

The first is the conviction that humans, when they control and manipulate other living organisms, devalue life itself. The second arises because biotechnology has proceeded hand-in-hand with claims of ownership to the building blocks of life. This proprietorship has been a prime motivation for companies promoting genetically engineered crops, but it has enraged biotechnology's most committed opponents.

These concerns often are hidden from view, like unfashionable and musty-smelling mementos of a bygone era. Yet they are good and proper reasons to subject biotechnology to special scrutiny.

Unfortunately, they don't offer clear judgments on the uses of biotechnology. Instead of obvious boundaries, there are many shades of gray. When it comes to the manipulation and ownership of living organisms, the spectrum ranges from the domestication of wheat on the one hand to extermination of people deemed inferior on the other. Somewhere in the middle lies an important ethical boundary, and it's up to us to find it.

I'd place the cloning of humans on the far side of that boundary, but I cannot quite manage to get agitated about the genetic manipulation of soybean plants growing in the fields of Iowa. I've come to accept the legitimacy of patents on some genetic constructions – the Bt genes are one example – that were built through human ingenuity, using elements found in nature. Yet I, along with many others, was repelled by Monsanto's rush to claim that genetic property and squeeze as much revenue as possible from it. The company's business ambitions, more then any other single factor, brought forth the backlash against agricultural biotechnology.

OPPONENTS OF biotechnology have succeeded for the moment in crippling the profit-making prospects of genetically engineered food. Many of their arguments amount to demagoguery, and this may be grounds for ridicule but not for moral outrage. The public welfare does not depend, to any significant extent, on the commercial success of Roundup Ready soybeans and corn. Nor is opposition to biotechnology depriving poverty-stricken parts of the world of crucial tools for solving urgent problems. If anything, the opponents have forced companies purely for the sake of public relations to share more tools and knowledge with researchers in the developing world who otherwise could not afford them. The biotech industry also has been forced to search more urgently for genetically engineered plants that are beneficial to consumers. In short, the chaos of public argument might actually yield an outcome that is both reasonable and wise.

Moreover, as the decades pass, genetic modification of plants will no longer seem quite so new and threatening. The risks of genetically engineered and conventional crops, one hopes, finally will be measured by the same yardstick. Less scrutiny will be aimed specifically at the effects of gene splicing, and more attention paid to the effects of agriculture in general.

For there is one aspect of the double standard affecting agriculture and biotechnology that I do want to abolish as quickly as possible.

It's the double standard of knowledge and passion. If genetic engineering is fascinating, or even ominous, then plowing, sowing, reaping, or breeding cannot be mundane.

So let genetic engineering be a window into things that ultimately are more important. Let us begin to learn where the myth of agriculture ends and reality begins. Let's try to understand why farmers do what they do to so much of Earth's surface. If we care about the health of the planet, particularly the part of it devoted to agriculture, perhaps we'll be willing to pay for what we value, either through direct purchases of food or through taxes. In the best of worlds, we might be able to create forms of agriculture that are good for all of the world's inhabitants.

# NOTES ON SOURCES

For the story teller and amateur historian of contemporary events, human memory is a blessing and a curse. In the assembling of this book, I often could rely on nothing else. Corporations rarely release detailed accounts of their internal deliberations, and scientific publications are a painfully dry accounting of history. Much of the information in this book, as a result, was culled from about three hundred interviews with scientists, business executives, political activists, and academic researchers, most of whom played a direct role in the fate of genetically engineered plants. At a distance of five, ten, or twenty years, however, memories become astonishingly fluid. Frequently, I heard contradictory accounts of the same event. I became all the more grateful, as a result, for the documentary records that do exist.

Fortunately, few of the people I interviewed could influence the course of events without leaving behind some record of their work, whether in the form of newspaper accounts or government documents. I owe particular thanks to the U.S. Patent and Trademark Office, the Securities and Exchange Commission, and the federal courts. The files of these institutions provided valuable clues regarding the chronology of innovation and deal making that dominates so much of this book. A description of selected sources, by chapter, follows.

## Prologue

For one example of technological enthusiasm, or the process of becoming "caught up in the fun of it all," see Robert Post's book, *High Performance: The Culture and Technology of Drag Racing, 1950–1990* (Baltimore: Johns Hopkins Press, 1994). Thomas Hughes has written the classic description of this phenomenon: *American Genesis: A Century of Invention and Technological Enthusiasm, 1870–1970* (New York: Viking, 1989). David Noble offers a very different interpretation in *The Religion of Technology* (New York: Knopf, 1997). Zoe Elford's statement in opposition to genetic engineering can be found on the Web site of genetix snowball, an activist group in Britain: http://www.fraw.org.uk/gs/statem/ 12.htm. I don't like to cite Web sites, because so many of them are here today and gone tomorrow, but in many cases I don't see any alternative.

## The First Transformation

Mary-Dell Chilton's account of the crucial discoveries regarding *Agrobacterium* was published in a special seventy-fifth anniversary issue of *Plant Physiology* in January of 2001 (Vol. 125, pp.9–14). The proceedings of the Miami Winter Symposium of 1983 were published as *Advances in Gene Technology: Molecular Genetics of Plants and Animals* (San Diego, Calif.: Academic Press, 1983). In 1997 Karen Keeler Rogers wrote a useful account of Monsanto's entry into biotechnology for the company's in-house publication, *Monsanto Magazine*. The two-part article, "Fields of Promise," is available as a brochure from Monsanto's public relations department. Jack Doyle's book *Altered Harvest* (Viking, 1985) includes an excellent portrait of David Padwa, the early biotech entrepreneur. One article that reflected the typical optimism of the day appeared in the Sunday magazine of the *New York Times* on October 25, 1981, titled "The Second Green Revolution." Crucial early patents include U.S. Patent 5,034,322 and U.S. Patent 5,352,605. In the case of these patents, I took the trouble to look through the entire file of correspondence that went back and forth between Monsanto and a series of patent examiners. Such files are available for inspection at the U.S. Patent and Trademark Office.

## Marching on Washington

Jeremy Rifkin's book *Algeny* (Viking, 1983) is a classic statement of fundamentalist opposition to biotechnology. For a hilarious profile of Rifkin, see "Biotech Gadfly Buzzes Italy" in the Sunday magazine of the *Washington Post* on January 17, 1988. Stephen Jay Gould, meanwhile, weighed in with his own critique of Rifkin ("On the Origin of Specious Critics") in the January 1985 issue of *Discover*. Far away on the other side of this debate is Henry Miller, formerly the coordinator of biotechnology policy for the Food and Drug Administration, with his own book, *Policy Controversy in Biotechnology: An Insider's View* (Austin, Tex.: R. G. Landes, 1997). The Monsanto archive at Washington University in St. Louis contains material that sheds light on the company's attitudes toward regulation during the early 1980s.

### "Everything Was Worth Doing"

The Monsanto archive contains a gallery of scientists who worked in Monsanto's early biotechnology program as well as several of Howard Schneiderman's annual self-evaluations, which make for fascinating reading. Shortly before his death in 1990, Schneiderman also wrote memoirs which Monsanto published several years later in a very limited edition as *Howard A. Schneiderman: A Brief Autobiography*. Schneiderman's personal notebooks are the property of his wife, Audrey.

The paper by Roger Beachy and his collaborators on virus resistance was published in *Science* in 1986. (Vol. 232, pp. 738–743) An interesting account of his collaboration with Monsanto was published in the *International Journal of Biotechnology* in 1999 (Vol. 1, No.1, pp. 67–81).

### The First Useful Gene

Anyone who wishes to learn more about the early history of research on *Bacillus thuringiensis* might attempt to track down *The Canadian Entomologist* from July/August of 1992. (Vol. 124, pp.587–616). The article includes a photo gallery of early Bt explorers. Scientists at Plant Genetic Systems published their triumph in 1986 in *Nature* (Vol. 328, pp. 33–37). The struggle to build a gene that would work well in plants is detailed in the testimony and ultimate verdicts of several court cases. They include *Monsanto Company* v. *Mycogen*

*Plant Science, Inc., Agrigenetics, Inc., and Novartis Corporation* (Civil Action 96–133-RRM) in the U.S. District Court for the District of Delaware, and in the same court *Mycogen Plant Science, Inc., and Agrigenetics, Inc.,* v. *Monsanto Company, DeKalb Genetics Corporation, and Delta and Pine Land Company* (Civil Action 96–505-RRM ). The saga of Mycogen's alleged misappropriation of the *tenebrionis* strain of the microbe was the subject of an article ("At Mycogen, it's a tale of intrigue") in the San Diego *Union-Tribune* on September 20, 1992.

## Gifts of God

Fred Gould's trail is strewn with publications. One of the earliest ("Evolutionary Biology and Genetically Engineered Crops") appeared in *Bioscience* in 1988 (Vol. 38, pp. 26–33). In 1998, the Union of Concerned Scientists published a small book containing papers by Gould and several other experts on insect resistance. The book, *Now or Never: Serious New Plans to Save a Natural Pest Control,* is available from UCS.

Proceedings of the first large conference on the wider ecological risks of genetic engineering were published as *Engineered Organisms in the Environment: Scientific Issues* (American Society for Microbiology, 1985). The Ecological Society of America's position on genetic engineering was published as a special report in *Ecology* in April 1989 (Vol. 70, No. 2, pp. 297–315). Rob Colwell's long essay on the philosophical underpinnings of his views was published as a chapter in *Scientists and Their Responsibility,* edited by William Shea and Beat Sitter (Canton, Mass.: Watson Publishing International, 1989)

## Genes That Love Poison

Luca Comai's success in creating Roundup-resistant plants, which so aroused Monsanto's competitive ire, was reported in *Nature* in 1985 (Vol. 317, pp. 741–744). Monsanto's long and tortuous path toward Roundup resistant plants is described in a succession of patents: U.S. Patents 4,940,835; 4,971,908; and 5,633,435.

The team at Plant Genetic Systems reported the first Basta-resistant plants in *The EMBO Journal* in 1987 (Vol. 6, No. 9, pp. 2513–2518). Günter Donn described the origins of this genetic trait more broadly in a paper delivered to a conference in Dijon, France, in December 1998.

## Triumphs of Tinkering

John Sanford's personal account of the origins of the gene gun appeared in *In Vitro Cellular and Developmental Biology—Plant* in September 2000 (Vol. 36, No. 5, pp. 303–308). The paper in *Nature* that finally gave the technique some respectability appeared in 1987 (Vol. 327, pp. 70–73). Dennis McCabe announced his success with soybeans in *Bio/Technology* in August, 1988 (Vol. 6, pp. 923–926). And DeKalb's researchers rushed into print with their genetically engineered corn plants in *The Plant Cell* (Vol. 2, pp. 603–617). The history of corn transformation has since been subjected to a veritable rugby scrum of patent lawyers. Anyone who wishes to dive into this morass can consult the records from the resulting court cases. One (Civil Action 96–505-RRM ) took place in the U.S. District Court for Delaware: *Mycogen Plant Science, Inc., and Agrigenetics, Inc., v. Monsanto Company, DeKalb Genetics Corporation, and Delta and Pine Land Company.* Another, *Plant Genetic Systems v. DeKalb Genetics Corporation* (Case number 3:96CV2015) was tried in U.S. District court in Hartford, Connecticut. And still another, *DeKalb Genetics Corp v. Pioneer Hi-Bred* (Case number 96 C 50112) was tried in February 2001 in the U.S. District Court in Rockford, Illinois.

## Forces in Opposition

Margaret Mellon and Jane Rissler, of the Union of Concerned Scientists, kindly gave me access to some of their old files, which greatly aided my reconstruction of the political dynamics of the late 1980s. Their activities, along with those of Rebecca Goldburg, provide an embarrassment of bibliographic riches. Most of their contributions, however, are collected in government publications which often are difficult to find. (The Web site of the Union of Concerned Scientists has a good collection of their writings, but it goes back only to about 1994.) Mellon and Goldburg have testified numerous times before Congress and submitted a blizzard of comments and criticisms to federal regulatory agencies. Mellon and her longtime colleague, Jane Rissler, did collect their views into a book, *The Ecological Risks of Engineered Crops* (Cambridge, Mass.: MIT Press, 1996). Many scientists who've worked in this field take great offense at the accusation, often repeated, that genetically engineered crops harbor unknown and unresearched risks to ecosystems. They insist that these issues have, in fact, been researched intensively, but that their opponents studiously ignore the results. Much of the research to which they refer has been published in obscure places such as the proceedings of international symposia on biosafety. Good luck tracking them down. I only saw them in the private collections of scientists who attended such meetings. In 2000 the U.S. National Research Council published a study called *Genetically Modified Pest-Protected Plants: Science and Regulation*. It also contains a helpful bibliography.

The issues that Goldburg and Mellon raised were debated during an excellent series of annual conferences organized by the National Agricultural Biotechnology Council. The proceedings of each conference have been published. Worthy of special note are NABC Report 3, *Agricultural Biotechnology at the Crossroads* (1991) and NABC Report 6, *Agricultural Biotechnology and the Public Good* (1994).

Jack Doyle's book, *Altered Harvest*, has been mentioned above. The questions that he posed in 1985 regarding ownership of seeds have since become a favorite of social scientists in academia. Jack Kloppenburg, Jr.'s *First the Seed* (New York: Cambridge University Press, 1988) includes a heavy dose of Marxist theory. Cary Fowler took a more empirical approach, with the benefit of first-hand experience, in his *Unnatural Selection* (Yverdon: Gordon and Breach, 1994). Calestous Juma focused particularly on the consequences for developing countries in *The Gene Hunters* (Princeton: Princeton University Press, 1989).

Wolfgang van den Daele's experiment in "participatory risk assessment" is described in detail in a book that he edited, together with collaborators Alfred Pühler and Herbert Sukopp, *Grüne Gentechnik im Widerstreit* (Weinheim: VCH Verlagsgesellschaft, 1996) A summary report is available in English from the Web site of the Berlin Social Science Research Center (www.wz-berlin.de). There have been numerous critiques of this process, all in German. They include Barbara Weber's "'Normalisierung' durch Vergleich?" *TA Datenbank-Nachrichten* (December 1996), and Bernhard Gill's "Wider die technokratische Engführung der Risikodebatte," *Wechselwirkung* (October 1996).

## Seed Wars

The origins of Pioneer Hi-Bred International are described well, if a bit adoringly, in Russell Lord's book *The Wallaces of Iowa* (Boston: Houghton Mifflin, 1947). Henry A. Wallace himself, a remarkable and fascinating man, finally has his own biography, *American Dreamer,* by John C. Culver and John Hyde (New York: Norton, 2000). For background on plant breeding, see an article by Donald Duvick, a former Pioneer breeder and research executive: "Plant Breeding, An Evolutionary Concept," in *Crop Science* (Vol. 36, pp. 539–548). The business dealings described in this chapter, though long the subject of rumor and gossip within the industry, cannot be confirmed through documented sources. There is one exception. When Pioneer sued Monsanto for breach of contract in 1997, Pioneer deposited a copy of its 1993 deal with Monsanto for Bt corn. The records of this case are at the U.S. District Court in St. Louis (Case No. 4:97CV1609 ERW).

## The Tomato That Ate Calgene

The people who used to work at Calgene are the most delightfully talkative collection of personalities in the entire industry, which eased the task of research immensely. Because the company courted press coverage so assiduously, it also left behind a rich lode of newspaper clippings. As this book went to press, a former Calgene scientist published her own account of the Flavr Savr saga, Belinda Martineau, *First Fruit: The Creation of the Flavr Savr Tomato and the Birth of Genetically Engineered Food* (New York: McGraw-Hill, 2001). A number of internal FDA documents relating to the FDA's approval of the Flavr Savr tomato are posted on the Web site of an antibiotech group, the Alliance for Bio-Integrity: http://www.biointegrity.org/FDAdocs/. They were obtained in the course of a lawsuit that the Alliance filed and lost against the FDA. The Web sites of the FDA, EPA, and USDA also hold a wealth of information on the government's regulation of biotechnology. The FDA's Web page (http://vm.cfsan.fda.gov/%7Elrd/biotechm.html) is a good place to start.

## Tremors of Anticipation

The events that led to Monsanto's reshaping of the seed business were shrouded by business confidentiality at the time and had to be reconstructed from the memories of the participants. The atmosphere within Monsanto during the mid-1990s, as Robert Shapiro took over as CEO, is evident in the pages of *Monsanto Magazine.* The magazine's third issue of 1995 was filled with accounts of the company's "global forum." I was also able to obtain videotapes of many internal meetings at which Shapiro spoke to the company's employees. Monsanto filed a statement with the SEC on February 7, 1996, which detailed the chronology of its negotiations to buy part of DeKalb.

## Summers of Triumph, Summers of Discord

The entry of Monsanto's genetically engineered crops into the marketplace was not heavily covered by the national press, outside of farm-oriented publications. Monsanto issued several brochures celebrating the growth of its biotech products; they contain useful facts and figures, and the most recent one is available from the company's public relations offices. The International Service for the Acquisition of Agri-Biotech Applications (ISAAA) compiles an annual report with estimates of the global area devoted to genetically engineered crops. One can retrieve summaries of these reports at http://www.isaaa.org.

Analyzing the rapid adoption of these crops, and their impact, has become a favorite occupation of agricultural economists. Studies of Roundup Ready soybeans and Bt corn have been carried out by researchers at the National Center for Food and Agricultural Policy (http://www.ncfap.org). ISAAA has published a study on who benefits most from Bt cotton. (Falk-Zepeda et al., "Rent Creation and Distribution from the First Three Years of Planting Bt Cotton," *ISAAA Briefs*, No. 13.) Fred Cooke, Jr., an economist with Mississippi State University's Delta Research and Extension Station in Stoneville, Mississippi, has monitored the success of Bt cotton at the local level, in the Mississippi Delta. Several of his reports have appeared in the proceedings of the annual Beltwide Cotton Conference organized by the National Cotton Council of America. Reports that are skeptical of the benefits of these crops have been released by the Leopold Center for Sustainable Agriculture (http://www.leopold.iastate.edu) and by Charles Benbrook, an independent consultant whose work often appears in an Internet-based library called Ag Biotech InfoNet (http://www.biotech-info.net).

Researchers and extension agents at agricultural universities have released their consensus recommendations regarding how best to prevent insects from developing resistance to Bt corn and cotton. The report on corn, "Bt Corn and European Corn Borer," was published as North Central Regional Extension Publication NCR 602, distributed by the University of Minnesota. The cotton report, "Bt Cotton and Management of the Tobacco Budworm-Bollworm Complex," was published by the USDA's Agricultural Research Service in January 2001 as ARS-154.

## Power Plays

The optimism of Monsanto's executives found full expression in the company's 1997 annual report, which promised continued exponential growth for agricultural biotechnology. The business dealings that resulted from that optimism and the consequences of those decisions are much more difficult to document. The bare facts are outlined, as usual, in documents that Monsanto, DeKalb, and Delta and Pine Land filed with the SEC. Most of the interpretation of these events comes from the memories of executives at Monsanto, and from Monsanto's direct competitors.

## Backlash

The explosion of opposition to genetically engineered crops coincided with the equally explosive growth of the Internet. As a consequence, an enormous amount of material was distributed and remains available electronically. (One can only hope for permanence in this electronic infrastructure.) Douglas Powell, a professor of agriculture at the University of Guelph in Canada runs a superb electronic clipping service called Agnet. Every day and sometimes several times a day Powell forwards a collection of newspaper articles, government announcements, and press releases related to environmental and health effects of agriculture. In recent years, the clippings have been dominated by the controversy over genetic engineering. These dispatches, going back to June of 1998, are archived at http://www.plant.uoguelph.ca/safefood/archives/agnet-archives.htm. The aforementioned Ag Biotech InfoNet (www.biotech-info.net) is also a helpful archive of the controversy, although it tends to lean heavily in the antibiotech direction. Monsanto currently maintains a Web site with a comprehensive archive as well (www.biotechknowledge.com). Friends of the Earth in the United Kingdom keeps an archive of its press releases on its Web site (www.foe.uk.co). They chronicle many events of the uproar over GM foods in Great Britain.

I obtained a copy of some of Monsanto's early polls in Europe from private sources. The analysis of British public opinion that was carried out by Robin Grove-White and his colleagues, with extensive use of focus groups, was published in March 1997 by the Centre for the Study of Environmental Change at Lancaster University under the title "Uncertain World: Genetically Modified Organisms, Food and Public Attitudes in Britain."

The literature related to each individual issue in this controversy is overwhelming. I'll list just a few sources. A chronicle of the outrage that greeted the Terminator is quite well archived on the Web site of the Rural Advancement Foundation International (www.rafi.org). The announcement of Pioneer's allergenic Brazil nut occurred in the *New England Journal of Medicine* in 1996 (Vol. 334, pp. 688–692). The same journal published in 1990 an account of the investigation into the deadly batches of L-tryptophan (Vol. 323, pp. 357–365). Arpad Pusztai's work was published in *The Lancet* on October 16, 1999 (Vol. 354, No. 9187), accompanied by critical commentaries written by other scientists. Pusztai has his own Web site, where one can read more than any reasonable person would want to know about his conflicts with the country's scientific establishment (www.freenetpages.co.uk/hp/a.pusztai/). For an example of the type of food safety studies carried out on genetically engineered food, see Monsanto's analysis of Roundup Ready soybeans, published in *The Journal of Nutrition* in March 1996 (Vol. 126, pp. 702–716 and 728–740). Studies carried out by industry are, of course, afflicted by conflicts of interest. One of the best independent laboratories carrying out studies related to the safety of genetically engineered food is in the Netherlands at the National Institute for Quality Control of Agricultural Products, Wageningen University and Research Center. As one example of their work, see their assessment of Bt tomatoes: (Noteborn, Bienenmann-Ploum, van den Berg, et al. "Safety assessment of the Bacillus thuringiensis insecticidal crystal protein CryIA(b) expressed in transgenic tomatoes," in Engel, Takeoka, Teranishi, eds., *Genetically Modified Foods: Safety Issues* [ACS Symposium Series 605, Washington DC, 1995]: pp. 134–47).

### The Wheels Come Off

As is typical of the purely business-related parts of this story, the primary sources for this chapter were news clippings, SEC filings, and interviews.

### The Deluge

The electronic archives mentioned above provide a good account of what happened in Britain during the first few months of 1999. The web site of the European Commission (europa.eu.int/comm/index_en.htm) provides much useful material, although it's sometimes hard to locate particular documents.

John Losey's original short paper on Bt corn's potential for killing Monarch butterfly larvae was published in *Nature* on May 20, 1999 (Vol. 399, p. 214). A collection of papers from all the follow-up studies was published on October 9, 2001, in *The Proceedings of the National Academy of Sciences*. These six papers can be found online at http://www.pnas.org/content/vol98/issue21/. A review of the controversy (indeed, of many controversies aroused by genetically engineered crops) has been published in *Genetically Engineered Organisms in Agriculture: Economics & Politics*, edited by Gerald C. Nelson (San Diego, Calif.: Academic Press, 2001).

Materials from the campaign against genetically engineered food as it unfolded in the United States can be obtained from the organizations involved in that campaign. Among the most prominent were Greenpeace (U.S.), Friends of the Earth (U.S.), the International Center for Technology Assessment, and the Institute for Agriculture and Trade Policy.

I acquired detailed minutes of the meeting between Monsanto executives and the Soil Association. Greenpeace provided a videotape of the conference at which Robert Shapiro spoke. Sources within Monsanto provided a videotape of the meeting at which Hendrik Verfaillie discussed Monsanto's merger with Pharmacia.

### Global Claims

The question of whether genetic engineering could be useful in improving the lives of people in the developing world has inspired an enormous amount of writing. For an optimistic answer, one can turn to the publications of the International Service for that Acquisition of Agri-Biotech Applications, which Clive James founded. ISAAA's reports describe a number of projects aimed at demonstrating the value of biotechnology in developing countries. One might also look at the mountain of publications from the various research centers of the Consultative Group on International Agricultural Research, which maintains a secretariat in the World Bank, in Washington,

D.C. The CGIAR has published the proceedings of a conference it convened on this topic, edited by G. J. Perseley and M. M. Lantin, called *Agricultural Biotechnology and the Poor.* Per Pinstrup-Andersen, the former head of a CGIAR research center called the International Food Policy Research Institute, has co-authored a book on this topic called *Seeds of Contention: World Hunger and the Global Controversy over GM (Genetically Modified) Crops* (Baltimore: Johns Hopkins University Press, 2001).

Organizations that take a decidedly negative view include the Rural Advancement Foundation International, the Spain-based Genetic Resources Action International (GRAIN), and Food First/Institute for Food and Development Policy. A representative statement of their critique, written by Miguel Altieri and Peter Rosset, was published in *Third World Resurgence,* Issue No.118/119 (June-July 2000).

The prime mover behind "golden rice," Ingo Potrykus, recounted the story behind his invention in the "Turning Point" section *In Vitro Cellular and Developmental Biology—Plant* (San Diego, Calif.: forthcoming). A critique of his invention appeared in *Seedling,* the quarterly publication of GRAIN, in March 2000 (Vol. 17, No. 1).

On Robert Shapiro's interest in sustainability, see an interview with him in the *Harvard Business Review* (January-February 1997)

Finally, on the question of the economics of the seed business worldwide, I am indebted to the writings of Michael Morris, an economist with CIMMYT, and Robert Tripp, an anthropologist at the Overseas Development Institute in London. Of particular relevance is a paper that Tripp presented at the 4th International Conference on the Economics of Agricultural Biotechnology, Ravallo, Italy, called "Can Biotechnology Reach the Poor? The Adequacy of Information and Seed delivery." It is currently scheduled for publication later in 2001 in *Food Policy.* A book that Morris edited, *Maize Seed Industries in Developing Countries* (CIMMYT, 1998) provides helpful background on the seed trade.

Also worthy of mention is *Food's Frontier,* by Richard Manning (New York: North Point Press, 2000). Only part of this book deals directly with genetic engineering, but that's as it should be.

## Perched on a Precipice

The path of the Starlink debacle can be traced through press releases and regulatory filings that are currently held on the Web sites of the U.S. Environmental Protection Agency (www.epa.gov/pesticides/biopesticides/) and Friends of the Earth—U.S. (www.foe.org).

## Infinite Horizons

I'm not aware of a satisfactory account written for outsiders of the innovations that led from genetics to genomics. For several somewhat technical articles on the current state of plant genomics, one could consult a special section on plant biotechnology that was published in *Science* on July 16, 1999 (Vol. 285, pp.367–389). *Technology Review* published a more popular account, "The Next Biotech Harvest" in its issue of September/October, 1998. For a review of attempts to produce pharmaceuticals or industrial enzymes in plants, see an article by Chris R. Somerville and Dario Bonetta in the seventy-fifth anniversary issue of *Plant Physiology*, in January 2001 (Vol. 125, pp. 168–171). One very good resource, for as long as it continues, is the National Science Foundation's plant genomics program, which maintains a Web site (www.nsf.gov/bio/dbi/dbi_pgr.htm) with links to many academic laboratories. The new genomics ventures, including Paradigm Genetics, Prodigene, and Maxygen, have their own Web sites.

# INDEX